'A MARVEL TO BEHOLD'

Gold and Silver at the Court of Henry VIII

TIMOTHY SCHRODER

THE BOYDELL PRESS

First published 2020
The Boydell Press, Woodbridge

ISBN 978-1-78327-507-6

The Boydell Press is an imprint of Boydell & Brewer Ltd
PO Box 9, Woodbridge, Suffolk IP12 3DF, UK
and of Boydell & Brewer Inc.
668 Mt Hope Avenue, Rochester, NY 14620–2731, USA
website: www.boydellandbrewer.com

A catalogue record of this publication is available
from the British Library

This publication is printed on acid-free paper

Typeset by BBR Design, Sheffield

For Malcolm Oxley

Contents

List of Illustrations viii
Acknowledgements xix
List of Abbreviations xxi
Glossary xxiii
Note to the reader xxviii
Preface xxx

1 Magnificence and Princely Virtue 1
2 The Jewel House 11
3 The King's Inheritance 27
4 'Heaven Smiles, Earth Rejoices' 39
5 'Defender of the Faith' 63
6 Royal Banquets 85
7 'Rich, Fierce and Greedy for Glory' 111
8 Thomas Wolsey, Patron of Goldsmiths 131
9 The Field of Cloth of Gold 153
10 Holbein and the 'Antique' 175
11 The Family Silver 203
12 Cromwell, the Tower and the Goldsmiths 229
13 Dissolution and Augmentation 259
14 'Most Avaricious of Men' 281
15 'Sic transit gloria mundi': The Fate of Henry VIII's Plate and Jewels 315

Notes 319
Bibliography 349
Index 355

Illustrations

Figures

1.1 David sending Uriah to the front (detail), from *The Story of King David*, Brussels, c. 1520. Tapestry. Showing the ubiquity of gold and silver at court: buffet of plate in background, regalia, jewelled armour, jewels and cloth of gold. Musée de la Renaissance, Ecouen. Photo © RMN-Grand Palais (Musée de la Renaissance, château d'Ecouen) / Gérard Blot. 2

1.2 Nathan reproaches David (detail), from *The Story of King David*, Brussels, c. 1520. Tapestry. Showing a procession of servants and nobles carrying plate into the royal presence: a covered cup, a cup of assay and a spice plate. Musée de la Renaissance, Ecouen. Photo © RMN-Grand Palais (Musée de la Renaissance, château d'Ecouen) / Gérard Blot. 3

1.3 Henry VIII with Jane Seymour and Prince Edward, detail from *The Family of Henry VIII*, British school, c. 1545. Hampton Court Palace. Royal Collection. Photo Royal Collection Trust / © Her Majesty Queen Elizabeth II 2019. 6

2.1 The jewel house at Westminster Palace, London. Photo © Timothy Schroder. 13

2.2 The Tower of London from a survey of 1597, John Howard and John Gascoigne. Showing the jewel house abutting the White Tower. British Library (Maps.K.Top.24.23.b). Photo © British Library Board 01/06/2020. 14

2.3 The imperial treasure of Maximilian I, Albrecht Dürer, 1515. Engraving. Metropolitan Museum of Art, New York. 14

2.4 *Sir Henry Wyatt*, Hans Holbein the younger, before 1537. Musée du Louvre, Paris. Photo © RMN-Grand Palais (musée du Louvre) / Hervé Lewandowski. 16

3.1 The duc de Berry dining, from the *Très riches heures of the duc de Berry* (fol. 1v), illuminated by the Limbourg Brothers, 1411–16. Detail showing a golden nef on the table before the duke. Musée Condé, Chantilly. Photo © RMN-Grand Palais (domaine de Chantilly) / René-Gabriel Ojéda. 28

3.2 *Das Goldene Rössl* (The golden horse reliquary), Paris, 1404. Gold, enamel, precious stones and pearls. Schatzkammer und Wallfahrtsmuseum, Altötting. Photo © imageBROKER / Alamy Stock Photo. 29

3.3 The French Royal Gold Cup, France, c. 1370–80. Gold, enamel and pearls. British Museum, London. Photo © The Trustees of the British Museum. 30

3.3a Detail of the French Royal Gold Cup, showing the martyrdom of St Agnes. British Museum, London. Photo © The Trustees of the British Museum. 31

4.1 Detail of Henry VIII's crown and sceptre from *King Charles I*, Daniel Mytens, 1631. National Portrait Gallery, London. Photo © National Portrait Gallery, London. 42

4.2 Henry VIII processing to the opening of Parliament in 1512. British Library (Add. MS 22306, section 6). Photo © British Library Board. 43

4.3 Henry VIII entering the lists, from the *Westminster Tournament Roll*, 1511. College of Arms. Reproduced by kind permission of the Kings, Heralds and Pursuivants of Arms. 46

4.4 The Beaufort beaker, London, 1507–08. Silver gilt. Christ's College, Cambridge. Reproduced by kind permission of the Master and Fellows of Christ's College, Cambridge. 56

4.5 One of three Beaufort salts, London, 1507–08. Silver gilt. Christ's College, Cambridge. Reproduced by kind permission of the Master and Fellows of Christ's College, Cambridge. 56

4.6 The Founder's cup, London, 1515–16. Silver gilt. Corpus Christi College, Oxford. By permission of the President and Fellows of Corpus Christi College, Oxford. Image © Ashmolean Museum, University of Oxford. 57

4.7 Pair of pots chased with feathers, London, 1660–61, attributed to James Beacham. Silver gilt. Royal Collection (Jewel House, Tower of London). Photo Royal Collection Trust / © Her Majesty Queen Elizabeth II 2019. 57

4.8 The San Lorenzo vase, London, 1511–12, maker's mark a cross. Silver gilt and enamel. Church of San Lorenzo, Florence. Photo © Timothy Schroder. 58

4.8a Detail of the marks on the San Lorenzo vase. Photo © Timothy Schroder. 59

4.8b Detail of putto on the San Lorenzo vase. Photo © Timothy Schroder. 60

4.8c Detail of enamelled roses on the San Lorenzo vase. Photo © Timothy Schroder. 60

4.9 Case to the Barbers' instrument box. Leather. Worshipful Company of Barbers, London. Photo © Timothy Schroder. 61

5.1 *Archbishop William Warham*, after Hans Holbein the younger, early seventeenth-century copy of a work of 1527. National Portrait Gallery, London. Photo © National Portrait Gallery, London. 65

5.2 Cope of cloth of gold embroidered with Tudor roses, crowned portcullises and a collar of esses, bequeathed by Henry VII to Westminster Abbey, c. 1510. Stonyhurst Abbey. Photo © Victoria and Albert Museum, London. Reproduced by kind permission of the Jesuits in Britain. 66

5.3 Image from the *Hallesches Heiltumbuch* (MS 14, fol. 2v) of the papal golden rose given to Cardinal Albrecht of Brandenburg, c. 1523, Hofbibliothek Aschaffenburg. 69

5.4 Sword of state with scabbard from the Honours of Scotland, Rome, early sixteenth century. Silver-gilt handle and scabbard. Historic Scotland. Photo © Crown Copyright reproduced courtesy of Historic Scotland. 70

5.5 Monstrance, early sixteenth century (the foot an early twentieth-century restoration), traditionally said to have been given by Henry VIII to the basilica of St Martin, Halle, near Brussels. Silver, parcel gilt. Basilica of St Martin, Halle. Photo © KIK-IRPA, Brussels. 76

5.6 Bishop Fox's chalice and paten, London, 1507–08, maker's mark a fleur de lis. Gold and enamel. Corpus Christi College, Oxford. By permission of the President and Fellows of Corpus Christi College, Oxford. Image © Ashmolean Museum, University of Oxford. 77

5.7 Virgin and child, southern Germany, 1486. Silver, parcel gilt, enamel and precious stones. Kimbell Art Museum, Fort Worth,

Texas. Photo © 2019. Kimbell Art Museum, Fort Worth, Texas / Art Resource, NY / Scala, Florence. 78

5.8 Diagram of arrangements for Prince Edward's christening in 1537, showing the silver font beneath a canopy. College of Arms, London (MS 6, fol. 82v). Reproduced by kind permission of the Kings, Heralds and Pursuivants of Arms. 82

6.1 *Banquet of Ahazuerius*, Antwerp or Bruges, c. 1520. Tapestry. Showing dishes of food being carried in, a jewelled covered cup being prepared for the king (at centre foreground), wine being diluted (to the right), and a buffet of plate and musicians playing (to right and left). Museo de Tapices de la Seo, Zaragossa Cathedral. 86

6.2 Six dishes in five sizes from the Armada service, London, 1600–01, maker's mark TE. Silver, parcel gilt. British Museum, London. Photo © The Trustees of the British Museum. 89

6.3 The huntsman salt, England, late fifteenth century. Silver gilt, rock-crystal and enamel. All Souls College, Oxford. Photo courtesy of the Warden and Fellows of All Souls College, Oxford. Image © Ashmolean Museum, University of Oxford. 90

6.4 Bishop Fox's ablution basin, London, 1514–15. Silver gilt and enamel. Corpus Christi College, Oxford. Image © Ashmolean Museum, University of Oxford. 93

6.4a Detail of spout beneath the brim of Bishop Fox's ablution basin. Corpus Christi College, Oxford. Image © Ashmolean Museum, University of Oxford. 93

6.5 One of a pair of pots with wild men finials and dragon handles, probably Nuremberg, late fifteenth century. Silver gilt and cold enamel. Metropolitan Museum of Art, New York. 95

6.6 Spice plate, London, 1532–33, maker's mark a cup. Silver, parcel gilt. Collection of the Goldsmiths' Company, London. Photo © The Goldsmiths' Company. 96

6.7 Spice plate with Saints Jerome and Andrew, Hinrich Grabow, Luneburg, c. 1515–20. Silver, parcel gilt and enamel. Kunstgewerbemuseum, Berlin. Photo © bpk-Bildagentur / Photographer: Karen Bartsch. 97

6.8 Flagon or bottle, Noël Delacroix, Paris, 1581–82. Silver gilt. Musée du Louvre, Paris. Photo © RMN-Grand Palais (musée du Louvre) / image RMN-GP. 103

6.9 *Henry VIII dining in his privy chamber*, school of Hans Holbein the younger, c. 1548. British Museum, London. Photo © The Trustees of the British Museum. 108

7.1 Image from the *Hallesches Heiltumbuch* (MS 14, fol. 7) of a jewelled reliquary cross from the treasure of Cardinal Albrecht of Brandenburg, c. 1523. Hofbibliothek Aschaffenburg. 113

7.2 A royal tent with a buffet of plate, from *The Story of King David*, Brussels, c. 1520. Tapestry. Musée de la Renaissance, Ecouen. Photo © RMN-Grand Palais (Musée de la Renaissance, château d'Ecouen) / Gérard Blot. 115

7.3 *The Marriage of Louis XII and Mary Tudor*, Tournai, c. 1525. Tapestry. Hever Castle, Kent. Photo reproduced by kind permission of Hever Castle & Gardens. 129

8.1 *Cardinal Thomas Wolsey*, Sampson Strong, 1610–11. Christ Church, University of Oxford (Accession number LP 11). Reproduced by permission of The Governing Body of Christ Church, Oxford. 131

8.2 Arms of Cardinal Wolsey from *Prince Arthur's Book*. College of Arms (MS Vincent 152, p. 93). Reproduced by kind permission of the Kings, Heralds and Pursuivants of Arms. 136

8.3 Wolsey's entourage setting out to Westminster, from a copy of George Cavendish's *Life of Wolsey*. Bodleian Library (MS Douce 363, fol. 52v). Photo © Bodleian Libraries, University of Oxford. 138

8.4 Bronze angel originally designed for the tomb of Cardinal Wolsey, Benedetto da Rovezzano, London, 1524–29. Victoria and Albert Museum, London. Image © Victoria and Albert Museum, London. 141

8.5 Plaster cast of the arms of Cardinal Wolsey, taken from the original, of terracotta, at Hampton Court Palace. Victoria and Albert Museum, London. Image © Victoria and Albert Museum, London. 145

8.6 The setting out of Wolsey's plate, from a copy of George Cavendish's *Life of Wolsey*. Bodleian Library (MS Douce 363, fol. 71). Photo © Bodleian Libraries, University of Oxford. 147

9.1 *The Field of Cloth of Gold*, British school, c. 1545. Hampton Court Palace. Royal Collection. Photo Royal Collection Trust / © Her Majesty Queen Elizabeth II 2019. 157

9.2 Designs for royal tents, possibly for the Field of Cloth of Gold, early sixteenth century. British Library (MS Cotton Augustus III, f. 18). Photo © British Library Board. 158

9.3 The St Michael cup, Josse Vezeler, Antwerp, 1532. Gold, enamel, pearls and precious stones. Kunsthistorisches Museum, Vienna. Photo © KHM-Museumsverband. 168

9.4 Design for a silver ewer, Enea Vico, 1533. Engraving. Private collection. 169

9.5 The Royal Clock Salt, attributed to Pierre Mangot, Paris or Blois, c. 1530. Silver gilt, glass clockwork, shell, enamel, agate, pearls and precious stones. Collection of the Goldsmiths' Company, London. Photo © The Goldsmiths' Company. 171

9.6 Francis I's book of hours, the cover of gold, enamel and precious stones, with a cornelian intaglio, Paris, 1532. Musée du Louvre, Paris. Photo © S. J. Phillips Ltd. 173

10.1 The Howard Grace Cup, London, 1525–26. Ivory, silver gilt, pearls and precious stones. Victoria and Albert Museum, London. Image © Victoria and Albert Museum, London. 176

10.2 Instrument case, perhaps given by Henry VIII to Thomas Vicary, serjeant-surgeon to the royal household and master of the Barbers' Company. England, c. 1530. Silver, parcel gilt and enamel. Collection of the Barbers' Company, London. Photo © Grant MacDonald. 177

10.2a Reverse of the Barbers' instrument case showing engraving of the murder of Thomas Becket. Collection of the Barbers' Company, London. Photo © Grant MacDonald. 177

10.3 Bronze candlestick with the arms and supporters of Henry VIII, England, c. 1525–30. Saint-Bavo's Cathedral, Ghent. Image: www.lukasweb.be–Art in Flanders, photo Hugo Maertens. 180

10.3a Detail of bronze candlestick, showing the arms and supporters of Henry VIII, England, c. 1525–30. Saint-Bavo's Cathedral, Ghent. Image: www.lukasweb.be–Art in Flanders, photo Hugo Maertens. 180

10.3b Detail of bronze candlestick, showing decorative mask, England, c. 1525–30. Saint-Bavo's Cathedral, Ghent. Image: www.lukasweb.be–Art in Flanders, photo Hugo Maertens. 180

10.4 Self-portrait medal, Michael Mercator, England, 1539. Silver. British Museum, London (M.6793). Photo © The Trustees of the British Museum. 183

10.5 Henry VIII's seal attached to the French copy of the Treaty of Amiens, probably designed by Hans Holbein the younger, 1527. Gold. Archives National, Paris. Photo © RMN-Grand Palais / Agence Bulloz. 185

10.6 Francis I's seal attached to the English copy of the Treaty of Amiens, France, 1527. Gold. The National Archives, London. Photo © The National Archives London. 185

10.7 Detail of *The Holy Family with Saint Elizabeth, the Infant Saint John the Baptist and Two Angels*, showing a golden crib comparable to one decorated by Holbein, southern Netherlands, c. 1520–30. Bilbao Fine Arts Museum, Bilbao. Photo © Bilboko Arte Ederren Museoa-Museo de Bellas Artes de Bilbao. 187

10.8 Design for the stem of a cup, Hans Holbein the younger, c. 1530–35. Drawing on paper. British Museum, London. Photo © The Trustees of the British Museum. 189

10.9 Design for elements of a silver vessel, Hans Holbein the younger, c. 1530–35. Drawing on paper. British Museum, London. Photo © The Trustees of the British Museum. 189

10.10 Design for a silver jug, Wenceslaus Hollar after Hans Holbein the younger, c. 1645. Engraving after an original of c. 1530–35. Victoria and Albert Museum, London. Image © Victoria and Albert Museum, London. 190

10.11 Design for a silver cup inscribed 'HANS VON ANT', Hans Holbein the younger, perhaps c. 1537. Drawing on paper. Kunstmuseum, Basel. Inv. 1662.165.104. 191

10.12 Design for a shallow cup or spice plate, Hans Holbein the younger, perhaps c. 1530–35. Drawing on paper. Kunstmuseum, Basel. Inv. 1662.165.102. 192

10.13 Design for a centrepiece or fountain, Hans Holbein the younger, c. 1533. Drawing on paper. Kunstmuseum, Basel. Inv. 1662.165.99. 193

10.14 Design for a fountain, Hans Holbein the younger, c. 1533. Drawing on paper. Kunstmuseum, Basel. Inv. 1662.165.89. 194

10.15 Design for the Seymour cup, Hans Holbein the younger, 1536. Drawing on paper. Ashmolean Museum, Oxford. Image © Ashmolean Museum, University of Oxford. 196

10.16 Design for a jewelled gold cup, Hans Holbein the younger, c. 1530–35. Drawing on paper. Kunstmuseum, Basel. Inv. 1924.64. 197

10.17 Design for a timepiece, Sir Anthony Denny's new year's gift to the king in 1545, Hans Holbein the younger, 1543. British Museum, London. Photo © The Trustees of the British Museum. 199

10.18 Design for the foot of a mounted glass, Wenceslaus Hollar after Hans Holbein the younger, c. 1645. Engraving after an original of c. 1540. Metropolitan Museum of Art, New York. 200

10.19 Design for a girdle prayer book, probably for Thomas and Jane Wyatt, Hans Holbein the younger, c. 1534–43. British Museum, London. Photo © The Trustees of the British Museum. 200

10.20 Girdle prayer book, with the judgement of Solomon and Moses and the brazen serpent, attributed to Hans of Antwerp, London, c. 1540. Gold and enamel. British Museum, London. Photo © The Trustees of the British Museum. 201

11.1 The Boleyn Cup, London, 1535–36, maker's mark three flowers. The finial formed as Anne Boleyn's personal badge, a falcon standing on a tree stump. Silver gilt. Church of St John the Baptist, Cirencester. Photo © Woodmansterne /Topfoto. 220

11.2 Design for a cup, from Hans Brosamer's *Neu Kunst-Büchlein*, c. 1530. Woodcut. Private collection. 221

11.3 *Jane Seymour*, Hans Holbein the younger, 1536–37. Kunsthistorisches Museum, Vienna. Photo © KMH-Museumsverband. 223

11.4 Letter from Henry Fitzroy, duke of Richmond, to Henry VIII thanking the king for a new year's gift in 1527. The National Archives (SP 1/40, fol. 207). Photo © The National Archives. 226

12.1 A folio from the 1532 jewel house inventory, detailing 'Layers, ewers and basones of golde'. National Archives (E 36/85, fol. 15). Photo © The National Archives. 230

12.2 *Thomas Cromwell*, after Hans Holbein the younger, early seventeenth century copy of a work of 1532–33 now in the Frick Collection. The National Portrait Gallery, London. Photo © National Portrait Gallery, London. 233

12.3 Cruse, London, 1533–34, maker's mark an arbalist (crossbow). Silver gilt. Corpus Christi College, Oxford. By permission of the President and Fellows of Corpus Christi College, Oxford. Image © Ashmolean Museum, University of Oxford. 238

12.4 *Henry VIII*, Hans Holbein the younger, c. 1537. Museo Nacional Thyssen-Bornemisza, Madrid. Photo © 2019. Museo Nacional Thyssen-Bornemisza / Scala, Florence. 239

12.5 Mary I blessing cramp rings, from a manuscript bound into a prayer book of c. 1550. Westminster Cathedral Treasury (Manuscript TMS 8, fol. 3v). Reproduced by kind permission of The Administrator, Roman Catholic Cathedral of Westminster. 241

12.6 *Robert Trappes, Alderman*, unknown artist, 1554. Collection of the Goldsmiths' Company, London. Photo © The Goldsmiths' Company. 242

12.7 Water pot, London, 1604–05, maker's mark of William Jefferies, possibly a copy of one of about 1530. Silver gilt. Kremlin Armoury Museum, Moscow. Photo © State Historical and Cultural Museum-Preserve, The Moscow Kremlin, 2020. Photographer: Baranov S.V. 244

12.8 Engraving of the impression of Henry VIII's third great seal, made by Morgan Wolf in 1542. Illustration for *The Pictorial History of England* (W. & R. Chambers, 1858). Photo © Look and Learn. 245

12.9 Gold sovereign, London, 1485–90. British Museum, London. Photo © The Trustees of the British Museum. 251

12.10 Map of London, Georg Braun and Frans Hogenberg, 1572. Engraving. British Library (Maps Crace Port.1.12). Photo © British Library Board. 254

12.11 *Sir Martin Bowes*, unknown artist, 1566. Collection of the Goldsmiths' Company, London. 256

12.12 London hallmarks for 1545–46, showing the crowned lion passant, taken from a standing cup in the collection of the Goldsmiths' Company, London. 258

13.1 The Dolgellau chalice and paten, probably Hereford, 1230–50, signed by Nicholas of Hereford. Silver gilt. Royal Collection, on loan to the National Museum of Wales, Cardiff. Photo Royal Collection Trust / © Her Majesty Queen Elizabeth II 2019. 266

13.2 The Ramsey Abbey censer, London or East Anglia, c. 1325. Silver gilt. Victoria and Albert Museum, London. Image © Victoria and Albert Museum, London. 267

13.3 The Ramsey Abbey incense boat, London or East Anglia, c. 1325. Silver gilt. Victoria and Albert Museum, London. Image © Victoria and Albert Museum, London. 267

13.4 Illumination of Henry VI praying at the shrine of St Edmund, late fifteenth century. British Library (Harley 2278, f. 4v). Photo © British Library Board. 270

13.5 The tower of Elsyng Spital, part of an Augustinian hospital and priory until 1536 and subsequently part of the home of John Williams, master of the jewel house. Author's photo. 273

13.6 *Mass of St Giles*, Master of St Giles, c. 1500. National Gallery, London. Photo © National Gallery, London. NG4681. 276

14.1 *King Henry VIII*, unknown artist, early seventeenth century after a work of c. 1542. National Portrait Gallery, London. Photo © National Portrait Gallery, London. 282

14.2 Drawing of a jewel offered for sale to Henry VIII and enclosed in a letter from Stephen Vaughan written at Antwerp in 1545. National Archives (SP 1/213 fol. 167). Photo © National Archives. 285

14.3 Watercolour of the Three Brothers jewel. Historisches Museum, Basel. Photo: P. Portner. 287

14.4 The Barber-Surgeons' Cup, London, 1543–44, maker's mark illegible. Silver gilt. Collection of the Barbers' Company, London. Photo © Timothy Schroder. 289

14.4a Cover of the Barber-Surgeons' Cup, London, 1543–44, maker's mark illegible. Silver gilt. Collection of the Barbers' Company, London. Photo © Timothy Schroder. 289

14.5 The Mildmay Bowl, Antwerp, 1541–42. Silver gilt. Emmanuel College, Cambridge. Photo reproduced by permission of the Master and Fellows of Emmanuel College, Cambridge. 291

14.6 Design for a ewer, Cornelis Floris, Antwerp, c. 1540. Engraving. Private collection. 292

14.7 Detail from *The Return of Sarah by the Egyptians* from *The Story of Abraham* series, attributed to Pieter Coeck van Aelst and Wilhelm Pannemaker, Brussels, c. 1540. Tapestry. Hampton Court Palace. Royal Collection. Photo Royal Collection Trust / © Her Majesty Queen Elizabeth II 2019. 293

14.8 Detail from *The Meeting of Abraham and Melchizidek* from *The Story of Abraham* series, attributed to Pieter Coeck van Aelst and Wilhelm Pannemaker, Brussels, c. 1540. Tapestry. Hampton Court Palace. Royal Collection. Photo Royal Collection Trust / © Her Majesty Queen Elizabeth II 2019. 293

14.9 The 'Holbein bowl', possibly southern Germany, c. 1545. Gold, rock crystal, enamel, pearls and precious stones. Schatzkammer der Residenz, Munich. Photo © Bayerische Schlösserverwaltung, Maria Scherf / Rainer Herrmann, Munich. 296

14.9a View of the inside of the 'Holbein bowl'. Photo Timothy Schroder, © Bayerische Schlösserverwaltung. 296

14.9b Detail of the central disc inside the 'Holbein bowl'. Photo Timothy Schroder, © Bayerische Schlösserverwaltung. 296

14.9c Cover of the 'Holbein bowl'. Photo © Bayerische Schlösserverwaltung, Maria Scherf / Rainer Herrmann, Munich. 297

14.9d Underside of the lid of the 'Holbein bowl'. Photo © Bayerische Schlösserverwaltung, Maria Scherf / Rainer Herrmann, Munich. 297

14.10 *Still Life*, Willem Kalf, 1678. National Gallery of Denmark, Copenhagen. 298

14.11 Coffer, Pierre Mangot, Paris, 1532–33. Silver gilt, mother of pearl and precious stones. Musée du Louvre, Paris. Photo © RMN-Grand Palais (musée du Louvre) / Michèle Bellot. 307

14.12 The Burghley nef, Paris, 1527–28. Silver gilt, nautilus shell and pearls. Victoria and Albert Museum, London. Image © Victoria and Albert Museum, London. 308

14.13 *Kunstkammer of the Dimpfel Family of Regensburg*, Joseph Arnold, 1668. Museum Ulm (1952.2611). Image © Museum Ulm. 313

Graphs

4.1 Approximate total expenditure on plate, jewels and cloth of gold during the period of the Chamber books, 1492–1521. 49

4.2 Royal goldsmiths during the period of the Chamber books, 1492–1521. 51

Plans

6.1 Speculative reconstruction of the buffet of plate at Westminster Hall in 1501 (not to scale). 102

6.2 Reconstruction of the plan for the Garter banquet at Windsor, May 1519. 106

Acknowledgements

This project has had a long gestation and has accrued many debts.

First of all, to my wife, Ellen, who has been constantly supportive and tolerant and who has even read the manuscript.

Dr David Starkey has been hugely encouraging from an early stage. He made frequent but ultimately only partly successful attempts to transform me from a historian of objects into a more general one. He read much of an early draft of the book, making many constructive suggestions concerning structure and detail. The book has been significantly improved as a result, even though its many remaining shortcomings are, of course, entirely my own.

Others who have read the entire text or large parts of it and have offered valuable criticism or asked perspicacious questions are Christopher Gayford, Professor Diarmaid Macculloch, Malcolm Oxley and Dr Dora Thornton. Martin Allen (Fitzwilliam Museum, Cambridge), Ivan Day, Professor Maria Hayward (Southampton University), Olenka Horbasch (British Museum), Professor Glenn Richardson (St Mary's University) and Professor Robert Turner have all read specific chapters. I am hugely indebted to them all and I would also like to record my thanks to the anonymous peer reviewer who read and commented on the entire final draft.

Special thanks go to my Research Assistant, Dr Charlotte Berry, who was involved with the project for a year and a half and whose contribution was transformative. Dr Berry is quicker and more accurate in her reading of sixteenth-century documents than I and was hugely efficient in providing transcriptions, chasing references and carrying out micro-research on whatever random queries I threw at her. She also undertook the necessary but joyless task of processing all the licences for the illustrations.

Dr Berry in turn triggers two other debts: to Dr Mark Merry (formerly of the Institute of Historical Research) for introducing us, and to the Goldsmiths' Company for generously funding her position. At the

Company I am especially grateful to the Wardens, to Sir David Reddaway, Clerk and Chief Executive, and to Eleni Bide, the Librarian.

I am further indebted to the Company and to the Silver Society for grants towards the costs of publication.

Friends and colleagues who have made other significant contributions are as follows: Raphael Beuing (Bayesches Nationalmuseum, Munich), Michèle Bimbenet-Privat (Musée du Louvre), Professor Eamon Duffy (University of Cambridge), Richard Edgecumbe (Victoria and Albert Museum), Philippa Glanville, Philip Hardie (University of Cambridge), Sabine Heym (Residenz Museum, Munich), Lisa Jefferson, Hanspeter Lans, David Mitchell, Lucy Morton, Dr Lorenz Seelig, Naomi Speakman (British Museum), Victoria West (Barbers' Company), Professor Timothy Wilson and Michael Winterbottom (Ashmolean Museum, Oxford).

At Boydell & Brewer, I am particularly grateful to Dr Michael Middeke. Also to Elizabeth Howard and Bonnie McGill.

Abbreviations

BL	British Library, London
BNF	Bibliothèque Nationale de France, Paris
Chamber Books	M. M. Condon, S. P. Harper, L. Liddy, and S. Cunningham and J. Ross, eds, *The Chamber Books of Henry VII and Henry VIII, 1485–1521*, http://www.tudorchamberbooks.org
CSP, Milan	Allen Hinds, ed., *Calendar of State Papers and Manuscripts in the Archives and Collections of Milan* (London, 1912)
CSP, Spain	G. A. Bergenroth, P. de Gayangos, M. A. S. Hume and R. Tyler, eds, *Calendar of State Papers, Spain*, 16 vols (London, 1862–99)
CSP, Venetian	Rawdon Brown, G. Cavendish Bentinck, Horatio F. Brown and Allen B. Hind, eds, *Calendar of State Papers Relating to English Affairs in the Archives of Venice*, 38 vols (London, 1864–1947)
Four Years at the Court	Rawdon Brown, ed. and trans., *Four Years at the Court of Henry VIII: Selection of Despatches Written by the Venetian Ambassador, Sebastian Giustinian, and Addressed to the Signory of Venice, January 12th 1515, to July 26th 1519*, 2 vols (London, 1854)
GC	Goldsmiths' Company, London
Great Chronicle of London	A. H. Thomas and I. D. Thornley, eds, *The Great Chronicle of London* (London, 1938)
Hall, *King Henry VIII*	Edward Hall, *King Henry VIII*, 2 vols, ed. Charles Whibley (London, 1904)
Inventory of Henry VIII	David Starkey, ed., *The Inventory of King Henry VIII: Society of Antiquaries MS 129 and British Library MS Harley 1419*, vol. 1 (London, 1998)

LP	J. S. Brewer and J. Gairdner, eds, *Letters and Papers, Foreign and Domestic, of Henry VIII*, 21 vols (1862–1920)
ODNB	*Oxford Dictionary of National Biography*
OED	*Oxford English Dictionary*
TNA	The National Archives of the United Kingdom, London
Trollope, 'King Henry VIII's Jewel Book'	Edward Trollope, 'King Henry VIII's Jewel Book', *Lincolnshire Diocesan Architectural Society*, 17, 2 (1883–84), pp. 155–229

Glossary

The author acknowledges drawing on the glossary of *The Crown Jewels: The History of the Coronation Regalia*, ed. Claude Blair (London, 1998) for some of the following definitions.

Aglette Decorated metal loops of tags worn as ornament on dress or on caps, often enamelled or set with stones or pearls.

Antique A range of ornament derived from classical antiquity.

Armill A ceremonial bracelet or armlet, often supplied in pairs, with one for each arm.

Assay A test. The term is principally used in this book in two senses, the testing of food or drink for poison, and the testing of gold and silver to ascertain that the alloys were of the correct legal standard.

Attainder A charge of treason carrying the death penalty and forfeiture of all goods and assets to the Crown.

Arras The finest and costliest type of tapestry, often embroidered with gold or silver thread.

Balase (or balas) ruby A red spinel, a gemstone found in Badakhshan, in what is now Afghanistan.

Bard A protective covering for the breast and flanks of a war-horse, made of metal plates, or of leather set with metal spikes or bosses, but sometimes (e.g. in tournaments) merely ornamental, and made of velvet or other rich stuff [*OED*].

Billet A short horizontal bar forming part of the thumbpiece to a pot cover.

Birral, beryl In Tudor documents the term is used promiscuously, referring usually to a transparent precious stone of various pale colours, but occasionally as an alternative term for rock crystal or fine glass.

Border Stones and pearls set in goldsmiths' work and sewn onto strips of fabric for stitching onto clothes.

Buffet of plate A tiered wooden structure, usually covered with carpet and damask cloth, for the display of plate.

Caparison An elaborate horse's harness.

Cabochon A stone cut with a smooth rounded top, with no facets, and highly polished.

Carbuncle A large precious stone of a red or fiery colour: in early use of unsettled identity, as a ruby, garnet, spinel, etc. [*OED*].

Censer A vessel for burning and wafting smoke from incense, usually with cup-like lower section and pierced cover of architectural form, suspended and swung from chains.

Chalice The vessel used for dispensing communion wine during the mass.

Chrism Chrism has two meanings, first, a compound of oil and balsam used in ordination and, in combination with holy oil, in the coronation; and secondly, a shawl of luxurious fabric in which a baby was wrapped during its christening.

Counterfeit An imitation precious stone, usually of rock crystal or glass and with a coloured foil backing to resemble a precious stone. Counterfeits in the sixteenth century were intended to impress but not necessarily to deceive.

Courser A large powerful horse, used on the battlefield or at tournaments.

Cruet One of a pair of covered vessels, in the form of miniature pots or ewers, one containing communion wine and the other water. Often distinguished from each other by initials V (vino) and A (aqua).

Crupper A leather strap buckled to the back of a horse's saddle and passing under its tail, to prevent the saddle slipping forwards. In Tudor tournaments the crupper was often a large decorative feature.

Cruse A small two-handled drinking cup, generally with a cover.

Curious Elaborately decorated.

Dentil In classical architecture, a row of spaced rectangular blocks forming part of an entablature. By extension, on plate, a distinctive decorative feature forming part of a moulding.

Denizen One who lives habitually in a country but is not a native-born citizen; an alien admitted to citizenship by royal letters patent, but incapable of holding public office [*OED*].

Ear A ring handle.

Ell A measure of length, varying from country to country. In England an ell was equivalent to 45 inches.

Fleur de lis, flower de luce A heraldic lily.

Gadroon A decorative motif formed of close-set rounded ribs; the reverse of fluting.

Gorget A piece of armour to protect the throat.

Grotesque A kind of decorative painting or sculpture, consisting of representations of portions of human and animal forms, fantastically combined and interwoven with foliage and flowers [*OED*].

Guilloche In architecture, a pattern of interlacing bands forming a plait and used as an enrichment on a moulding.

Hallmark The marks struck on plate at Goldsmiths' Hall to indicate that a gold or silver object had been assayed and found to be of the correct legal standard. During the early sixteenth century three marks were used: the leopard's head (indicating the correct standard); the maker's – or master's – mark (identifying the goldsmith who had presented it for assay); and the date letter (showing the year in which it was marked). The date letter was changed each year on St Dunstan's day, in May, so any given date letter staggers two calendar years. In 1544 a fourth mark was introduced, a lion passant (see p. 258).

Hippocras Wine flavoured with spices, generally sweet.

Image In sixteenth-century documents, normally a sculptural or painted representation of the human form, especially saints.

Incense boat A small vessel, often in the form of a miniature boat or ship, used to hold incense.

Knop A decorative bulbous moulding, usually placed at the mid-point of the stem of a chalice or cup; also used in sixteenth-century documents to mean a finial.

Layer A kind of decorated ewer.

Livery The distinctive dress or uniform worn by a royal or noble servant or a member of one of the trade guilds of London. The term has many extensions: livery can refer also to an item of such uniform (such as a livery badge) or even to a distinctive colour scheme (such as the Tudor livery colours of white and green). In livery companies, 'the livery' might also refer to the senior members of that company (as distinct from 'the freedom' or 'freemen').

Mark A weight (chiefly for gold and silver), the equivalent of eight ounces. In accounting terms, two-thirds of a pound or 13s 4d.

Monstrance A large object, often of architectural form, used to display the host or wafer, either on the altar or in procession.

Moresque Linear decoration of Islamic origin, composed of scrolling stylised foliage.

Owche A brooch, generally used as a fastening as well as an ornament.

Parcel gilt Partly gilded (see Silver gilt).

Paten A small plate, usually paired with a chalice, used to distribute communion wafers during the mass.

Pattern In Tudor documents, usually signifying a design or model to be followed by a maker.

Pattern book A group of designs for objects or ornament, usually in the form of engravings or woodcuts.

Pax A small tablet with a religious scene or device, for exchanging the kiss of peace during the mass without physical contact. It was kissed in turn by those present.

Plate A generic term for wrought vessels and other objects made of gold or silver, derived from the Spanish word *plata*, meaning silver.

Pommel The shaped knob at the bottom of the hilt of a sword, serving as a counter-balance to the blade.

Prasinus A variety of quartz; dark or pale green jasper.

Pyx A small box, usually for containing the host. In a secondary sense the term refers specifically to the box that was used in the mint for sample coins of precious metal set aside for testing for correct purity at the 'Trial of the Pyx'.

Quillons The arms extending from the bottom of a sword or dagger hilt to protect the user's hand.

Rock crystal A clear and colourless quartz crystal.

Sallet In armour, a light headpiece, with or without a vizor.

Shapwe A chapeau, or war hat.

Silver gilt Silver applied with a thin layer of gold plating to the surface. The process involved mixing powdered or granulated gold with mercury, painting it onto the surface and then burning off the mercury in the fire, leaving the gold bonded to the surface.

Simar A robe or loose light garment worn across the breast.

Spangle A jewelled embellishment to clothing, usually sewn on and applied in large numbers.

Stranger In the sixteenth century, the term used for someone from another country (as distinct from a 'foreigner', who was someone from another part of England).

Strapwork A form of decoration resembling cut and curling strips of leather, invented for the decoration of Francis I's palace at Fontainebleau.

Table In gemmology, a stone cut from an octahedral stone by removing the points to leave a flat, square or rectangular surface at the top.

Tablet A rectangular panel supporting relief or two-dimensional imagery in metal or paint. The term is used in Tudor inventories and other documents quite inclusively and can sometimes mean diptychs or triptychs.

Tilt Part of a tournament; the combat between two horsemen armed with lances, riding towards each other at speed with the object of unhorsing the other.

Ton (tun) A barrel.

Touch Marks struck on a piece of plate, indicating its town of origin.

Trapper A defensive or decorative metal or leather covering for a horse.

Traverse A temporary enclosure, generally in a church and made of fabric covering a wooden frame, to provide the most important participants with privacy.

Trencher A plate for eating off. Of any material (Henry VIII had one of gold), but most commonly of wood.

Vessel Normally any hollow container, but in sixteenth-century inventories and documents generally used in the more restricted sense of plates, dishes, platters and saucers.

Note to the reader

Any study of plate based on documents will be full of numbers. These mostly relate to money, weights and purities of alloy. The following is a brief guide to help the reader through these often confusing units of measure.

English money is expressed in *pounds*, *shillings* and *pence*, but occasionally in *marks* as well. Before the decimal system (introduced in 1971) the pound sterling was divided into 20 shillings and the shilling into 12 pennies (or pence). These units are abbreviated in documents to *L*, *s* and *d* (for *libra*, *solidus* and *denarius*, the notionally equivalent units of ancient Roman coinage). The penny could be broken into fractions of a half (ha'penny) or a quarter (farthing). There were gold or silver coins corresponding to these units or fractions thereof (such as the groat, which was worth 4d or a third of a shilling). The mark was a unit of account rather than a coin and equalled two-thirds of a pound or 13s 4d.

Foreign currencies are often mentioned too. The most frequently encountered are the *ducat* (mainly used in Italy, Spain and the Holy Roman Empire) and the *crown* (in France). Exchange rates fluctuated but as a broad rule of thumb, for most of Henry VIII's reign the crown and ducat were of similar value and worth between 4s and 5s or between a fifth and a quarter of a pound. In 1525, for example, the ducat was exchanged at 4s 6d, making 800 ducats worth £180.

Inventory clerks and others compiling records of plate tended to keep scrupulous records of weight because weight related directly to value. In England precious metals and gemstones were usually weighed in troy measure. The *troy pound* (as distinct from the avoirdupois pound which was used for other commodities and was slightly heavier) was divided into *ounces*, *pennyweights* and *grains*. There are 12 troy ounces to a troy pound, 20 pennyweights to an ounce and 24 grains to a pennyweight. Weights in inventories and goldsmiths' bills are normally expressed in ounces (*oz*) and pennyweights (*dwt*). A troy ounce is the equivalent of about 30 grams, and a kilogram is a little over 32 ounces. Occasionally plate is weighed in *marks*, a unit that related to the troy pound as the monetary mark does to the monetary pound: it equated to about 8 ounces or two-thirds of a pound. Inventories and goldsmiths' bills express weights as precisely as possible and often in fractions of ounces, such as 'xix oz di' (19½ oz) or 'ij oz iij quarters di' (2 oz ¾ and a half, or 2⅚ oz). In most cases, I have rounded weights to the nearest ounce.

The other essential quotient for plate was the purity of its alloy. Throughout the period of this book (and long before and after too) the legal standard for silver plate in England was sterling, or 92.5 per cent silver mixed with 7.5 per cent base metal. Apart from a brief period, this was the same standard as the coinage. The relationship between gold plate and coinage was more complicated but for plate the required standard was 18 carat or 75 per cent pure. The term 'crown gold' refers to 22 carat, named after the crown coin that was introduced in 1526.

With occasional exceptions I have modernised spelling in quotations. In addition, the original documents are almost devoid of punctuation, sometimes obscuring meaning. Where it is helpful to do so, I have occasionally inserted punctuation.

Preface

The seeds that led to this book were planted long ago. In the autumn of 1994 I went to a small exhibition about Lorenzo de' Medici at the Accademia Italiana in London. I might well have missed it. Its opening hours were not ideal and the reviews had not been compelling, but I found myself passing and I popped in.

It turned out that I recognised many of the objects from existing publications, but one always looks with new eyes when seeing familiar objects 'in the flesh' for the first time. Among the exhibits was a silver-gilt mounted and enamelled rock-crystal reliquary that was labelled 'Italian, probably Siena, c. 1490'. My first thought on peering at it in the showcase was that the mounts did not look obviously Italian. I wondered if it might in fact have been made north of the Alps and maybe a little later than the suggested date. And as I looked I spotted what appeared to be hallmarks of some sort on the cover. Had the piece been turned around the other way I would not have seen these and would probably have given it no further thought. But it occurred to me that it might, just might, be possible to identify the marks if one considered possibilities other than Italy. So I asked for permission to examine it.

Consent was eventually given and the piece was made available to me after the exhibition closed. I went along with my assistant, Lucy Morton, and we looked, first of all, at the marks. These were not easy to read as they were partly struck on an uneven surface. But it soon became clear that they were in fact those of London, with the date letter for 1511–12 and the maker's mark of a cross in a shield. I then turned to the enamelled decoration and realised that it comprised red and white roses and pomegranates: Tudor royal badges and the personal badge of Katherine of Aragon. And it dawned on me that I was holding in my hands nothing other than a major piece of royal plate dating from the very start of the reign of Henry VIII. Not only that but, as I later discovered, possibly the only surviving piece of goldsmiths' work that we can be quite sure was made in England for the king.

Subsequent research towards my publication of the reliquary in *The Burlington Magazine* led me to explore an extraordinary wealth of documentation surrounding Henry VIII's now vanished accumulation of plate and jewels. A series of inventories from across the reign describe its quantum and character, lists of payments show what it cost and dispatches by foreign ambassadors give vivid accounts of the impression it made on contemporaries.

As I worked through these sources it gradually became clear to me what a remarkable story there was to be told of plate at this most colourful of royal courts. Nearly all of this splendour has disappeared; indeed, it had mostly disappeared within decades of the king's death. We cannot recreate this lost world, but we can at least evoke an idea of the impression it made and the role that it played.

This is an important subject and overlooking it simply because the material no longer exists skews our understanding of early Tudor court culture. Yet that is exactly what most historians, novelists and film directors have done. Few acknowledge its crucial role in projecting a sense of royal wealth and power. Hilary Mantel's fictional evocations of Henry's court only hint at it; and the widely praised 'authentic interiors' of the BBC adaptation of the same novels contained virtually no plate (or none that looked plausibly sixteenth-century anyway). Today we acknowledge the part played by tapestries, princely armour and palaces in promoting the Tudor regime; we also recognise the importance of pageants, tournaments and other 'performances', so how can we not take account of the vast displays of gold and silver that contemporaries found so striking?

This book attempts to put the record straight. It is primarily about plate, but gold and silver reached deep into the fabric of court life and it is not easy to know where to draw the line. There is an obvious affinity between plate and jewellery, in that precious stones were set in gold, while gold cups and other wares were often enriched with gems; whole walls were hung with cloth of gold on which enormous sums were spent, and clothes were embroidered with gold thread and stitched with jewels set in gold. So gold and silver had a much broader profile than just plate.

The following chapters paint a picture of this many-layered phenomenon, how it worked and why it mattered. But they also ask questions. Perhaps the most important of these is why princes (for Henry VIII was not alone) spent such prodigious sums on these materials. And the answer, as will emerge, is not that they were reckless or profligate (though it is true that they were not always prudent); it is because they had a different world view, one that actively required such expenditure and that is summed up in a single word, 'magnificence'.

One

Magnificence and Princely Virtue

We were conducted to the presence, through sundry chambers all hung with most beautiful tapestry, figured in gold and silver and in silk, passing down the ranks of the body-guard, which consists of three hundred halberdiers in silver breast-plates and pikes in their hands [...] We at length reached the King, who was under a canopy of cloth of gold, embroidered at Florence, the most costly thing I ever witnessed: he was leaning against his gilt throne, on which was a large gold brocade cushion, where the long gold sword of state lay [...] Very close round his neck he had a gold collar, from which there hung a round cut diamond, the size of the largest walnut I ever saw, and to this was suspended a most beautiful and very large round pearl. Beneath the mantle he had a pouch of cloth of gold, which covered a dagger; and his fingers were one mass of jewelled rings.

Piero Pasqualigo, 1515[1]

One of the treasures of the Musée de la Renaissance at Ecouen is a set of tapestries depicting the *Story of King David*. Woven in Brussels during the 1520s, this is among the most remarkable surviving sets from the period and almost certainly belonged to Henry VIII.[2] The subject was important to Henry. David, the anointed of God, was the biblical figure with whom he most closely identified and in one of the illuminations in his 1540 psalter Henry is depicted playing the harp, surely a reference to David.

As with most medieval and Renaissance depictions of biblical subjects, the events in the tapestries are made more real by being set in the present. They are in effect a panorama of contemporary court life. The architecture is a fusion of late gothic and Renaissance styles, as it would have been at the time; the costumes are courtly and contemporary; and the armour is in the latest fashions. Among the many things about them that would have been familiar to a courtier of the time was the ubiquitous presence of gold and silver and the tapestries show goldsmiths' work in almost every scene: in buffets and dining wares, in shrines and altar plate, in gold chains,

Figure 1.1 David sending Uriah to the front (detail), from *The Story of King David*, Brussels, c. 1520. Tapestry. Showing the ubiquity of gold and silver at court: buffet of plate in background, regalia, jewelled armour, jewels and cloth of gold. Musée de la Renaissance, Ecouen.

Figure 1.2 Nathan reproaches David (detail), from *The Story of King David*, Brussels, c. 1520. Tapestry. Showing a procession of servants and nobles carrying plate into the royal presence: a covered cup, a cup of assay and a spice plate. Musée de la Renaissance, Ecouen.

collars and jewels, in clothes, cloth of gold, weapons and precious horse harnesses. The first tapestry shows the arc of the covenant being transported to Jerusalem. A large gilded and jewelled structure like a church, it is borne by four men; servants carry golden maces and staffs of office, courtiers wear hat badges and heavy gold chains. In others architectural and sculptural details are embellished with gold leaf. The tapestry with David sending Uriah to the front line (fig. 1.1) shows the king enthroned, wearing a jewelled gold collar and jewel-encrusted robes of cloth of gold; in the background is a buffet set with silver and silver-gilt vessels. The seventh tapestry, with the prophet Nathan reproaching David for his treatment of Uriah, shows a procession of magnificently dressed courtiers carrying in dining plate of gold or silver-gilt (fig. 1.2).

Away from the palace, the last two tapestries show the magnificence that incongruously accompanied the horrors of warfare. The one of King David after the siege of Rabah (fig. 7.2) depicts him as a contemporary ruler: he stands in full pomp before his tent, inside which is a handsome buffet of plate; his vanquished enemies kneel before him, surrendering crown, gold chains and plate. This was just the start of the harvest and the last tapestry shows David's general, Joab, directing the systematic looting of plate and jewels which his soldiers carry before him in great chests. War was as much about profit as about territory and honour.

Around the biblical narrative, the David tapestries and others like them show a series of court ceremonies and protocols that would in broad terms have been familiar throughout Europe. Underlying these is an appearance of super-abundant wealth that to modern sensibilities might seem excessive, even absurdly so. But although this was partly driven by princely competition (and none more so than that between Henry VIII and his almost direct contemporary, Francis I of France), such magnificence was not just about showing off; on the contrary, it was perceived as one of the most important and necessary of princely virtues.

Magnificence

To understand in what sense such flagrant extravagance could be seen as moral, we need to turn to the origins of the 'doctrine of magnificence', first expounded by Aristotle in the *Nicomachean Ethics*. There it is discussed under the heading of 'other moral virtues'. Aristotle starts with liberality in relation to money. Liberality is a finely judged quality that sits between avarice and prodigality; 'the liberal man will give with a fine end in view, and in the right way; because he will give to the right people, and the right amounts at the right time'. Not only that, but he 'will do it with pleasure'.[3] This leads to a discussion of magnificence itself, which is 'a virtue that has to do with money' and which he contrasts with pettiness. The magnificent man 'will spend gladly and generously, because precise reckoning over the cost is petty'. From this it follows 'that the magnificent man must also be liberal'. Aristotle gives some examples of this, such as 'entertaining the whole city to a banquet', laying on 'entertainments to mark the arrival or departure of foreign guests, or the exchange of complimentary presents', commenting that 'it is also characteristic of him to furnish his house in a way suitable to his wealth'.[4]

This is a virtual blueprint for princely magnificence in late medieval Europe and it found more current expositions too. Edward IV's *Black Book of the Household*, compiled in 1478, is prefaced with a discussion of magnificence and liberality, in which we read that a ruler must

> know how to spend in proportion to what the expense is for; he will spend greatly and properly on good, honourable things; he will spend happily, not calculating the expense; he must spend appropriately and be liberal, according to what is fitting; what he spends should result in admirable and excellent work; [but] the magnificent man must avoid vulgarity or over-excess.[5]

Sir John Fortescue, arguably the father of English constitutional history, wrote on similar lines, that 'it is necessary that the king has such treasure that he may [...] buy himself rich stones, cloth, belts, and other jewels and ornaments [...] as befits his royal majesty'.[6]

But is that which 'befits royal majesty' necessarily the same thing as moral obligation? According to Gordon Kipling, Guillaume Fillastre's influential treatise *La Toison d'Or* (The Golden Fleece), written around 1470, left no room for doubt and set magnificence at the head of all princely virtues, ahead, even, of justice. This was a philosophy that John Skelton picked up on in his satirical play *Magnificence*, dating from about 1519.[7]

But magnificence was not only about expenditure. Aristotle argues that it had an equal and opposite face, namely receiving. This was a reciprocal process, 'because right giving implies right receiving'.[8] There was, therefore, as much virtue in receiving as in giving. As a result, gifts played an important part in oiling the wheels of courtly and international relations and their exchange was almost as ubiquitous as magnificence itself. In the course of this book we will see gifts as a fundamental component of diplomacy, rites of passage, and the expression of favour and loyalty between king and court.

Any prince worthy of the name took magnificence immensely seriously. This was manifested in many forms and materials, such as tapestry and spectacular armour, and in exotic materials like rock crystal, ivory or glass. Among this diversity, however, precious metals had a special place, spreading across the entire panorama of court life. Gold and silver were deployed in almost everything. The finest tapestry, known as 'Arras', was embroidered with gold or silver thread that glittered in the light. This was extraordinarily luxurious and could cost fifty times as much as ordinary wool tapestry.[9] Cloth of gold was exactly that: a sumptuous velvet, generally made in Italy, heavily brocaded with thread painstakingly wound around with gold foil.[10] It was used for wall hangings, clothes, upholstery, ecclesiastical vestments and altar frontals. It was, in short, everywhere. It was also extremely expensive. Cloth of gold, depending on its quality, ranged from 28s 4d per yard to as much as £6 (the rate paid for twenty-four yards of 'crimson cloth of gold of tissue' in April 1513).[11] And the quantities held

Figure 1.3
Henry VIII with Jane Seymour and Prince Edward, detail from *The Family of Henry VIII*, British school, c. 1545. Hampton Court Palace. Royal Collection.

in store were prodigious: a royal wardrobe inventory from early in the reign lists over 4,400 yards of cloth of gold and silver.[12]

No less ubiquitous was gilding: the embellishment of a metal, wood or plaster surface with a thin layer of gold. This could cover large areas and costs ran very high. In 1514 the king's armourer, Paul van Vreland, was paid £121 6s 8d for the gold, mercury and workmanship involved in gilding the royal armour.[13] Plate, furniture, ceilings and even the ephemeral props and stage machinery for pageants and revels were routinely gilded. A sense of these opulent interiors can be gained from the dynastic (and fictive) portrait of Henry VIII with Jane Seymour and Prince Edward in the Royal Collection (fig. 1.3), where the fabrics are heavily embroidered with gold thread and the pillars and architectural mouldings richly gilded. A reported conversation between John Wallop, Henry's ambassador to France, and Francis I suggests that Henry had a reputation for 'bling' that exceeded even the demands of magnificence. 'I declared', writes Wallop in a dispatch to the king, 'the magnificence of [your houses], especially Hampton Court. He [Francis] was interested, and said he heard you used much gilding in your houses, especially in the roofs; for his part he preferred natural wood, as ebony, brasell etc., which was much more durable.'[14] The gibe is unmistakable.

Plate and jewels

Despite the jaw-dropping impression of these interiors, the most extravagant comments of visitors were always reserved for plate and jewels, the sheer quantity of which was obvious to all. Plate was the dominant component of banquets, but gold and silver were also conspicuous in church services, at pageants and tournaments. Altars were set with gold and silver 'images' and crosses, clergy wore jewelled mitres and copes, and on the tilt-yard horse harnesses were fashioned in silver-gilt. All this was calculated to impress and phrases such as 'a marvel to behold'[15] or 'the most stupendous sight in the world' occur repeatedly in the sources.

A different sort of goldsmiths' work was the jewelled collars, brooches and hat badges worn at court. These too were made to impress and one of the earliest surviving Milanese ambassadorial dispatches from the reign of Henry VII describes a visit to the king at Woodstock, where

> the royal seat was adorned with cloth of gold [...] His Majesty, in addition to his wonderful presence, was adorned with a most rich collar, full of great pearls and many other jewels, in four rows, and in his bonnet he had a pear-shaped pearl, which seemed to me something most rich.[16]

We have a clearer idea of the role of jewels in promoting royal magnificence than we do of plate, not because the jewels survive but because of their careful depiction in portraits. Holbein's universally familiar image of Henry VIII standing astride shows him in a doublet embroidered with silver thread and sewn with rubies or garnets in gold settings. He has rings on his fingers, a jewelled gold collar and his hat is sewn with further jewels and pearls, while a rich gold or silver-gilt mounted dagger hangs from his belt. But what this and other portraits show is just the tip of the iceberg; the precious stones and pearls he acquired in his lifetime numbered in the thousands. Nor were they worn only by himself and his family. In the first decade of his reign he spent several thousand pounds on 'spangles' (small gem-set jewels sewn into clothes) for the yeomen of the guard,[17] and the establishment in 1539 of his personal body guard, the gentlemen pensioners, was marked once again by huge expenditure on spangles.[18] But his acquisitiveness – and his father's before him – is not explained purely in terms of his luxurious taste in adornment. Jewels, like plate, were a semi-liquid asset and when bought cheaply, as they sometimes were, were a valuable investment. The inventory of Henry's possessions compiled after his death lists huge numbers of jewels and loose stones kept in coffers that could easily have been disposed of for ready money.

Magnificence sent messages: it presented the court as a centre of patronage and power; it demonstrated the king's wealth; and from that it followed no less clearly that he was powerful and not to be crossed. Sir Thomas Elyot, author of *The Boke Named the Governour*, captured this when he wrote in 1531 that 'like as the sun doth his beams, so doth [Majesty] cast on [its] beholders and hearers a pleasant and terrible reverence'.[19] 'Terrible reverence', or intimidation, was exactly what the king inspired, and intended to inspire, when he came in person to judge the London apprentices after the Evil May Day riot in 1517, and when he had Westminster Hall 'hung with tapestry of cloth of gold, with the canopy of brocade'.[20] So was it in 1541 when Henry transported the court on a stately progress to York in the aftermath of a northern rebellion and when, according to the French ambassador, he 'brought from London his richest tapestry, plate and dress, both for himself and his archers, pages and gentlemen', adding that 'this seems to betoken some extraordinary triumph'.[21]

In addition to their obvious use as a measure of wealth, plate and jewels had special features that set them apart. Not least, they were recyclable and there are many references to jewels being given new settings and stones being recut, or to old plate being 'new made'. Equally, plate was usually esteemed for its intrinsic worth and was frequently melted down and transformed into coin. Henry, by and large, preferred other means of meeting his cash requirements, but even he was not immune to emergencies and when the northern rebellion, known as the Pilgrimage of Grace, flared up in 1536 he met the crisis by sending some £17,000 worth of plate to the mint.[22]

Conveying a sense of the modern equivalent of such sums is fraught with difficulty since the relative value of commodities has changed completely. Even the value of gold relative to silver was very different from today. Nowadays the ratio of sterling silver to 22 carat gold is approximately 1:100, ounce for ounce, but in the sixteenth century it was closer to 1:10. As two other random examples, timber was plentiful in Tudor times and, to our eyes, very cheap, while the cost of sending a letter from London to Rome was huge. So, calculating the modern equivalents of the costs of plate and jewellery is inevitably misleading and is not attempted in this book. But comparisons with other contemporary costs can be helpful and are introduced from time to time. For example, the £12,000 value put at the time on a silver-gilt buffet shown at Westminster Hall in 1501[23] is thrown into stark relief when compared with the £15,000 recently paid by Henry VII for the complete rebuilding of Richmond Palace, or the £8,700 paid by Henry VIII for his great warship, the *Henri Grace à Dieu*, and three attendant barques in 1514:[24] to the modern mind, for a display of silver vessels – even a large one – to cost nearly as much as a palace or more than a warship is scarcely credible.

By the end of the reign Henry had accumulated more than six tons of plate, comprising several thousand objects or sets. This was probably more than any other English king, before or since, and as large or larger than any of the great accumulations formed over multiple generations by the Habsburgs or the other ruling houses of Europe. Almost all of Henry's plate has gone and today only four objects are known to survive, but its loss is compensated by a wealth of documentation. Several major inventories of royal plate survive from across the reign, while the state papers, diplomatic dispatches and contemporary chronicles paint a rich picture of its conspicuous presence at court. In addition, we have a spectacular cache of designs by Hans Holbein that radiantly illuminate the court style of the 1530s. But there are limitations to these resources. Most of the inventories are incomplete and anyway they give us only a very limited sense of what the wares actually looked like. Surviving documentation is patchy; some contemporary sources are biased and others are limited by the position or interests of their authors. Edward Hall's *Triumphant Reign of Kyng Henry the VIII*, for example, is an important source by someone who probably witnessed many of the events he described. But in Hall's eyes the king could do no wrong and his account is something of a hagiography. The same may be said of the first biography of Thomas Wolsey, written by George Cavendish, his gentleman usher. Then there is the issue of what the accounts do *not* tell us. Resident diplomats like Charles V's ambassador, Eustace Chapuys, were often given privileged access, but not even they were invited into the privy chamber, the innermost sanctum of the king, and can tell us little of the king's life behind its closely guarded doors. Nor can they tell us what sort of objects he surrounded himself with or how they were deployed. (Anyway, Chapuys does not seem to have been much interested in plate and seldom bothers to mention it. The Venetian ambassadors, on the other hand, were fascinated by it.) Another sense in which contemporary observers fail to paint a perfect picture is what they assume. No chronicler or ambassador reported the things they assumed their readers knew already, or expected, and as a result much of the basic context of plate and jewels at court goes unmentioned. What wares were used on the table, what people ate and drank with, how the altar was dressed: these were questions that only seemed to be addressed when what was seen was unusual or special; normality was normally unreported.

This book tells a story. It examines the place of plate and jewels in court ceremony, in the church, in diplomacy and in relations between the king and his court. It also looks at the repertoire and styles of royal plate, at the artists, goldsmiths and merchants who made it or who supplied it and at the influence of figures such as Cardinal Wolsey and Francis I on forming the king's taste and aspirations. But Henry himself is at the heart of the story, as is the way in which goldsmiths' work and his attitudes towards it shed light on his changing character during the course of the reign. Early commentators called him 'virtuous', seeing his behaviour in the light of correct princely magnificence, but later observers saw a very different Henry. They refer to his cruelty and his greed. Philip Melanchthon, the German evangelical reformer, pulls no punches and calls him a monster,[25] while Charles de Marillac, the last resident French ambassador of the reign, said '[the king] is so covetous that all the riches in the world would not satisfy him'.[26] This decline from virtue into vice can be clearly seen not only in persecutions and executions, but through the parallel prism of plate and jewels. The liberality that characterised the young Henry appears in the carefree delight he took in spectators making off with gold spangles lost from the clothes of courtiers at a tournament in 1511, or in the way in which he spontaneously presented the French ambassador with his sumptuous robe in 1518. Later on, plate and jewels become an equally clear mirror of a more grasping, manipulative character: far from satisfying his appetite for riches, the treasure of the dissolved monasteries seems to have stimulated it yet further; equally, the cruelty and spitefulness of his late dealings with Katherine of Aragon are given an extra twist by his appropriation of her jewels as an instrument of humiliation. The final years of the reign were marked by colossally expensive war waged on two fronts, by the government becoming saddled with huge loans and by the disastrous policy of debasing the coinage. Yet at the eye of this perfect financial storm sat the king, adding new jewels and plate to his already bloated holdings right up until the end.

Two The Jewel House

The provision and management of much of the magnificence on which the king depended was the responsibility of the master of the jewels. Sitting at the centre of a complex web of suppliers and administrators, he controlled the care, transport, procurement and disposal of royal plate. The jewel house, over which he presided, was both an institution and a place. As a place, it was the repository in the Tower of London for royal plate and jewels not in daily use, but as an institution it stood within the royal household and it is with the household that we should start.

The household and the jewel house

The great household was one of the key political units of the late medieval world. This is a big subject and can only be discussed here to the extent that it relates to our theme. Composed of dozens or even hundreds of people, depending on the rank of its master, it was a community and a power base. The royal household was not fundamentally different from those of other great noblemen, except that it was larger and that it interacted with the court.

But the two were not the same. According to Simon Thurley, the difference was that the household provided for the king, while the court was 'part of the setting of kingship, [giving it] a sense of spectacle'.[1] Not that the household itself was without spectacle, not least because of its sheer numbers. Edward IV's *Black Book* of court protocol laid down that a duke's household would number up to 240 servants and the king's as many as 500. By the reign of Henry VIII its numbers had swelled to as many as 1,500.[2] These retainers, most of whom had to be fed, placed a significant burden on royal finances but were justified as yet another manifestation of magnificence, enhancing the king's status in the eyes of his subjects and of foreign ambassadors. The court, by contrast, was much smaller than the household; it was not a constant community and its members swelled or contracted according to circumstances. Nor were the two entirely separate. Various senior members of the household, such as the master of the jewels or the lord chamberlain, were household servants but were courtiers too.

Such numbers needed structure. Each man (for the king's household was predominantly a male world) had his place and his role within a clearly defined hierarchy. The medieval household was essentially binary, its two divisions, as David Starkey points out, each reflecting the precepts of magnificence by being 'given a characteristic virtue': the lord chamberlain's division was the *Domus Magnificentiae* ('the Household of Magnificence') and the lord steward's the *Domus Providentiae* ('the Household of Providence').[3] Roughly the equivalent of 'upstairs' and 'downstairs', the lord chamberlain's role was to ensure that all the requirements of magnificence were correctly observed and that the honour of the king was properly upheld within the household; the steward's was to provide victuals and other daily necessities. With hundreds of mouths to feed and the additional factor that for significant parts of the year the household (or part of it) was itinerant, this was a huge job.

The household structure evolved significantly under Henry VII through the creation of the privy chamber, a third tier of spatial hierarchy that was carved out of the *Domus Magnificentiae*. This gave the king greater privacy and protection, as well as resulting in the creation of what amounted to a 'private office' which gradually took control of many of the royal revenue streams formerly administered by the exchequer or the Chamber. This in turn had major implications for the procurement and visibility of plate, jewels and other luxuries. Beyond the reach of the chamberlain, the king's innermost rooms were now 'effectively off limits'[4] to all but a small cohort of trusted royal servants headed by the most personal of them all, the 'groom of the stool' or, as he was later known, 'chief gentleman of the privy chamber'.

The frequent references to plate in the *Black Book* show how important it was, both as a ware and as an asset that needed proper control. Within the household were various separate departments, each with their own functions and allocations of plate. The pantry (which provided bread) looked after salts and spoons, the confectionery held spice plates and the ewery ewers and basins. A sub-department, the pitcherhouse and cuphouse, looked after vessels concerned with wine, 'the chief yeoman of [which] hath in charge under the sergeant of cellar the keeping of all the pots and cups of silver', while the page was 'to help keep and attend, to bear and wash [them]'.[5] In order to check that nothing had gone astray, there was to be an annual audit in which the clerk of controlment was 'to call the plate hither, to prove the waste and to know if any lack thereof'.[6] When

Figure 2.1 The jewel house at Westminster Palace, London.

on progress, the groom of the king's mouth had to share responsibility for the travelling plate and 'to help truss and keep them safe in carriage'.[7]

Most of this household plate was provided by the jewel house. This was a sub-department of the Chamber, but it was also a place. The first mention of the jewel house as such was when Edward III ordered the construction of a purpose-built facility at the palace of Westminster around 1365. This three-storey structure still stands and is the only part of the medieval palace to survive (fig. 2.1). But the Tower of London, three miles east of Westminster, remained the principal royal stronghold and in 1497, as the Cornish rebels advanced towards London, the royal plate was moved from Westminster to the Tower for safety.[8]

Around 1507 Henry VII decided that the Tower, rather than the palace, should become the main repository for the growing accumulation of royal plate and jewels (apart from the coronation regalia, which remained at Westminster Abbey). At the time this would not have seemed a radical proposal, since the Tower remained one of Henry VII's regular residences. A new jewel house was built, abutting the White Tower and in the most secure part of the fortress. In keeping with its function as a secure location, it had few windows and the exterior of the building, as far as we can tell, was unprepossessing. A 1597 bird's-eye view of the Tower of London (fig. 2.2) suggests a two-storey building and this is confirmed by the 1649 inventory of the jewel house, which divides the list into the upper and lower

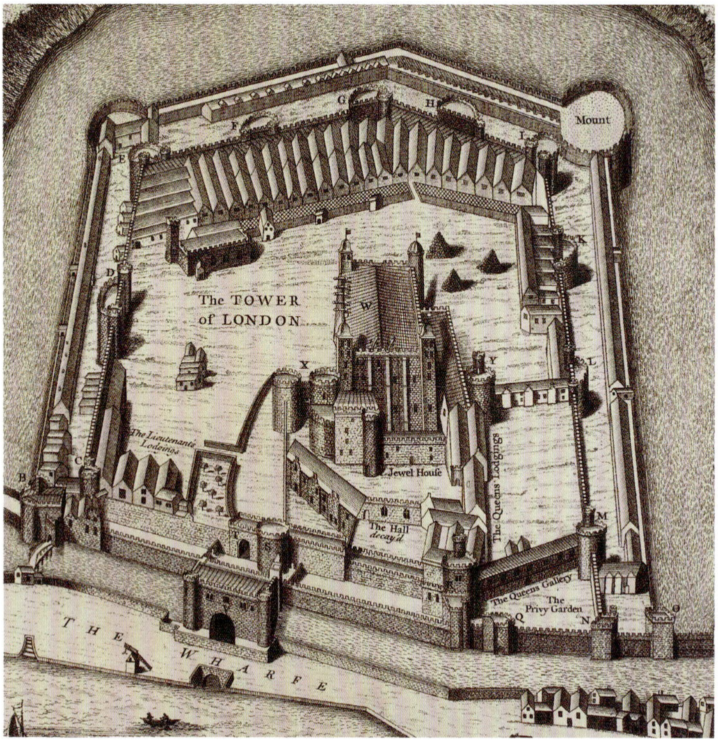

Figure 2.2
The Tower of London from a survey of 1597, John Howard and John Gascoigne. Showing the jewel house abutting the White Tower. British Library (Maps.K.Top.24.23.b).

Figure 2.3
The imperial treasure of Maximilian I, Albrecht Dürer, 1515. Engraving. Metropolitan Museum of Art, New York.

jewel house. We have no clear idea what it looked like inside, although a woodcut by Albrecht Dürer, supposedly representing part of the Holy Roman Emperor Maximilian's treasury, might give us a clue (fig. 2.3): a secure vault with thick walls and iron bars across the window, housing a mixture of sacred and secular plate and jewels, while more treasure is in the coffers on the floor. The full imperial treasury would have occupied several such rooms and according to a Venetian document of 1495, Maximilian, more truly peripatetic than English kings, needed twenty-one carts and sixty-three locked chests to move all his plate to Nuremberg.[9]

According to the *Black Book*, the jewel house was administered by 'an architectour called clerk [...] or keeper of the king's jewels, [who had] a clerk under him, a groom and yeomen'.[10] But the title 'master' did not come in until later; it first appears in 1485 as the role became more prestigious, with the jewel house staff taking part in the coronation and in royal funeral processions. In the *Black Book* the roles of 'keeper' of the jewels and treasurer of the Chamber are combined.[11] This made sense and reflected the enormous value of the plate, which amounted to a significant proportion of the Crown's liquid assets. But the creation of the new Tower facility had, over time, two effects: it separated the wares in daily use from what was essentially a store of wealth,[12] and it loosened the ties between the Chamber and the jewel house.

Masters of the king's jewels

At the start of Henry VIII's reign these effects were still taking shape and the role of master depended largely on the character and circumstances of its appointee. Like the master of the mint, it was – or could be – a sinecure rather than an executive role. It was moderately prestigious and it provided its holder with an income of £50 a year, plus 'the usual profits of office'[13] – a handsome sum, especially in comparison with the twenty marks salary of the subordinate clerk or the 6d a day paid to the yeomen. Nor was that all. The master also had the right to appoint royal goldsmiths, for which he extracted a heavy fee, and a right to £20 a year on signing the royal goldsmiths' account.[14] It was, therefore, a desirable position, especially as it was normally held in conjunction with other court appointments.

The jewel house had a total of six masters during Henry VIII's reign, the last four of whom are discussed in Chapter 12. The first Tudor master was Sir William Tyler, who was appointed in 1485 but seems to have held it as a sinecure.[15] He was not made treasurer of the Chamber and there is little evidence of his having had any direct impact on the running of the jewel house either. The real work was done by the subordinate clerk.[16]

Sir Henry Wyatt (c. 1460–1537), who was in post at the time of Henry VIII's accession, was appointed subordinate clerk in 1486 and promoted to master a few years later. A loyal supporter of Henry VII, Wyatt was a busy man, leading a number of military and diplomatic missions for both Henrys and being rewarded with a string of official titles. In addition to the jewel house, he held positions at the mint, culminating in comptroller, but the extent of his direct involvement with either institution is unclear

Figure 2.4
Sir Henry Wyatt,
Hans Holbein the younger, before 1537.
Musée du Louvre, Paris.

and his military duties must have kept him away for extended periods. In Henry VII's funeral procession it was John Heron, subordinate clerk of the jewels as well as treasurer of the Chamber, who headed the list of seven jewel house staff, not Wyatt.[17] It is possible, however, that Wyatt became more directly involved under Henry VIII, since he was specifically charged with transporting the royal plate to Canterbury and Calais in 1520, for the king's meetings with Charles V and Francis I.[18] He must, in any case, have been an able administrator and in 1521, at the age of about sixty, he succeeded Heron as treasurer of the Chamber. Wyatt finally retired from the jewel house in 1524 and from the Chamber four years later. By the time he sat for Holbein (fig. 2.4) he must have been close to death. He looks weary and wary, as well he might. His fur-lined black velvet gown and gold chain speak of one who has reaped the rewards of a lifetime's loyal service to the Crown, but his chain supports a large gold cross, held in his hand, almost as if to conceal it. By now, living in a world where the dissolution of the monasteries was in full swing and religious changes were starting to encroach on the lives of ordinary people, he was a man of an earlier generation, increasingly out of step with his times.

Wyatt's more famous son, Thomas, looked set to follow his father in the jewel house and was made subordinate clerk in 1524, but the mastership went instead to Robert Amadas (c. 1480–1532). Another busy man, though of a quite different stripe, Amadas had done very well for himself and qualified for the appointment not as a courtier but as a successful goldsmith. Like his predecessor, he was also much involved with the mint, though in an unambiguously working capacity. In 1510 he was appointed deputy to the master of the mint, Lord Mountjoy, by which time the Chamber accounts show that he had also become the leading supplier of goldsmiths' work to the Crown.[19] We will look more closely at his lucrative career as a goldsmith in Chapter 4 but as master of the jewel house he would also have had plenty of opportunity to enrich himself, through his ability to control the distribution of commissions and through his entitlement to 'the usual profits' of the office. But quite how attentive he was to managerial minutiae is another matter; when Thomas Cromwell took over after Amadas's death in April 1532 and a new inventory of the jewel house was taken, £1,771 19s 10d worth of plate was found to be 'lacking'.[20] This was an enormous quantity, equivalent to some 9,000 oz of silver plate and it is unclear in what circumstances it had gone missing. What is clear, however, is that his widow was held accountable.

The work of the jewel house

The master, whether hands-on or hands-off, headed a well-oiled administrative machine whose chief responsibilities were the security, maintenance and procurement of royal plate and jewels. Each of these roles was multifaceted, involving sensitive relationships with the goldsmiths' trade, the Chamber and the court.

Security is a broad umbrella that had several aspects: the custody of plate within the Tower, its transportation between royal residences, and its allocation to the various royal households. The last of these, as we have seen, also involved an annual audit 'to call the plate hither [...] to know if any lack thereof'. Just how critical this was is shown by the discovery, in 1530, when Amadas and Sir Henry Guildford, comptroller of the household, carried out an audit of the scullery, that some 800 oz of platters had gone missing.[21] Even more seriously, David Starkey recounts how Sir William Compton abused his position of trust as groom of the stool by embezzling plate to the value of £579 2s 6d.[22]

Less dramatically, audits were also an opportunity 'to prove the waste thereof', in other words, to check that everything was in good repair. This was not considered necessary for plate kept in the jewel house itself – as bullion, it was worth as much broken as whole – and many of the entries in the jewel house inventories note that plate was 'broken', 'worn', or 'wanting certain stones'. But plate in active service was a different matter and the Chamber accounts note frequent payments to goldsmiths for 'mending of plate in diverse offices in the king's house'.[23]

The movement of the entire court from one place to another was one of the greatest logistical challenges to face the household and the author of the *Receyt of the Ladie Kateryne* gives a flavour of the scale of operations when the celebrations for Katherine of Aragon's arrival in 1501 moved from London to Richmond:

> the king's officers of household busied themselves in all their diligence and power to truss and stuff their great and huge standards, coffers, chests, cloth sacks, with all other vessels of conveyance, every officer with such things as he had in his governance and rule, and this sent forth by many carts and chariots by land, and also by divers boats and wherries by water.[24]

Such operations would have been a particular headache for the jewel house because of the huge quantity and value of plate involved. But plate often had to be moved from one royal residence to another and it was the job of the groom to 'truss the chariot' and accompany it and its team of 'seven horses' [riders] on its journeys to and from the jewel house. At the time of the *Black Book* these journeys were routine and 'betwixt the treasurer of the household and this office be many interchanges of silver vessels, whole and broken, received or delivered by officers by indenture, as it will appear in the account of [the] household'.[25] The Chamber accounts show many payments for this purpose: the hire of horses and carts to take plate from London to Woodstock, the jewel house cart from Greenwich to Eltham and so on. In October 1528 three yeomen were paid for 'giving attendance on the king's plate at the Tower'; in the following July Robert Draper and another were paid board wages for 'lying at Bridewell two several times with plate when the king was at Greenwich'.[26]

Sometimes the team had to take plate much further afield. Serious quantities went to France in 1520 and 1532 for summit meetings with Francis I, when a warrant for packing materials gives an idea of what was involved. Quantities of canvas were needed to make bags, broad cloth to wrap plate in, 'eighty yards of white Walshe frees [fleece?] to lay between gilt bowls etc. to save the gilding', twelve new coffers and eight refurbished ones, 'certain cases of leather for the trussing of cups and bowls of gold' and 'two new bare hides for the covering of the carts with the said jewels and plate'. A final item was 'a load of hay for trussing the said jewels and plate into the said coffers'. The total cost of these materials was £35 3s 4d,[27] a considerable sum when set against the £15 it cost to send three jewel house yeomen to accompany the plate and jewels over a fifty-day period.[28] Once safely back across the Channel, the yeomen were instructed to requisition 'so many sundry carts or waynes and cart horses' in Sandwich and

Dover, and as many 'honest and able persons nightly to watch the same' as were needed for the onward journey to London.[29] Nor was it only for the king that large-scale movements of plate were arranged. When Anne of Cleves and her vast entourage travelled to England in 1539, Thomas Cromwell busied himself with drawing up lists of 'money to be sent to Calais for defraying the Lady Anne's train' and sending 'plate to Calais, Dover, Canterbury, and all other places',[30] so that she could be received with magnificence appropriate to her imminent status as queen at the various staging posts on her way to London.

'Per indenturam': the 1521 inventory

These precious things were not only moved between the jewel house and the king. Plate was periodically sent out to be remade into new wares, because it was old-fashioned or worn out; jewellery too was sent to the goldsmiths for remaking, or for the stones to be recut, reset or stitched onto new clothes. The value of these consignments could be enormous and the normal method of keeping track of them was through indenture – essentially two copies of the same list signed off by both parties to acknowledge the transfer.

The greatest transfer of all was that between the king and the master of the jewel house and his appointment was, or should have been, marked by the compilation of a complete inventory of everything in his charge. We know what this amounted to from the one compiled in 1521 as an indenture between the king and Sir Henry Wyatt. Once again, this followed the *Black Book*, which required that the 'architectour' of the jewel house 'taketh *per indenturam* between him and the king all that he findeth in this office of gold, silver, and precious stones';[31] this would then be reconciled with what remained in the master's charge at the end of his tenure and any discrepancies – such as the £1,772 shortfall when Amadas retired – properly accounted for.

From our point of view, the surviving jewel house inventories are valuable in a quite different sense. Two are known from Henry VIII's reign, that of 1521 and another of 1532,[32] and they form the basis for much of our knowledge of early Tudor royal plate. The 1521 inventory has had a chequered history, if, indeed, it still exists. It belonged in 1734 to one John West, who inscribed his name in the book and wrote that 'he had bought it of Fletcher Gyles in Holbourn'.[33] At some stage thereafter it was acquired by the duke of Portland and preserved for many years in the library at Welbeck Abbey. Around the end of the nineteenth century, however, it seems to have disappeared and nothing has been seen of it since. What would have been a serious loss to scholarship, however, was largely averted by the fact that Edward Trollope, an antiquarian bishop of Nottingham, made a careful transcription of it, which was published by the Lincoln Diocesan Architectural Society in 1884.[34] The inventory covers fifty-eight paper folios, bound in vellum, and comprises nearly 900 entries, many of which are for multiple pieces, such as pairs of pots, sets of six or twelve bowls, or sets of spoons. Large numbers of dishes and plates are covered by single entries, one of which gathers in 'seventy-one platters of various sorts' weighing 2,745 oz.

The carefully recorded weights against each entry in the inventory enable us to take a view of the overall quantum and value of the precious metal in the Tower. The gold items come to a total of around 4,770 oz, the silver-gilt to 77,000 oz and the silver and parcel-gilt to a little under 40,000 oz.[35] At 40s an ounce the gold would, in round terms, have been worth around £9,500. The silver-gilt, at 5s an ounce (valued more highly than silver because the gilding was largely recoverable), came to around £19,250, and the white silver, at 4s, to about £8,000.[36] Adding these numbers together gives us a bullion value of about £36,750. But the unquantifiable value of the stones and pearls that embellished the crown jewels and many items of plate would have been huge. To take just three items, the king's crown alone was set with twenty-seven diamonds, thirty-three balases, twenty-one rubies, eleven sapphires, four emeralds and 105 pearls; the 101 oz gold image of St George contained six balases, fourteen rubies and 107 pearls; and a 42 oz gold cup 'chased with waterflowers' was enriched with fourteen balases, four rubies, fourteen sapphires and ninety-four pearls.[37] Altogether some fifty-eight pieces, almost all of gold, were embellished with stones and pearls. And we get a sense of how much these huge numbers of gemstones added to the value of an object from the price achieved by a jewelled gold layer when it was sold in 1649: the object weighed 160 oz; without the stones it would not have been worth more than about £350, but with them it made £2,390 (see p. 317), nearly seven times as much.

The list is divided into sections. It opens with the regalia then moves on through the different categories, with gold wares followed by silver-gilt and silver. The gold, including the regalia, account for just under twenty per cent of the items (although only about four per cent of the total weight) and have quite a narrow range. About fifteen per cent are sacred; the rest are divided into drinking vessels, salts, spoons and 'layers'.

The silver-gilt wares are much more varied. About twenty per cent are sacred and there are several types of secular plate that have few or no equivalents in gold. These include pots, flagons, bottles, candlesticks, and ewers and basins. In some cases this was because they were utilitarian wares, in others it was because they were much larger than even Henry VIII could have aspired to in gold. All of the secular gold weighed around 2,980 oz, the equivalent of just a few pairs of the largest silver-gilt pots or sets of bowls. But quite apart from their weight, the sheer numbers of wares held in the Tower are impressive. To cite just three categories, there were 86 salts, 204 pots and 250 bowls.

We will consider the objects themselves in more detail at a later stage, but for now we focus not so much on the list as on the amendments to it, which were made over the following few years. Like any indenture, there would have been at least two copies and the Portland version was presumably the office one, since it was marked up as objects came and went. A more detailed record of movements in and out would have been kept in the books of *infra* and *extra* (in and out) that are referred to in other sources but which have not survived.[38] In their absence, however, the inventory amendments provide a remarkable 'way into' the workings of the jewel house and show us much more than simply what was there at a particular moment. They show us allocations to the household, they show us ingress and egress, previous owners (sometimes) and, occasionally, the onward destination of objects or the names of the goldsmiths who had supplied them.

On the side of the *infra*, many items came in as gifts, both at new year and at other times. Those exchanged between the king and the queen were regularly dispatched to the jewel house, as were those from leading members of the nobility. A golden rose from the pope was consigned there years after it was originally received. Some incoming assets came through attainder (most notably from the duke of Buckingham) while others, like a gold cross and salt recovered after the battle of Flodden, were the spoils of war. But the jewel house was a two-way street and a significant proportion of its holdings would have figured in the book of *extra*. Items assigned to the household are duly noted and a group of wares weighing some 338 oz were marked 'with Sir William Compton': as groom of the stool Compton was in charge of the king's day-to-day plate, so these wares – flagons, bowls and pots – were probably for the king's own use in the privy chamber. Others were given away as christening presents or diplomatic gifts, and yet others (though not many) assigned to royal servants like Sir Thomas More. The inventory carries the occasional whiff of politics too, such as the annotation of a 24 oz salt that was 'appointed for the Lord Bergavenny's new year's gift in *anno* 15 [1524] but not delivered'.[39] George Nevill, third Baron Bergavenny (1469–1535), was one of Henry VIII's councillors but fell from favour by association with the duke of Buckingham and was imprisoned in the Tower for a year after the duke's arrest in 1521. The withholding of his gift in 1524 is an indication, perhaps, that he was still not fully rehabilitated.

Even where the inventory is silent we can draw conclusions: the fact that significant numbers of items disappear from the record between 1521 and 1532 is telling in itself and probably means either they had been refashioned into something more up to date, or that they had been sent to the mint.

Procurement

If security in the broadest sense was the chief responsibility of the jewel house, most of its work was concerned with procuring new plate. This was costed at fixed rates of so much per ounce for the metal and so much per ounce for the 'fashion', or work, and, except for the most highly wrought wares, the metal cost far more than the work.[40] The most predictable and regular of these orders, in a tradition that went back at least to the reign of Henry III (r. 1216–72), was the king's new year's gifts to his family and to the court. Nearly all of these were of plate, and in the early years of his reign Henry VIII spent between about £800 and £1,000 on this largesse each year, rising gradually to over £1,700 by 1521. A covered cup at Corpus Christi College, Oxford (fig. 4.6), discussed on p. 56, was probably such a gift (to the bishop of Winchester) and would have been a fairly standard object. But the overriding principle of new year's gifts was reciprocity; it was always a good idea for courtiers to err on the side of generosity and the Venetian ambassador, Sebastian Giustinian, had no doubt that the king generally got the better of the exchange.[41] Most of the incoming gifts would have been sent straight to the jewel house and many of those recorded as such in the 1521 inventory were of gold, ranging from a 103 oz basin given by the queen, down to spoons weighing just an ounce or two.

At the time of the *Black Book* the king received his gifts in the royal bed chamber.

> On new years day in the morning, the King, when he cometh to his foot-schete [a narrow sheet spread across the foot of a bed], an usher of the chamber to be ready at the chamber door; and say: 'Sire, here is a years gift coming from the Queen.' And then he shall say: 'Let it come in, Sire.'[42]

This first gift was followed by a steady procession of messengers bringing in others from the court, all in order of precedence.

Lists of these gifts would have been compiled for the record but the earliest to have come down to us is a partial list of eighteen given by the king in 1513.[43] These were all of silver-gilt, ranging in weight from 34 oz (for the archbishop of Canterbury) down to just 4 oz. The weight bands were probably long established and later lists follow a similar pattern. The exception was the king's gift to the queen, a pair of 'great pots' weighing a colossal 575 oz, which dwarfed all the others combined. Apart from these, the gifts were mostly of just three sorts: covered cups, 'little pots' and 'proper bottles for rose water'. Supplied by William Holland, these cost £212 11s 10½d and were largely paid for by the exchange of old plate, with a small balance being paid in cash by John Heron from the Chamber.[44] Everything was charged at the same rate of 5s an ounce. This was a satisfactory enough arrangement, except when something more customised or elaborate was required and Holland amended his bill on this occasion with an appeal to the king to reward him more generously for the queen's pots 'for he cannot live to make such curious [elaborate] work at the price within written'.[45] His plea was rewarded with a topping-up payment of £6 13s 4d. But what Holland supplied would only have been a small part of the gifts that year and the rest of the order would have been distributed among several other goldsmiths. In practice, they worked on these steadily through the year and received a series of interim payments. The Chamber accounts show periodic payments of £333 6s 8d, normally in April and November, 'for advancement of the king's new year's gifts', followed by a final settlement in January.[46]

New year's gifts were expensive. But in practice the cost, in terms of bills to be paid, was much less. The settlement of Holland's bill in 1513 with old plate was probably normal procedure and anyway the total cost of the presents would have been more than covered by the value of the incoming ones. New year's gifts, therefore, were very good business for the king, for the goldsmiths and for the master of the jewel house. For courtiers, on the other hand, they were a significant outgoing, especially since gifts were expected not only by the king but by other members of his family and sometimes by his ministers too. This annual obligation, for example, was one of the largest items of expenditure in the countess of Devon's expenses and in 1523 cost her £49 17s.[47] In 1537 the bishop of Salisbury wrote to Cromwell apologising for not giving more than £20 to the king, but saying he could not afford to do so.[48]

Nor was that all. The gifts were usually delivered by messengers, who expected a reward. These could be very substantial, depending partly on the value of the gift, but mostly on the status of the donor and the messenger. The *Ryalle Book*, a late fifteenth-century manuscript of court ceremonial,[49] sets out the going rates at the time:

> The messenger that bringeth the Queen's gift, [if] he be a knight, the sum of x marcs; and he be a squire, viij marcs, or at the least 100s […] and those that come from the king's brothers and sisters, every each of them vj marcs: and to every duke and duchess, each of them v marcs; and every earl & countess xl s.[50]

In 1529 the king paid rewards of 66s 8d and 53s 4d respectively to the servants who brought Wolsey's and Warham's gifts and in 1535 Anne Boleyn paid out a total of £254 16s 8d in rewards for the new year's gifts that were brought to her.[51]

There was more to procurement than new year's gifts, however. Other regular orders included plate for foreign ambassadors, new domestic plate for the household, and repairs. A reading of the Chamber accounts between 1509 and 1521 gives an insight into the range of activities the jewel house was either directly or indirectly concerned with.[52] A small but representative cross-sample of these includes payments to Amadas in July 1513 of £2,000 for 'furnishing of horse harness and trapp[er]s of goldsmith work', and in September of the following year of £1,906 8s 4d 'for certain gold work for the king's grace'.[53] Payments for repairs and orders for new plate were often shared among two or more goldsmiths; in June 1517 John Twyselton and William Holland collaborated on a £125 order for plate given to the queen of Scotland and in 1518 Holland, Twyselton and Amadas shared a payment of £1,829 for plate for the French ambassadors.[54] Then there were routine administrative expenses. In 1513 the Chamber paid out 15s 8d for 'three great books of paper royal of the largest size [...] for the king's rich jewels and plate'; this sounds very like one of the indenture inventories that have not survived.[55] Other costs were incurred in transport. In May 1518 Wyatt was reimbursed 5s 'for the hire of a horse from London to Woodstock with three crosses of silver and gilt with the staves' and in June 1519 Robert Draper, yeoman of the jewel house, was paid £6 19s 4d 'upon a bill signed for certain parcels laid out by him by Master Wyatt's commandment for certain necessaries for the jewel house stuff'.[56] The year 1520 saw exceptional expenses in connection with the Field of Cloth of Gold; in May of that year Draper received £20 'for certain necessaries to be employed for and upon the king's business touching his jewels', and in August £6 6s 11d for the expenses of getting the king's plate to Calais.[57]

It is important to realise, however, that the jewel house was not the only store of royal plate nor the only conduit through which it was purchased. It probably never had been, but the development of the privy chamber under Henry VII and its consolidation in the next reign gave the latter an increasingly important role in the purchase and custody of royal plate. The groom of the stool became keeper of the king's jewels and plate in daily use (in other words, those *not* in the jewel house) and in 1509 the treasurer of the Chamber reimbursed him £152 11s 9d for jewels bought;[58] in 1526 Compton's successor, Henry Norris, took delivery of around sixty items of plate weighing some 1,200 oz. This was paid for out of funds under his control and the jewel house appears not to have been involved. The groom of the privy chamber's accounts for the early part of the reign do not survive but had they done so they would have shown high levels of expenditure, especially on luxuries for the king's personal use.

So we can be sure that the plate listed in the 1521 inventory did not represent the totality of royal plate at the time and indeed, as we shall see in Chapter 14, at the end of the reign, when we have the only full inventory of Henry VIII's plate, as much as a third of what he owned was not kept in the jewel house.[59] But exactly what the jewels and plate in daily use comprised, unless assigned by the jewel house, we do not know. Much of it would have been utilitarian, but other, more interesting, objects would have been for display.[60] The latter, by and large, would have been items that pleased the king aesthetically, while old-fashioned objects might have been relegated to the jewel house because they were not to his taste. It is ironic, therefore, that on this interpretation we know more about the plate that did not appeal to the king than did.

This is an issue that we will explore further in later chapters. But this preliminary discussion of the jewel house and its centrality in all matters to do with royal plate has already taken us well into the reign of Henry VIII. It is now time to wind the clock back, to return to the beginning and to ask what the young king would have found when he came to the throne in 1509.

Three The King's Inheritance

Kings did not just inherit (or win) crowns; they also acquired assets. In the case of Henry VIII these were enough to cause widespread speculation. A Venetian in London at the time of his accession wrote that the late king 'had accumulated so much gold that he is supposed to have more than well nigh all the other kings of Christendom'[1] and the chronicler, Raphael Holinshed, wrote that 'unto no king at any time before, was left greater or the like riches, as well in ready coin, as in jewels and other moveables'.[2] Henry VII's accumulation of riches had been a matter of interest for some time and as early as 1497, with more than a decade of his reign still to run, the Milanese ambassador wrote that he 'has upwards of six millions of gold and it is said that he puts by annually more than 500,000 ducats'.[3] The millions in question would have been ducats rather than pounds, equivalent to about £1.3 million, but a huge sum even so and more than enough to support Holinshed's assessment.

The ambassador went on to say that this rate of accumulation was easy, 'for his revenue is great and real [...] nor does he spend anything'. It was observations such as this, coupled with Henry's close scrutiny of the royal accounts and his policy of maximising revenues, that led to an early and extraordinarily resilient reputation for parsimony. But 'nor does he spend anything' was very far from the truth and when substantial expenditure was called for by a national emergency or by a need to enhance his image as a powerful and wealthy prince, he did not hesitate. The enormous stocks of plate, jewels, cloth of gold and other splendid trappings built up by the first Tudor king were all inherited by his son and enabled him, from the moment of his accession, to bask in epithets such as 'magnificent' and 'descended from heaven'.

This chapter considers what Henry VIII's inheritance of plate and jewels consisted of and how much of it can be traced back to earlier reigns than his father's, for, although the royal treasury that Henry VII acquired in 1485 was depleted by nearly thirty years of intermittent civil war, it was not empty.

Richard II and his successors

Our knowledge of pre-Tudor royal plate is patchy. We have, for example, partial lists from the time of Edward II and III and also from the early to mid-fifteenth century. But within this relative darkness, an extraordinary pool of light is cast by an apparently complete inventory of Richard II's plate, compiled in 1399.[4] Written in French, it lists some 2,300 items in 1,206 separate entries. It is arranged under the principal headings of gold, silver-gilt and silver and, within these categories, under types of wares, a surprisingly high proportion of which were of gold.

The inventory is impressive, not only for its extent but also for the evident visual richness of the things it describes. Ewers and salts of sculptural form abound and many objects incorporated costly hardstones like rock crystal and jasper, or exotic natural materials such as ivory, mother of pearl, horn, ostrich egg and coconut. Many more were decorated with enamels and gemstones or with badges, such as a large golden ship model set with jewels and known as 'the Tiger'. This was given to Richard by Charles VI of France (r. 1380–1422), but was previously a gift to Charles from his uncle, the duc de Berry. It was supported by a bear (the duc's badge) and

Figure 3.1
The duc de Berry dining, from the *Très riches heures of the duc de Berry* (fol. 1v), illuminated by the Limbourg Brothers, 1411–16. Detail showing a golden nef on the table before the duke. Musée Condé, Chantilly.

Figure 3.2
Das Goldene Rössl (The golden horse reliquary), Paris, 1404. Gold, enamel, precious stones and pearls. Schatzkammer und Wallfahrtsmuseum, Altötting.

featured tigers (Charles VI's badge) in the castles at the prow and stern.[5] A simplified version of this type of object appears in an illumination from the *Très riches heures*, showing the duc de Berry dining (fig. 3.1).

Spectacular and imposing though much of this must have been, only a small proportion of Richard's plate survived far into the fifteenth century. It was in the nature of plate to be periodically recycled and further inroads were made as a result of wars and pledges for loans. A few pieces, such as the 'Tiger', survived into Edward IV's reign (1461–70 and 1471–83), but just one piece from the 1399 inventory, a gold and jewelled 'tablet' of the crucifixion, weighing 74 oz, can still be recognised in Henry VIII's first inventory.[6] Apparently of architectural form, it was modelled in two tiers and surmounted by pinnacles. The crucifixion scene was on the upper part, supported on five pillars, with the figures enamelled in white. The lower part had a green enamelled 'terrace' with six white harts (Richard II's badge) and bushes. It was enriched with many precious stones and an indication of its sumptuousness is that the harts are described as having small pearls on their antlers. But that was not all. It had a Pietà at the front and St John the Baptist at the back.[7] We have no image of this extraordinary work but an analogous piece, giving a clue to its appearance, might be the famous 'golden horse' reliquary at Altötting in Bavaria (fig. 3.2), which stands 62 cm high and is made of gold, enamel and precious stones. Created

Figure 3.3 The French Royal Gold Cup, France, c. 1370–80. Gold, enamel and pearls. British Museum, London.

Figure 3.3a
Detail of the French Royal Gold Cup, showing the martyrdom of St Agnes. British Museum, London.

in Paris, this was a new year's gift to Charles VI from his queen in 1404; it came to Altötting a hundred years later and has been there ever since. If Richard II's crucifixion was anything like the quality of the reliquary, which it almost certainly was, it would have been extraordinary. The 1399 inventory records that it was given to Richard by Thomas Mowbray, duke of Norfolk; later pawned by Henry V, it was redeemed in 1423 and pledged once more just a year later, to Cardinal Beaufort (d. 1447). Its survival into the sixteenth century and throughout Henry VIII's reign, by which time it was a hundred and fifty years old, is remarkable; but by 1574, when Queen Elizabeth I's inventory was compiled, it too had gone, a victim of Edwardian or Elizabethan iconoclasm, or perhaps just because the time had come to cash in its gold, stones and pearls. The repeated pledging and less frequent redeeming of such treasures was symptomatic of the fragile state of royal finances in the fifteenth century and stood in stark contrast to the early Tudor regime, when there was less need for such hand-to-mouth financing.

Despite the erosion of Richard II's treasures, the store of royal plate was regularly replenished (even if at a lower rate) and one spectacular object acquired by Henry VI (r. 1422–61 and 1470–71) remained in the jewel house throughout the Tudor period. The so-called royal gold cup, surviving to this day and preserved in the British Museum (fig. 3.3), had a similar roller-coaster history to the golden crucifixion and its survival is little short of miraculous. In 1391, four years before the 'Tiger', the duc de Berry gave it to Charles VI; in 1434 it was acquired by John, duke of Bedford

(d. 1435), who bequeathed it to Henry VI. Henry pawned it in 1449, then redeemed it, after which it was held in the jewel house until 1604, when James I presented it to Juan Fernández de Velasco, leader of the Spanish delegation to the Somerset House conference. Velasco presented it in turn to the convent of Medina de Pomar near Burgos, where it remained until shortly before the British Museum acquired it in 1892.[8]

The cup is 23.5 cm high and has a relatively shallow bowl and cover and a spreading foot and stem. Its chief glory is the spectacular translucent enamels depicting the beasts of the evangelists and the story of St Agnes (fig. 3.3a). Further enamelled roundels of Christ in blessing and St Agnes receiving instruction are inside the cover and bowl. The technical and artistic quality of these depictions has arguably never been surpassed in enamel. The enamels themselves are extraordinarily thin but the figures are modelled through tiny variations in the depth of the engraved ground that dictate the thickness of the enamel and the amount of light that is reflected back from the underlying gold. At the same time the plain surface of the areas not bearing enamel has been articulated by finely pricked scrolling foliage. The cup is not entirely in its original condition, however. Two disfiguring areas of damage are the replacement of the finial with a simple ring and the heavy damage to the border of the cover, which would originally have matched the pearled crown-like gallery around the foot. In 1521 there were sixty-two pearls; today there are fewer than thirty.[9] The stem has two extensions, one with enamelled red and white Tudor roses on a crudely worked ground, and the other with an engraved inscription recording its presentation to Juan de Velasco. The ring on the cover replaces what was described in 1521 as a crown imperial (itself probably a Tudor replacement). But that cannot be the full extent of the changes, since the present weight of the cup is just over 67 oz, 12 oz less than it weighed in 1521. The finial and pearled gallery are unlikely to have weighed quite so much, so perhaps some other element has been lost from the stem.

Another notable piece in Henry's inheritance was the 'tablet of Bourbon', a gold reliquary weighing 177 oz and described as being 'garnished' with the four evangelists and set with sapphires and balases. In this case, its condition was probably the main reason that it was assigned to the Tower, for the inventory tells us that 'the glass of the leaves [was] broken in many places and diverse of the relics shaken out, lacking one clasp'.[10] It was, however, an important and historic piece, even if its significance had been forgotten by the sixteenth century. The 'diverse relics' included the blood of Christ, a fragment of the True Cross and various relics of saints. It dated from at least the second quarter of the fifteenth century, when Henry VI pledged it to Cardinal Beaufort. Together with the royal gold cup, Beaufort bequeathed it back to the king, who then presented it to his foundation of Eton College. But Edward IV stripped the college of most of its assets and repossessed the tablet for the crown, hence its descent to Henry VIII.[11]

Finally, there was the 'salt of gold with a Moryon [moor] garnished with rubies, diamonds and pearls, the knop but coarse rubies', weighing 46½ oz. A. J. Collins, in his monumental account of the 1574 jewel house inventory, established that this had been in the royal treasure from at least the time of Richard III by reference to an indenture of November 1485. Signed by Henry VII, this acknowledged receipt of the salt from alderman Richard Gardyner, who had had it from 'the said late pretended king, in pledge for £46 13s 6d'.[12] At just one pound per ounce, this was only about half the salt's melt value (quite apart from its stones and pearls) and clearly explains why Henry VII wanted to redeem it. The Moryon salt was one of the great survivors of the medieval treasure, remaining in the royal collection until 1649, when it was described as 'an old salt and cover supported by a blackmore' and sold for £140.[13]

Although these are the only demonstrably pre-Tudor objects in the inventory, there would certainly have been others. In some cases an earlier date is suggested by their ornament and the most telling in this respect is badges (quasi-heraldic marks of ownership), which can give a clue to original ownership (even if seldom proof). The 'five white harts' decorating the body and cover of a 19 oz gold layer suggest that it could possibly have been Richard II's,[14] while another item may have dated from earlier still: 'two great silver-gilt spice plates with two covers' weighing 495 oz were 'chased with roots and two griffins'.[15] This is a very unusual combination but griffins and roots were two of Edward III's (r. 1327–77) badges and were also used by the same duke of Bedford who had owned the royal gold cup, so they may indicate a late fourteenth- or early fifteenth-century date. In other cases the clue to age lies in condition, as it did with the Bourbon tablet. Damage dominates the description of one of the most impressive gold cups in the inventory: the 'Dream of Paris' cup had an intricate miniature sculptural group on the cover, but was 'wanting of the garnishing under the cover', while various flowers, stones and other decorative details were missing from the figures of Venus, Juno and Pallas and from Paris's horse.[16] As Collins observed, 'this list of defects implies that the cup was far from new in 1521'.[17] The same might be said of another seeming masterpiece, 'a salt of gold called the Moresdaunce', again with a sculptural group, which was richly set with stones and pearls, although many were missing in 1521.[18]

These ancient royal objects were surely not preserved simply because of their artistic merit. The very fact of their descent from kings who had reigned a century of more earlier gave them a dynastic significance or, in Thomas Campbell's phrase, an 'associative value' that enhanced the credentials of the Tudor monarchy and helps to explain their survival into the seventeenth century when so much royal plate of more recent manufacture had been disposed of.

Henry VII and magnificence

Throughout the medieval period the royal holdings of plate and jewels were chronically unstable. Edward IV had inherited little, but was praised by the *Croyland Chronicle* 'for collecting [more] vessels of gold and silver, tapestries and decorations of the most precious nature' than any of his predecessors.[19] Under Richard III the holdings were eroded once again and the *Great Chronicle of London* tells us that 'King Richard in this past time had spent and given largely away the treasure and goods of King Edward to purchase him friends'.[20] It cites Edward's helmet 'with the garnish of gold, stone and pearl', jewel-encrusted gold cups, 'and the xii apostles of silver and overgilt'. One particularly choice object, 'a flat cup with a cover of gold [worth a hundred marks] garnished with certain balases, diamonds and pearls', had been given to 'the Chamber of London' for the 'kindness showed unto him by the citizens', presumably as security for a loan.[21]

For a king, power and visible wealth went hand in hand and to be secure it was essential to be seen to be rich. One of Henry VII's first priorities, therefore, was to restock the jewel house. This was partly achieved as a by-product of strengthening his grip on the throne, through the automatic forfeiture of the assets of those found guilty of treason.[22] But this was not nearly enough and Henry's expenditure on plate and jewels, certainly in the latter part of his reign, was colossal. The surviving Chamber accounts from 1492 to 1509 show his total spend on plate, jewels and cloth of gold to have amounted to more than £200,000.[23] Some of the individual entries in the accounts are extraordinary: 'for diverse and many jewels brought out of France against the marriage of my Lord prince [Arthur, in 1501] £14,000', 'for diverse precious stones and other jewels that come from beyond the sea £30,000' in 1504, and so on.[24] Frustratingly, it is impossible to separate these categories out as many of the entries bunch plate, jewels 'and other stuff' (luxury textiles like cloth of gold) together, but there is little doubt that a high proportion of the 120,000 or so ounces of plate listed in 1521 were acquired during Henry VII's reign. This had come from a variety of sources. The jewel house ordered large quantities of plate from the royal goldsmiths but French and Flemish plate was also bought through foreign merchants and jewellers. Another source was jewels bought on the cheap from impecunious foreign princes: in 1507 the Spanish ambassador wrote to Ferdinand of Aragon that 'Henry VII has the reputation of possessing immense riches. Both the kings of Naples, Alfonse and his son Ferdinand, and beside them some other princes, have therefore sent their jewels to the king of England, who has bought them very cheaply.'[25]

By 1501 Henry had accumulated a huge amount of plate. We have no inventories from this time, but this is quite clear from the accounts of the festivities laid on to mark the arrival of Katherine of Aragon. According to the *Great Chronicle*, the mayor of London, Sir John Shaa, who happened to be one of the king's goldsmiths, was invited by Henry Wyatt to inspect the two 'cupboards' (open displays of plate). The first had five shelves 'set thoroughly with gilt plate as flagons, great pots, standing cups and bowls' and which he valued at £12,000.[26] The other comprised a similar range of wares but would have made a very different impression. Not only were they entirely of gold, but they were enriched with stones and pearls, 'the which the mayor and other expert in valuing of such jewels prized above £20,000'. These are impressive sums and suggest enormous quantities. Assuming the silver-gilt was valued at, say, 5s an ounce, £12,000 implies a total weight of some 48,000 oz. This is not impossible, either in terms of the king's resources, or of what might have been displayed on a single structure, given that a pair of pots or a set of bowls could weigh as much as 500 oz and that it was spread over five levels. The £20,000 gold display would have been smaller and more concentrated: at 40s per ounce, this would have equated to around 10,000 oz, but these items were also 'garnished with stone and pearl', which would have been factored into the valuation, so the amount of gold on display would have been less.[27]

But in 1501 the reign still had eight years to run, a period during which the royal stocks of plate continued to grow. In addition to frequent payments to the royal goldsmiths, the Chamber accounts continue to record substantial purchases from abroad: £1,058 in December 1505 for jewels and plate from France and Flanders, £4,000 in November 1508 for 'diverse jewels and plate' from France, and in October 1508 an astonishing £26,000 for 'diverse and sundry jewels and gilt plate' from France.[28]

Henry VII was as controlling in death as he was in life and his will is extraordinarily detailed in its provisions for the completion of projects left unfinished during his life, most notably his chapel at Westminster Abbey. He also left specific bequests of church plate. Remarkably, he left money for silver-gilt pyxes 'garnished with our arms, and red roses and portcullises crowned' to be provided to every parish church in the land that, 'to our inward regret and displeasure', had to keep the sacrament in 'simple and inhonest pixes, specially pixes of copper and timber'.[29] More predictably, he left munificent bequests of vestments and plate to Westminster Abbey and St George's Chapel, Windsor. Some of the vestments bequeathed to the Abbey still survive and are discussed in Chapter 5 (fig. 5.2); the plate has fared less well but included

> our great piece of the Holy Cross set in gold and garnished with pearls and precious stones [...] the precious relic of one of the legs of St George, set in silver parcel-gilt [...] a gold chalice value 100 marks [... and] the greatest image of Our Lady that we now have in our jewel house.[30]

Specifically for the shrine of Edward the Confessor, he ordered 'an image of a king, representing our own person'. This was to be of timber covered in sheet of fine gold and was to show him kneeling in armour, enamelled with the arms of England and France and holding the crown that he had won at Bosworth. It was to be on a silver-gilt base, to stand three feet high and to be enamelled around its base *REX HENRICUS SEPTIMUS*. On a much smaller scale but perhaps analogous is the gold reliquary of St Lambert, commissioned by Charles the Bold of Burgundy in about 1470 and preserved in the treasury of Liège Cathedral. Here the golden figure of the duke, also kneeling and in armour, holds a reliquary containing the saint's finger and is supported on a silver-gilt base. The quality of this work of precious miniature sculpture is astonishing.[31] As a final example, the 'College of Windsor' (St George's Chapel) was also to receive 'a great image of St George, of gold, peysing [weighing] 240 oz, garnished with rubies, pearls, sapphires, diamonds, and other stones, the which image is now in our jewel house'.[32]

Other than these specific legacies, all of Henry VII's plate was inherited by his son, and Philippa Glanville has estimated that of the 887 items listed in 1521, only 152 had been acquired since the start of the new reign.[33] Nor would these 735 items have been the full extent of his inheritance. There would also have been what he inherited from his grandmother, Margaret Beaufort, and what his father had kept at Whitehall or at Richmond rather than in the jewel house. Amongst these would have been domestic wares for the king's daily use (doubtless including gold), devotional objects and mounted pieces of the sort listed in Richard II's inventory. Exotic materials mounted in precious metal, such as hard stone, mother of pearl, coconut and horn, were standard princely fare and, although they are largely absent from the 1521 inventory, they would certainly have existed.

Turning our attention back to the jewel house, a number of inherited items can be recognised from their inscribed initials, 'H and E', which are surely for Henry VII and his queen, Elizabeth of York (d. 1503). Others can be inferred from their badges: items with just red roses rather than red and white were probably made for Henry VII,[34] while pieces bearing portcullises combined with margarets likely belonged to Margaret Beaufort.

The H and E group includes a gold and jewelled holy water bucket and sprinkler of 24 oz and a pair of 'great' silver-gilt pots weighing 426 oz; among the items with red roses is a jewelled gold cup and cover of 55½ oz.[35] Then there are entries with the names of donors who died before the new reign started, such as a 39 oz 'cup of gold chased with tonnes [...] with a ring upon the cover set with a sapphire given by Dr Moreton the late archbishop of Canterbury'.[36] John Morton (whose name is alluded to by the 'tonnes' in the decoration) was appointed archbishop in 1486 and died in 1500; the cup was presumably a new year's gift to Henry VII. In one case it is the name of the silversmith rather than the donor that alerts us to its date: 'twelve parcel-gilt bowls without covers [weighing 436 oz], of Sir John Shaa's making'[37] are among the few items attributed to a specific maker, but Shaa died in 1505. Other demonstrably inherited items include another pair of large gilt pots and basins, weighing 409 oz and 188 oz, which had been given to Prince Arthur by the mayor and aldermen of London on 31 October 1499.[38] The inventory does not mention their source but the weights tally exactly with those given by the *Great Chronicle* in an account of the events of that day. According to this, Arthur (then aged twelve) was received into the City and presented with the gifts, whose weights are carefully noted. The recorder 'besought his Grace to accept that little and poor gift, trusting that after[wards] they should remember his Grace with a better', to which the prince replied:

> Father mayor I thank you and your brethren here present, of this great and kind remembrance, which I trust in time coming to deserve, and for as much as I cannot give unto you according thanks, I shall pray the king's grace to thank you, and for my part I shall not forget your kindness.[39]

Beyond inheriting crowns and assets, kings also inherited customs, advisors and suppliers. In the case of Henry VIII, certain high-profile advisors, such as the much-maligned councillors, Empson and Dudley, were sacrificed to send a message that the new regime was going to be less rapacious than its predecessor, but others below the parapet continued in post, such as John Heron, treasurer of the Chamber, or Henry Wyatt. Among these were a small group of wealthy merchants and goldsmiths.

More than a dozen goldsmiths are named in the Chamber accounts from 1494 to 1509. Of these the most important of the older generation were John Shaa and Bartholomew Rede, who were themselves successors to an earlier pair, Shaa's uncle, Edmund, and Rede's master, Hugh Brice. All four were wealthy men, all served as mayor, and all were knighted. The younger Shaa and Rede were both upper wardens of the Goldsmiths'

Company as well as holding the lucrative position of joint masters of the mint. As royal goldsmiths they received substantial payments for new year's gifts and for other plate and jewels. But they played a wider role too: they lent the king money and helped regulate the coinage, buying in huge quantities of silver coins from the king and exchanging them for gold, his preferred metal. Shaa, in particular, seems to have had his finger in other pies too and in 1496 received large payments for supplying lead and timber for various royal building projects.[40] Equally importantly, they facilitated relations between the Crown and the City. As mayor in 1501, Shaa welcomed Katherine of Aragon to the City. Not only that, but he held a great banquet for the Scottish ambassadors who came to negotiate Margaret Tudor's marriage to James IV, earning a poetic tribute from William Dunbar, who described him as

> [...] exempler, loode-ster, and guye;
> Principall patrone and roose orygynalle,
> Above all Maires [mayors] as maister moost worthy[41]

For all these reasons, S. P. Harper maintains that these goldsmiths, more than other tradesmen, were indispensable to the king (especially early on, when he needed money) and as a result had easy access to the royal presence.[42] But by 1505 Shaa and Rede were both dead and a new generation of royal goldsmiths followed, including John Mundy, Nicholas Warley, Thomas Exmew and Robert Amadas. These names figure just as prominently in the Chamber accounts as Shaa and Rede but, Harper argues, the relationship was different; they were 'merely suppliers, and there is little evidence that they served the king in any other capacity'.[43] The important thing, however, is that they continued in post well into the next reign, helping bridge the transition and ensuring that, despite the new king's youth, the first years of the reign were marked more by continuity than by change.

Four 'Heaven Smiles, Earth Rejoices'

The accession of the eighteen-year-old Henry VIII was greeted with more than the customary enthusiasm. Not only was his legitimacy beyond question (he was 'the undubiate flower and very heir of both lineages'),[1] but he was young, handsome and energetic. Those close to the court were struck by his beauty, his liberality and his virtue. Foreign ambassadors sent ecstatic dispatches and Lord Mountjoy, master of the mint, was positively lyrical when he wrote to his friend Erasmus that 'heaven smiles, earth rejoices; all is milk and honey and nectar'.[2] Not only that, but he commented that 'liberality scatters wealth with boundless hand. Our king does not desire gold or gems or precious metals, but virtue, glory and immortality.'[3]

The irony of Mountjoy's characterisation is not far to seek, for there can be few monarchs who have been more obsessed with the accumulation of such treasures than Henry VIII. But in the early years observers were more impressed by his carefree and liberal scattering of it than by his urge to acquire more of it.

Young Henry's apparently carefree attitude towards wealth was remarked upon because it was in such stark contrast to his father, as was almost everything else about him. The message of rejuvenation was sent as clearly in spontaneous acts of generosity as it was in the carefully planned expenditure directed towards court festivities and in the more cynical execution of two of Henry VII's most trusted ministers – Empson and Dudley – in order to underline the new order.

But such messages could only be sent because they were underpinned by immense wealth. In terms of territory England did not compare with France, Castile or the Holy Roman Empire, but the sovereigns of those lands were perennially short of cash and in terms of ready money, plate and jewels the newly crowned Henry VIII was widely regarded as the richest monarch in Europe; by 1516, having fought a hugely costly and entirely avoidable war, he brashly claimed that he was richer than ever.[4]

This chapter looks at plate and jewels in Henry VIII's early years, from their role in the coronation, to the euphoria and glamour of court pageants and tournaments. It also looks at the sources and policies that contributed to the accumulation of treasure. In most respects these years were marked more by continuity than by innovation: pageants and tournaments continued as before, as did attainder and new year's gifts, and the new king continued to patronise the same goldsmiths and merchants as his father. All of these factors helped to ensure that styles and usage remained, at least at first, much as they had been before.

Coronation and the regalia

The first spectacle of Henry VIII's reign was the coronation. This took place on 24 June 1509, just nine weeks after the accession and plans had to be drawn up in very short order. It could not have been more important. Politically it legitimised the king's claim to the throne and the power that flowed from it, but spiritually it conferred God's grace, through the anointing with holy oil. The date was chosen deliberately. It was the Feast of St John the Baptist, associated with the descent of the Holy Spirit and reinforcing the gift of grace and the parallels between the king and Christ himself.

Everything about the coronation was strictly choreographed and informed by tradition. The proceedings began with the royal procession from the Tower of London to Westminster Abbey, which was vividly described by Edward Hall:

> the streets where his grace should pass, were hanged with tapestry and cloth of Arras [and] with cloth of gold [...] [And] every occupation [trade guild] stood, in their liveries in order, beginning with the base and mean occupations, and so ascending to the worshipful crafts: highest and lastly stood the mayor with the aldermen [...] The priests and clerks, in rich copes, with crosses and censers of silver, [censed] his grace and the queen also as they passed.[5]

Hall goes on to describe the splendour of the young king and his entourage. His robe was 'of crimson velvet, furred with ermines, his jacket or coat of raised gold, the placard embroidered with diamonds, rubies, emeralds, great pearls, and other rich stones'. Not only that but he wore a great 'bauderike' (a girdle worn diagonally across the chest) set with 'great balases'. Behind Henry came Queen Katherine in a litter, dressed in white, with her hair loose, symbolising her virgin purity, and wearing a jewelled coronal.[6] Then came a procession of gentlemen wearing surcoats with the arms of the sainted kings, Edmund and Edward the Confessor, and of St George and France.[7]

In the abbey, the order of the coronation service broadly followed the fourteenth-century *Liber Regalis* and Henry VI's *Ryalle Book*. At its start the coronation regalia, also known as the regalia of Edward the Confessor (although surely much younger), were carried to the high altar. Every aspect of the service and the regalia was replete with religious symbolism and designed to reinforce the sanctity of kingship. And although coronation was not one of the seven sacraments, it was, as Alice Hunt points out, 'nonetheless sacramental, meaning that supernatural grace was imparted'.[8] The central mystery of the ritual was not so much the crowning as the anointing. This was performed with chrism and holy oil, poured from silver-gilt and silver phials and which were not merely 'a symbol of God's grace' but were actually 'God's grace in material form'.[9]

Having received 'unction', as the act of anointing is known, the king was vested with the regalia – the robes, spurs, sceptre, rod, armil and sword – before the crowning itself. Each of these items had its own mystical significance: the sword is blessed and consecrated to the defence of the Church, the armil (bracelet) signifies sincerity and wisdom, and the mantle that the king's earthly power is derived from God. The sceptre and rod are the symbols of his regal office and the crown of the 'manifold graces' he has been granted.[10]

The coronation itself was followed by the mass, for which the 'stone chalice' and paten of St Edward the Confessor were used. No images of the chalice survive, but an inventory of 1433 describes it as 'of onyx stone with a foot, mounts and paten of excellent gold, all which are held to be precious relics'.[11] For a possible sense of its appearance we could do worse than to turn to the twelfth-century chalice of Abbot Suger, now in the National Gallery of Art in Washington DC.[12] This too is of onyx, but mounted in silver-gilt rather than gold; it has two scroll handles, is set with precious stones and pearls and is enriched with filigree and gold reliefs.

It followed from the regalia's deep spiritual significance that they could only be used for the coronation itself, and it also followed from their accepted status as relics of the Confessor, whose shrine was in the abbey, that they should never leave that place. It was therefore important for the king to have another set for use on other occasions; it is this second set, with the 'imperial' (closed) crown, that is described in the 1521 jewel house inventory.

These were deployed almost immediately. At the end of the service the coronation regalia were laid on the altar of St Edward's shrine and the king, walking beneath a canopy of cloth of gold supported by six silver-gilt staves, processed out of the abbey wearing the imperial crown and carrying the orb and sceptre.

From the abbey, the royal party moved directly on to a sumptuous banquet in Westminster Hall. The *Great Chronicle of London* refers to the 'exceeding richness of the cupboard garnished with weighty and massy flagons, pots and cups of gold and of silver and gilt'.[13] The original sources do not discuss the feast in detail but Hall is at pains to describe two of the 'coronation claims', the customary gifts made by the king to various individuals who contributed to the ceremony of the occasion.[14] The first was to the king's champion, Sir Robert Dimocke, who proclaimed the honour of the king against would-be challengers. For his pains he received a gold cup and cover. Next came the mayor of London, Sir Stephen Jenyns, who served the king with hippocras (a sweet wine) in a gold cup, 'which cup, after his grace had drunken thereof, was with the cover, given unto the said Sir Stephen'.[15] Amongst the other recipients of plate at the banquet[16] was the earl of Oxford, who, as lord great chamberlain, received the basins and towels used by the king to wash at the feast. Together with a 9 oz 'cup of assay', these appear in the earl's 1513 probate inventory, where they are described as 'two basins silver all gilt with the king's arms in the bottom, which my lord had at the coronation of King Henry the eight by reason of his office', weighing 96 oz.[17]

Unlike the coronation regalia, the imperial regalia are well described in the inventory. Not only that, but the chief items – the king's crown, orb

Figure 4.1
Detail of Henry VIII's crown and sceptre from King Charles I, Daniel Mytens, 1631. National Portait Gallery, London.

Figure 4.2 Henry VIII processing to the opening of Parliament in 1512. British Library (Add. MS 22306, section 6).

and sceptre – are all depicted in Daniel Mytens's portrait of Charles I in the National Portrait Gallery (fig. 4.1). These images correspond remarkably closely to the inventory descriptions, suggesting that they are studiedly accurate. The inventory describes the crown, the round ball with a cross and the gold sceptre with a dove, together with a pair of jewelled bracelets, a rod, and the queen's crown, sceptre and circlet. But the most impressive piece by far is the king's closed imperial crown. This has alternating fleurs de lis and crosses, each set with precious stones, and is surmounted by an orb and cross. Its most interesting feature is the 'images', probably shell or agate cameos, which are set at the base of the rising arches. According to the inventory, one of these (the one visible in Mytens's portrait) depicts 'our Lady and child' and another St George, while the other two are said to be both of Christ. Two depictions of Christ on one object seems unlikely and the 1574 jewel house inventory reinterprets them as 'kings'. Ronald Lightbown, in his study of the medieval regalia, considers this much more likely, proposing that they actually represented 'the two sainted English kings, Edmund and Edward the Confessor'.[18]

If conferring the Holy Spirit through coronation could only happen once, its core message – that the king was the anointed of God – could be reaffirmed as often as it was expedient to do so, by wearing the crown. That, at least, was the theory and the *Ryalle Book* sets out the so-called crown days, when 'the king ought to go crowned and in his robes royal' and walk in solemn procession beneath the canopy of estate.[19] It goes on to say that the regalia 'ought to be hallowed and no temporal man to touch it but only the king; and an esquire of the body to bring it in a fair kerchief, and the king to put them on himself'.[20] What is less certain, however, is whether Henry VIII did in fact ever follow this custom. True, he is depicted in several images wearing a crown,[21] but this may just be conventional royal iconography and none of the chroniclers or contemporary observers ever mention him wearing it. One image with a strong sense of authenticity, showing the king processing towards the opening of Parliament in 1512 (fig. 4.2), depicts him under his canopy, carrying the sceptre, but instead of the crown he is wearing a cap with a jewel. Moreover, the 1521 inventory invites the same conclusion, since it is annotated to the effect that several of the crown's stones had been taken out and were 'with the king'.[22] Eleven years later the 1532 inventory again notes that 'several collets [were] without stones'.[23] It is hard to imagine that the king would have borrowed stones from the crown if he was regularly wearing it.

Rejuvenating the court

The solemnity and spirituality of the coronation was very different from the carnival atmosphere that characterised much of court life in the early years of the reign. This focused on hunting, tournaments and having fun. The tournament – an elaborately choreographed dual between pairs or groups of knights – was the pinnacle of medieval chivalry. Originally conceived for training purposes in horsemanship and the martial arts, it had developed by the fifteenth century into a great spectacle and 'a form of artistic expression in its own right'.[24] But it was not usually a stand-alone event; the tournament was just one component of a sequence of festivities that included pageants, banquets, disguisings and religious observance. All of these came at huge cost, and intentionally so. As Sydney Anglo puts it, these lavish court entertainments 'should be regarded not so much as idle extravagance but rather as the outward show of Henry VIII's desire to impress Europe with his wealth, taste, and accomplishments, and to make England, culturally and militarily, a power on the Continent'.[25]

Tournaments were a familiar sight in England and Henry VII had marked many great events in this way, such as when he made Prince Henry duke of York in 1494. But the difference between Henry VII and his successor was that while the older king had generally been present on these occasions, it was, certainly in his later years, as an observer, whereas his son was itching to take part. And, indeed, it presented an irresistible opportunity for a young and energetic monarch, especially one who had not yet had an opportunity to prove himself in war, because while all court festivities promoted the regime, only the tournament and the king's participation in it could show his personal valour and prowess. And there was a further advantage, namely, that whereas other festivities were acted out before a carefully chosen audience, the tournament was performed before a much larger crowd and was an opportunity to present the young and glamorous king and his rejuvenated court.

Much of the cost of these events arose from the involvement of goldsmiths' work in almost every aspect. Huge sums were spent on splendid gilded armour for the competitors, on gold chains and 'spangles' for their support teams, and on silver-gilt harnesses, bells and cruppers for the horses. The stunning visual impact of these occasions is clear from the account by the papal nuncio, Francesco Chieregato, of a tournament held in 1517. He describes a procession led by the king, who was followed by footmen, trumpeters and gentlemen.

> The horses were all white, and all caparisoned alike, having cost the king a mint of money, as during the last four months all the London goldsmiths have wrought nothing but these trappings. The bridles, pectorals, girths and cruppers of the horses, together with the pommels of the saddles, were of pure silver, on which were chiselled all the royal emblems, none of the materials being either of leather or silk.[26]

He adds that the king himself wore a surcoat of cloth of silver wrought with emblematic letters and pearls and that his horse's bridle and pectoral were studded with jewels and immensely valuable.[27]

The most celebrated tournament of the reign (other than the Field of Cloth of Gold) was that held at Greenwich in 1511 to celebrate the birth of Prince Henry. Sadly, the little prince, born on the first of January, lived just a few weeks. Had he survived, the reign might have panned out very differently, but for the moment everything was rapturous joy. Hall and other chroniclers left vivid accounts of the spectacle and the ubiquitous presence of goldsmiths' work. The *Great Chronicle*, for example, describes the king's horse with its cloth of gold trapper 'wrought with goldsmith work and garnished with gold roses'. Further gold roses embellished the cruppers at the back which 'as a goldsmith reported that had the oversight of the making of that horse harness [...] weighed either of them above fifty ounces in gold'.[28]

Our knowledge of this spectacular event is not limited to written accounts, however, and we have a rare pictorial record of it in the

Westminster Tournament Roll, which is preserved in the College of Arms.[29] The roll is wonderfully detailed and gives an extraordinary visual reference to many of the features mentioned by the commentators. The key image, from our point of view, is that showing the king processing through the tilt-yard on his horse (fig. 4.3). The tilt-gallery is hung with the Tudor green and white livery, with red roses and other royal badges; the footmen all wear impressively heavy gold chains; the king has a sumptuous robe of cloth of gold trimmed with sable, and a magnificent gold and jewelled collar. His horse is hardly less magnificent. It has a dazzling bard sewn with gold letters of K, pomegranates and Katherine's personal motto for the occasion, 'Loyall'. Before the king rides a knight – either Lord Bergavenny or Thomas Howard – bearing the king's helmet. Sydney Anglo describes the knight as holding a white staff on which the silver helmet is balanced. 'The gorget-plates are of gold and set with red and green gems. The helmet is surmounted with a crown of gold and crimson set with gems'; his horse is 'trapped in gold hung with golden bells [and there is a] golden pomegranate and cluster on the crupper'.[30] Another of the many horses depicted on the

Figure 4.3 Henry VIII entering the lists, from the *Westminster Tournament Roll*, 1511. College of Arms.

roll is shown in a bard of cloth of gold and ermine and has stirrups exquisitely modelled with gothic tracery.

Are we really to believe that such lavish ornaments, both human and equine, were actually made of precious metal, or might we suspect that this is an example of observers simply repeating official propaganda, designed once again to give an inflated sense of royal wealth? Fortunately, there can be no doubt about this, for we have detailed corroborating evidence. The Chamber accounts, which cover not only the last seventeen years of Henry VII's reign but the first twelve of his son's, contain references to a number of items of exactly this kind. These include a colossal payment to Robert Amadas in 1513 of £2,000 for 'horse harnesses and trappers of goldsmiths work', another of £462 4s 2d for 'garnishing a headpiece with crown gold, garnishing a salet and mending a shapwe'[31] and, in 1516, a third of £481 5s 1¼d for 'four saddles for fourteen horse harnesses, wrought with spangles and tassles of silver'.[32]

Other aspects of courtly performance included pageants and revels. Pageants enacted through the streets of the City of London, such as that devised for Katherine of Aragon's arrival in 1501, were largely paid for by

the City, but those held at court were entirely funded by the king and were the responsibility of Richard Gibson, master of the revels. One of the greatest regular festivities in the court calendar was 'twelfth night' and that held in January 1511 must have been especially splendid, given how soon it was after the birth of Prince Henry. Hall describes it succinctly:

> Against the xii. day or the day of the Epiphany at night, before the banquet in the hall at Richmond, was a pageant devised like a mountain, glistening by night, as though it had been all of gold and set with stones, on the top of which mountain was a tree of gold, the branches and bows frysed with gold, spreading on every side over the mountain, with roses and pomegranates, the which mountain was with [de]vices brought up towards the king, and out of the same came a lady, apparelled in cloth of gold, and the children of honour called the henchmen, which were freshly disguised, and danced a morice before the king. And that done, re-entered the mountain, and then it was drawn back, and then was the wassail or banquet brought in, and so brake up Christmas.[33]

Gibson's accounts for this occasion confirm what we might have assumed: that although the mountain appeared 'as though it had been all of gold', the illusion was in fact achieved with gold foil. But for the costumes of the performers no such economies were made and a sampling of the Chamber accounts during the opening years of the reign gives a flavour of the extraordinary use of gold and silver on these occasions: in 1510 Robert Amadas supplied 590 gold 'pieces' of sheaves of arrows and castles, forty-five enamelled gold roses and fifty-six gold pomegranates, weighing 141 oz. The next year he delivered 477 gold letters of H and K weighing 170 oz, followed soon after by yet more.[34]

The scale of this expenditure was partly due to high losses, either through 'liberality' or carelessness. On one occasion the king casually gave away four ounces of letters 'to lords and ladies off his jacket', but the £8 15s that Gibson noted as the cost of this spontaneous gesture was of very little consequence compared with the 225 oz of gold apparently lost when the king's and Sir Thomas Knyvet's 'dresses were damaged and lost' in February 1511.[35] This was perhaps the same scene of controlled mayhem colourfully described by Hall:

> After the king and his companions had danced, he appointed the ladies, gentlewomen and the ambassadors to take the letters of their garments, in token of liberality, which thing the common people perceiving, ran to the king, and stripped him of his hosen and doublet, and all his companions in likewise [...] The ladies likewise were spoiled, whereof the king's guard came suddenly, and put the people back [... But] all

these hurts were turned to laughing and game, and thought that, all that was taken way was but for honour and largesse: and so this triumph ended with mirth and gladness. At this banquet, a shipman of London caught certain letters which he sold to a goldsmith for £3 14s 8d by reason whereof, it appeared that the garments were of great value.[36]

Royal expenditure on plate and jewels

Our main source for royal expenditure on luxury goods over the first decade of the reign is the Chamber books. These show the young king, once fully established on the throne, spending at an even greater rate than his father. In comparison with Henry VII's outlay of some £200,000 on plate and jewels between 1492 and 1509, by 1521 his son had in a much shorter period paid out around £175,000 (see graph 4.1). But impressive though this sum is, it is almost certainly not the full picture. For, as we have seen, this was a period when the privy chamber was taking on an increasing share of royal discretionary spending, but its accounts for the early part of the reign do not survive. Had they done so, they would doubtless have added considerably to the total.

Closer examination of the Chamber books shows the young king continuing his father's policy of spending heavily with foreign merchants. The dominant names were all Italian: the Frescobaldi of Florence, Bruges and Antwerp, Lorenzo Bonvixi, Antonio Cavallari of Lucca, and Guido

Graph 4.1 Approximate total expenditure on plate, jewels and cloth of gold during the period of the Chamber books, 1492–1521.

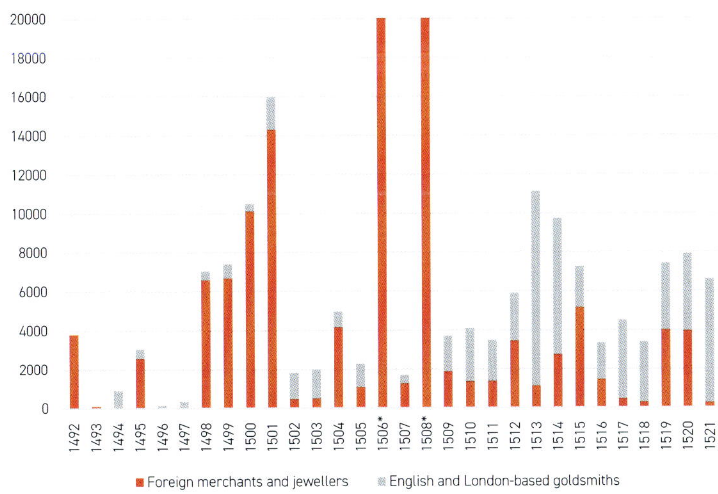

* In 1506 and 1508 exceptionally large sums were spent overseas: £88,000 in 1506 as a combined total for French jewels, precious stones, plate and a loan to the Spanish king, and £30,000 in 1508 for French plate and jewels alone.

Portinari (related to Tomasso Portinari, the Medici banker in Bruges).[37] Their connections gave them access to the finest goods and in return they enjoyed special privileges, such as customs concessions on condition of giving the king first refusal. Although mostly associated with luxury textiles, especially cloth of gold, they also supplied plate and jewels: in 1509 Frescobaldi supplied Henry VIII with an order of new Flemish plate[38] and in 1510 another Italian, Lodovico della Fava, was paid £766 for two separate consignments of plate.[39] Like most of the others, 'Lewes dela Fava' provided a wide range of goods and services, from jewels, cloth of gold and 'diverse things' to currency exchange and couriering money to the king's ambassadors abroad. French merchants, such as Jacques Maryne, Jacques Langeloys and Jenyn Lengeam, also figure prominently, especially in connection with jewels. The last of these was paid nearly £4,000 for jewels in 1519.[40]

The special privileges extended to these merchants were not only on account of the desirable things they could offer. They were in touch with other princes and were in possession of information that made them useful. Giovanni Cavalcanti, for example, a senior member of the Bardi firm and the Medici factor in London, was an usher of the Apostolic Chamber and was a channel of communication between London and Rome.[41] Such usefulness worked both ways and in 1533 Eustace Chapuys, the imperial ambassador at Henry VIII's court, wrote to the emperor with some politically sensitive news, saying that he had heard it from 'a very worthy and creditable man' who had got it from 'the king's own silversmith and jeweller'.[42]

These rich and influential merchants were not the king's only access to foreign goods, however. In December 1517 the Venetian ambassador, Sebastian Giustinian, wrote that galleys from Venice were expected in England and 'I am informed the king longs for their coming, and that his Majesty means to go to [South]Hampton, saying he shall purchase many articles of luxury.'[43] Two years earlier the same ambassador had reported a conversation with Thomas Wolsey when the cardinal confirmed a rumour that substantial funds had been remitted to Germany and claimed this was 'for the purchase of [the king's] personal ornaments, both weapons and other things' and that several princes 'whether in France, in Germany or in Italy, have pledged a quantity of beautiful jewels of great value, which we hope to obtain at no great cost'.[44] Purchases like these were probably funded by the privy purse rather than the Chamber but even when they do figure in the Chamber accounts the entries are frustratingly vague. Given the substantial sums involved – £1,300 to Jenyn Lengeam 'for certain jewels', £811 3s 8d to 'Jacques Langeloys, jeweller of France', or £533 6s 8d to Cavalcanti 'for a diamond set in a gold ring' – the descriptions are thin at best.[45] Cavalcanti's ring, in particular, at such a price, must have been a remarkable jewel.

The king's goldsmiths

We have a rather clearer idea about the work done for the Crown by the goldsmiths of London, not least because the Chamber payments are backed up by the jewel house inventory. Regular orders mainly revolved around domestic wares for the household, spangles and accessories for court festivities, and gifts for courtiers and foreign ambassadors.

Five names appear most frequently in the first decade of the reign (see graph 4.2): Robert Amadas, Thomas Exmew, John Mundy, John Twyselton and Nicholas Warley. William Holland, an important figure later on, first appears in 1513, and at least three strangers, Paul van Vreland, John van Delft and Henry Holtesweller, appear several times. Over the period 1509 to 1521 the Chamber books show payments of some £53,000 to this group, but they are spread very unevenly, with expenditure starting at a lower level than under Henry VII and gradually rising to eclipse it.

Other than Amadas, all of the London goldsmiths in the group were fully trained and independently working by the turn of the century; two of them, Mundy and Warley, had direct links with earlier royal goldsmiths, having been trained under Edmund Shaa and Hugh Brice.[46] Two of them had distinguished civic careers as well: Exmew and Mundy were both elected mayor of London (in 1517–18 and 1522–23) and were subsequently knighted.[47] Exmew, Mundy and Warley also became powerful figures in the Goldsmiths' Company, serving either as warden or as upper warden. They were not all entirely alike, however. Mundy was probably the wealthiest of the four, contributing £500, half of the entire Goldsmiths' Company's contribution, to a forced loan to the king in 1521.[48] He was also connected

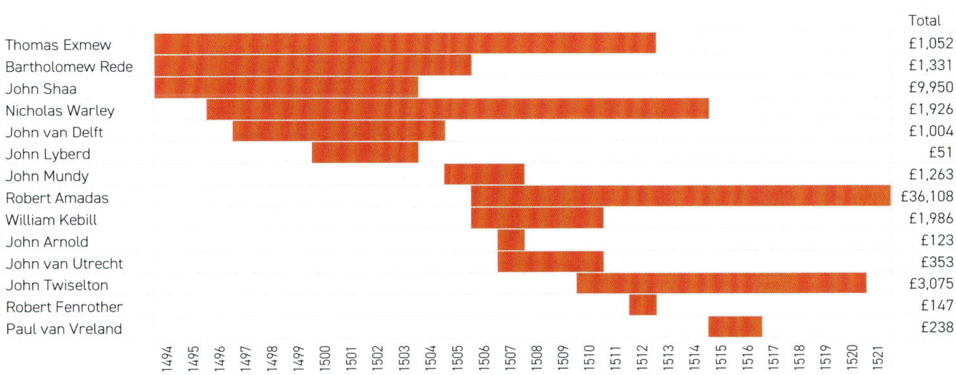

Graph 4.2 Royal goldsmiths during the period of the Chamber books, 1492–1521.

* Totals exclude mint-related currency exchanges but include purchases for materials other than plate and goldsmiths' work.

to the duke of Norfolk through the marriage of his daughter to the duke's third son, a rare alliance between trade and aristocracy, and his will shows him bequeathing a gold salt to the duke.[49] The interest of Exmew's children lay not in their marriages but their calling. Both chose the religious life, his son being among the Carthusian monks executed by Henry VIII in 1535 for refusing the oath of royal supremacy, and his daughter a nun of Dartford Priory, Kent who fled the country to continue her vocation in Bruges.[50]

John Twyselton was the odd man out within the group. He was something of a rebel within the Goldsmiths' Company and regularly clashed with the authorities.[51] Despite this, he provided plate for Princess Mary when she married Louis XII in 1514 and was a regular supplier of new year's gifts from 1519 to 1523.[52] It was perhaps on account of his position as a royal goldsmith that, despite his tempestuous relations with the company, he became a warden in 1517.[53]

As we have seen, the most important figure by far among the royal goldsmiths was Robert Amadas and the £36,000 of payments to him in the Chamber books between 1506 and 1521 vastly exceed the combined total paid to all the other London goldsmiths over the same period. Many of Amadas's payments were for what are vaguely described as 'diverse things', but a few are more specific. Orders include 'gold stuff for the disguising', domestic plate, letters and spangles, horse harnesses and 'a great seal of silver'.[54] The largest category was spangles and 'ornaments for jackets'. These included 'gilt and white spangles' and 'letters, wreaths, harts and roses of fine gold'.[55] The ornaments for jackets referred to the rich uniforms of the king's guard, which seem to have been refurbished each year and for which, over the period of the Chamber books, he received more than £6,750. This was the equivalent of around 3,000 ounces of wrought gold plate or 27,000 ounces of silver-gilt.[56] Amadas's career continued until his death in 1532 and became even more profitable during the years when he combined the roles of royal goldsmith, deputy master of the mint and master of the jewel house.

The scale of Amadas's operations by the end of his life was enormous and we get a sense of his wealth through the probate inventory compiled after his death.[57] By then he had houses in London and in Essex. The house in Lombard Street was his residence and his business premises. It had a hall and a chapel, as well as a workshop, a warehouse and a counting house. The workshop and warehouse contained some goldsmithing tools – bellows, tongs, ladles, melting pots, leads and scales – though apparently not enough for large-scale production. The counting house, however, in addition to tools of his trade like 'piles great and small of troy weights of brass', contained a serious quantity of jewels and gold and silver plate of all sorts, including 'broken gold' and 'broken silver'.

This was either stock or precious metal held in pledge; it was valued at around £850 and was quite separate from his own household plate. The most impressive figures, however, related to the debts that remained outstanding at his death. These were categorised as 'sperat' (hopeful) and 'desperat' (hopeless – essentially written off). The 'sperat' debts totalled £3,845 but the 'desperat' ones came to a colossal £6,564, including a clearly irrecoverable sum of £1,600 owed by the now long dead Cardinal Wolsey. On the other side of the balance sheet were sums that Amadas owed to others: £3,524, including the £1,772 owed to the king on account of the missing plate from the jewel house.

For the other royal goldsmiths the main sources of business were gifts, domestic plate for the household and repairs. The plate they supplied was not all new, however, and in April 1514 Mundy received £443 7s 'for plate late [of] the Earl of Wiltshire';[58] Henry Stafford, first earl of Wiltshire, had presumably been obliged to sell in order to raise money for his participation in the 1513 French war. Other names crop up too, such as one John Smyth, who supplied twelve bowls weighing 650 oz 10 dwt at 3s 6d per ounce.[59] This was a low price so presumably the bowls were second-hand.

These thumbnail sketches of royal goldsmiths, drawn from the Chamber books and the records of the Goldsmiths' Company, are revealing in certain respects but tell us little of the workshops that supplied the plate. The £452 paid to John Twyselton in 1516, for example, would have equated to about 1,800 oz of new silver-gilt and have required a team of journeymen and apprentices working under the master. Robert Amadas's vastly greater payments (£9,666 in 1513, £2,029 in 1517, £2,356 in 1519, etc.) imply either a much larger workshop or subcontracting to other goldsmiths (as we know he did). In this respect it is curious that we know more about the businesses of stranger goldsmiths than of natives because of the strangers' requirement for licences to employ journeymen (see p. 178).

Other sources of plate

Direct purchase was only one of the means through which the stock of royal plate was increased. Other sources remained as they had been under Henry VII, namely new year's gifts, gifts from other princes, and dowries. But the most lucrative source was attainder. Early inflows of attainder plate included that of the unpopular ministers, Richard Empson and Edmund Dudley,[60] and the plate of Lady Hungerford, hanged for the murder of her first husband in 1522.[61] But the biggest catch of the early years was the duke of Buckingham. Edward Stafford, third duke (1478–1521), was directly descended from Edward III, as well as being nephew of Edward IV's queen,

Elizabeth Woodville. He was, therefore, close to the throne and claimed the roles of lord high constable and lord high steward as his hereditary right at the coronation. As the wealthiest peer in England he lived in great style and his personal magnificence in the coronation procession, according to the *Great Chronicle*, was barely less than that of the king himself.[62] This was sailing dangerously close to the wind and when his loyalties came under suspicion so did his magnificence. Perhaps sensing that something was up and trying to buy himself out of trouble, the duke issued detailed instructions to his chancellor in November 1520 'to have a goblet of gold made for a new year's gift to the king, a pomander and chain of gold for the queen, and a cup of gold with a cover for the cardinal'.[63] The 'goblet' was perhaps that described in the 1521 inventory as engraved with roses and pomegranates, with a red and white rose on the cover and weighing 14¾ oz.[64]

Buckingham might have been lulled into a false sense of security by receiving gifts himself from the king and queen and he tipped the servants that brought them with handsome rewards of 100s each.[65] But later in the year he was accused of treason and imprisoned in the Tower. His elevated status accorded him certain privileges despite the gravity of his indictment and the jewel house inventory includes a list of plate that he was allowed to retain in his quarters while he awaited trial: a ewer and basin, a covered salt, pots, bottles, cups and jugs, together with half a dozen spoons and some chapel plate.[66] But this was as nothing compared with the plate that was appropriated by the king after his death. This is all annotated in the inventory as 'parcel of the plate that was the late duke of Buckingham's the king's Rebel'; it contributed several thousand ounces of silver and 81 oz of gold to the jewel house.[67] Nor can we be sure that even this impressive quantity was the totality of his plate. The low ratio of gold to silver, in particular, is surprising and suggests that more gold might either have gone directly to the privy chamber or been sent to the mint.

Court style in the early years of the reign

Although popularly seen as the Renaissance prince *par excellence*, Henry VIII inherited a throne still essentially medieval in its artistic tastes. That this was as true of plate as it was of other artistic media is clear from the repertoire of ornament described in the 1521 inventory. As we have seen, this seldom mentions shapes or general decorative characteristics, but it does include a rich vocabulary of specific motifs. These are of two kinds, pure decoration, and a range of motifs that come under the general heading of heraldry and badges.

Pure decoration is limited in range but include motifs such as 'drops' (or 'doppes'), 'bullions' (raised bosses), branches and feathers; lozenges or 'lozenged' patterns appear repeatedly too, as does the term 'wrethen' (twisted): spoons are described as having 'wrethen steles' (or handles) and pots, salts, bowls and even altar crosses are 'chased wrethen'. All of these might be loosely categorised as part of the language of late gothic architecture and decoration and have parallels in German and Flemish plate as well as surviving objects made for highly placed English patrons. What distinguishes the royal plate in the jewel house is its heraldic and quasi-heraldic ornament. Many pieces are engraved or enamelled with the 'king's arms', but many more carry initials or badges. Badges reflected an aspect of late medieval society, inelegantly dubbed 'bastard feudalism'. Unlike coats of arms, badges could be used by retainers as a mark of affinity or loyalty. Senior members of a household might wear their master's badge on a gold chain (the origin of today's mayorial chains); servants of lower rank wore them sewn to their uniforms (as the yeomen warders at the Tower of London still do). The language of badges was complex. When shown on your own property they demonstrated ownership, but when displayed on a gift, such as a piece of plate, they served a different function, reminding its recipient of obligation or relationship. Under the Tudors, badges became an obsession. They appeared on the exterior and interior of buildings, on arms and armour, on furniture, clothes and documents and, of course, on jewels and plate.

The repertoire of early Tudor badges was extensive: the most common in the first half of Henry VIII's reign were pomegranates (for Katherine of Aragon) and red and white roses (signifying the houses of Lancaster and York, united through Henry VII's marriage to Elizabeth of York). Henry VII preferred the red rose, whereas his son normally combined the two. Other badges also appeared on plate: a castle and sheaf of arrows were secondary badges for Katherine; the portcullis and daisy (or 'margaret') signified Lady Margaret Beaufort, Henry VII's mother, but were also adopted by Henry VIII. As the reign progressed, still more badges appeared, such as the falcon on a tree stump for Anne Boleyn and the phoenix for Jane Seymour. In addition to badges, elements from the royal arms were sometimes used in a way that was not strictly heraldic: fleurs de lis often appear as a decorative motif and the royal supporters (a dragon and greyhound for Henry VII and a dragon and lion for Henry VIII after about 1525) are occasionally made to serve as stems, handles or finials on plate. Less obvious is the martlet, which appears on more than a hundred items in the 1521 inventory, most of which were bowls. This was not one of the commoner Tudor badges but was one of the charges of the arms of Henry VII's father, Edmund Tudor, and his uncle, Jasper.[68]

Figure 4.4 The Beaufort beaker, London, 1507–08. Silver gilt. Christ's College, Cambridge.

Figure 4.5 One of three Beaufort salts, London, 1507–08. Silver gilt. Christ's College, Cambridge.

Of the 900 or so entries in the 1521 inventory only the French royal gold cup survives. But several other pieces with royal associations also survive and give some visual clue to the wares that lined the shelves of the jewel house. Of particular interest are two of the bequests of Lady Margaret Beaufort (d. 1509) to Christ's College, Cambridge, a covered beaker and a salt (figs 4.4 and 4.5), both hallmarked for 1507–08. These are very different from each other but are united by their ornament. The beaker is engraved with a trellis pattern (or lozenges) containing roses, daisies and portcullises, while the finial is modelled with the same motifs. Its high rose-shaped foot, where only holes remain, would have been set with stones, pearls or badges, probably attached with butterfly clips. The covered salt, one of three in the bequest, is less sophisticated but is modelled on the stem with gothic pinnacles and embossed with roses. A third object of the same genre is a small cup and cover of 1515–16 at Corpus Christi College, Oxford (fig. 4.6). This was given to the college by its founder, Bishop Richard Fox (d. 1528), and is embossed all over with 'bullions', but the engraved roses, fleurs de lis and pomegranates on the cover and finial are royal and the cup may well have been a royal gift to him, perhaps at new year.

Another remarkable object, not royal but surely of comparable stature, is the Leigh cup in the collection of the Mercers' Company. Hallmarked for 1513–14, it is of similar profile to the covered cup seen in figure 1.2. It is decorated with trelliswork like that on the Beaufort beaker, but in relief, the interstices of which are filled with applied badges.

Clear though the ornamental parallels are between these survivals and plate in the jewel house,[69] it is harder to relate them to actual objects in the inventory, because the latter gives so little away in terms of form. Perhaps, for example, the Fox cup resembled 'a [silver-gilt] cup with a cover and a rose upon the knop' weighing 23 oz',[70] or the beaker 'a goblet with a cover gilt graven with roses portcullises fleurs de lis pomegranates and sheaves of arrows' weighing 28 oz';[71] we will never know for sure.

One other group described in the inventory could be said to survive, if only in surrogate form. The term 'feather fashion' occurs ten times in the inventory, in relation to salts, bowls, pots and flagons. A pair of silver-gilt pots, weighing 332 oz, is described as 'chased wrethen feather fashion' and another pot, at 103 oz, as 'chased with feathers'.[72] There is no indication of their shape, but such pots in the early sixteenth century were usually pear-shaped, exactly like a group made for the coronation of Charles II in 1660 (fig. 4.7).[73] The latter are not in the style of that time and both their form and chased feathers suggest that they are copies of much older ones. One particular detail leans towards this conclusion: their distinctive thumbpieces are again not typical for 1660, but correspond exactly to a known early sixteenth-century type that is described here and there in the inventory as, for example, 'knops strawberry fashion behind

Figure 4.6 The Founder's cup, London, 1515–16. Silver gilt. Corpus Christi College, Oxford.

Figure 4.7 Pair of pots chased with feathers, London, 1660–61, attributed to James Beacham. Silver gilt. Royal collection (Jewel House, Tower of London).

Figure 4.8
The San Lorenzo vase, London, 1511–12, maker's mark a cross. Silver gilt and enamel. Church of San Lorenzo, Florence.

the lids'.[74] The 1660 pots are 52 cm high and weigh about ten per cent more than the larger of the two pairs in 1521, so here again, perhaps, is a useful point of reference for visualising the scale of much of the vanished royal Tudor plate.

The single most spectacular surviving royal object from the early years of the reign, however, has no direct parallels in the inventory and reminds us that there was another body of holdings, closer to the king and perhaps less formulaic than most of the more routine plate in the jewel house. This is a silver-gilt mounted rock-crystal vase, or cup (now serving as a reliquary), in the church of San Lorenzo in Florence. Standing 32.3 cm high, the elaborately mounted vase may be assumed to epitomise court style around the start of the reign (fig. 4.8).[75] It bears London hallmarks for 1511–12, just two years into the reign, and the unidentified maker's mark of a cross on a shield (fig. 4.8a).

The embossed motifs on the foot and stem, alternately burnished and engraved with matting, are 'drops', the cover is 'wrethen', and the badges are the same as those that appear throughout the inventory: the foot is embellished with alternating pomegranates and roses and the vertical straps encasing the rock crystal are enamelled with alternating red and white roses, interspersed with a third flower, a blue pansy or 'heartsease' (fig. 4.8c). The ogee-profiled cover has a hemispherical finial ('knop' in the inventory), the top of which is roughly formed and enamelled with translucent green to resemble a grassy mound. The element that surmounted it is lost but we know from a sixteenth-century illustrated inventory of the reliquaries at San Lorenzo that it was in the form of a standing figure of St George and the dragon. St George, of course, was the patron saint of England and of the Order of the Garter.

In two ways, however, the vase is not typical. The small kneeling putti on top of the handles (fig. 4.8b) have no known parallels in surviving English plate and nowhere does the inventory seem to refer to such a motif. This is an early nod towards the Renaissance style and marks the

Figure 4.8a
Detail of the marks on the San Lorenzo vase.

Figure 4.8b Detail of putto on the San Lorenzo vase.

Figure 4.8c Detail of enamelled roses on the San Lorenzo vase.

vase out as a fashion leader. Their most famous contemporary occurrence is the gilded bronze putti that flank the royal arms on Henry VII's tomb in Westminster Abbey. These were by the Italian artist, Pietro Torrigiano, who started working on the tomb at exactly the same time as the cup was made, in 1512.

The other atypical feature is the crystal itself. The vase with its mounts weighs some 77 oz,[76] more than twice as much as the only possibly comparable piece in the jewel house, which was 'a goblet of berall with a cover garnished with silver and gilt'.[77] The San Lorenzo crystal is Italian and probably dates from the fourteenth century; it is of very similar form to a group of hardstone vessels once owned by Lorenzo the Magnificent and may have come to England as a gift to Henry VII, or as one of his many purchases from Italian merchants. Quite aside from its mounts, the crystal vase itself would have been regarded as an object of exceptional preciousness. Rock crystal was highly prized, especially when cut and turned into elegant vessels, and could be as valuable as gold. Margaret Countess of Richmond's executors valued 15 oz of beryl and jasper at 30s an ounce;[78] larger specimens would have commanded a higher price and the San Lorenzo vase might have been worth as much as £40. Presumably it travelled to Florence as a sumptuous gift to one or other of the two

Medici popes, Leo X (r. 1513–21) or Clement VII (r. 1523–34), since it has been in their family chapel since 1532.

Aside from the finial, another lost element of the San Lorenzo vase is the leather case that would almost certainly have been supplied with it. These have been mentioned before and were essential for the protection of fragile plate as it was moved around from one place to another. Almost none of these survive and they are even rarer than plate itself. Virtually the sole English survivor from this period is the case for the surgeons' instrument case discussed in Chapter 10 (fig. 4.9). Carefully shaped to conform to the object itself, this is made of wood panels wrapped in leather. But it is more than a utilitarian protective container and the decorative foliage tooling that covers much of the outside transforms it into a modest work of art in its own right.

What do these few and arguably unrepresentative survivals of royal plate tell us of the state of goldsmiths' work in England in the early sixteenth century? And what inference should we draw from Henry VII's and perhaps the young Henry VIII's predilection for plate from abroad? The Fox cup at Corpus Christi College is competently made but has a certain formulaic and routine quality. The castings, stamped ornament and engraving lack flare or invention. This is hardly surprising, for it would have been one of many, valued more for their bullion than their artistry. The same criticism – or worse – might be levelled against the Beaufort salt, and while the beaker sets an altogether higher standard of silversmithing and engraving, it is let down by its coarse finial. Even the San Lorenzo vase, whose mounts were created for a vessel of undoubted preciousness, lacks outstanding artistry. The decoration is standard, the enamelling unsophisticated and the modelling of the putti sculpturally weak.

Figure 4.9
Case to the Barbers' instrument box. Leather. Worshipful Company of Barbers, London.

The levels of skill attained by native English goldsmiths seldom equalled those of the greatest foreign masters and help explain both Henrys' appetite for good quality German, Flemish and French plate. A chronic problem that drew complaints right through to the eighteenth century, this was largely attributable to the relatively low standards of training demanded by the Goldsmiths' Company.[79] Such a deficit created real opportunities for 'stranger' goldsmiths coming to England with more finely developed skill-sets, but it also led to tensions within the goldsmithing community as the company tried to exclude the strangers and protect their own. For those working under the patronage of the king, however, regulations could be circumvented. This is an issue that we will look at more closely in later chapters.

Five 'Defender of the Faith'

The relationship between Church and Crown in medieval England was symbiotic. The king's unique status as the anointed of God was enacted at the coronation through – and only possibly through – the agency of the Church. The very symbols of kingship, the coronation regalia, tied the two together through their association with a sainted king and were kept and guarded not by the king but by the Church, in Westminster Abbey. But equally, the Church depended on the Crown and enjoyed its privileges and wealth only so long as it continued to have the king's goodwill. As the events of the 1530s were to show, without that it was powerless.

The Church was central to the life of the court and no great royal event was complete without a magnificent religious service. On such occasions the high altar would be set with gold or silver-gilt and jewelled crosses, candlesticks and 'images' (silver busts or figures of saints). The performance of the liturgy required chalices, paxes, censers and so on, and the clergy wore vestments of embroidered cloth of gold. Bishops and abbots processed in jewelled mitres with golden croziers; further magnificence would be provided by altar frontals and cloth of gold draped over the desks of the king and queen. At a less public level, life at court was marked out by a daily round of masses and other offices performed by the Chapel Royal, and the king himself would often hear more than one mass a day.

This chapter looks at some of the most spectacular church services of the early part of the reign, their importance in contributing to the perception and self-perception of the king, and the spectacular religious plate that he had at his disposal. It also considers the centrality of Henry's relationship with the pope until matters matrimonial changed that for good.

Church and Crown

There was another, more practical, link between the Church and the Crown, in that the Church had traditionally provided many of the king's leading councillors. The Church had long been a powerful magnet for brilliant minds and a promising ecclesiastical career could lead to a place on the king's council. Men like Cardinal Bainbridge and Bishop Fox were typical high-fliers of their time. Bainbridge climbed the ecclesiastical ladder quickly, moving swiftly from dean of Windsor to archbishop of York and then to Rome as ambassador to the pope. There Julius II made him a cardinal in 1512, but he died two years later, allegedly from poisoning. On his death he was reputed to be worth 50,000 ducats (around £11,250) and left 'much ready money and plate'.[1] None of this survives, other than a pair of snuffers in the British Museum, probably made in Rome but enamelled with his arms and, as Henry VIII's ambassador, with those of the king as well.

Richard Fox's career was ecclesiastical and political in equal measure. In 1487 he was made keeper of the privy seal as well as bishop of Exeter; by 1501 he was appointed bishop of Winchester, the wealthiest diocese in England. In parallel with this, he remained a councillor to both Henrys until retiring in 1516. As bishop of Winchester he received about £4,000 a year and, with a total annual income of about twice that, was probably as wealthy as any nobleman.[2] Today he is best remembered for his foundation of Corpus Christi College, Oxford, which still preserves some of his plate, including his crozier, two ablutions basins and a gold chalice and paten, as well as the covered cup we considered in the last chapter (fig. 4.6).

These 'princes of the Church' were exactly that. Not only were they men of wealth and power but, like secular princes, they had insignia to denote their office. For a bishop these included a ring, crozier and mitre, together with precious vestments. Some of these were extraordinarily splendid. One bishop's or abbot's insignia – perhaps Cardinal Wolsey's – found its way to the jewel house and is included in the 1532 inventory. The mitre was spectacular. Described as 'gold and garnished with stone', it was set with sixty sapphires, fifty-four balases, more than 270 pearls and an unspecified number of diamonds.[3] A hint of its magnificence can be gleaned from the rather less sumptuous pearl and stone-set mitre in the National Portrait Gallery's portrait of Archbishop Warham (fig. 5.1). This also includes his golden processional cross, set with stones and enamelled with his arms, while his hands rest on a cushion covered in luxurious cloth of gold. Similarly, the richness of vestments can be seen in the superb cloth of gold cope bequeathed to Westminster Abbey by Henry VII and preserved at

Figure 5.1 *Archbishop William Warham*, after Hans Holbein the younger, early seventeenth-century copy of a work of 1527. National Portrait Gallery, London.

Figure 5.2 Cope of cloth of gold embroidered with Tudor roses, crowned portcullises and a collar of esses, bequeathed by Henry VII to Westminster Abbey, c. 1510. Stonyhurst Abbey.

Stonyhurst College (fig. 5.2). Richly embroidered with crowned portcullises, Tudor roses and a collar of esses, it epitomises the presence of the Crown in the Church.

Immensely rich though these prelates were, the Church itself was wealthy too, owning huge tracts of land, plate and jewels, and receiving donations from pilgrims visiting the shrines of saints. But impressive altar plate was not only a mark of the Church's wealth; it also had a theological role, as exempla that would move the spirit to contemplate higher things. Abbot Suger, head of the great royal Benedictine abbey of St-Denis near Paris, expressed this idea in his twelfth-century tract *De administratione*, in which he argued that gold and precious stones reflected the glory of God and gave the faithful a vision of his perfection.[4] Typical of his attitude towards precious materials was the effect that the great golden altar cross had on his own perceptions:

> when […] the loveliness of the many-coloured gems has called me from external cares, and worthy meditation has induced me to reflect, transferring that which is material to that which is immaterial, on the

> diversity of the sacred virtues: then it seems to me that I see myself dwelling [...] in some strange region of the universe which neither exists entirely in the slime of the earth nor in the purity of heaven.[5]

There was another string to Suger's bow and that concerned gold as the ideal material for the chalice, because it symbolised the divine nature of its contents.

> To me [...] one thing has always seemed pre-eminently fitting: that every costlier or costliest thing should serve first and foremost, for the administration of the Holy Eucharist. If golden pouring vessels, golden vials, golden little mortars used to serve [...] to collect the blood of goats or calves or the red heifer: how much more must golden vessels, precious stones, and whatever is most valued among all created things, be laid out, with continual reverence and full devotion, for the reception of the blood of Christ![6]

This is nothing less than a theological exposition of the doctrine of magnificence and it was put in more prosaic terms in Henry VIII's own day by Sir Thomas Elyot in *The Boke Named the Governour*, when he wrote that 'ornaments dedicated to God were necessary for [the] augmentation and continuing of reverence'.[7]

An even more potent focus of Church wealth was the shrines of saints, which pilgrims travelled great distances to venerate. The incentive for these pilgrimages was the pious hope of spiritual gain or a cure for some debilitating disease and the odds in favour of saintly intercession were much improved by the gift of a jewel to embellish the shrine. The most famous shrine in England was Thomas Becket's at Canterbury and Erasmus's account of his visit gives a vivid impression of what a treasure it was:

> a coffin of wood covering a coffin of gold, which being drawn by the ropes and pulleys, an invaluable treasure was discovered. Gold was the meanest thing to be seen there. All shone and glittered with the rarest and most precious jewels of an extraordinary bigness; some were larger than the egg of a goose. When this sight was shown, the prior, with a white wand, touched every jewel, one by one, telling the name, the value and the donor of it.[8]

Unlike the Crown, the Church was a multi-faceted institution. It was composed of many different elements, with the secular Church in England headed by the archbishop of Canterbury and each of the monastic orders with their own head. The ultimate authority for all was the pope and it was this that gave the relationship between Church and Crown an international aspect.

The pope was a temporal as well as a religious ruler, with territories, political ambitions and strategic alliances. For a young prince like Henry VIII, politically ambitious himself but also a true son of the Church, there was a delicate path to be trod and his relationship with the pope was critically important. At the start of his reign this was very close and, in a remark that he might have come to regret had he remembered making it, Henry was quoted by the Venetian ambassador in 1515 as saying that 'I [...] am [the pope's] good son, and shall ever be with his Holiness and with the Church, from which I never mean to depart'.[9] It would be decades, however, before the irony of this became clear, and a measure of the warmth of his initial relationship, across four papal reigns, is the series of gifts received by Henry VIII between 1510 and 1524. One of these, a hundred parmesan cheeses sent by Julius II in 1511, strikes a rather homely note,[10] but more notable were two kinds of specifically papal gifts, the golden rose and the sword and cap of maintenance.

These were given each year to a Christian prince as a special mark of favour and were invested with great spiritual significance. The golden rose was blessed on the fourth Sunday of Lent as a symbol of the hope aroused by the approach of Easter. Henry VIII received this great honour on two occasions, from Julius II in 1510 and from Clement VII in 1524. Julius wrote to Warham at the time saying 'we now send him [Henry] the Golden Rose, anointed with the Holy Chrism, sprinkled with odiferous musk, and blessed with our hands [...] which we would have you, brother, to give him, with our Apostolical Benediction, during the solemnity of the mass'.[11] The arrival of Clement's rose was described by Edward Hall:

> This year the first day of September, was received into London [... an] ambassador from Clement bishop of Rome, which brought with him a rose of gold, for a token to the king [...] After a solemn mass sung by the cardinal of York, the said present was delivered to the king [... The rose] was a tree forged with fine gold, and wrought with branches, leaves and flowers, resembling roses: this tree was set in a pot of gold, which had three feet of antique fashion: the pot was of measure half a pint, in the uppermost rose, was a fair sapphire loupe pierced, the bigness of an acorn, the tree was of height half an English yard, and in breadth it was a foot.[12]

The rose was promptly passed to the master of the jewels and listed as an addition to the 1521 inventory: 'Received from the pope's holiness by Doctor [Thomas] Hannibal, a rose of gold with ix branches standing upon iij lions' feet and a coarse sapphire in the top'.[13] There it joined two others, Julius II's and a third, given to Prince Arthur by Alexander VI. They all weighed between nineteen and twenty-one ounces and were presumably quite similar, although with different feet. Alexander's and Julius's had oxen and acorn feet, alluding to the Borgia and della Rovere arms; the lion feet of Clement's made no such allusions and were probably just classicising motifs. We have no images of these roses but Hall's description of Clement's being 'set in a pot of gold, which had three feet of antique fashion' corresponds exactly to one given by Leo X in 1520 to Cardinal Albrecht of Brandenburg. This is painstakingly depicted in a remarkable illustrated inventory of Albrecht's jewels and plate (fig. 5.3).[14] Clearly, papal roses were made to a standard pattern and did not greatly differ from one year to another.

The sword and cap of maintenance were blessed on Christmas Eve and awarded to a secular ruler for his defence of Christianity. Leo X gave them to Henry VIII in 1513 and they were received at a great service in St Paul's. The Venetian ambassador, Andrea Badoer, reported that 'great honour was paid [to the papal emissary] and the ceremonies were performed in St Paul's church, in the presence of the king'.[15] Two particularly vivid but different

Figure 5.3
Image from the *Hallesches Heiltumbuch* (MS 14, fol. 2v) of the papal golden rose given to Cardinal Albrecht of Brandenburg, c. 1523, Hofbibliothek Aschaffenburg.

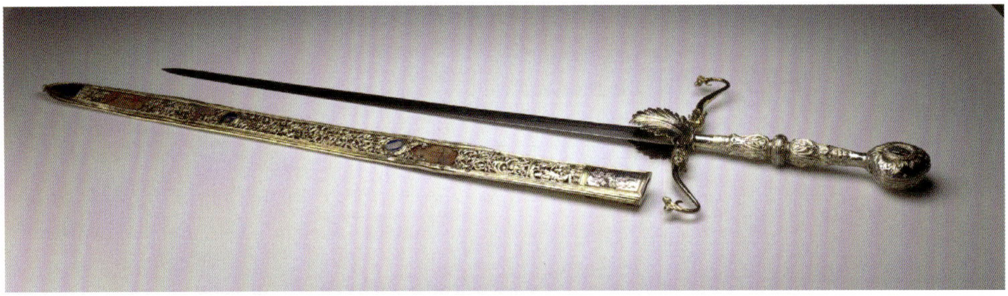

Figure 5.4 Sword of state with scabbard from the Honours of Scotland, Rome, early sixteenth century. Silver-gilt handle and scabbard. Historic Scotland.

accounts of the occasion survive, one by Nicola di Favri, a member of the Venetian delegation, and another by an anonymous Italian observer. Di Favri was mainly interested in the gifts themselves and the wealth of the assembled court:

> The weapon was long, with gilded guard and scabbard, and the cap seemed to be of purple satin [...] covered with embroidery and pearls [... The nobles] bore such massive gold chains that some might have served as fetters for a fellon's ankles, and sufficed for his safe custody, so heavy were they, and of such immense value.[16]

The other account focused on the ceremony, describing the solemn procession and the archbishop of Canterbury vesting the king with the sword and cap after the mass.[17]

Henry's sword does not survive but three others of the period do, including one given to James IV of Scotland in 1507 (fig. 5.4).[18] Like the golden roses, they follow a standard pattern. The quillons of the silver-gilt-handled sword are formed as dolphins and the hilt as a double baluster with acanthus leaves above and below a central knop. The pommel is formed as a laurel wreath that originally surrounded an enamel plaque. James's sword, part of the 'Honours of Scotland', is a remarkable survival. It has suffered some damage but retains its scabbard and leather belt with its silver-gilt and enamel buckle and is decorated with the arms of Julius II. They must have made a considerable impression, not least because they were in the fully developed 'antique' (or Renaissance) style which would have been quite unfamiliar in England at the time.

Revelatory though they may have been aesthetically, such gifts were more of symbolic than financial value. The golden roses equated to a bullion value of around £40 (plus the sapphire) and Leo X, writing to Henry VIII before the arrival of the sword, told him that the gift was 'not so valuable for the matter as for the mystery'.[19]

Gifts of plate and jewels continued to mark Anglo-papal relations and flowed in both directions. A high point was the first of two legatine visits by Cardinal Campeggio in 1518 when he came to promote Leo X's doomed project for a crusade against the Ottomans. The cardinal stayed for several months and was showered with presents when he left. The Venetian ambassador reported that 'His Majesty bestowed on him £7,000 in money, and plate to the value of 700 marks'[20] and Campeggio wrote to Henry thanking him and Wolsey for their 'kindness and liberal gifts of plate'.[21] A further letter, written by Leo after Campeggio arrived in Rome, also thanks Henry for his gifts, so it is possible that some of these were for the pope.[22] What exactly they comprised we do not know. The Chamber accounts record a payment in November 1519 of £298 10s to Amadas and Holland 'for plate delivered to the Cardinal of Rome'[23] but there may have been other pieces too and it is possible that these included the mounted rock-crystal vase now in the church of San Lorenzo in Florence (fig. 4.8).

In his early years, however, Henry had hankered after some other sort of gift from the pope than swords and roses. He wanted a title. It irked him that the kings of France and Spain were styled 'Most Christian King' and 'Catholic King', while the king of England had no such epithet. Wolsey had recommended this to the pope as early as 1515 but nothing came of it until 1521,[24] when the situation changed as a result of Henry's refutation of Martin Luther's doctrines in his *Assertio septem sacramentorum* (The Assertion of the Seven Sacraments), which he dispatched to the pope, bound in cloth of gold. Luther was becoming an increasingly irritating thorn in the pope's side and Leo was grateful to Henry. Whether the book was written entirely by the king or, as seems more likely, composed with theological advice did not matter. It was presented as the king's work and it had the desired effect: Leo responded by investing him with the title *Fidei defensor* (Defender of the faith).

Magnificentia ecclesiae

The central and most visible conjunction of Church and Crown was the great set-piece services held in St Paul's, Westminster Abbey and Canterbury Cathedral to mark key moments in the reign. Apart from coronations, these focused on events such as dynastic marriages, royal funerals, 'summit' meetings and the ratification of treaties.

Plate must have been conspicuous and magnificent at weddings and funerals, especially in processions, but in most cases specific evidence is not there. One exception to this was Katherine of Aragon's wedding to Prince

Arthur in 1501, surely one of the greatest spectacles of the previous reign. The anonymous *Receyt of the Ladie Kateryne* describes how St Paul's, in which a raised walkway had been erected to give the congregation a clear view, was decorated 'with the most excellent ornaments appertaining unto the worship of God and honour of this joyful marriage [...] first the altar with their plates, jewels, and relics of wonderful riches and preciousness', then the copes and vestments 'of great value' and, finally, the choir hung with cloth of Arras.[25]

Prince Henry, as the ten-year-old duke of York, had attended this service and it set the standard for many that followed in his own reign. Contemporary accounts of two in particular make the point. One was the mass in Canterbury marking the brief visit of the Emperor Charles V in the summer of 1520:

> Their Majesties went to the cathedral, preceded by the ambassadors and upwards of 600 lords and ladies, who were all sumptuously clad in cloth of gold and silver, and wore massive gold chains around their necks [...] The simar [a kind of robe] of the king of England was entirely of cloth of gold, lined with very beautiful lynx's fur, and around his neck he wore a very valuable jewelled collar [...] On entering the cathedral they were met by the archbishop with cross and censer, and on arriving at the high altar found three traverses [small enclosures]. The first [...] was of gold brocade, lined with silver brocade embroidered with roses, the king's badge, and carpeted with crimson velvet [... This] was destined for the two sovereigns, who knelt to hear mass, their kneeling desk being of cloth of gold, and the ledge covered with cloth of gold.[26]

If this account is telling in terms of the general magnificence of the decorations, the other tells us much more about the role of plate and jewels, particularly images. This was a service held two years earlier at St Paul's. It was staged to ratify the so-called general peace and to mark the betrothal of the infant Princess Mary to the dauphin; it was presided over by Cardinal Wolsey:

> The large chapel and the choir were hung with gold brocade, wrought with the king's arms. Near the altar was a traverse formed of cloth of gold, for the king, and in front of it a small altar quite crowded with golden images one foot high, with a cross of pure gold to correspond; all the rest of the ornaments being of silver-gilt. At this altar two low masses were said before the king, whilst High Mass was being sung [...] All the bishops and abbots wore jewelled mitres [... The king] had a tunic of purple velvet powdered with [...] rubies, sapphires, turquoises and diamonds, all of the best water and sparkling. The king wore a collar thickly studded with finest carbuncles as large as walnuts.[27]

Another kind of service, underlining the interdependence of Church and Crown, was that traditionally held as part of the ceremonies for the opening of Parliament. The so-called mass for the Holy Ghost took place at Westminster Abbey and began with a long procession of mitred abbot, monks and clergy, with 'four monks bearing a rich canopy of gold which they set over the king, and [in which] the abbot censed the king, and delivered him a sceptre of gold in his hand, which was St Edward's the Confessor'.[28] This event (or its equivalent, twenty-four years earlier) is represented by the image in the British Library of the procession in 1512 (fig. 4.2): the king walks beneath the canopy with its 'wrethen staves plated with silver', carrying the sceptre and preceded by the sword and cap of maintenance, a herald and Archbishop Warham.[29]

The rich visual impact of these occasions, especially the great services of 1518 and 1520, was created not by the painted walls, polychrome sculpture and stained glass that were permanent features of the churches, but by gold, jewels and sumptuous fabrics: vestments, hangings and cushions of cloth of gold and the extraordinary wealth of jewels and plate on the altars and in the processions. But what can we say of these 'golden images', 'silver-gilt ornaments' and 'crosses of pure gold'? It is not clear whether they belonged to the cathedrals or the king, although the resources of the jewel house were certainly sufficient. Of the roughly 900 entries in the 1521 inventory, twenty items of gold and 151 of silver-gilt fell into the category of sacred plate. The gold wares included several crosses and two substantial images weighing 101 oz and 62 oz. In addition, there were forty silver-gilt images (excluding eight that came from the duke of Buckingham). Most of these weighed under 100 oz, although a few were much heavier. The jewel house also held a large stock of other church plate.

The Chapel Royal

The heart of royal religious observance was not these great services that attracted so much attention, but the relative privacy of the Chapel Royal. This was where the liturgical calendar was scrupulously observed from Christmas through to Easter and through the rest of the year. Daily masses were celebrated in the royal presence and holy days were marked with specific protocols and standard offerings of a gold noble or more.[30] Normally the king was unseen, but on certain days he was more visible. At Candlemas he carried a blessed taper to signify the purification of the Virgin; on Good Friday he crept to the cross at the high altar and distributed gold rings, and on Easter Sunday he kissed the cross. On certain other holy days he processed from the privy chamber to the chapel in purple robes, with the sword of state carried before him.

The Chapel Royal, however, was not so much a place as a department of the household. Each of the main royal residences had a physical chapel but the Chapel Royal as such comprised the personnel and paraphernalia required to perform the religious offices wherever the king happened to be. The personnel consisted of the dean, chaplains and choir and the equipment included vestments, altar frontals, hangings and plate. Chapel personnel and equipment would generally follow the same peripatetic pattern as the rest of the household and accompany the king on his itinerary from residence to residence. But the more frequently occupied houses, those that later came to be known as 'standing houses', were permanently furnished and the amount of chapel plate held in each at the end of the reign, including Whitehall, Hampton Court, Windsor and Greenwich, was a measure of the relative importance of the house: the 1547 inventory lists gold crosses at Whitehall and Hampton Court but silver-gilt ones elsewhere; images were kept at all the houses, but many more were at Whitehall, as was the case with altar candlesticks, chalices and all the other categories of liturgical plate.[31]

At the start of the reign the most prestigious royal residence was Richmond and it was probably the most sumptuously furnished. Henry VII's chapel there, newly built after the previous one was destroyed when the old palace of Sheen burnt down, was inaugurated for Katherine of Aragon's arrival in 1501 and is described in the *Receyt of the Ladie Kateryne*:

> [It was] well paved, glazed, and hanged with cloth of Arras; the body and choir with cloth of gold; and the altars set with many relics, jewels and full rich plate [...] In the right side of the chapel is a goodly and privy closet for the king, richly hanged with silk, and traverse, carpet and cushions, for his noble grace. The altar is also hanged and plated with rich relics of gold and precious stone [...] In the other side of the chapel other like closets for the queen's grace and the princess my lady the king's mother, with other states and gentlewomen.[32]

The closets were in effect privy chambers for the king and queen to observe and participate in the mass without being exposed to the general gaze. The finest surviving example is that in St George's Chapel, Windsor, which is placed between the choir and the altar and looks down on both. It served more than one purpose, however; devout though the king may have been, he was not fanatical, and hearing three masses in a day, in the privacy of the closet, was an opportunity not only to worship but to conduct business discretely too.

The chapel plate fell under the jurisdiction of the master of the jewel house, which is why it is listed in the 1521 and 1532 inventories. But the former is helpfully annotated to show which pieces were 'out' for use in the household. In the absence of the original document we cannot take a view on when exactly any of these movements took place but most probably where an object is noted as being 'in the chapel' or 'in the closet' this was its normal location for the time being. A significant proportion of the jewel house church plate was assigned to the chapel, either for the high altar or for one or other of the closets.

The fact that James IV lost his gold 'cross of the holy cross' (and his life) on the battlefield in 1513 did not prevent it from being used in Henry's chapel; in addition, some fifty further items are marked as 'in the chapel': eight crosses, nine images, six chalices and patens, and all the other equipment needed for the mass, including monstrances, cruets, censers, incense boats, paxes, candlesticks and basins. A close reading of the inventory shows that they were selected with care. The allocated crucifixes mostly weighed more than 100 oz and included all the heaviest ones on the list, the largest weighing 261 oz. The same is true of the images. Six of the nine weighed more than 200 oz and the largest of all, 'an image of Our Lady standing upon a foot garnished with imagery [...] and having her son on her arm and a sceptre in her hand and a crown upon her head', weighed 415 oz and must have been very large.[33]

The closets were similarly equipped and there was a close correspondence between the contents of the king's and the queen's closets: eight images for the king and eight for the queen (although the king's were slightly bigger); a silver-gilt cross, two candlesticks, a holy water bucket, cruets and a bell for each. The only significant differences were that the king had six chalices, while the queen apparently had just one; the king also had a gold crucifix and a little coffer containing four relics. Katherine had plate of her own, however, brought from Spain, which had never been absorbed into the jewel house and which might have brought the equipment of her chapel into line with his. In addition to chapel plate as such, the inventory also notes that the 'vj wrethen staves plated with silver to bear the canopy [and] weighing together 512 oz' were kept in the king's closet, presumably so that they were on hand for use in processions.[34]

Three monstrances were consigned to the chapel (though none to the closets, for the monstrance was used to display the consecrated host to the congregation). The inventory tells us little of their appearance, but one surviving piece with some claims to a direct connection with Henry VIII – a monstrance in Halle basilica near Brussels (fig. 5.5) – may offer some clues. The basilica is the mother church of the cult of the Virgin of Halle, which had a long association with English royalty going back to Edward III,[35] and the monstrance is traditionally said to have been given by Henry around 1510. This is not impossible, although 1513 is a much more likely

Figure 5.5
Monstrance, early sixteenth century (the foot an early twentieth-century restoration), traditionally said to have been given by Henry VIII to the basilica of St Martin, Halle, near Brussels. Silver, parcel gilt. Basilica of St Martin, Halle.

date, when he besieged the town of Tournai, just forty miles from Halle, during his brief French military campaign.

The monstrance is 73.5 cm high and is of elaborate gothic form with the upper part designed as a three-tiered openwork tower with pinnacles, flying buttresses and tracery. At the centre of the tower stands a silver-gilt Virgin and child; the place for the missing wafer crescent is flanked by two angels and the architecture is embellished at various points with figures of apostles. Unfortunately, the monstrance is in very far from its original condition. The present hexafoil base dates from 1910 and is a spirited attempt to create a more plausibly late gothic profile than the previous one. This is known from an early photograph and was itself clearly a nineteenth-century restoration. The upper part, however, although not untouched by the restorations, appears to be much closer to its assumed original appearance.[36]

Is the monstrance English? Conceivably but improbably. Nothing like this survived the Reformation purges, so we have no English monstrances with which to compare it, but its overall form and details are close to those of German examples of around 1500. True, the small figures of saints embellishing the architecture are not unlike the finials of English apostle spoons, but they do not correspond *exactly* to known spoon finials as, for example, the apostle figures on Bishop Fox's crozier do.[37] The piece has no marks, which, if they ever existed, were probably on the base, and we have no good reason to suppose that it was made in England.

For other clues to the appearance of the religious plate in the jewel house we have to resort to imagination and to analogous objects. The inventory gives only a generic idea of what these objects looked like, although the prevalence of roses and portcullises suggests that most were not old. The inventory lists just a single gold chalice and paten (in addition to fifteen of silver-gilt). It is described as a 'chalice of gold chased with branches and iiij images enamelled, with a paten graved with the Trinity'.[38] The only surviving objects to open a window onto their possible appearance are Bishop Fox's chalice and paten, hallmarked for 1507–08 and preserved at Corpus Christi College, Oxford (fig. 5.6). These are the earliest known hallmarked English gold plate. The chalice is 15.2 cm high and is of conventional form, with a sexfoil foot and pierced knop. Its design is unremarkable, apart from the fine engraving on the foot and the enamel on the knop. The engraving comprises a crucifix, the Virgin and child and

Figure 5.6
Bishop Fox's chalice and paten, London, 1507–08, maker's mark a fleur de lis. Gold and enamel. Corpus Christi College, Oxford.

four saints, each contained within crossed arch surrounds. The enamel on the knop is quite minimal but is in translucent red, of a similar intensity to the red on the fifteenth-century royal gold cup (fig. 3.3a). This was a colour which, as Marian Campbell points out, was 'an enameller's *pièce de résistance*, [that] could only be achieved on gold'.[39] How might this chalice have compared with the royal one? Fox's chalice is smaller – the two pieces weigh just 16¼ oz compared with 25 oz – and is simpler too: the branches on the royal chalice were chased and the figures enamelled, rather than engraved. It would have been an altogether more sumptuous object, but even so the Fox chalice is a remarkable pointer that can quite easily be enriched in the mind's eye to evoke an image of the lost royal one.

Turning to the largest category of chapel plate in the jewel house, many

Figure 5.7
Virgin and child, southern Germany, 1486. Silver, parcel gilt, enamel and precious stones. Kimbell Art Museum, Fort Worth, Texas.

of the silver-gilt images described can be invoked by comparison with survivors too. Nearly all seem to have been of standing figures, identified through their conventional attributes: Mary Magdalene with a box and reed, John the Baptist with a lamb, Barbara with a tower and so on. The great 415 oz image of Our Lady may have been similar in appearance (although entirely gilt) to a late fifteenth-century German one in the Kimbell Art Museum, Fort Worth (fig. 5.7). But the Kimbell image is 53 cm high and weighs just 101 oz,[40] so the one in the chapel must have been significantly larger, unless it had a wooden core which was included in the weight.[41]

For other categories of church plate – paxes, censers, incense boats, cruets and so on – we are helped by various analogous survivals, such as the Ramsey Abbey censer and incense boat (figs. 13.2 and 13.3), the hauntingly beautiful pax at New College, Oxford, with its applied crucifixion scene within an engraved border of branches, and Bishop Fox's crozier at Corpus Christi.

In trying to understand exactly how some of these objects were deployed in the chapel and the closets, particularly the images which existed in such large numbers, we are helped by an improbable source, namely Henry VII's will. This gives detailed instructions for the exact placing of some of his bequests, particularly for the images on the altar before his tomb:

> We will that our executors [...] cause to be made for the overpart of the altar [...] a table of the same length of the same altar [...] and that in the midst of the overhalf of the same table, be made the images of the crucifix, Mary and John, in manner accustomed; and upon both sides of them, be made as many of the images of our said advouries [patron saints] as the said table will receive; and under the said crucifix, and images [...] be made the xij apostles. All the said table, crucifix [and other images] to be of timber, covered and wrought with plate of fine gold.[42]

This suggests an altar arranged in two tiers (rather like a buffet) and that would have been just as 'crowded with images' as the one at St Paul's in 1518.

Royal christenings

An especially important function of the Chapel Royal was royal baptisms. These were occasions of immense dynastic significance and were attended by the greatest nobility and by foreign ambassadors (but not by the parents of the child). Most of the royal baptisms of Henry VIII's reign were held in the Franciscan friars' church at Greenwich, adjacent to the palace. The church, a building chosen for its convenience rather than its splendour, was transformed by tapestries and cloth of gold and a brilliant array of plate, for the altar, for the baptism itself and also in the form of the godparents' gifts. The baptism, the processions to and from the church and the other associated ceremonies were all controlled by strict protocol. This can be pieced together from a variety of sources. The *Ryalle Book* sets the ground rules:

> The child must be borne in a rich mantle of cloth of gold furred with ermine [...] then must be borne before the child two hundred torches [...] and when they come to the church, the torches to stand unlit all about the font [...] and when he is christened then all the torches to be lit.[43]

The clearest descriptions we have of royal baptisms from Henry VIII's reign were those of Princess Elizabeth and Prince Edward, in 1533 and 1537. Elizabeth's took place at Greenwich and followed the same pattern as previous ones. According to Edward Hall,

> all the walls between the king's place [palace] and the Friars, were hanged with Arras, and all the way strawed with green rushes: the Friars church was also hanged with Arras. The font was of silver and stood in the midst of the church, three steps high [...] Then came the earl of Essex, bearing the covered basins gilt, after him the marquis of Exeter with the taper of virgin ware [wax], next him the marquess [of] Dorset, bearing the salt, behind him the lady Mary of Norfolk, bearing the chrism which was very rich of pearl and [precious] stone, the old duchess of Norfolk bare the child.[44]

After the christening 'the trumpets blew, then the child was brought up to the altar, and the Gospel said over it: and after that immediately the archbishop of Canterbury confirmed it'. The presentation of gifts came next, 'then was brought in wafers, comfets, and hippocras in such plenty, that everyman had as much as he would desire. Then they set forwards [... and] the gifts [...] were borne before the child.'[45]

The godparents' gifts were appropriately munificent. Louis XII of France, godfather to the sadly short-lived Prince Henry in 1511, gave a gold cup and a gold salt weighing 48½ oz and 51 oz, as well as further gifts to the lady mistress and the midwife. By 1521 Louis' cup (but apparently not the salt) was in the jewel house, where it was described as 'garnished with roses, fleurs de lis, H and R with a crown about the cover [and] the knop a crown imperial'. Such ornament sounds exactly like a standard Tudor jewel house commission and yet the inventory states clearly that it was 'given to the queen's grace at the christening of the prince by the French king'.[46] Either the cup was bought from a London royal goldsmith by the French ambassador, or its ornament was carefully chosen to compliment the king. Either way, the French ambassador described the gifts as 'such as are usual here' and reported that they 'gave great satisfaction to the king and queen of England and the council'.[47] But christening gifts were not always the same. Princess Elizabeth's godparents, in 1533, gave her three gold cups, one 'fretted with pearl', and three silver-gilt and engraved standing bowls with a cover; Prince Edward (baptised at Hampton Court), being the long-awaited heir, did rather better and received a gold cup, six great bowls, six great pots and two great flagons.[48]

Unlike the gifts, the plate used for the baptism itself was prescribed. Basins were used to pour the water into the font and a cup to perform the assay (ceremonial testing for poison) before it was administered. Salt had a special function as a symbol of purity. The Old Testament prophet Ezekiel describes rubbing with salt as part of the ritual cleansing of a new-born child[49] and in the pre-Reformation service of baptism blessed salt was placed in the mouth of the infant 'to signify the spiritual salt, which is the word of God, wherewith he should be seasoned that thereby the filthy savour of stinking sin should be taken away'.[50] It was perhaps in reference to the purifying qualities of salt and water that Louis XII gave the presents he did.

For these reasons the liturgical plate was treated with great reverence. According to *The Northumberland Ceremonial*, an early sixteenth-century manuscript in which the exact form of an aristocratic baptism is described, the bearer of the salt should have a towel on his right shoulder and hold the salt in both ends of the towel; 'the other gentleman which beareth the covered basins with water [...] to bear them in both his hands and upon them the cup of assay and upon the cup of assay the towel folden'.[51]

One aspect in which royal christenings differed from others was the font. From at least the late fifteenth century considerable extra expense had been incurred by having a silver font brought specially to the church from Canterbury. In 1516, for the christening of Princess Mary, 6s 8d was paid for 'riding with a letter to the prior of Christ Church, Canterbury, for the font of silver to be conveyed to Greenwich', and shortly afterwards £4 was paid to 'the servants of the Prior [for] carrying and recarrying the font between Canterbury and Greenwich'.[52] The same sum had been paid out in 1511 for Prince Henry's christening and at other times too, in preparation for christenings that never took place because of the still birth of the child.

The font itself is a mystery. To have cost so much to transport, it must have been large and heavy. The last time its carriage from Canterbury is mentioned is in 1516 and nothing like it appears on the 1530s inventories of Christ Church,[53] so it is possible that it had already been surrendered or sold by then. Conceivably this costly loan was rendered unnecessary by

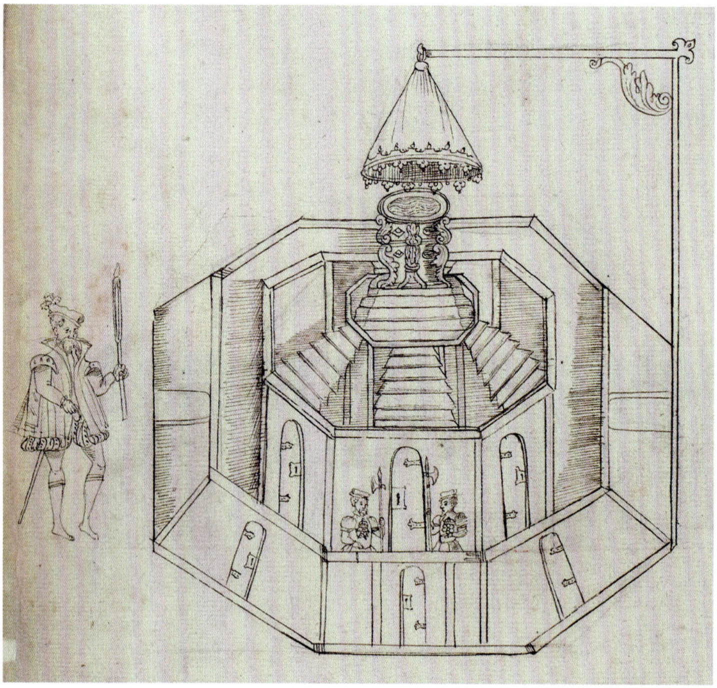

Figure 5.8
Diagram of arrangements for Prince Edward's christening in 1537, showing the silver font beneath a canopy. College of Arms, London (MS 6, fol. 82v).

the addition of a substantial silver font to the holdings of the jewel house, noted in a rather strange amendment to the inventory:

> Received of the queen's grace for a font called in her indenture a 'wyder' [voider] or a dish chased with beasts men and fowls half gilt without a cover weighing in the said indenture 174½ oz, to which font one William Holland hath made a cover gilt chased with men beasts and fowls weighing 100½ oz and weigheth now together all 275 oz.[54]

This impressive hybrid object, augmented by Holland's new cover, is perhaps represented in a schematic drawing of the staging erected for Prince Edward's christening (fig. 5.8). It shows a large and impressive font with a canopy above. But it is not easy to interpret and if accurate we must assume that the elaborate scroll supports are quite separate from the font and of another material, such as gilt wood.

The Northumberland Ceremonial is a revealing source of information on some of the finer details of the ceremonial which are glossed over or assumed in the account of Princess Elizabeth's christening. After the confirmation, for example, the godparents were to wash and 'if they be of estate to have covered basins [...] and if they be not then to have a single basin and a ewer'.[55] This distinction is significant, as is the fact that the company were then to move in order of precedence to another part of the church for wafers and hippocras, for these details make it clear that this was the liturgical mirror image of the 'void', the highly ritualised concluding part of a great banquet such as we will turn to in the next chapter.

Turning to the account of Prince Edward's christening, this tells us more than the form of the service, the gifts and the *personae dramatis*. It also states that the plate used for the ceremony itself was provided not by the chapel or the jewel house but by the household. The basins and cup of assay came from the ewery, the tapers from the chaundry and the salt ('richly garnished with pearl and stone') from the pantry. But on one important detail it is almost silent, telling us only that 'the high altar [was] richly garnished with stuff and plate'.[56] What exactly was this 'stuff and plate'? One might imagine no more than the regular paraphernalia of the altar, perhaps 'crowded with images' for good measure, but another document altogether gives us grounds for thinking again: an account in Leland's *Collectanea* of a christening thirty years later at Whitehall Palace, when Queen Elizabeth herself happened to be godmother, describes a ceremony structurally similar to Edward's (although now evangelical), but where the loading of the altar (or, by then, 'communion table') is minutely described:

> The communion table was richly furnished with plate and jewels, viz. a fountain and basin of mother of pearl; a basin and fountain gilt, rayed with gold; a rich basin, garnished with stones and pearls; a ship or ark garnished with stones; two great layers, garnished with stones, and two lesser layers, garnished with stones and pearls; a bird of agate furnished with stones; a cup of agate, furnished with stones and pearls; a bowl of corral, garnished with pearls; a bowl of crystal, with a cover; two candlesticks of crystal; two ships of mother of pearl; two pair of candlesticks of gold; two great candlesticks, double gilt, with lights of virgin wax; and a cross.[57]

Objects answering to these descriptions can certainly be found in the 1547 inventory and might well have graced the altar at Hampton Court a decade earlier, although obscured by contemporary understatement.[58] This was the stuff of a princely *Kunstkammer* rather than the normal dressing of an altar and shows, as do the hippocras and wafers, the domestic baptismal plate, the gifts and the trumpets, that a royal christening was as much a courtly event as a liturgical one.

Six
Royal Banquets

Great banquets were the climax of any embassy or important royal occasion. They were feasts not only for the body but for the mind and the eye; they were an opportunity for opulent display and they were meant to astonish. Indeed, as a central plank in the promotion of the regime and its wealth and power, it was essential that they did astonish. When the papal nuncio, Francesco Chieregato, attended a feast given for the Spanish ambassadors in 1517 he concluded his report with the observation that 'the wealth and civilization of the world are here; and those who call the English barbarians appear to me to render themselves such. I here perceive very elegant manners, extreme decorum, and very great politeness'.[1]

Great royal banquets, as we have already noted, were not held in isolation. They were set within a sequence of events that included tournaments, pageants and church services; they were hugely costly and were an essential feature of princely magnificence. The principal guests were usually foreign ambassadors and because an account of such an event, which they attended as their masters' representatives, would inevitably have been written up in their dispatches, we have more evidence of what they were like than most other kinds of courtly spectacle.

No two banquets or feasts (terminology was fluid and 'banquet' also had a more restricted sense) were exactly alike, but the basic elements did not change much. The hall, or banqueting house, was always hung with rich tapestries and cloth of gold, the meal was always punctuated by elaborate ceremonies, and the serious business of eating was invariably accompanied by extravagant entertainments. But, other than the food, the feature that usually attracted most comment was the plate. This comprised wares used for the service of the meal itself and, more impressively, rows of gold and silver-gilt vessels displayed on tiered structures called buffets or cupboards.

This chapter looks at the spectacle of banquets and the extravagant rituals that attended them. It concentrates on the huge quantities of plate that were deployed and the uses to which it was put. Sources include accounts

Figure 6.1 *Banquet of Ahazuerius*, Antwerp or Bruges, c. 1520. Tapestry. Showing dishes of food being carried in, a jewelled covered cup being prepared for the king (at centre foreground), wine being diluted (to the right), and a buffet of plate and musicians playing (to right and left). Museo de Tapices de la Seo, Zaragossa Cathedral.

by ambassadors and chroniclers, as well as depictions of similar events in contemporary tapestries, which we will consider through the lens of the 1521 inventory. But it also explores a very different sort of banquet – the Garter feast of 1519 – and the evidence we have for royal dining in the more intimate setting of the privy chamber.

Royal banquets: display and performance

The best way to describe an early Tudor royal banquet is to plunge into one through contemporary eyes. There are many to choose from: the feasts at Whitehall and Richmond for the arrival of Katherine of Aragon in 1501, the receptions of 1517 and 1518, or the great banquet for the French ambassadors at Greenwich in 1527. All of these were described by contemporary observers. We open, however, not with a real banquet but with a fictive one, shown in an early sixteenth-century Flemish tapestry (fig. 6.1). This is preserved in Zaragossa Cathedral and depicts the biblical Feast of Ahazuerius. The king is seated beneath a cloth of estate and is flanked by four nobles, dressed in cloth of gold and sumptuous fabrics. To the right stands a buffet loaded with plate. The table is covered with a fine diaper cloth laid on top of a costly carpet. On the table before the king is a gilded dish with a stuffed peacock; two nefs (vessels in the form of ships) are to either side, and covered cups stand on the near side of the table. The king and his companions sit at the centre of a maelstrom of activity. A procession of servants led by the chamberlain with his staff of office bring in dishes of food, their entry announced by a fanfare of trumpets; behind the diners a crowd of courtiers look on, while in the foreground household officers and servants busy themselves with the preparation of food and drink.

The designer of the tapestry knew nothing of a biblical feast, but he knew very well what a contemporary one was like and this is what he depicts. It puts visual flesh onto the bones of the otherwise more matter-of-fact descriptions of royal banquets such as the one Chieregato witnessed in 1517:

> There was a buffet set out [...] with silver gilt vases and vases of gold, worth vast treasure [...] All the small platters used for the table-service [... the] dishes, basins, plates, saltcellars, and goblets were all of pure gold. The large vases were all of silver gilt, very costly and precious [...] The removal and replacing of dishes the whole time was incessant, the hall in every direction being full of fresh viands on their way to table.[2]

Leaving aside for now the question of whether all of these wares really were of 'pure gold', our first task is to consider Chieregato's impressions against the evidence of what the jewel house would have been able to provide. We do not know exactly how many attended this banquet but it was clearly many more than we see in the tapestry and the procession of dishes alone would have accounted for a large proportion of the plate deployed. Dishes came in four sizes, called chargers, platters, dishes and saucers. These were listed in the jewel house inventory under the generic term 'vessel' and were usually supplied in sets (or 'garnitures') comprising two chargers and twelve of everything else. In all, the jewel house held around 1,220 of these wares, of which just 162 were in silver-gilt and would have been reserved for high-ranking guests. One reason for needing so many dishes was the manner in which the meal was served. Each course consisted of a range of different items, served on separate dishes and placed within reach of several people. These groups of dishes were known as a 'messe'; guests helped themselves and ate off 'trenchers', which might have been of silver but were more usually of wood. The number of dishes provided was another measure of status and Anne Boleyn alone, at her coronation banquet in 1533, was served with twenty-four dishes for the second course and thirty for the third. Another reason for the huge number of dishes in the jewel house was that they did not have purpose-made covers and food was kept warm by inverting one dish over another as it was carried in. A single, incomplete, garniture survives from the Tudor period, the so-called Armada Service in the British Museum, which comprises twenty-six pieces in all four sizes, mostly dating from 1600–01 (fig. 6.2).[3] All are of exactly the same shape, quite deep, with a flat rim and slightly domed centre; that those in use sixty years earlier were probably very similar is confirmed by the identical form of a set of pewter dishes found on the *Mary Rose*.

The tapestry does not only depict plenty; it is also rich in ceremony, much of which would have been entirely recognisable at the English court. While the carefully choreographed procession of dishes enters from the left, more elegant ceremonies are also being enacted in the foreground. A youth (probably of high rank because he is wearing a sword) kneels before a gentleman in authority, perhaps the carver. The latter – doubtless a nobleman, to judge by his rich clothes and hat jewel – is receiving two plates to set before the king, while the cupbearer stands with a covered cup, probably of gold, and enriched with jewels, also ready to be proffered to the king; further to the left, another cup is being filled with wine, or perhaps the wine is being diluted.

Covered cups were among the most prestigious vessels and a mark of elevated social status. Those described in the 1521 inventory were more diverse in form and ornament than any other category than salts. They were about fifty in all, twenty-eight of which were of gold. Some of the most magnificent pieces in the jewel house were gold cups, including the French cup discussed on p. 32 (fig. 3.3) and the extraordinary 'Dream of

Figure 6.2 Six dishes in five sizes from the Armada service, London, 1600–01, maker's mark TC. Silver, parcel gilt. British Museum, London.

Paris' cup (see p. 33). Many were set with pearls, rubies and other gemstones but most were evidently less inventive and feature the standard range of Tudor dynastic ornament.

One of the most conspicuous objects in the tapestry, standing at the extreme left of the table, is a cylindrical vessel, chased with spiral flutes ('wrethen') and with a cover. Its function is ambiguous; it may be a covered beaker (like the Beaufort beaker, fig. 4.4) or it may be a salt. If the latter, then it represents what in England was one of the most imposing types of table ware, to which great ceremonial importance was attached.[4] Like cups, great salts symbolised rank and the cover was a mark of honour. Much store was set by the manner in which the saltcellar was placed on the table and the *Northumberland Ceremonial* says that on twelfth night the earl's table should have 'a great standing salt of gold or silver-gilt, with a small salt of gold for the assay'.[5]

The jewel house held around sixty gold and silver-gilt salts and they were among the most striking objects in the inventory. Most of the gold ones were quite small and the most impressive by far was the 'salt of gold called the Morris Dance'. This weighed 147 oz, three times more than any other, and was highly sculptural. The description is not very clear and it is better described in the 1547 inventory: the main part was a group of five 'Moresdancers' and a tabrell (a drum), together with a 'lady holding the salt' (presumably above her head and around whom, one imagines, the morris men danced). All of the figures were set with stones and pearls, while the salt container itself, also gem-set, was shaped like a small cup, apparently with a cover. Altogether this sumptuous object was enriched with nine sapphires, fifty-two diamonds, ninety-six rubies and 153 pearls.[6] The closest surviving analogue to this (and a pale one at that) is the magnificent salt at All Souls College, Oxford, known as the Huntsman, which is formed as a standing figure on an enamelled base and supporting a covered rock-crystal salt above his head (fig. 6.3). Other sculptural gold salts in the inventory include one modelled as a 'Morean' (or moor) and others as a black dragon, a mermaid, and a castle. Amongst

Figure 6.3
The huntsman salt, England, late fifteenth century. Silver gilt, rock-crystal and enamel. All Souls College, Oxford.

those made of silver-gilt the familiar repertoire of Tudor ornament tended to predominate over innovative forms. Very few of the salts, whether gold, silver-gilt or silver, were completely plain, although a number were small, had no cover and were clearly not intended to convey any special sense of honour to their user.

Returning once more to the tapestry, one feature we have not mentioned is the three elaborate carving knives lying on the front edge of the table. Carving was considered a courtly art,[7] normally performed at the royal table by a nobleman, and carving knives were accordingly often sumptuous and beautiful works of art. They had etched and gilded steel blades and handles incorporating costly materials such as ivory, amber and gilt bronze. One such carving knife appears to survive, since it was exhibited to the Society of Antiquaries in 1897 by J. C. Robinson. Its present whereabouts are unknown but Robinson described it in the Society's proceedings as about 40 cm long, with a long, pointed blade and silver-gilt handle. The handle was partly enamelled and divided into three sections, one decorated with a rose within a garter, the second inlaid with panels of carnelian and the third with 'a somewhat rudely drawn' portcullis. The edges of the handle were decorated with gilt roses and letters SS, alluding to a livery collar.[8] The knife was not illustrated but for a clear sense of the ornament, though in a different context and on a different scale, we only have to look at the Stonyhurst cope, the main part of which depicts portcullises and roses, with letters SS around the edge (fig. 5.2).

The Ahazuerius tapestry, like any other image, depicts a single moment. A banquet, however, was a sequence of events that included many other ceremonies, such as the handwashing with which it began, the 'void' with which it concluded, and 'assaying', which occurred repeatedly. Some of these had a quasi-religious dimension that arose from the unique status of the sovereign, as the anointed of God.[9] This lay behind much of the complexity of royal dining ceremonial, underpinning magnificence with a religious substratum and giving it what amounted to a semi-eucharistic character, with the anointed king taking on a priest-like role in a mass-like event. Thus, the ritualistic handwashing before the banquet, using pairs of basins, closely mirrored the ablutions during mass, as did the mixing of wine and water. And so, again, did the character and role of some of the plate. The form of the covered cup alludes to the chalice and its elaborate administration to the mass itself, while the majestic scale of the standing salt, a particular feature of English and French courtly plate, alludes to the theological symbolism of salt. These vessels took on such a stature, not, as has often been claimed, because salt was very expensive (it was not) but because, as we have seen (p. 81), it was a symbol of purity.[10]

The complex handwashing ritual is captured in a carefully observed account by the Venetian ambassador at the start of a banquet held for Charles V on his visit to Canterbury in 1520:

> The emperor and the king and queen of England washed together by themselves. The duke of Suffolk brought a large gold basin with a cover bearing a crown, in the centre of which was a small cup, and when this had been removed by the duke of Buckingham, the marquis of Brandenburg's brother [...] took off the cover, handling it under the basin borne by the duke of Suffolk; whereupon the duke of Buckingham gave the water in the cup to the duke of Suffolk to drink, who having thus made the assay then poured the water from his basin, which had an aperture or mouth at the side, over the hands of the sovereigns, to whom the brother of the count palatine of the Rhine presented the towel. The emperor and the king and queen then sat down to table.[11]

The covered gold basin – if it was actually gold – does not appear in the inventory, although several pairs in silver-gilt are listed, including one with a spout.[12] These weighed 174 oz and are described as having 'sunbeams in the bottom and enamelled with blue flowers'. Two apparently very similar basins, enamelled in the centre with Bishop Fox's arms, are among the founder's plate at Corpus Christi College, Oxford (fig. 6.4). Measuring 43 cm across, they weigh just over 126 oz together, smaller than the royal ones but well within the range of most pairs of basins in the jewel house. The most important point of similarity, however, is that one of them has just such a spout under the rim, modelled like a gargoyle (fig. 6.4a). In all probability, therefore, they would have borne a close resemblance to others deployed at royal banquets. Pairs of basins like this were also used for the ritual ablutions during the mass, where water was poured through the spout of one basin, over the hands of the celebrant and into the other.

There were repeated handwashing moments during the course of a banquet and according to Edward Hall, splendid provision was made for this purpose at the great banquet held at Greenwich in 1527. Here there were three 'ewery boards', one for the king, another for the queen, and the third for Princess Mary. The princess's board was set with ewers and basins, whereas the king's and queen's had pairs of basins and no ewers, gilt basins for the queen and (allegedly) gold for the king.[13] Quite apart from the obvious fact that the king's basins were more precious, there was a hierarchy in the provision of basins or ewers. This was the same distinction that we noted in the *Northumberland Ceremonial* protocol for christenings, where godparents, 'if they be of estate', should wash with covered basins 'and with ewers and basins if they be not'.[14] Clearly the princess *was* of estate, but less so than her parents. The inventory gives very little clue as to the shape of the ewers, although a number are described as 'of helmet

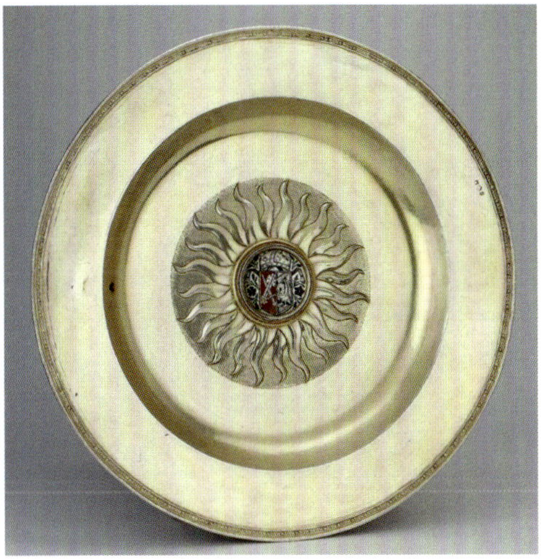

Figure 6.4 Bishop Fox's ablution basin, London, 1514–15. Silver gilt and enamel. Corpus Christi College, Oxford.

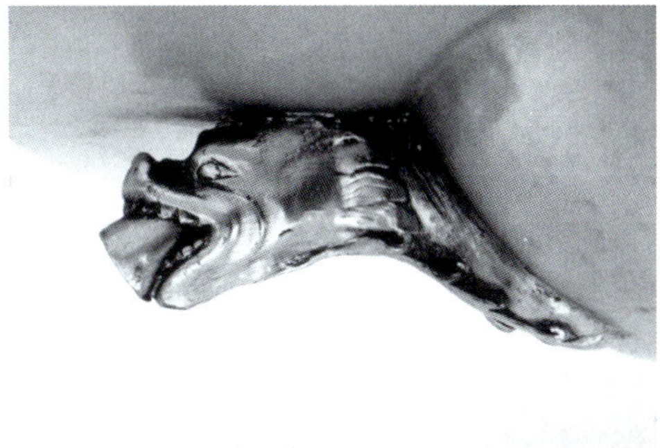

Figure 6.4a Detail of spout beneath the brim of Bishop Fox's ablution basin. Corpus Christi College, Oxford.

fashion' and presumably resembled the one of 1545 given by Archbishop Parker to Corpus Christi College, Cambridge, so-called because it looks a little like an inverted helmet.[15]

Some of the most complex choreography came at the end of the proceedings. The 'void' or 'spice' was largely composed of artfully prepared, sugary delicacies and was served with sweet wine called hippocras.[16] By convention, the void was usually taken standing up, a custom that perhaps made it more socially fluid than the hierarchical seating plan of the earlier courses. But there was no lack of ceremony in its service. According to one of the descriptions in the *Receyt of the Ladie Kateryne* in 1501, after dancing,

> began the void to enter [...] At the which void came in five score couple [200], earls, barons and knights, over and beside squires, having collars and chains of gold, every each of them throughout bearing the one of them a spice plate and the other a cup, beside yeomen of the guard that followed them with pots of wine according to fill the cups. The spice plates were furnished in the most bounteous manner with spices.[17]

But this only hints at the complexity of the ceremony, which is set out in both the *Ryalle Book* and the *Northumberland Ceremonial.* Apart from the fact that the former stipulates that the king was to be served by the 'greatest estates'[18] (the most senior noblemen), the two are very similar, although the protocol is rather clearer in the *Ceremonial.* Each 'set' required three servers, one for the spice plate, another for the cup and the third for the towel. The lord's and lady's plates were to be covered and everyone else's *un*covered. One server took off the cover and passed it to another; then, having taken the assay, he was

> to step to the lord with it and when the lord hath done, then he to cover it again and [...] retreat back and stand still. Then the cupbearer to step to the lord with the cup and first uncover and take the assay and then cover it again, and then uncover it and proffer him the cup to drink and when the lord drinketh he is to hold the cup of assay under the cup and when he hath drunken to cover it again and then to retreat back unto the lord's spice plate. Then he that holds the towel to proffer it to the lord to wipe his mouth.[19]

The whole process is repeated for the lady, then for the rest of the company.

Clearly, all of these ceremonies were immensely time-consuming and are one of the reasons for feasts being such protracted affairs. One of those in 1501 lasted four or five hours and Chieregato wrote in 1517 that 'the guests remained at table for seven hours by the clock'.[20]

The void involved several different types of plate, most of which were required in great quantities: pots (to bring in the wine), cups of various kinds, and spice plates. Pots were one of the largest categories of domestic plate in the jewel house. The inventory lists some 125 in silver-gilt and eighty-three in parcel-gilt or silver, most of which came in pairs. The parcel-gilt ones must have been fairly standard and utilitarian; they mostly had a capacity of half a gallon (known as 'pots poteller') and weighed around 50 oz. The silver-gilt ones, on the other hand, came in a much wider range of sizes, weighing from around 50 oz to more than 200 oz. They were also generally more highly decorated, featuring Tudor badges and heraldry, 'men hunting wild beasts' or, as we have seen, feathers (fig. 4.7). Tantalising sculptural features are sometimes mentioned, such as 'a castle on the top and a vane and men of arms in the castle', or 'with a handle and a dragon ... and a coronet under [presumably, that is, around] the base'. The shape of these vessels is seldom mentioned, although the few surviving examples from the period, as well as those depicted in contemporary Flemish and German paintings and tapestries, are generally of the same bellied form as the 1660 'feather pots'. The latter are 52 cm high and weigh 180 oz each. By comparison, the heaviest of the pots in the inventory weighed 300 oz or more and so would have been significantly taller, say 75 cm.[21] In all of these respects a tantalising analogue to these Tudor pots is a pair of German pots of around 1500 in the Metropolitan Museum, New York. These feature just such dragon handles and a very similar 'castle on the top' (fig. 6.5). Standing 63.5 cm high and weighing around 100 oz each,[22] it is difficult to see these as utilitarian vessels and they, like the more massive wares gracing the Tudor banquets, were surely made for display.

Figure 6.5
One of a pair of pots with wild men finials and dragon handles, probably Nuremberg, late fifteenth century. Silver gilt and cold enamel. Metropolitan Museum of Art, New York.

Standing cups we have considered already, but another kind of cup was also used in the void (and throughout the banquet), namely the cup of assay. Frustratingly, we have very little visual reference for these. They were, however, essential to the ceremonial testing for poison carried out before offering the king, queen or great nobleman anything that would pass their lips or touch their hands. When Henry VIII and Charles V met in 1520 the duke of Suffolk 'took the assay' of the water before they washed, and when the void was served to the earl of Northumberland on twelfth night repeated assay was taken of the spice and wine before it was consumed; salt, too, had to be assayed. The descriptions of these procedures always mention 'a small cup' but neither they nor the inventories tell us exactly what they looked like. The jewel house held a single gold one, 'chased with a double rose', and four of silver-gilt, two of which had 'a little ring in the bottom'. But other than that, and the fact that they all weighed between 6 and 11¾ oz, we have no clue as to their appearance, although Ronald Lightbown suggests that they were perhaps like small beakers.[23] One such vessel, an unusually shallow beaker of 1525–26 in the Gilbert Collection, weighs six and a half ounces and may, possibly, be a cup of assay.[24]

One type of ware was specific to the void: spice plates. These could be particularly splendid and contemporary accounts often pick them out for special praise; at the celebrations for Katherine of Aragon, for example, 'the number of the spice plates were goodly and marvellous' and in 1518 Hall says of the sixty spice plates borne in at the end of the evening that they were as 'great as men with ease might bear'.[25] Some sixty-eight, some weighing more than 100 oz each, were listed in 1521. Most were unremarkable, but a few must have been extraordinary. The list is topped by 'two great spice plates with two covers enamelled with two naked men on the covers with two shields', which weighed 1,041 oz together;[26] it is difficult to form an idea of their appearance but they were obviously showstoppers. It is also difficult to form a view of how old they were at the time. Naked men may hint at the new 'antique' style, but not necessarily; they could equally well have been 'wild men', such as appear on the top of the Metropolitan Museum's pots. Another, 'wanting five pinnacles on the foot and on the top', sounds gothic and, in view of its losses, seems to have been in poor condition.[27]

Figure 6.6
Spice plate, London, 1532–33, maker's mark a cup. Silver, parcel gilt. Collection of the Goldsmiths' Company, London.

Figure 6.7
Spice plate with Saints Jerome and Andrew, Hinrich Grabow, Luneburg, c. 1515–20. Silver, parcel gilt and enamel. Kunstgewerbemuseum, Berlin.

No English spice plates of the early part of the reign have survived or have been recognised as such, although three slightly later vessels with strong claims to this function do. Two, the so-called Rochester tazzas, are in the British Museum and the third is in the collection of the Goldsmiths' Company (fig. 6.6).[28] Their shallowness seems to suggest food rather than drink and the Latin inscriptions inside their lips also hint at the eucharistic connotations of the void.[29] That on the Goldsmiths' piece reads 'Benedictus deus in donis suis et sanctis in omnibus', probably a contraction of Pope Benedict XII's grace, meaning 'Blessed be God in his gifts and holy in all [his works]'.[30]

The vessels date from between 1528 and 1532 and are relatively simply decorated; for a sense of the style and variety of some of those described in the inventory we turn to two other sources, one fictive and the other real. The first is one of the David tapestries we have looked at already (fig. 1.2) and the second one of a remarkable group of ten German spice plates formerly belonging the Luneburg town council (fig. 6.7). The tapestry shows a covered cup, what is probably a cup of assay, and a large spice plate being carried to the king. The spice plate, covered with an embroidered cloth, is gilt and set with jewels. It stands on a high stem and is filled with sweetmeats. The Luneburg spice plate weighs 35 oz and is dated c. 1515–20. In what might be termed the late gothic style, it has a 'wrethen' foot and stem and a sculptural group of Saints Jerome and Andrew in the centre. It is not the largest of the group but it is the closest in date to the banquets we have been discussing and is probably as good an analogue for those that were deployed at the royal voids as we are likely to find.

Two other categories of plate should be mentioned, even though the direct evidence for their use at Henry VIII's court is thin: the alms dish and the nef. The enormous quantities of food procured for banquets were part of magnificence. But it was not all intended to be eaten and it was equally part of magnificence that what was left should be given away. The alms dish was the vessel from which the leftovers were distributed to the poor and that a specific vessel had formerly been designated for this purpose is clear from the household ordinances of Edward IV, in which the sergeant of the cellar is charged with being responsible for the king's alms dish.[31] Sometimes these were in the form of a ship and a partial inventory of Henry VI's plate includes one described as 'a great alms dish of silver and overgilt in the manner of a ship full of men of arms fighting upon the ship side weighing 67 lb 9 oz [813 oz]'.[32]

What is less clear is the extent to which these things were still current in Henry VIII's time. The commentators and chroniclers make no mention of them but there are occasional intriguing references elsewhere, such as a letter from the council of the household of Princess Mary to Wolsey in 1525 asking about the arrangements for Christmas and in particular 'to let us know your gracious pleasure concerning as well a ship of silver for the alms dish requisite to her high estate [...] to be sent'.[33] The 1521 inventory lists two obviously imposing but quite undescribed items called 'the king's great alms dish', at 559 oz and 'the queen's great alms dish' at 256 oz. These were still extant in 1532 when a third piece, a 278 oz 'great alms dish like a ship', was also listed. In terms of regular usage, however, it is perhaps significant that they were now kept in the jewel house rather than being closer to hand.

Royal banquets: the wider context

So far, we have considered banquets in the context of plate, and we shall do so again when we discuss the buffet of plate. But it is important to realise that there was much more to these occasions than ceremonious consumption. As we noted at the beginning of the chapter, they were as much a feast for the mind and the eye as for the body.

What was probably the most spectacular banquet of the entire reign was that held at Greenwich in May 1527 for the French ambassadors, in England for the signing of a treaty of perpetual amity. We have two angles on this event, through the eyes of observers with rather different interests. Gasparo Spinelli, a member of the Venetian ambassador's entourage, was particularly interested in the entertainments, while Edward Hall was more focused on the banquet itself and the decorations created for it.[34]

It was clearly different from any that came before, not only for its scale and expense, but also because it seems to have been entirely conceived in the 'antique fashion'. This is a term that has been mentioned before and will be discussed in Chapter 10; it crops up increasingly often in documents from the 1520s onwards and refers to a decisive move away from gothic design and towards a style that drew its inspiration from classical antiquity. A temporary structure was erected, comprising two separate but connected buildings, one for the feast and the other for the entertainments. The walls of the dining hall, which measured about one hundred by thirty feet,[35] were hung with the David tapestries[36] and the ceiling was decorated with 'purple cloth full of roses and pomegranates'. Light was provided by rows of torches. The royal table was at one end of the room, where the king sat beneath 'a large canopy of tissue [cloth of gold]', with the queen and his sister Mary (the widowed French queen) to either side. The French party sat at one of two long tables and the Venetian and Milanese ambassadorial parties at the other, each joined by lords and ladies.

An equally striking feature was 'a very lofty triumphal arch, fashioned after the antique, beneath which were three vaulted entrances [… Above these] was a spacious balcony for the musicians, bearing the arms of the king and queen, with sundry busts of emperors.'[37] (Hall adds that 'the arch was all of gold [leaf] burnished, swaged and graved full of gargoyles and serpents'.)[38] This was very possibly designed by Hans Holbein the younger, who was paid £4 10s 'for the painting of the plat of Tirwan, which standeth on the backside of the great arch'.[39] It must have been one of the most spectacular elements of the whole event.

Both writers were impressed by the vast quantities of food. There were three courses, each with ten or twelve dishes to a messe. The recently discovered menu for the banquet shows that there was an extraordinary variety of food and many of the recipes, designed to maximise their visual impact, called for costly imported ingredients like oranges, pomegranates and Flemish fowl.[40] Huge quantities of sugar were used in the cooking and elaborately shaped jellies would have been a major feature.

The main part of the feast completed, the evening led seamlessly on as the company moved through to the second space, a sumptuously decorated theatre. Taking elements from both accounts, we learn that 'the floor was covered with cloth of silk embroidered with gold lilies', that the room was fitted with tiered seating and decorated with 'pillars of azure, full of stars and fleurs de lis of gold [and that] every pillar had at the top a basin [of] silver, wherein stood great branches [candelabra] of white wax'. The whole of the flat ceiling was painted with a map of the world and the signs of the zodiac, 'these paintings being supported by giants'. Some way down the hall was a gilded triumphal arch painted with classical heroes and what Hall describes as 'very strange work, with leaves, balls and other garnishes, all gold'.[41]

Hall's account stops at this point but Spinelli continues with a detailed report of the entertainment that followed. A key feature was its classical and martial themes, such as Jupiter and Mercury appearing and asking Henry to resolve a dispute between them. Others were its cloth of gold costumes decorated with gold spangles, the beauty of its performers and its use of cleverly contrived mechanical devices. The entertainment concluded with a masked dance (the 'disguising'), after which everyone returned to the dining hall for the void. Spinelli ends his letter on a rather lame poetic note, telling us that 'the sun, I believe, greatly hastened his course, having perhaps had a hint from Mercury of so rare a sight; so showing himself already on the horizon'.[42] In other words, time had flown and dawn had broken.

The costs of this event are recorded in Sir Henry Guildford's and Sir Thomas Wyatt's list of payments and came to £761 4s 7d, including a small but significant sum for gold and silver foil used to decorate the arches and other parts of the structures. The gold foil came in two qualities, 'fine gold' and 'party gold', costing 50s and 20s per 1,000 leaves, while 'fine silver' cost 7s 6d. No less than 31,700 party gold leaves were applied to the ceiling alone. There is also a payment of £14 6s 8d 'for eighty basins and the silvering of them, and the setting them up'. These are presumably the 'basins silver' mentioned by Hall, 'wherein stood great branches of white wax', but which turn out not to have been silver after all, but base metal covered in silver foil.[43]

These prosaic documents are an essential check to the more colourful eye-witness reports which are often intentionally or unintentionally exaggerated: the whole supper was almost certainly *not* 'served in vessel of gold'; the wall lights were not made of 'basins of silver'; and the buffets were probably not 'all of massive gold'. That they were enormously impressive, however, is not in any doubt.

The buffet of plate

The focal point of any feast was the buffet, or 'cupboard', of plate, normally a stepped structure, made for the occasion and formed of wooden boards covered with special carpets and damask cloth. The 1547 inventory of Henry VIII's possessions includes a number of 'cupboard carpets', which were mostly between nine and ten feet long.[44] Ordinarily, the plate seen on the buffet was used to serve the meal, but on great occasions it was purely for display. Commentators repeatedly noted, not only that it was 'worth vast treasure', but that 'none of it was touched'.[45] Such buffets were status symbols and their size reflected exactly that. Part of a typical, although by Tudor royal standards very modest, buffet is shown in the Ahazuerius tapestry. Fifteenth-century Burgundian sumptuary laws tied their permitted size to rank, with a sovereign entitled to five tiers, a prince to four and a count to three.[46] No such rules applied in England, however, and the scale of those erected at the Tudor feasts was enormous.

Banquets staged in 1501 and 1527 will serve as examples. At one of those held in Westminster Hall for Katherine of Aragon's arrival:

> The cupboard [of] seven shelves and stages of height, furnished and fulfilled with precious and sumptuous plate of most pleasant fashion, was erected and set, continuing all the breadth of the Chancery. The plate thereof were great and massy pots, flagons, standing cups, goodly bowls and pieces – for the most part clean gold and all the residue gilt.[47]

At a supper at Richmond a couple of days later, the buffet was differently configured and set up 'in a bay window of nine or ten stages and haunches of height'.[48] At Greenwich in 1527 the configuration was different again and Spinelli describes two buffets 'reaching from the floor to the roof, forming a semicircle';[49] Hall, while not mentioning this innovative shape, tells us rather more of what was on them. One had seven shelves, was thirteen feet long and set exclusively with gold plate, 'some garnished with one stone and some with other stones and pearls'. The other cupboard, with silver-gilt, was larger and 'so high and so broad that it was [a] marvel to behold'.[50] These and other accounts like them are all imprecise in one way or another. Not least, they seldom give a clear idea of their size and therefore of the amount of plate that could have been displayed. In the case of Westminster Hall in 1501, however, the Chancery court normally occupied the south end of the hall and its 'breadth' was about thirty feet (see plan 6.1).[51] This would have been room enough to show many pieces on each of the seven shelves, suggesting a total of well over a hundred items. The jewel house would surely have been able to provide enough plate for such a display, and indeed, the sheer number of vessels deployed on such occasions is part of the explanation for the great quantities of plate it held in store.

Their principal purpose, of course, was to impress and after the 1527 banquet at Greenwich was over, the king ordered, unusually, that 'these two houses with cupboards, hangings and all other things [...] should stand still, for three or four days, that all honest persons might see and behold the houses and riches, and thither came a great number of people, to see and behold the riches and costly devices'.[52] It became, in other words, for a short time, an open public display of magnificence.

Plan 6.1
Speculative reconstruction of the buffet of plate at Westminster Hall in 1501 (not to scale).

The security of these displays was a constant concern and it was usual for them to be guarded by an official, even though not always very effectively. Tapestry depictions of buffets sometimes include such a guard and in one, an early sixteenth-century tapestry in the Musée Lorrain in Nancy, he looks decidedly the worse for wear.[53] At the entertainment laid on for the French admiral in 1546 it was ordered that two officers had to stand guard at each of the four buffets.[54]

As to how exactly these displays were arranged and how much they varied from occasion to occasion, most of the sources are thin on detail. Terms such as 'great and massy pots, flagons, standing cups, goodly bowls and pieces' are impressionistic but give little idea of quantity or appearance. Once again, in the absence of firm information about the royal buffets, we turn to the detailed instructions in the *Northumberland Ceremonial* for guidance. This describes the buffet as it was to be set for the feast of twelfth night, the most ceremonial occasion in the earl's calendar: it was to be five stages high, 'the first stage with pots, the second stage with flagons, the third stage with bowls, the fourth stage with goblets. And the fifth standing cups.'[55] The overriding principle here, of course, is that each shelf had one category of wares, so it is a fair assumption that the royal buffets were done in a similar way. But these had more stages than the earl of Northumberland's, so they probably included other types of plate as well, such as ewers, basins or spice plates.

We have discussed some of these categories already, but what of flagons and bowls? Flagons follow pots on the 1521 inventory and come immediately before bottles, which seem to have been similar but smaller (the median weight of flagons is somewhere between 150 oz and 350 oz per pair, whereas most of the bottles are much lighter). Their distinguishing features were their bellied form, slender neck and stopper, together, in most cases, with a distinctive carrying chain. But flagons and bottles were greatly outnumbered by pots and only about fifty are listed, mostly in pairs. Several can be seen standing on the second tier of the Ahazuerius buffet; surviving examples from the period include two French pairs, one from the early fifteenth century at All Souls College, Oxford,[56] and another of 1581 in the Louvre (fig. 6.8). As with pots, it is the larger, gilt flagons that tend to be more highly decorated.

Figure 6.8
Flagon or bottle, Noël Delacroix, Paris, 1581–82. Silver gilt. Musée du Louvre, Paris.

The next tier of the Northumberland buffet was loaded with bowls, which were part of the wider family of drinking vessels. Those displayed on the royal buffets had two special features, namely that they were mostly very large and came in sets. The inventory includes nearly 260 in gilt and parcel-gilt, many grouped in sets of six or even twelve. As with other categories, the gilded ones seem to have been the more richly decorated, but there were other differences too: the gilt sets mostly had a single cover, implying that they were meant to be stacked together for display, and they were generally much heavier. The parcel-gilt bowls mostly weighed between 30 oz and 50 oz each, whereas the gilt ones seldom weighed less than 60 oz and could be more than 120 oz.

The inventory tells us next to nothing of the basic form of these vessels but the Rochester tazzas (1528 and 1532) perhaps give some indication of their general character. These are very like the Goldsmiths' spice plate but have a single shallow cover. They might be compared with the two bowls, stacked together, that we see in the image of Wolsey's plate from Cavendish's biography (fig. 8.6). The tazzas weigh about 30 oz each, giving a measure of how much bigger the largest ones in the jewel house must have been. The British Museum's vessels have short, stubby stems, but this is not necessarily the only form that they could take. Some of the descriptions refer to 'standing bowls' and some just to 'bowls', implying that some had stems while others did not. The *Ryalle Book*, in the instructions for 'the void on twelfth night and wassail', says that the usher is 'to come in with piles of cups;'[57] it is difficult to imagine the Rochester tazzas being carried in 'piles', so perhaps the 'piles' were of smaller vessels such as the group of seven shallow cups placed upside down at the front of the buffet in the Ahazuerius tapestry (fig. 6.1).

A Garter feast

Significantly different from the great banquets for foreign ambassadors, but hardly less impressive, were the annual feasts for the knights of the Order of the Garter. One of these, held at Windsor in May 1519, is drily but clearly recorded in a protocol that helps fill in some of the gaps left by the more sensational reportage of the others.[58] It took place over three days, interweaving church services and feasting, but the feasts were rather different from the great ambassadorial events. Attended only by the king, the knights themselves and certain other individuals, it was an all-male affair, without any of the accompanying entertainments that were found elsewhere.

Two meals are described, one held on the Saturday evening and the other on the following morning. The account describes the layout of the tables, the plate that was used and the ceremonial service. The grander of the two (but only slightly so) was the second, which was held in the hall rather than the chamber of estate. This took place after mass. The king's board was on a raised platform and was occupied only by the sovereign and the prelate of the order, Richard Fox. Below this were two long tables, one for the knights and the other for a party comprising three French noble 'hostages',[59] the dean and canons of the Chapel Royal and the heralds. The tables were set with plate before the company entered, all of which carried nuances of hierarchy. The king's board was laid with a 'saltcellar [of] fine gold set with pearls and precious stones to a rich value, the spoons of gold, three carving knives for the carver and one for the king on his trencher, the hafts [handles] of fine gold';[60] at the knights' board every mess (each shared by two knights) had one gold salt (but not jewelled) and trenchers; and the noble hostages, at the upper end of their table, were provided with trenchers and gold salts (in their case, *with* stones), while the heralds and chapel personnel further down the table made do with silver-gilt.[61] In addition to the wares set on the tables, there was a six-stage buffet 'furnished with [plate …] of fine gold for the king's board only' and a seven-stage buffet of silver-gilt for the knights. There was also a ewery board 'replenished with basins of fine gold for the king and also other basins and ewers gilt to serve the knights of the Garter'.[62] This shows the now familiar distinction between pairs of gold basins for the king but silver-gilt ewers and basins for others. The account clearly describes the placing of each of these elements within the hall, the plan of which is represented in plan 6.2.

But with the buffets there is an important difference. For these are not – as they were on the other occasions we have discussed – purely for display; they are functioning buffets that appear to have been used during the course of the meal. The gold buffet was 'for the king's board only' and the other 'for the knights'. The descriptions of the service during the meal imply that the gold buffet was used as a staging post for the cup on its way to the king's board as, for example, when the gentleman usher 'took with him an esquire for the body to bear the king's cup to the cupboard'.[63]

The event started with washing, much as it would in Canterbury a year later, followed by grace. We are told that there was one ewer and basin to each mess, which means that, in addition to the king's gold basins, there must have been around twenty-five ewers and basins on the ewery; it so happens that there were slightly more than this in the jewel house.

Exaggerated rituals of service at the king's board were constantly in evidence:

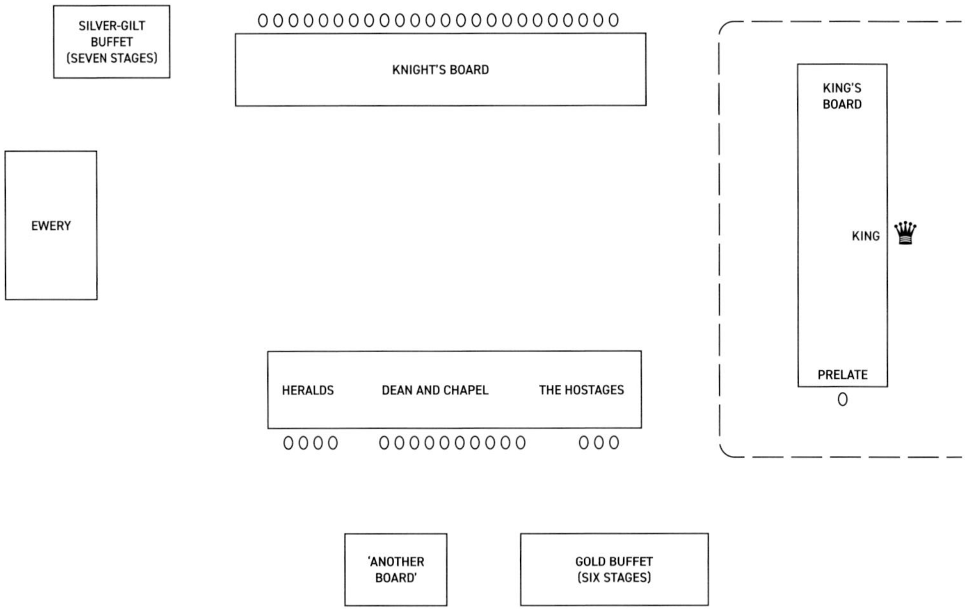

Plan 6.2 Reconstruction of the plan for the Garter banquet at Windsor, May 1519.

> Then entered the king's sewers in the hall and thirteen bachelor knights in gowns of velvet and great gold chains about their necks; every one of them bore a dish of gold. A lord bore the king's pottage, the henchmen bore the king's sauce, the serjeants at arms went before the sewers. And when the sewers came in the midst of the hall they made the first curtesy and against the king's cupboard they made the second obeisance and at their coming before the board they made the third. And there before the board kneeling they took the assay and so set the meat upon the board.[64]

Rank and its degrees were observed through gesture, assay and plate: the king was served in gold, always from a kneeling position, and had the assay taken before anything passed his lips; trumpets were sounded throughout the act of serving him (as they were for the washing); Fox, who shared his table, was also served in gold but had no assay; and while he and the king had the honour of being served with covered cups and spice plates, those deployed at the lower tables had no covers, even though 'that some were dukes':[65] their shared membership of the order levelled the field on this occasion and normal distinctions in rank were set aside.

Both banquets concluded with a void of wafers and hippocras, the eucharistic echoes of which are hard to miss. On the Saturday night the lord chamberlain, accompanied by torches and 'three of the greatest estates', approached the king's board with the towel, spice plate and cup. He uncovered the spice plate and performed the assay.[66] The king was then served, followed by the rest of the company. Something like this happened on Sunday too, followed by washing and grace. The final ceremony involved each group rising in order of precedence and paying their obeisance to the king. At this point the king's cup and wafers were 'voided' (cleared away) and things loosened up, as the king 'talked and paused a while' before everyone filed out to evensong.[67] Evensong was followed by a second performance of the void, this time taken standing up in the great chamber. It was perhaps less formal than the other, but no less ceremonial. In preparation, the gentleman usher and the king's cupbearer went to the cellar 'and there received certain bowls and plates [...] the sewer received a covered spice plate for the king [and] went on the left hand of the cupbearer and somewhat behind him'.[68] The ceremony reached its climax with a procession into the chamber: the usher 'went before them all having in his hand the cup of estate'.[69] He was flanked by serjeants at arms carrying maces and followed by bachelor knights with spice plates and henchmen and sewers of the chamber with cups. 'When the king had taken his pleasure of spices and hippocras the king's cup was again covered' and the knights were served.[70]

Privy dining

Dining in the great hall or even the chamber was in decline during Henry VIII's reign, except on special occasions, such as the Garter feast. The king's preference for privacy was expressed in his retreat to the privy chamber, access to which was very restricted. It was here that he would normally dine, but we know frustratingly little about how or where this was conducted, for the obvious reason that there were few witnesses and certainly none whose business it was to write about it.

An intriguing drawing (fig. 6.9) shows the king dining alone beneath a cloth of estate, in the presence of a few courtiers and with a small buffet of plate against the wall. Despite its inscription 'Holbein inven', this is probably not by Holbein, but it does appear to date from the mid-sixteenth century and may well depict something reasonably close to reality. If so, it shows how life in the king's private quarters had moved on since Henry VII's day. Then, according to 'directions for different officers about the court',[71] one of the duties of the gentleman usher was to ensure that 'no manner [of] man do set any dish upon the king's bed for fear of hurting the king's rich counterpoints that lie thereon'. In other words, the king ordinarily ate in the bedroom. By now he would have been eating elsewhere in the privy apartments, perhaps even in a designated dining room. But arrangements

Figure 6.9 *Henry VIII dining in his privy chamber*, school of Hans Holbein the younger, c. 1548. British Museum, London.

for the provision of plate at night time may have changed less from those set out in the 'directions', which stipulate that in preparing for the night, the usher had to collect the king's cup from the cellar, together with two pots of wine, the basin and water from the ewery, and a 'pricket' (candlestick) from the groom porter; all of these had to be returned first thing in the morning to the various departments responsible for them.

What did the king eat off and what were the wares on that small buffet? As we have seen in the case of chapel plate, we can piece together at least a partial list of these from the annotations to the inventory. Most of the plate 'loaned out' by the jewel house would have been for general use across the household,[72] but when it comes to gold wares we can be fairly sure that we are looking at things specifically intended for the king. This included a cup (weighing 50 oz and decorated with roses and sheaves of arrows, one of Katherine of Aragon's badges), the cup of assay, four goblets (including one of mounted birrall and another of glass), two salts (one of chalcedony, with rubies and pearls, weighing 21 oz and another smaller), a 19 oz layer and two spoons (one with a diamond in the end).[73] Spoons are seldom mentioned in accounts of royal dining but the jewel house held no fewer than 175 of silver and thirty-three of gold. The latter were presumably similar in shape to silver ones, many of which survive, but several had been received as new year's gifts and were decorated with Tudor dynastic motifs; some were enamelled, and three were embellished with a ruby or a diamond.

It is surely significant that several of the pieces gracing the king's table incorporated exotic materials like chalcedony, birrall and glass (at that time still relatively rare in England). These were objects that would have been prized not just for their bullion but as things of beauty and hint at a taste for *Kunstkammer* objects that only becomes completely clear with the inventories from the end of the reign. The gold layer was evidently a strikingly virtuoso object too, enamelled as it was with white harts, pearls and blue flowers.

An important question that repeatedly crops up during these accounts of banquets concerns gold. It is likely that the king's own table would have been set with gold, and indeed we have seen the evidence for that. But if the chroniclers and ambassadors are to be believed, it was deployed much more widely. The buffet plate in 1501 was said to be 'for the most part clean gold', the *vasi* on a buffet in 1517 were 'of gold, worth vast treasure', and the plate on one of the buffets in 1527 was 'all of fine gold'. Gold was said to be much in evidence on the tables too: in 1515 a member of the Venetian ambassadorial party wrote that 'we attended High Mass […] and afterwards we accompanied the king to table, where he chose us to see the service of the courses, contained in sixteen dishes of massive [solid] gold with sixteen covers;'[74] in 1527 'the whole supper was served in vessel of gold'. But the problem with these accounts is that they are not entirely supported by the jewel house inventory. The 1527 gold buffet was thirteen feet long and had seven shelves. If one assumes a density of, say, twelve pieces per shelf, that would suggest eighty-four pieces. This is rather more than the jewel house could have provided and even though we can be confident the inventory does not represent the totality of royal gold plate, the references to gold dishes and plates are particularly problematic, as there is no inventory evidence for these at all. And even though one might expect such wares to be kept with the king rather than in the jewel house, it is odd that, with the exception of a single 27 oz trencher, there is no sign of them in the supposedly complete inventory of 1547 either.[75]

There are two possible explanations for this. One is that these additional holdings were melted down or spirited away before the final inventory was compiled, and the other is that the ambassadors were simply mistaken or misled. In support of the second are occasional hints of silver-gilt being passed off as gold. Gilding on silver was done by mixing gold with mercury, applying it to the surface and then burning off the mercury in the fire; this left a lemony yellow plating of gold that was prized for its beauty although quite easy to distinguish from solid gold. But when given a second layer of gilding the resemblance was much closer. This was, of course, expensive – a chalice in the 1521 inventory described as double gilt weighed 51 oz, but the description tells us that 'the gold that went to the garnishing of the same' weighed 5 oz, ten per cent of the whole.[76] A number of other items in the inventory were 'double gilt', including a pair of 139 oz pots described as being 'made for the cupboard of gold',[77] and Collins recounts how, in 1588, Lord Burghley had been deceived into buying some plate as gold but which subsequently proved to be silver-gilt.[78] But what of the other hypothesis, that gold wares were melted down or spirited away before the 1547 inventory was compiled? This is also possible, but the evidence is not decisive and will be considered in Chapter 14. In all probability, more gold had existed outside the jewel house, but it is also likely that the ambassadors were sometimes deceived.

Seven 'Rich, Fierce and Greedy for Glory'

Even though he never met the king, Niccolò Machiavelli's description of the young Henry VIII as 'rich, fierce and greedy for glory' exactly summed up the man and his ambitions.[1] Unlike his father, who avoided war whenever possible, the young Henry VIII wanted to make his mark on the world. This chapter does not discuss his foreign aspirations in any detail. Instead, it focuses on the means by which he pursued them. These were essentially threefold: through loans, through warfare and through dynastic marriages. In each of these plate and jewels played a conspicuous role. As another essential element of princely interaction, we will also look at diplomacy. This covered a broad spectrum, from the spectacular embassies dispatched for some special purpose, to the altogether lower-key system of resident ambassadors that was in its infancy in the sixteenth century. We have already looked at the extravagant receptions laid on for embassies; here we focus on the munificent gifts of plate that were integral to them and the much lower level of gifts that a resident ambassador might expect at the end of his term.

Banker to princes

Henry VIII's inherited liquidity immediately made him a force to be reckoned with, for Henry had huge cash reserves, which continental rulers often did not, especially when it was most needed. Cash could buy military force and Nicola di Favri, a member of the Venetian diplomatic delegation, recognised this when he wrote in 1513 that 'for gold, silver and soldiers not another king in Christendom can be found to compare with him'.[2] But money could be used to influence events in other ways too; it could be used to extend loans to his more cash-strapped fellow princes. This had been a major plank of Henry VII's policy and he lent large sums to Philip the Fair of Burgundy and Louis XII of France. As we have seen, he also passed money to impecunious rulers by buying jewels and other assets from them at advantageous rates.[3]

Henry VIII's loans during the early years of the reign were, therefore, a continuation of existing policy and the sums involved were very substantial. In September 1510 the Venetian ambassador, Andrea Badoer, reported to the Signory that Henry was willing to lend the Republic 150,000 ducats. By November the offer had increased to a million, in both cases 'provided jewels to that amount were consigned to [the king] as security'.[4] In 1517 Pope Leo X requested 200,000 ducats[5] and two years later Francis I approached Henry for 100,000 crowns.[6] Such loans were viewed strategically and were not always granted. Nor were they granted without adequate security, which Henry always preferred in the form of jewels. When Charles V requested 200,000 ducats in 1522 he offered a choice of jewels, merchants' bonds or cities as security but Henry and Wolsey opted firmly for jewels, on the grounds that they were portable and tangible and, in case of default, easily realisable.[7]

One of the most protracted and complex of these was a loan of 50,000 crowns advanced by Henry VII to the Emperor Maximilian in 1508. This was secured against a splendid gold reliquary known as the 'fleur de lis', which remained in England until long after the emperor's death and is described in great detail in the 1521 jewel house inventory.[8] The 'fleur de lis of gold with certain relics' was an impressive object, apparently of cruciform shape, with terminals formed as fleurs de lis. These terminals contained fragments of the true cross, the uppermost one of which was enriched with a crucifix. In addition to the holy wood, one of the nails that had fixed Christ to the cross was set in the base. Two other embellishments were 'a little ball or apple silver and gilt wrought with fire brands and fire irons' and a jewel-set crown, perhaps above the crucifix. The glory of the piece was the extraordinary wealth of gems that adorned it. These were very numerous and included fifty-four diamonds, seventy-three balases, fifty-six sapphires, twenty emeralds and more than 200 pearls. Weighing over 211 oz with the relics and stones, it was by far the largest (or heaviest) gold object in the jewel house at this date. We have no image of this cross but a sense of its bejewelled magnificence is perhaps conveyed by an equally sumptuous cross, itself enclosing a fragment of the true cross, from the 1523 illustrated inventory of Cardinal Albrecht of Brandenburg's treasures (fig. 7.1).

This precious reliquary was part of Maximilian's Burgundian inheritance, the clue lying in the 'fire brands and fire irons', the personal badges of Charles the Bold (1433–77). The detailed audit of stones, as with all the jewelled objects in the inventory, was essential, given that they accounted for a large part of its value and could easily be removed. Indeed, that is exactly what happened to the fleur de lis and an annotation to the inventory notes that in December 1514, on the king's instructions, most of the pearls and

Figure 7.1 Image from the *Hallesches Heiltumbuch* (MS 14, fol. 7) of a jewelled reliquary cross from the treasure of Cardinal Albrecht of Brandenburg, c. 1523. Hofbibliothek Aschaffenburg.

stones were unset and delivered to the king. This was probably connected with his sister Mary's marriage that October to Louis XII of France: her dowry included many stones which had possibly been borrowed from other objects and which needed to be replaced. We gain an idea of the extent of this 'borrowing' from the fact that when the still denuded cross was reweighed in 1521 it came to just 190 oz: 21 oz short of its original weight.

In 1527 the fleur de lis was still in Henry's possession and became a pawn in a protracted three-way negotiation. Francis I was negotiating with Charles V for the release of his sons, held hostage in Spain as a result of Francis's defeat at Pavia in 1525. Charles demanded a substantial ransom from Francis, but he was also indebted to Henry. A complex deal was proposed whereby Charles would release the princes but would also cede Burgundy to Francis in exchange for two million crowns, part of which would be used to settle Charles's debt to Henry. It was further proposed that the fleur de lis should go to France as security for the safe deliverance of the princes, and that it should be delivered to the French ambassador, the bishop of Bayonne.[9] Very correctly, Henry declined to comply without first getting Charles's consent but in preparation had the jewel cleaned and the missing stones replaced. Several months of procrastination ensued. The imperial ambassador, Eustace Chapuys, smelt a rat. He complained to the duke of Norfolk who assured him that all the stones had been replaced 'with larger and finer ones'. 'Besides,' Norfolk added, 'between the king and the emperor, a matter of 300 or 400 ducats, more or less, is not worthy of consideration.'[10] Things dragged on and some months later, in February 1530, Joachim de Vaux, a member of the French delegation, wrote colourfully to Francis that 'we have not yet seen this jewel, but by all accounts it is so large and heavy that it is a horse-load so to speak'.[11]

The final chapter in the saga was that Chapuys insisted on having the jewel professionally examined, after which, he wrote,

> it should be carefully packed, and [the king's] own royal seal affixed to the packet, mine being likewise appended so that no tampering with its contents should be possible, and that then, as soon as the promised security should arrive from the bishop of Bayonne he (the king) would dispatch his ambassador to France with the jewel.[12]

This, finally, is what transpired and in February 1530 the Chamber accounts record a payment of £170 to Francis Bryan for being 'sent to the diet to be kept on the confines [borders] between France and Spain with a certain jewel called the fleur de lucye'.[13] This would seem to indicate an end to the matter, except that in May de Vaux writes again to Francis complaining that further difficulties were being raised about the quality and weight of the gold. He suspects that 'these excuses are only made to put off the delivery till such a time when it may suit the emperor's convenience'.[14] After that the jewel fades from the English records. It does not end there, however. Margaret of Austria maintained that the jewel belonged with the Burgundian dynasty and urged that it be returned to the treasury of the former dukes. Between 1536 and 1545 it resided in the chapel at the palace in Brussels and in 1558, on his abdication, Charles V took it with him to Spain. He bequeathed it to his son, Philip II, and in 1605 it was designated a dynastic heirloom and an integral part of the crown jewels, but it was subsequently lost in the fire of 1734 that destroyed much of the Alcázar palace in Madrid.[15]

War and peace

Wars (especially Henry VIII's) were about honour and glory. These required more than just military prowess; they required magnificence, and when Henry went to war he was abundantly equipped with jewels, plate and gilded armour. In this respect he was not much different from other princes. In 1513 James IV of Scotland took huge quantities of plate to the battle of Flodden,[16] as did Francis I to Pavia twelve years later. One of the French tents there was said to have been 'full of silver and gold vessels, cups, flasks and so forth',[17] a sense of which we can glean from the depiction

Figure 7.2 (opposite) A royal tent with a buffet of plate, from *The Story of King David*, Brussels, c. 1520. Tapestry. Musée de la Renaissance, Ecouen.

of a battlefield tent in the David tapestries (fig. 7.2). As it happened, the Scots and the French were both routed at these battles; James was killed at Flodden and his plate was seized by the English. Some found its way to the jewel house where it was recorded in the 1521 inventory. We have already noted the gold reliquary cross found around James's neck after the battle (see p. 21) and the inventory also identifies a hexagonal gold saltcellar with St Andrew on the cover as having been recovered from the battlefield.[18]

From the outset Henry was determined to mount a campaign in France to recover England's lost possessions. Two years into his reign Pope Julius II provided him with a pretext by excommunicating Louis XII and recognising Henry as king of France. Needing no further encouragement, Henry embarked for Calais in June 1513 with an army of some 24,000 men. It was an impressive display and an Italian based in London noted that 'the valuables they took with them were incredible; the housings [harness] of the king's charger and the jewels around his head piece were worth 15,000 crowns. Never had a finer sight been seen.'[19] Edward Hall adds that Henry's armour was 'gilt and graven [...] full of borders, and in all places traversed with branches in running work of fine gold, the branches were of hawthorne wrought by goldsmith's craft, wound with a branch of roses, and every flower, leaf and berry were embossed'.[20] But the most fulsome account of the king's magnificence in war was written by a member of the entourage of Henry's ally, Emperor Maximilian, whom Henry met near Thérouanne. This describes the king's rich attire, his liberality and magnificence:

> [the king] rode clad in his armour without the helmet, wearing a surcoat of cloth of gold; his hair bound in a rich golden cap in which were set many rich precious stones [...] He sat [on] a beautiful brown stallion, the bridle and harness laid with pure beaten gold plates. There hung [...] many golden bells, each about two ounces in weight, some of which were so loosely fastened that when he made his stallion bound, one or other of the golden bells fell off and he called to a German to pick it up and keep it, and none of his own people might pick up any.

The account goes on to describe his royal tent:

> All over from the ground to the roof, [this] was covered with rich cloth of gold of pure drawn gold thread. There is also therein here and there a beautiful gilded sideboard of very large vessels and flagons, among them some drinking cups all of gold, which are looked after by certain persons who are thereto appointed [...] The outside of the tent was likewise from the ground to the summit overlaid with good cloth of gold [...] Above it stood a lion of gold holding the arms of England in its paws.[21]

Henry's meeting with Maximilian also allowed for a more relaxed exchange between the two allies, when the conversation turned to a subject close to Henry's heart. Paolo de Laude, Milanese ambassador to the emperor, wrote to his master that

> immediately after dinner I hear that these princes talked of rings and jewels, and that the king showed some very fine ones to the emperor and in the end gave his Imperial Majesty an eagle to wear at his neck, holding in his claws a large carbuncle, and at its breast or perhaps in its beak, a large cluster of diamonds, and a great pearl at its throat, so that this eagle is estimated to be worth more than 30,000 gold florins [...] Some say that this eagle formerly belonged to Duke Charles of Burgundy.[22]

Henry's personal magnificence was mirrored, though less brightly, in the magnificence of the English nobility. The same German commentator writes that 'the king of England's servants and lords riding with him [...] wore coats completely covered with gold and silver plates bound together with rings instead of seams, others of cloth of gold, velvet and rich clothing';[23] Hall tells us that the duke of Buckingham cut a fine figure 'in purple satin, his apparel and barde full of antelopes and swans of fine gold bullion and full of spangles and little bells of gold marvellous costly and pleasant to behold',[24] and the list of the earl of Northumberland's baggage opens with 'a sumpter horse for the coffers with my Lord's plate'.[25]

Taking huge quantities of valuables in the baggage trains was about more than showing off. Any military campaign depended on its army being paid on time and this required cartloads of coin. According to one account, Henry went to France with fourteen wagons of gold and silver coin,[26] but underestimating the amount of cash needed for this purpose could spell disaster unless other liquid assets were available. In Milan in 1526, for example, the imperial troops threatened mutiny when their pay was delayed and the situation was only saved by various nobles pledging the plate and jewels that they had with them.[27] The royal and aristocratic plate and jewels in France in 1513 were more than a portable token of status and would undoubtedly have been used for this purpose had the need arisen.

Diplomacy

Compared with its huge cost, the outcome of Henry's French campaign was underwhelming. Two towns were captured, Thérouanne and the more important city of Tournai. But these brought little glory and were hugely expensive to garrison. In the long term this was unsustainable and by the end of 1515 Henry had made serious inroads into his inheritance. Thomas Wolsey, by now effectively the king's chief minister, sought to leverage the king's influence through other means. An opportunity arose in 1518 when Pope Leo X proposed a united Christian crusade against the Turk, which Wolsey used as a means of settling Henry's differences with Francis: Tournai was sold back to France, a substantial annual 'tribute' was agreed, and the bargain sealed by the betrothal of the two-year-old Princess Mary to the dauphin. A great French embassy came to England to swear the Treaty of London and was received in magnificent style. Such delegations were hugely expensive to send and also to receive, but they were much cheaper than war.

All of this was achieved through diplomacy, which took two distinct forms: on the one hand there were high-profile embassies sent for some specific purpose, such as the ratification of a treaty, and on the other there was the system of exchanging permanent ambassadorial representation. The two systems were entirely different. The special embassies were extremely high-level delegations; the visiting ambassadors were some of the greatest in the land – in the case of England, figures like the duke of Suffolk and Cardinal Wolsey – and they were treated with great honour. As a result, these embassies were very opulent. They called for the most extravagant hospitality and for the presentation of costly gifts. Resident ambassadors, by contrast, were professionals. They enjoyed privileges such as immunity from arrest and relatively free access to the royal court, but in other respects they were not well provided for by their hosts or by their masters and sometimes struggled to keep up appearances. At the end of their residence the gifts they could expect were relatively modest.

The great embassies were vast undertakings involving huge entourages, long trains of baggage carts, and dozens or even hundreds of horses. The Spanish embassy to London in July 1517 was 'accompanied by so noble a train of men and horses that, had the king of Spain himself come in person, he could not have been more honourably attended [...] They had with them some hundred horses and twenty-four baggage waggons.'[28] The following year the admiral of France, Guillaume Bonnivet, led the embassy for the Treaty of London and came with 600 horses and seventy mules.[29] Not only that, but Hall adds that the official entourage was accompanied by 'great number of rascals and peddlers and jewellers' bringing 'hats and caps, and diverse merchandise uncustomed [without customs duties being paid], all under the colour of the trussery of the ambassadors'.[30]

The giving of gifts was usually left to last, after the formal business of the embassy and after the rich programme of church services, tournaments and banquets. Gifts were governed above all by reciprocity and it was essential that what was given was roughly equivalent to what was received, either at the same time or by a subsequent return embassy. The preferred material was plate, because this was easy to value and easy to cash in. An amusing story from the end of the reign describes what must have been quite common practice. The English ambassador to France, Nicolas Wotton, wrote of how he sold Francis I's present to him almost immediately after receiving it. He judged that none of the items were newly made and, indeed, recognised two of the cups as ones that he had himself sold in Paris a while before (presumably having just been given them) and 'since I had them as cheap first as now, I will sell them again trusting that they love me so well that they will not be long away'.[31]

What could be sold, of course, could equally well be passed on to a third party to satisfy an obligation and in 1513 we read of the recycling of two gold cups previously given by Henry VIII to Cardinal Adrian Castellesi, who in turn presented one to the emperor and the other to the doge of Venice.[32] Again, this was probably not unusual.

The best documented of all Henry VIII's ambassadorial gifts were those presented to the ambassadors from Cleves who accompanied Henry's fourth bride to England in 1540.[33] In addition to the total cost of £1,405 16s 5d, we also have a full list of the recipients and the individual items each received. The plate was all gilt and was divided between twenty-five members of the delegation, from the ambassadors down to a 'messenger'. At the bottom of the list, 'messenger Guillum' received two items, a cup and a cruse (a small two-handled cup), weighing 38 oz. At the other end of the scale the five ambassadors each received more than 300 oz in identical parcels: a pair of pots, three bowls, a cup, two jugs and salts and a ewer and basin; 'gentlemen' received around 150 oz each and 'Master John' the surgeon 77 oz. The gilded plate was costed at 5s 2d per ounce, and the parcel-gilt ewers and basins at 4s 6d. Altogether 191 objects were presented, weighing between ten and sixty ounces each.

But the Cleves gifts were not the most munificent of the reign. The order for the 'diverse parcels of plate given to the French ambassadors' in 1518 was split between William Holland, John Twistelton and Robert Amadas and cost £1,829 14s,[34] about thirty per cent more than the other. Beyond its total cost, however, the evidence is anecdotal: Hall tells us that the admiral alone received 'a pair of covered basins gilt, twelve great gilt bowls, four pair of great gilt pots, a standing cup of gold, garnished with great pearl'[35] (much more than the ambassadors from Cleves), and a Venetian wrote that the plate, all set out on a buffet, comprised 'fifty-two large silver vases or drinking cups, more than five *palmi* [about 75 cm] high each, all gilt'.[36] In addition to the plate, the same source tells us that Bonnivet also received a valuable robe from the king.

Setting out these gifts on a buffet in order to maximise their impact seems to have been usual practice and when the imperial ambassador, Jehan de la Sauche, came to discuss arrangements for Charles V's impending visit in 1522 he wrote to the emperor that Cardinal Wolsey had 'led me to a room where there were displayed, on a buffet, about eighty pieces of plate, most of them beautifully gilt, which he presented to me'.[37]

Precedent was always an important concern and when the French admiral, by now Philippe de Chabot, arrived in November 1534 Thomas Cromwell wrote himself an *aide memoire* 'to know the value of the last gift given to the admiral at Calais'.[38] On that occasion, in 1532, Henry and Francis had met in person and the gifts had been particularly lavish, setting the bar high. After being richly entertained in London, Chabot was duly presented, according to Chapuys, with gifts to the value of 8,000 ducats (£1,800), in addition to the presents given to other members of the delegation.[39] But values could also be adjusted downwards to send a message and in 1533, when Jean du Bellay, bishop of Paris, came to explain Francis's latest diplomatic manoeuvres with the pope, Henry was not pleased and, as a result, according to the rumour Chapuys passed back to the emperor, the bishop 'has only had at parting, as I am told, half the present the king at first thought of giving him'.[40]

Personal gifts between princes were less formulaic than those given to ambassadors and were of two sorts: strategic gifts intended to seal an agreement, or gifts chosen as special expressions of friendship. An example of the former was the marquis of Mantua's gifts to Henry of mares, falcons and an oriental scimitar, which resulted in his ambassador reporting that the king was 'so pleased with the present that the marquis might rely on his support on all occasions'.[41] A more blatantly strategic gift came from Ferdinand of Aragon, Henry's own father-in-law, when in 1515 he sent Henry magnificently caparisoned horses and a fabulous sword worth, in Cardinal Wolsey's opinion, 100,000 ducats. Henry wrote to Ferdinand that 'great as the value of the presents is, I value them principally because they show [your] love and benevolence towards me'.[42] Katherine of Aragon, perhaps more acutely, or just more candidly, wrote to her father saying that 'the king of England is very proud of the splendid presents come to England [and] it is due to his presents that the treaty with England is concluded and the alliance renewed'.[43]

Some of the most notable gifts came from France. The evidence for believing that the surviving clock salt (fig. 9.5) was a personal gift from Francis is discussed in Chapter 9, but there were many others. Of some we have only a vague idea, such as the four mules 'loaded with most handsome effects' sent in 1529,[44] but others were described more fully. In 1531 Chapuys told the emperor that Francis had sent 'a very fine and artistic clock, on the dial of which the movement of several celestial spheres and planetary systems can be distinctly observed'. He quips that 'I fancy that if Jehan Jocquin [the French ambassador] has been the inventor of this device, Mars is sure to predominate over Mercury'.[45] Even more striking were two portraits, received in December 1526. These were carefully described by Gasparo Spinelli, who happened to see them. Each was essentially a diptych, with a finely worked gold cover, opening to reveal a painted miniature, one of Francis and the other of his two sons. The image of Francis faced a beautiful *impressa* of two columns separated by water but joined at the top, with a Latin motto to the effect that the two lands separated by sea are joined by friendship. Spinelli goes on to say that 'it would be difficult to express the delight these gifts caused his majesty, for the demonstration was extreme and will testify eternally to the Most Christian King's obligation to him'.[46] The gift was almost certainly in thanks for Henry's role in his release from captivity after Pavia, but it would have conveyed an obligation of its own, probably repaid by Henry's own gift to Francis six months later of a double portrait of himself and Princess Mary. This went down very well and Francis wrote to Henry that he 'found it so perfect that it could not be more so'.[47] Even more telling is the account that Henry's envoy, Bishop John Clerk, wrote immediately after presenting the gift:

> at the first sight of the king's physiognomy he took off his bonnet, saying he knew well that face, and further, 'Je prie Dieu que il lui done bone vie et longue' [I pray God to give him a good life and a long one]. He then looked at the Princess's, standing in contemplation and beholding thereof a great while, and gave much commendation and laud unto the same. He kept it for some time, without showing it to any creature, and then sent it by the Grand Master to his mother.[48]

Ambassadors in residence

The life of a resident ambassador abroad was altogether less glamorous than that of aristocratic envoys with their vast entourages. Permanent diplomatic representation varied depending on the general state of relations between the two princes but during the reign of Henry VIII the most established delegations were those from Venice, France and Spain (which, under Charles V, was part of the empire). These delegations were small, normally comprising the ambassador and a small staff, and they were relatively inexpensive to maintain. Indeed, quite frequently *too* inexpensive and the evolving nature of the system is reflected in the difficulties resident ambassadors sometimes encountered. These usually centred around money and maintaining the dignity that their position required. Money was usually short and the ambassador's salary was seldom enough to cover unexpected expenses. Foreign ambassadors in England and English ambassadors abroad struggled to keep up appearances, although there is evidence that this situation gradually improved as the reign advanced.

The individual circumstances of ambassadors very often depended on the help they received from their resident compatriot merchants and it was not all bad. When Raimondo de' Raimondi, the new Milanese ambassador, arrived in London in 1498 he wrote to the duke that '[they] took me to a house which Agostino Spinola had prepared for me, decorated with his hangings and plate'.[49] Spinola was a Genoese merchant and the duke of Milan's agent in London. But not all ambassadors had such a soft landing. The Venetian Signory, recognising plate as an essential mark of status, always allowed their ambassadors to take table wares to the value of 400 ducats 'at the Signory's risk' (enough, say, for a dozen plates and a modest group of other wares). But there is no firm evidence of them receiving a salary until 1525 when Lorenzo Orio was appointed on 140 golden ducats a month.[50] As a result, things were not always easy and when Andrea Badoer was sick in 1509 he wrote to his masters that he had had to pawn his plate, 'being unable to find anyone who would give him money on bills of exchange'.[51] Chapuys had a more dramatic setback in October 1533 when,

> without knowing how to account for it in the least, fire broke out in one of the towers of my house containing my plate, wearing apparel, best house furniture, and, in short, almost every valuable I possessed in this world [... It is an] almost irreparable blow to me, who must be completely ruined in consequence! [...] But I have found no small comfort from the alacrity with which both Spaniards and Germans residing in this city have placed at my disposal more money and silver plate than could be held in one large room.[52]

Even in normal circumstances ambassadors often complained of the cost of living in London,[53] but ambassadorial life was not without its compensations. Ambassadors were at the heart of power; they frequently had audiences with the king and were invited to court festivities and banquets. And when they returned home they could expect to receive a present from the king, although a much smaller one than those given to aristocratic ambassadors. It was the custom in England for the retiring Venetian ambassador to receive a gold chain, normally to the value of around £100. These were as close to money as they could be without being actual cash and were probably formed of simple links, like those worn around the necks of the attendants in the *Westminster Tournament Roll* (fig. 4.3). But gifts of plate were also sometimes given and in 1533 two papal nuncios received presents, one a gold cup and the other unspecified silver plate.[54]

Whether such gifts were normally retained by their recipient or accepted in the name of their master is not always clear, but in the case of Venice the situation was indisputable and the former ambassador had to petition the senate to be allowed to keep it. These petitions were not always successful and in 1535 returning ambassador Capello failed to secure the required four-fifths majority and had to hand his chain over to the state.[55] Eustace Chapuys, the long-serving imperial ambassador, occasionally grumbled that he never received anything from Henry (other than a haunch of venison in 1529). On one occasion his complaints were perhaps tactlessly audible and the duke of Norfolk had to take him aside and tell him that

> the king commands me to say in his name that you must not think it strange that the Flemish ambassadors who have left this court have received the customary presents on parting, whereas you have received none. It is no great fault of the king, or of his ministers, but the custom in this country is to give such presents only on parting.[56]

The life of an English ambassador abroad was no easier and lack of money and plate is a recurring theme. Richard Sampson, the English ambassador to Spain, appealed to Wolsey for financial assistance in 1523. He was 'desirous always to act for the king's honour [...] but has no plate nor other things convenient'. His real problem was that he had no 'vessel but of tin [pewter], which prevents him from entertaining personages of estimation'.[57] John Hackett was in a similar situation ten years later when he complained from Brussels that he needed money 'to spend it on some serving silver vessel, more for the king's honour than otherwise'.[58] To cite one more example, Richard Vaughan, also writing from Brussels in 1538, complained to Cromwell that he was almost out of money due to the high cost of maintaining his dignity as ambassador.

> I must buy at least a dozen horses and have as many servants, and buy household things and pompous apparel [...] I have already bestowed over 200 marks in plate here, and this I write to show how willingly, to my power, I bestow my money to serve the king.[59]

English ambassadors abroad had their fair share of unexpected calamity too. Richard Pace was burgled when serving in Venice in 1522 and lost thirty-two silver cups, though he was partly compensated on his departure some months later by receiving a gold chain worth 800 ducats (£180) 'by reason of the trouble taken by him [...] and to keep him well disposed towards the Signory'.[60] Thomas Wriothesley and Vaughan, travelling through France together in 1538, faced a lesser irritation when they found themselves in Cambrai having to entertain a guest with 'as good cheer as we could, none of our stuff or plate being come because one of our carts broke two leagues out of the town'.[61]

One diplomat who ran the gamut of such experiences was Sir Robert Wingfield, who spent much of the 1520s in Calais and Flanders. His brother Richard was ambassador to France at the time of the Field of Cloth of Gold in 1520 and received a munificent service of plate from Francis I.[62] Robert was not so fortunate and Richard advised Wolsey in 1521 that his brother 'has little desire for the post [of ambassador to Charles V], especially as the little plate he has is either sold or pawned'.[63] His circumstances must have oscillated, however, since a year later he was evidently able to lend some of his kitchen plate to the bishop of Utrecht;[64] three years after that he suffered a setback, writing to Brian Tuke in the summer of that year that 'I must ride to Antwerp to seek friends, or money or plate, as I get no remittance from England', and to Wolsey that he 'has this year sold 200 marks of plate, so that now I eat in pewter, as I have not done these dozen years past, being the king's ambassador'.[65] Some respite came from Richard Gresham, who lent him £50 to save him having to sell his plate.[66] But this can only have been a stop-gap and by January 1528, a year before his death, he wrote in desperation to Wolsey from Calais, saying that he would pawn or sell his plate to pay off his debts but could not find a buyer.[67]

There were signs, however, of a growing acceptance that it was in the king's interests to provide for his ambassadors. In 1532 Nicholas Hawkins, archdeacon of Ely, succeeded Thomas Cranmer as ambassador to Charles V. Hawkins wrote to the king informing him that Cranmer had departed and that 'he [Cranmer] has delivered me your plate and other things'.[68] This is the first clear indication we have of ambassadors being entrusted with the king's plate. Hawkins was not entirely happy with it, however, and a month later complained to Cromwell that 'I have much plate here of the king's, but, except the salt, the basin and ewer, two flagons, and the spoons, all unprofitable [unsuitable]'. The problem was he had no 'vessel'. 'All other ambassadors have their meat vessels for their tables of silver, as Cranmer can inform you. Howbeit, he had none, nor have I. Judge you how they are content to be served in tin or pewter, who are accustomed to dine at home off silver.' He asks if he might be permitted to 'turn the unprofitable plate into profitable' and is prepared to bear the refashioning cost himself.[69]

Among other references to ambassadorial plate, the cases concerning Sir John Wallop and Bishop Bonner are particularly interesting. Wallop was resident ambassador to France from 1533 to 1537 and again from 1540 to 1541. His predecessor in 1533 was Sir Francis Bryan, after whose recall the royal goldsmith, John Freman, submitted a bill to the jewel house for erasing Bryan's arms on eighteen silver dishes 'of the king's vessel' and replacing them with Wallop's. Freman charged 20s for the job, of which Wallop himself paid 9s 8d.[70] Clearly, therefore, the dishes belonged to the king but were being 'rebranded' for the new ambassador. What subsequently happened to them is not clear and the evidence is confusing. Wallop's two successors in the role were Stephen Gardiner (1537–38) and Edmund Bonner (1538–40), but while Bonner cheerily wrote to the king on his appointment that he 'has received, according to the king's pleasure, [certain] plate and stuff from Dr Thirlby [a member of Gardiner's delegation]',[71] Wallop was evidently less content when he himself was reappointed in 1540. At that stage he asked Cromwell to write to Bonner 'that he may have his silver dishes', adding that 'he sold those he had when last in France to supply his necessities'.[72] Was he referring here to the jewel house dishes or to some of his own? We do not know. But if the situation there is unclear, what Bonner did in a later diplomatic role is anything but. Now bishop of London, he resumed his diplomatic career as ambassador to Charles V in 1542, evidently taking an impressive service of jewel house plate with him, which he duly returned in 1544. This we know from an oddly placed entry in the jewel house accounts of plate 'received from monasteries and cathedrals, shrines etc'. This records the receipt of just under 900 oz of plate from Bonner 'at his return from ambassage from the emperor'. This, it clearly states, had been 'lent and delivered unto him by order and commandment of the late Lord Cromwell'.[73] But Cromwell was executed in July 1540, which begs the question of when exactly and in what capacity it had been lent to him in the first place.

The clearest evidence of all that by the end of the reign a system was in place relates to Lord Lisle's appointment as ambassador to France in June 1546, when he was provided with 982 oz of jewel house plate. The preamble to the list states that the plate is issued 'by way of loan' and goes on to require that Lisle 'bind himself [to return it] at his next return out of France, safe, whole and in like fashion'.[74]

Dynastic marriages

One of the most sensitive and important fields of diplomacy concerned dynastic marriages. This was a long game and, when it came to a successful conclusion, was tantamount to a declaration of supposedly permanent alliance. It involved lengthy and careful negotiations, public celebrations and huge expenditure on dowries and presents. Frequently centred on children who were well beneath any conceivable age of consent and who were pawns in their parents' strategy, it was preceded by formal betrothal and proxy-marriage. Love had very little to do with it, even though such marriages, given their relatively low level of emotional expectations, were often surprisingly successful.

Typical of the use and abuse of potential young brides was the story of Henry VIII's first daughter, Mary. She was not the son that Henry and Katherine had so badly wanted but she was the first child to survive infancy and she was much loved. A princess in early modern Europe, however, was also an asset and potential dynastic alliances would be explored from (by modern standards) an indecently early age.

Mary was first betrothed in 1518, at the age of two, to the dauphin, who was himself just eight months old. But the engagement was terminated when war broke out three years later and the asset was promptly reinvested by her betrothal to her much older cousin, Charles V. This also eventually failed when Charles chose to marry Isabella of Portugal instead. Several more fruitless negotiations were conducted and for a betrothal that went the distance, Mary had to wait until her eventual marriage to Charles V's son, Philip II of Spain, in 1554.

The two most famous dynastic marriages of the early Tudor period were Prince Arthur's to Katherine of Aragon in 1501, and Henry VIII's sister Mary's to Louis XII of France in 1514. Arthur and Katherine's marriage was the result of more than twelve years of negotiations. Embassies shuttled backwards and forwards between Spain and England as the details were worked out. From the beginning Henry VII had insisted that Ferdinand and Isabella 'are to dress their daughter suitably to her rank and to give her as many jewels, & c. for her personal use, as becomes her position'.[75] By 1496 detailed specifications of the dowry were on the table. This was set at 200,000 scudos, some parts of which were to be in specific forms: 15,000 was to be in gold (presumably coin), another 15,000 in plate and 20,000 in diamonds and other precious stones. Nothing was fudged and Henry insisted that the plate and stones be appraised by sworn valuers, according to the price for which such things could be sold in England;[76] 15,000 scudos converted to around £3,125, which in turn would have equated to nearly 12,500 oz of silver-gilt plate. This would ensure, at the very least, that Henry would not be put to the expense of providing for that part of his daughter-in-law's dignity. But Ferdinand and Isabella were suspicious and three months before Katherine's departure they wrote to their ambassador in London, Dr de Puebla, for the terms to be amended so that

> the 35,000 crowns which the princess is to take with her in jewels and gold and silver, should be received as an instalment of the first payment ... [but] that the princess be not despoiled of the said jewels, gold and plate [...] Still the plate and jewels must belong to the princess, who takes them for her own use and enjoyment.[77]

Katherine's entourage, in addition to courtiers and ladies-in-waiting, included numerous household officers, two of whom, Saravia and Pedro de Solozano, were responsible for the plate and jewels.[78] Clearly, these were seen as a major asset that needed proper care and indeed, following Arthur's death in the following year, one of Ferdinand and Isabella's first concerns was for their safety. They wrote instructing Katherine's officers to 'keep all the gold, silver, jewels &c. of the princess with the greatest care. Not the smallest portion of them ought to be sold.'[79] But it was not so easy to control events from afar, as we will see in Chapter 11.

The marriage of Henry's eighteen-year-old sister Mary to the fifty-two-year-old Louis XII was not her first foray into the marriage market and in 1508 she had been betrothed to a very different potential husband, the eight-year-old Charles of Habsburg, the future Holy Roman Emperor. But shortly before the date set for their marriage the political ground shifted and in May 1514 Charles's grandfather, Maximilian, suddenly called it off. Saving face, Henry moved with extraordinary speed to capitalise on the new amity between France and England, betrothing her within weeks to the recently widowed Louis.

Part of the rationale for this was that it was a means of settling Louis' long-standing debts to Henry and although Henry agreed to pay a dowry of 200,000 crowns in jewellery and 'furniture' (a very similar sum to Katherine's), Louis agreed to the much higher contra-payment of a million in reparations.[80] Moreover, the dowry was subject to 'restoration' in the event of Louis' early death.[81]

The wedding took place in France in October of that year, but was preceded by a proxy-marriage at Greenwich in August and – bizarrely – a 'proxy-consummation'. For the marriage, 'the duke [de Longueville] delivered a gold ring which the princess placed on the fourth finger of her right hand'.[82] In a characteristic gesture of largesse he was awarded the sum of £2,000 for his pains (either in plate or money) and Henry's costly gown. The latter was described as 'embroidered with beaten gold [and] worth 300 ducats'.[83] In the strange ceremony that followed, the marquis de Rothelin 'touched the princess with his naked leg [and] the marriage was declared consummated'.[84]

Mary embarked for France two months later with a huge entourage of noblemen, knights and ladies. According to the Italian merchant, Lorenzo Pasqualigo,

> there are so many gowns of wove gold and with gold grounds, housings for the horses and palfreys of the same materials, and chains and jewels, that they are worth a vast amount of treasure [... The queen of France] wore a gown in the French fashion, of wove gold, very costly [...] On

> her neck was a jewelled diamond, as large and broad as a full-sized finger, with a pear-shaped pearl beneath it, the size of a pigeon's egg, which jewel had been sent her by the king of France.[85]

This jewel, probably the so-called 'Mirror of Naples', was to become a major bone of contention in the negotiations that followed Louis' death.

The shortcomings of Edward Hall's economical account of Mary's plate ('great was the riches in plate, jewels, money, apparel, and hangings that this lady brought into France')[86] are more than compensated by Henry Wyatt's inventory, written in French.[87] This lists a great many jewels (including the 'Mirror of Naples') and a large consignment of plate. There are twenty-two gold items – a chalice, cups, salts and other vessels – some of which were of gold-mounted rock crystal set with jewels and weighing together some 405 oz. The list of silver and silver-gilt amounts to around 10,450 oz and covers the familiar repertoire. The chapel plate includes chalices, a cross, candlesticks, six images (including St George and St Thomas of Canterbury), a covered basin and a holy water bucket. Table and buffet plate include fifteen pots (one pair weighing an impressive 425 oz), bottles, ewers, cups, goblets, sets of bowls and three garnishes of 'vessel', which weighed around 3,000 oz. Among the more unusual items is 'une mestier d'argent a besonguer de Soye', weighing 97 oz. This was apparently a silver loom (*métier*) for weaving silk and was presumably for the queen's personal use. The list hints here and there at the decoration of her plate, which echoes the 1521 inventory – initials H and R, roses and fleurs de lis, martlets and portcullises[88] – and the impression is that much of it was simply pulled from the shelves of the jewel house. Some pieces have red roses (rather than red and white), implying that they date from the previous reign.

This impression is strengthened by the surprising survival of another document, a list of plate drawn up in preparation for Mary's aborted wedding with Charles of Habsburg.[89] The two lists are generically similar but not the same. The later list is longer, but a more important difference is that, while the French one is clearly a record of actual objects, the Habsburg one seems to be more of a 'shopping list': weights are all in round numbers and the list is annotated with notes such as 'to be new made here', 'of her own', 'of the king's own' or 'to be provided'. In other words, the plate was clearly intended to be a mixture of jewel house stock and specially made pieces. A specific difference between the two lists is that the French one includes a huge 463 oz parcel-gilt nef, whereas the Habsburg one does not, a telling reminder of the special importance of the nef as a mark of status in France.

Despite a stormy crossing, in which one ship foundered and 'much plate and property was lost',[90] Mary arrived safely and was grandly received in

Figure 7.3
The Marriage of Louis XII and Mary Tudor, Tournai, c. 1525. Tapestry. Hever Castle, Kent.

Abbeville in a series of ceremonies reminiscent of Katherine's reception in 1501 (fig. 7.3). She was also showered with gifts by her doting husband, as is clear from a letter from the earl of Worcester to Wolsey:

> My lord I assure you he hath a marvellous mind to content and please the queen [...] He showed me the goodliest and richest sight of jewels that I ever saw [...] And when he had showed me all, he said that all should be for his wife. And another coffer also was there that was full of goodly girdles, collars, chains, bracelets, beads of gold, and other diverse goodly jewels: but merrily laughing he said, 'My wife shall not have all at once, but at diverse times; for he would have many and at diverse times kisses and thanks for them.'[91]

Louis was generous to Mary's noble escort too, some of whom returned to England with gifts of plate amounting to 30,000 francs each.[92]

Such diplomatic initiatives required huge organisation and enormous administrative ability. The mastermind behind most of those during the second and third decades of the sixteenth century was Thomas Wolsey and it is to him and his extraordinary career that we turn next.

Eight

Thomas Wolsey, Patron of Goldsmiths

Much of the courtly magnificence that we have looked at so far – the great church services, the banquets, dynastic marriages and so on – were planned and overseen, directly or indirectly, by one man, Thomas Wolsey (c. 1470–1530) (fig. 8.1). Other than the king himself, Wolsey is the biggest figure of the first half of the reign. His administrative genius and extraordinary capacity for work led to rapid promotion and escalating wealth and with this went a growing obsession with the trappings of power. This chapter is not a biography of Wolsey, but it does look at him through the lens of magnificence, in both its ecclesiastical and secular contexts, and it considers his role as a patron of goldsmiths.

Figure 8.1
Cardinal Thomas Wolsey, Sampson Strong, 1610–11. Christ Church, University of Oxford (Accession number LP 11).

Wolsey owed everything to the king, a fact that he acknowledged through his new year's gifts, which were always more costly than those of other courtiers. But Henry owed something to him too. Through his artistic patronage he played a major role in bringing the Italian 'antique' style to England. He also brought over Italian artists whose work would ultimately benefit the king. Henry benefited directly from his fall too, in that Wolsey's houses, his accumulated wealth and his unparalleled holdings of plate and works of art all went to the king. About ten per cent of all the plate in the 1532 royal jewel house inventory is identified as 'late the Cardinal's'.

Wolsey is a difficult figure to judge because contemporary opinions of him were so polarised: some (notably his usher and biographer, George Cavendish) idolised him; others (such as the contemporary historian Polydore Vergil and the imperial ambassador, Eustace Chapuys) despised him and saw his every action in the worst possible light. As a result, the truth is sometimes hard to get at. He was undoubtedly haughty, covetous and endlessly ambitious, but that is not the whole picture. His covetousness and ambition must be set against his energy and exceptional ability. No one could have been a better judge of that than his former master, Richard Fox, bishop of Winchester, who, on retiring from the council, told Wolsey that 'more diligence and labour for the king's rights, duties and profits [...] be in you than ever I see in times past in any other'.[1] Equally, it was expected that the king's great and powerful minister should be hardly less magnificent than the king himself, because this reflected on the greatness of his master. Henry himself recognised this when he wrote to Leo X, thanking him for making Wolsey a cardinal and saying,

> nothing has given the king so much pleasure in all his life as the breve announcing the election of Wolsey into the College of Cardinals [...] He has outdone all the king's expectations, who esteems the distinction thus bestowed upon a subject, for whom he has the greatest affection, both for his eminent gifts and most excellent services, as done to himself.[2]

But there was a fine line between being hardly *less* magnificent than the king and being slightly *more* so, and Wolsey came perhaps too close to overstepping that line.

'More as pope than legate'

Thomas Wolsey's administrative abilities were the making of him and explain his rapid rise through the ranks of Church and court. After escaping his relatively humble Ipswich origins by excelling at Oxford, he became a tutor in the household of Sir Richard Nanfan, a minor courtier. There, proximity to the king gave him an opportunity to make himself useful; Henry VII noticed him and appointed him a royal chaplain, then almoner. The almoner was officially responsible for dispensing royal alms but it was an open-ended role that led to wider opportunities within the household.

Like so many medieval statesmen, Wolsey's career began in the Church. From royal chaplain he became secretary to Richard Fox, then in 1511 a canon of Windsor. A meteoric rise followed, during which he became bishop of Lincoln in 1514, then archbishop of York. With the last of these came York Place, the archbishop's London residence, adjacent to the royal palace of Westminster. That he never added Canterbury to his list of titles was due to the longevity of William Warham, who was appointed primate of England in 1503 and outlived Wolsey, remaining in office until his death in 1532. But Wolsey found a way to outrank even Warham. In 1515, just twenty months after becoming a bishop, he was raised to cardinal by Leo X and finally, in 1518, made papal legate. This was the pinnacle of his ecclesiastical preferment and although he entertained the idea of putting himself forward as pope on the death of Leo in 1521, the chances of this actually coming to pass can never have seemed strong, even to him. By 1529, shortly before his fall, he had added bishop of Winchester – the richest see in England – and abbot of St Albans *in commendam* to his long string of titles; at previous stages he had also enjoyed the titles (and revenues) of bishop of Bath and Wells, and of Durham.

In parallel with these went his inexorable rise in the royal service: from the outset he realised that the key to ingratiating himself with Henry VIII lay in immersing himself in the minutiae of royal business, encouraging the king not to concern himself with such trivia and leaving him to enjoy himself. It was, in the words of Cavendish, 'the very vein and right course to bring him to high promotion'.[3] He was made a royal councillor in 1511 and by 1515 was effectively the king's chief minister. At the end of that year, soon after his elevation to cardinal, Warham recognised that Wolsey had eclipsed him in the king's service and resigned the Great Seal. As a result, at the age of forty-five, Wolsey added lord chancellor to his many dignities and emerged as the most powerful man in England after the king himself.

Wolsey's wealth rose in tandem with his escalating status. Sybil Jack has estimated that from around £1,000 a year in 1511 (already enough for a minor nobleman) his income had risen by 1519 to as much as £9,500 (making him the wealthiest subject in the land).[4] By the time of his fall, once all his legatine and legal fees, his bribes, his presents and his French and German pensions had been added in, it must have been approaching £30,000 a year.[5] Needless to say, his expenses rose too. As archbishop of York his household numbered some 160 people and his wages bill alone came to around £2,000 a year; his elevation to legate would have brought with it a further escalation in expenses. The greatest costs, however, would have come through the obligations of magnificence which, given his position, would have been considerable. But in the eyes of his contemporaries Wolsey took these to excess and the huge levels of income at his disposal made it possible for him to spend on a lavish scale. The Venetian ambassador, Ludovico Falier, said that Wolsey 'spent his whole income' and that, as a result, 'his court was far more magnificent than that of the king'.[6]

In the last decade and a half of his life the cardinal spent considerably more on building projects even than the king;[7] spending on luxury commodities like plate and tapestry was on a commensurate scale. The result, by the end of the 1520s, was a concentration of material wealth that was virtually unparalleled in England. In his 1519 report on the state of England, the retiring Venetian ambassador, Sebastian Giustinian, wrote of Wolsey that he

> has a very fine palace, where one traverses eight rooms before reaching his audience chamber, and they are all hung with tapestry, which is changed once a week. He always has a sideboard of plate worth 25,000 ducats, wherever he may be; and his silver is estimated at 150,000 ducats [£33,750]. In his own chamber there is always a cupboard of vessels to the amount of 30,000 ducats.[8]

More poetically, the same observer described the banqueting hall at York in 1518 as 'so decorated with huge vases of gold and silver, that I fancied myself in the tower of Chosroes'.[9] Eight years later, either his holdings had significantly increased or Giustinian had understated them in the first place, for the then ambassador, Marc Antonio Venier, wrote that Wolsey had invited the French ambassador to Hampton Court 'to see at his leisure the Cardinal's sideboards of gold plate, estimated in England at 300,000 golden ducats',[10] twice as much as before.

As with the king, purchase was not the only source of Wolsey's luxurious goods. Many came as gifts, either freely given or solicited. In France in 1527, for example, he received 'great presents [from Francis I]; most beautiful tapestries worth 30,000 ducats or crowns; a handsome chalice and paten both of gold; an image of the Virgin; an altar service, containing 88 marks of gold; besides other cloths of silk'.[11] Freely given though these might have been, there was never any question of such gifts being simple expressions of goodwill. They were bribes, if not to achieve specific ends then at least to buy favourable attitudes. Polydore Vergil, no fan of Wolsey, wrote that Francis I, in order to secure Henry's friendship, had his ambassadors 'mollify Wolsey with gifts and magnificent addresses'.[12] And Wolsey himself understood perfectly the way the world went in this respect, as Vergil reveals later in the same passage when he recounts how, none too subtly, Wolsey would on occasion share with Henry some of the gifts he had received from Francis. 'For he would bring some little present, such as a dish of fine workmanship, or a jewel, a ring, or something of the kind, and while the king closely examined and admired it, he would artfully bring up what he had in mind.'[13] But not all such gifts were so freely given and in 1519 Wolsey reminded the Venetian ambassador, Antonio Surian, of his predecessor's promise of sixty 'beautiful and choice' carpets. Despite their high cost of 600 ducats, Surian advised the Signory to deliver; having previously described Wolsey as 'a fish not to be caught save with a golden hook',[14] he tells them 'it would be well to make a present to this individual, who might [so great was his power] be styled the king of England'.[15] Ten years later, just months before his fall, the Republic found itself having to make the cardinal a further gift of 'forty-five yards of the handsomest tawny coloured damask there be'.[16]

Like any prince of the Church, Wolsey was keen to perform magnificence as well as to display it. The Greenwich banquet was not the only one staged for the French ambassadors in 1527 (see p. 98) and it was preceded by another, comparably magnificent event, hosted by Wolsey at Hampton Court. Cavendish describes the banquet itself in great detail and the enormous logistical complications of staging it away from London, including the 'carriage and re-carriage of plate, stuff, and other rich implements'.[17] He describes the buffet of plate ('very sumptuous and of the newest fashions'), the sugar table sculptures, and some conspicuously splendid objects, such as 'two great candlesticks of silver and gilt, most curiously wrought (the workmanship whereof, with the silver, cost 300 marks)', and 'a bowl of gold, which was esteemed to the value of 500 marks' and in which he proposed a toast to the two kings.[18] When the guests returned to their chambers they found them, too, well provided with plate: 'Every chamber had a basin and a ewer of silver and more besides.'[19]

One question repeatedly raised by Cavendish's text (as it is by other eye-witness accounts of such events) is to what extent we should believe the huge reported valuations of some of these objects? Aside from the generalisations, was the gold bowl in which Wolsey toasted the two kings really worth 500 marks (£333)? Did the 'two great candlesticks of silver and gilt, most curiously wrought' really cost 300 marks (£200)? And can we really believe that all the guest rooms (and there were a great many) were equipped with a silver ewer and basin? We should certainly doubt the last of these: there is no corroborating evidence, although we do know that Wolsey had purchased a large number of *pewter* pots and basins 'for chambers',[20] so perhaps Cavendish had misremembered. As to the gold bowl, for it to have been so valuable it must have weighed something like 160 oz (unless it was set with precious stones, in which case Cavendish would probably have said). But we will never know for sure since, according to Cavendish, Wolsey presented it immediately afterwards to the French Grand Master as a gift. On the silver-gilt candlesticks, however, the 1532 jewel house inventory comes to our aid. These too must have been exceptionally large, and so it proves, for the inventory includes 'two candlesticks gilt with griffins on the base, with the king's arms in the midst, with bolts of iron in them, weighing altogether 880 oz'. Although now rebranded with the royal arms, their provenance is betrayed by the griffin feet, Wolsey's heraldic beast (fig. 8.2). At 4s 8d per ounce, the normal price charged by Amadas for silver-gilt, these would have cost £206, or just over 300 marks.[21]

Displaying magnificence on such a scale came close to upstaging the king himself, but Wolsey was careful to stop short of this point. Indeed, Cavendish concludes his account by observing that 'it is not to be doubted that the king was aware of all this worthy feast, and intended far to exceed the same, giving a special commandment to all his officers to devise a far more sumptuous banquet for these strangers than they had at Hampton Court'.[22] And we have seen the extent to which his entertainments at Greenwich did indeed 'far exceed the same'.

Figure 8.2
Arms of Cardinal Wolsey from *Prince Arthur's Book*. College of Arms (MS Vincent 152, p. 93).

Wolsey came even closer to matching the king, and quite deliberately so, when he led an embassy to Amiens to meet with Francis I a few months earlier. Exceptionally, Henry had appointed Wolsey his lieutenant general. This was quite different from the normal status of an ambassador. Rather than being the king's representative, he was as if the king himself. This was intended as a compliment to Francis, but it upped the stakes for Wolsey, who announced on arriving in Calais, that '[I must] assume and take upon me, in all honour and degrees, to have all such service and reverence as to His highness's presence is meet and due: and nothing thereof to be neglected or omitted by me that to his royal estate is appurtenant'. Wolsey meticulously exacted every extreme detail of ceremony and deference during the visit, while in terms of plate 'he showed them more gold and silver than the king [of France]'.[23]

Wolsey's parallel role as the most high-ranking prelate in England called for magnificence and deference of a different kind. Like the crown jewels, his ecclesiastical regalia played a potent role in conveying his authority within the hierarchy of the English Church. No sooner had he heard of his elevation to cardinal than he wrote to Silvestro de' Gigli, absentee bishop of Worcester and protector of English interests in Rome, requesting that 'the hat be sent with all due diligence'.[24] According to Hall, this was 'brought to London with such triumph as though the greatest prince of Christendom had been come into the realm. And on a Sunday at [Westminster Abbey] he received the habit, hat, and pillar, and other vainglorious trifles, appertaining to the order of a cardinal.'[25] Another source describes how Wolsey immediately used his regalia to demonstrate his new precedence over Warham by noting that in the procession out of the abbey he had 'next before him the cross, preceding it the mace [pillar] such as belongeth to a cardinal to have, and then my Lord of Canterbury, having no cross borne before him'.[26] His elevation to legate changed things again by adding a second cross to his processional regalia, 'whereof one was for his archbishopric and the other for his legacy'. Cavendish's description of the impressive retinue with which he was regularly seen in public is captured by an Elizabethan drawing (fig. 8.3). Another version of the drawing shows the cardinal setting out on his embassy to France in 1527 with a much longer procession snaking before him.[27] After the mounted household servants come the mace bearer, another pair perhaps bearing the Great Seal and the cardinal's hat, then the pillars and, immediately before Wolsey himself, the two crosses. He even brought his regalia when attending the king, 'his crosses commonly standing, during the time of his abode at court, on one side of the king's cloth of estate'.[28]

In church his pre-eminence was symbolised by his insistence on processing under the canopy and with cross and censer, 'not as usual for

Figure 8.3 Wolsey's entourage setting out to Westminster, from a copy of George Cavendish's *Life of Wolsey*. Bodleian Library (MS Douce 363, fol. 52v).

a mere legate', wrote Gasparo Contarini, but 'as if the pope in person had arrived'.[29] Such systematic self-aggrandisement might have aroused derision in certain quarters but more dangerous was that 'within a few days [of becoming legate] he began [...] to employ bishops and abbots, dukes and earls as his acolytes to pour water over his hands and hold his napkins' during mass.[30] At the service at St Paul's to solemnise the treaty of 1518, for example:

> the cardinal of York sang high mass, and had his cloth of estate of tissue: his cupboard set with basins all gilt covered: his place was five steps high. And at the first lavatory [ablutions], three earls served him, and at the second two dukes and a marquis, and with the [as]say taken, they gave him wine, and after water.[31]

Understandably, this was perceived as humiliating and the duke of Buckingham complained bitterly that Wolsey 'would undo all noble men if he could'.[32] There was little love to be lost between them and, according to Neville Williams, 'once in a public ceremony, when he was holding the basin for the king to wash his hands, Buckingham deliberately spilt water into Wolsey's shoes'.[33] But Wolsey's use of regalia, and perhaps of the nobility too, was complicated: he used them to extol himself, no doubt, but also to honour the dignity of his office (which was different from himself), and of the king, the Church and the pope.

Different again from Wolsey's regalia and insignia were his vestments. These, too, were extraordinarily sumptuous and even though contemporary accounts of them are vague at best, we get a powerful sense of their magnificence from the description of the jewelled mitre in the 1532 inventory (see p. 229). The mitre was accompanied by two gold bracelets, a ring, a pair of gloves and a crozier. The bracelets were set with balases, counterfeit stones and large numbers of pearls, and the gloves with an enamelled gold cross and a flower, with diamonds, rubies and sapphires. The crozier too was elaborately worked with images, pinnacles and angels, one 'holding a great counterfeit stone, lozenged [and] set in gold'.[34] Elsewhere we read of his magnificent copes and of a pair of bejewelled sandals.[35]

Patronage of artists and goldsmiths

Wolsey's taste in luxury goods was wide-ranging and voracious and he has been described as 'indisputably one of the greatest patrons of the arts in English history'.[36] His interest in exotic goods was well-known to his contemporaries and we have noted already his fondness for carpets and damask and the grasping pressure he put on the Venetian ambassadors to procure them as gifts. Wolsey's greatest claim to fame as a patron probably lay in his tapestries, which were arguably the most impressive collection ever formed in England, other than Henry VIII's. But he sought out, either as gifts or as purchases, foreign goods across a much broader spectrum: he was a major patron of stained glass from the Low Countries; in 1515 Anthony Spinelli wrote from Antwerp that he had found him a painting for an altar 'which was made by the best master of all this land';[37] a year later he acquired a sophisticated clock from Brussels;[38] and in 1526 he received silver-gilt mounted glasses from Germany.[39] The year 1515 also saw Wolsey buying Paris plate through the English ambassador, Richard Wingfield, and a month later he received a letter advising him that the vessels were about to be delivered 'with a goldsmith to unpack them'.[40] This unusual precaution can only mean that they were delicate objects, perhaps of mounted rock crystal or some other fragile material. It is unfortunate that we do not have more direct evidence for this side of Wolsey's collecting, although two objects on the 1547 inventory of the king's possessions may be indicative: a 21 oz silver-gilt mounted glass and cover 'having upon the knop the late Cardinal's arms' and a 27 oz silver-gilt mounted 'cup or jug of crystal [...] with the Cardinal's arms in the top thereof of gold'.[41]

Many of his overseas purchases were negotiated by English agents or diplomats, but Wolsey also patronised foreign artists directly, inviting them to work on various projects and bringing, in the process, their own Italian style to England. Among the Italian sculptors working in England in the early sixteenth century were Giovanni da Maiano and Pietro Torrigiano. Apart from breaking Michelangelo's nose, Torrigiano is most famous for Henry VII's tomb in Westminster Abbey and for a group of remarkable terracotta portrait busts, including those of Bishop Fisher and Henry VII. We do not know if he worked directly for the cardinal, but Wolsey did commission Giovanni da Maiano to make the series of terracotta medallions of Roman emperors at Hampton Court and for which he charged £2 6s 8d a piece in 1521.[42]

Giovanni returned to Italy but was back in England by 1524 when he started work, in collaboration with Benedetto da Rovezzano, on Wolsey's tomb. This project was largely managed on Wolsey's behalf by an able Italian speaker of whom we will hear much more later, Thomas Cromwell.[43] It continued for the rest of the decade, involving a team of Italian carvers and Flemish gilders, and periodic payments are recorded, right up to 1529 when Antonio Cavallari was paid the large sum of £380 13s for gilding.[44] By this time significant parts of the scheme had been completed, not least the black marble sarcophagus, later repurposed as Admiral Nelson's tomb at St Paul's. Also completed and surviving are Benedetto's four recently discovered bronze figures of kneeling angels, now in the Victoria and Albert Museum (fig. 8.4). All of these works are in an uncompromisingly contemporary Italian style and must have made a very strong impression on their untravelled English observers.

No complete list of Wolsey's possessions at the time of his fall survives, but several extensive documents do give us some idea of the range and character of his plate and the roles that it played. By far the most interesting and revealing of these is the running account maintained by his principal goldsmith, Robert Amadas. This covers the years between 1517 and 1527, when Wolsey was at the height of his powers. But he had clearly had dealings with the goldsmith before that and the account begins by noting that 'at Michaelmas' of that year is 'due to me Robert Amadas by my said Lord's Grace £356 17s 3d'.[45]

From our point of view the account leaves much to be desired: it offers almost nothing by way of descriptions and it is not always clear on what date a transaction took place. But it does show the levels of Wolsey's expenditure with a single supplier, the kinds of plate he was buying, and the range of business being transacted. A careful reading provides various other kinds of information too and throws shafts of light on different aspects of Wolsey himself, even if the account is occasionally ambiguous.

The overwhelming impression is that Wolsey's plate was a constantly evolving resource, with wares being given away or exchanged almost as fast as new ones arrived. The headline figure is that over the period of the account Wolsey spent £5,002 0s 9d with Amadas, but this was only partly paid in cash and many of his bills were settled by recycling old plate. The net figure, therefore, was rather less. A good example is a substantial order delivered around the second half of 1521.[46] It comprised 1,982 oz, made

Figure 8.4
Bronze angel originally designed for the tomb of Cardinal Wolsey, Benedetto da Rovezzano, London, 1524–29. Victoria and Albert Museum, London.

up of twenty-nine pots and bowls, and costing £363 9s 2d. But rather than paying in money, Wolsey met most of the bill by trading in some seventy-one redundant vessels and a quantity of spoons.[47] A few of these are described as 'old' but the main point was that the new items were fewer and heavier than the old. Wolsey would have been familiar with the massive plate seized from the duke of Buckingham earlier that year, and perhaps decided to up his game. Similarly, in 1524 Amadas supplied 'two fair gilt flagons of silver' weighing 208 oz, 'whereupon [I] received one pair of old gilt flagons sore worn pois [weighing] 183 oz, so my flagons weigheth more than my Lord's by 25 oz':[48] not only newer, but heavier.

The list covers a wide range of wares from church plate and ecclesiastical regalia to jewels and presents. The largest category for his own consumption is domestic plate. Most types of dining and drinking wares are included: cups, 'great bowls', 'great gilt pots', candlesticks, spice plates, salts and so on. Most of these were decorated with royal badges or charges from his own arms, and the way this repertoire made for a distinctive 'Wolsey look' emerges from some of the descriptions in the 1532 jewel house inventory. The cover of a gold bowl weighing 103 oz had 'a liberde's [leopard's] head rising out of a crown [...] and within the cover [...] the cardinal's arms enamelled under a cardinal's hat';[49] the finial of a gold cup was formed as 'an angel kneeling within five pillars, holding a cardinal's hat';[50] six bowls had 'great martlets [...] and two leopards holding a cardinal's hat';[51] the cover of a cup had two naked children (his heraldic supporters) holding up his arms';[52] and a 145 oz holy water bucket and sprinkler were engraved with 'a griffon, a lion, and a Cornish chough, cross keys [for York] and cardinals' hats'.[53] This was exactly the same use of heraldry that we have seen in the royal plate to create a visual language or ownership and affinity, but the repertoire is quite different.

Not all of the plate that Amadas was supplying was new and Wolsey was evidently content for the lower tables to be served with second-hand plate, such as a 'garnish of silver vessel [weighing 1,080 oz] bought of Sir William Fitzwilliam of the Court'[54] or two garnishes 'which were bought of my Lord Durham's executors for my Lord Cardinal's use'.[55]

The most revealing feature of the account is the light it shines on costs. As we noted in Chapter 2, prices were based on bullion and 'fashion', each of which were charged at so much per ounce. The bullion price was relatively consistent, depending on the alloy, while 'fashion' varied according to the type of ornament required. But however elaborate the decoration, the cost of the metal was usually the lion's share. This is important to our understanding of pre-modern attitudes to plate because it explains why patrons thought so little of melting down redundant or old-fashioned wares and starting again: in relation to the retained value of the metal, it was cheap to do so, especially for plain domestic wares.

While the account tells us almost nothing directly about decoration, a higher fashion charge usually implies more elaborate design. For example, a pair of 'goodly altar candlesticks of silver and gilt' were charged at 4s 8d per ounce while a 'pot new made unto a match' (that is, copying another) cost just 3s 8d an ounce.[56] In each case the metal would have accounted for 3s 4d per ounce, so while it cost just ten per cent on top of the metal to make the pot, the fashion charge and gilding of the candlesticks added nearly thirty per cent. Very occasionally fashion charges are higher still, such as the 'four knops for a bed of silver and gilt' which weighed 54 oz and which Amadas supplied in 1525.[57] These were charged at 6s 8d per ounce, a premium of one hundred per cent over the metal, which suggests they must have been exceptionally elaborate. Gilding was a costly embellishment, normally based on the weight of the object itself and charged at 12d (one shilling) an ounce for gilding all over and less for parcel gilding.

For gold the costs were much higher. A gold cup and cover supplied in 1525 was priced at 33s 4d per ounce for the gold and 5s for the work,[58] each about ten times the rate for silver-gilt. There are several reasons for this higher 'fashion charge'. One is that it simply reflected the greater prestige of gold; another is that a higher level of finish would generally be expected than for silver, often including settings for precious stones; but a third is that gold is harder and riskier to work than silver, requiring meticulously maintained tools in order to avoid problems arising from contamination from silver or other metals.[59]

Amadas's account also has much to tell us about other aspects of the goldsmith's trade. Many of the commissions were evidently subcontracted to other goldsmiths. This may be because his own workshop did not have the capacity to fulfil all these orders. But equally, it could be because stranger goldsmiths, trained to a more rigorous technical standard on the continent, were better able to produce the sort of specialist work required for Wolsey's finest commissions.[60] Goldsmiths mentioned by name include George Huxor[61] (entrusted with some of the more prestigious orders for gold cups and altar plate), John Beynarde[62] (supplier of a silver-gilt harness for Wolsey's mule), Robert Cowper[63] and John Harlam.[64] By 1526 a new name, Cornelis Hayes, starts to appear in the account; by the end he is undertaking much of Wolsey's work and is described as 'my Lords Graces goldsmith'.[65]

But the London trade was not Wolsey's only source of new plate. We have already noted what appear to be fragile works being sent from Paris and around 1521 Amadas supplied 'six new great gilt bowls' and 'six great gilt candlesticks, made at Bridges' (Bruges), together with a 'case of leather to the same'.[66] These were clearly custom-made, since they were chased with martlets, leopards' heads and cardinals' hats, but if Wolsey or his agent had ordered them in Bruges it is unclear why Amadas was involved, unless he was acting as a broker. This is quite possible and the account includes many services beyond the supply of new and second-hand plate: jewels are supplied or reset, repairs were carried out, transport of plate organised and financial services provided.

Certain entries in the account are unexpectedly revealing of Wolsey's personal attitudes, particularly those relating to his ecclesiastical regalia. In May 1519 Amadas delivered 'one great pillar of silver and gilt' and a processional cross. The pillar, presumably the second one that Wolsey was now entitled to as legate, weighed 156 oz and cost 12d per ounce to make; the cross was charged at the slightly lower rate of 10d an ounce and was described as 'new made after the fashion of the cross of the Cardinal Campeggio'.[67] Presumably Wolsey had decided that his own did not compare well, or that the two legatine crosses should be exactly alike and equal. The following years see Wolsey's pillars going back several times for repairs (probably because they got dropped), but a later twist in the story concerns Campeggio's second visit to England when he came to adjudicate over the royal divorce. According to a memorandum of October 1528, shortly after his arrival, Amadas supplied Campeggio with 'a pillar of silver and most part gilt', which Wolsey paid for.[68] Quite why Campeggio should suddenly have needed a new one and why Wolsey should have paid for it is not clear, but one might speculate that Campeggio had only brought one with him and that Wolsey, disinclined to reduce his own regalia but wanting to appear equal, paid for his fellow legate to have a second. Two weeks later a further two pillars 'most part gilt' were delivered to Wolsey himself. If my explanation for Campeggio's pillar is correct then it would follow that the design of the new ones probably copied Campeggio's original one, which was presumably Italian. All three, at around 80 oz each, were much lighter than Wolsey's old ones but, at the much higher price of 6s an ounce (inclusive of the metal: £73 6s 9d altogether), were presumably more elaborately worked.

Unsurprisingly, many of Wolsey's commissions were for altar plate. Most of these were of a routine nature but some stand out as more exceptional. Two in particular, both farmed out to Huxor, were a 147 oz silver-gilt crucifix and 'an image of Our Lady in a tabernacle'.[69] The first of these seems to be identical with one in the 1532 jewel house inventory (although one ounce heavier) and must have been a very rarefied object. It was made of jasper, chased on the foot with 'antikework', and its gilt mounts were set with 'porcelains',[70] enamels and a whole range of precious stones and pearls. The tabernacle was evidently a more troubled commission, perhaps because the specification was changed. Huxor was initially given 300 oz of silver to make it with, but some time later (it is unclear exactly how much later) he was provided with a further 100 oz 'towards the making of the Salutation of Our Lady in a tabernacle begun and not finished'.[71] By the time it was described in the 1532 inventory it had evolved into an extraordinarily sculptural object described as 'Our lady with her son in her arms naked, with angels crowning her, and angels playing on instruments before her; and on the other side a lily pot, and she sitting in a throne, with the cardinal's hat, arms and antique work'. Its total weight by then was 536 oz.[72]

A significant recurring item in the account is new year's gifts and the absence of any mention of gifts for the queen is a sure indication that the account can only be a partial picture of Wolsey's patronage. But there are regular annual gifts to the king and at least one to the duke of Richmond. The first of the king's is intriguing. This is a 'flower of gold with a great table diamond and three pearls which his Grace gave to the king at Windsor for his new year's gift [in 1518], price £80'.[73] Wolsey, by then a cardinal for three years, stood on the brink of becoming legate and perhaps, in his own mind, was as close to pope as made no difference. It is revealing therefore that he should have chosen to give something that, whilst not necessarily in the form of a rose as such, was nonetheless obviously suggestive of the traditional papal gift that Henry had himself received from Leo X. Such a highly charged gift, with all its implications of the spiritual relationship between prelate and sovereign, may have been a step too far and it does not appear to have been repeated. For subsequent new year's gifts Wolsey stuck to the altogether safer formula of gold cups and covers, generally costing about £120.[74] But Wolsey's status as a most important fount of patronage other than the king ensured that the total value of the new year's gifts he received from others comfortably exceeded what he spent, and in 1519 the Venetian ambassador claimed that he made 15,000 ducats each year through his incoming gifts.[75]

Gifts of a quite different nature were the quantities of plate with which Wolsey endowed St Alban's Abbey and the two colleges he set up in Ipswich and Oxford. Some 2,400 oz went to St Alban's and 2,040 oz to Cardinal College in Oxford. In both cases the benefactions were partly made up of 'old plate new dressed up [refurbished] and amended [altered]' and paid for by the exchange of old plate, either Wolsey's own or, in the case of St Alban's, old abbey plate. In addition to some 1,160 oz of 'dressed up' altar and table silver, the college in Ipswich also received four images of saints. These were newly made by Amadas and weighed 310 oz, but they were paid for with twelve older images weighing 349 oz, so once again, we see Wolsey replacing old images with new ones that were fewer in number but bigger and more impressive.[76]

Cavendish tells us that Wolsey's plate was 'very sumptuous and of the newest fashions' and while Amadas gives frustratingly little insight into what these fashions were, he does drop occasional hints of their newness. His 1522 new year's gift to the king, for example, weighed 66 oz and cost £135 11s 1d. The wording of the entry is unusual, describing it as 'a standing cup [of gold ...] as appeareth by one counterpiece of lead'.[77] This must mean that the goldsmith, George Huxor, was given a lead model to copy,

Figure 8.5
Plaster cast of the arms of Cardinal Wolsey, taken from the original, of terracotta, at Hampton Court Palace. Victoria and Albert Museum, London.

which surely means that the cup was not of a standard design but something different and – presumably – more advanced in taste. But the question remains: what exactly were these 'newest fashions' seen by Cavendish and the French ambassadors? The term 'antique' does not appear in Amadas's account although it is used in the 1532 inventory, sometimes in relation to items formerly belonging to Wolsey. And a hint of what it meant can perhaps be gleaned from other things made for the cardinal. The terracotta relief of his coat of arms at Hampton Court, made in about 1525 (fig. 8.5), is entirely 'antique'. The arms, superimposed on a jewelled cross beneath a cardinal's hat, are placed between two naked putti; the composition is framed by Corinthian columns beneath an entablature and above an egg-and-dart moulding which is itself supported by scroll brackets overlaid with acanthus: it is the essence of the Italian Renaissance and would have been very new to England.

Fall

Cardinal Campeggio's second visit to England, when Amadas provided him with a new silver pillar, turned out to be the beginning of the end for Wolsey. He was gambling that by having Campeggio join him in judging the validity of Henry's marriage to Katherine this would enable them to declare it invalid. Henry, perhaps on Wolsey's advice, reminded Campeggio of the desired outcome by presenting him with a munificent gift at Christmas said to be worth 2,000 marks.[78] But the process was doomed to failure. The Italian was secretly instructed by the pope to drag the proceedings out as much as possible and the court did not actually sit until the following summer. Then Katherine refused to recognise its authority and finally the case was withdrawn to Rome and Wolsey lost control. Signs of Henry's impatience were evident in various ways and in September he refused to grant the cardinals an audience except that 'they come without any sort of pomp or ceremony, without their crosses preceding them as usual, or that arrogant display of retainers which the two cardinals were wont to show in public, but with only ten or twelve servants each'.[79]

The referral of the case to Rome left Henry frustrated and placed Wolsey in an impossible position. The least bad outcome would have been for Campeggio's official mission to have been accomplished and for the king to have got his way, but this was far less desirable – for international relations, for tensions at home and for Wolsey himself – than if the situation had never arisen in the first place. As Ambassador Falier wrote to Venice in May 1529, 'Cardinal Wolsey does not wish the divorce to take place, because, should the king take to wife the daughter of Sir Thomas

Boleyn, according to his intention, her father, one of the chief personages in England, will deprive Wolsey of his repute.'[80]

By now events were moving apace. Campeggio left London on 5 October and almost immediately Wolsey was indicted for *praemunire*, an ancient statute prohibiting the aiding and abetting of a foreign power within the realm; two weeks later, on 18 October, he was ordered to surrender the Great Seal and deprived of his seat on the king's council. Cavendish takes up the story, telling us that after surrendering the seal, Wolsey

> called all the officers of his household before him, to take account of all such stuff as they had in their charge [...] There he had two chambers adjoining the gallery, the one called the gilt chamber and the other called, most commonly, the council chamber. In each were set two broad and long tables upon trestles, whereupon was set such a quantity of plate of all sorts as was almost incredible [see fig. 8.6]. In the gilt chamber was set out upon the tables nothing but all gilt plate; and the cupboard standing under a window was garnished wholly with plate of clean gold, whereof some was set with pearl and rich stones. And in the council chamber was set all white plate and parcel gilt. And under the tables, in both the chambers, were set baskets with old plate, which was not esteemed but for broken plate and old, not worthy to be used. And books containing the value and weight of every parcel were laid by them ready to be seen. And books were also set by all manner of stuff, containing the contents of everything.[81]

Figure 8.6 The setting out of Wolsey's plate, from a copy of George Cavendish's *Life of Wolsey*. Bodleian Library (MS Douce 363, fol. 71).

It was as if the plate had been set out as Wolsey's abject surrender to the king. Sadly, these books have not survived.

Meanwhile, the ripples were widening out and a diplomatic spat took place at Dover when the locks on Campeggio's coffers were broken open on suspicion that he was smuggling some of Wolsey's valuables out of the country. Nothing was found.[82]

The ground was fast crumbling under Wolsey's feet. Cavendish wrote that 'my lord was of necessity compelled to borrow from the bishop of Carlisle and from Sir Thomas Arundell, both dishes to eat his meat in, and plate to drink in, and also linen cloths to make use of'.[83] Robert Amadas lost no time in positioning himself among the creditors and on 20 October, two days after Wolsey resigned the seal, he submitted an account showing that his patron had an outstanding balance of £275 19s 1d owing. Rumours were rife and the Italian merchant Pierfrancesco di' Bardi wrote four days later that 'of everything, he has been despoiled; the value of his silver vases and furniture amounting to £40,000, his ready money to £30,000, besides other jewels and household goods'.[84] But this was pure speculation and there was plenty of that during the days immediately following Wolsey's dismissal: the French ambassador, Jean du Bellay, quoted quite different figures, writing that Wolsey's goods were valued at 500,000 crowns, or around £125,000.[85]

It was not only Wolsey's personal possessions that were in jeopardy; his grandiose colleges in Oxford and Ipswich, too, looked likely to be smothered at birth. As early as December 1529 Chapuys heard that 'the vestments and other church ornaments which he once presented to his college at Oxford have been brought [to London], and I hear from an embroiderer, who lives opposite my house, that some [of them have had] the Cardinal's escutcheon removed therefrom'.[86] This was just the start. Ipswich was entirely disbanded and its assets seized by the Crown; Cardinal College in Oxford would have suffered the same fate had the king not been persuaded to re-found it himself, as King Henry's College, although with a much smaller endowment. (In 1546 it was reconstituted as Christ Church, combining the college with the cathedral for the new diocese of Oxford.)

Henry, however, was delighted by his windfall and Chapuys wrote that 'yesterday the king came by water from Greenwich to view the said effects, bringing with him only his lady friend [Anne Boleyn], her mother and one gentleman of his chamber; [...] the king was much gratified and found the present more valuable even than he had expected'.[87] Steps were immediately taken to consolidate his ownership and there are various records of transfers of plate, as required by the king. The Chamber accounts record a payment of 7s 2d in January 1530 to Robert Draper, yeoman of the jewel house, for taking plate from York Place to the Tower;[88] in the following December he and two colleagues were paid for 'giving attendance in the Tower of London to receive the cardinal's plate and for conveying it from the Tower to the Court'.[89]

But in parallel with this narrative there were signs of a thaw in Henry's attitude: in October 1529, shortly after the charge of *praemunire* was brought, the king dispatched Henry Norris, groom of the stool, to Wolsey with 'a ring of gold, with a rich stone'. Cavendish explains the significance of this gesture, which was not lost on Wolsey. 'This ring my lord knew very well, for it was always the private token between the king and him whensoever the king would have any special matter dispatched at his hands.' Wolsey was palpably moved and gave Norris a reward, saying

> 'I have nothing left me but the clothes on my back. Therefore I desire you to take this small reward of my hands'; the which was a little chain of gold, made like a bottle chain, with a cross of gold hanging thereat, wherein was a piece of the Holy Cross, which he wore continually about his neck next his skin.[90]

The ring was the prelude to much greater concessions and shortly before Christmas, while staying at Esher, 'the king caused to be sent him three or four cart loads of stuff, and the most part thereof was locked in great chests [...] wherein was both plate and rich hangings and chapel-stuff'.[91] A document dated 14 February itemises 'the money, goods and chattels given by the king's Grace to the Lord Cardinal [...] First, in ready money £3,000. Item, in plate, 9,565¾ oz at 3s 8d the oz, amounting to £1,753 3s 7½d.' This is followed by £800 worth of furniture and hangings, 'apparel for his body' at £300, and various other gifts amounting to a total of £6,374 3s 7½d.[92] But there were conditions attached and by a second indenture three days later Wolsey agreed, in exchange for the gifts, to cede to the king all his ecclesiastical revenues except York.[93] It restored a measure of his dignity as a great prelate, but at a high price.

And it was anyway only a measure. William Capon, master of the not-quite dissolved Ipswich college, wrote to Wolsey in April to say that he had managed to pay the wages, but only by borrowing against the plate. By now Wolsey's formerly reliable tradesmen closed ranks. His wine merchant declined to supply any more and Amadas said he would deliver no new plate 'unless Wolsey send him old'.[94] But at least he had the assets Henry had restored to him and, armed with these, he began a slow progress towards York, where he settled down at his archiepiscopal residence at Cawood to plan his enthronement as archbishop, postponed for nearly fifteen years. Once there he faced considerable calls on his cash reserves, with the costs of his coming enthronement and for repairing dilapidations at Cawood. His health was also in decline and it was perhaps as well, in a way, that this inexorable process was accelerated by his summons to London to answer charges of treason and by his death at Leicester before facing his judges. For there is no doubt that all the deference Wolsey had demanded of the nobility in former times would have come home to roost. They would surely have been out to get him.

The charge of treason was based on certain intercepted letters from Wolsey to Francis I and Charles V which suggested that he had been negotiating without the king's knowledge and perhaps not in his best interests. It was arguably far-fetched but it was enough for him to be deprived, once again, of his 'plate and stuff', and the following January jewel house staff were paid for 'weighing the plate that came from Cawood, late the Cardinal's'.[95] But by this time Wolsey was dead.

The plate inventory taken at Cawood after Wolsey's departure lists a total of 8,424 oz and gives a clear picture of what Wolsey had to support his reduced circumstances at the end (he doubtless took some with him for the journey to London, which might account for the 1,141 oz shortfall).[96] Altogether, it is not unimpressive. The majority was silver-gilt and only about a quarter was white (mostly 'vessel'). The gilt wares included eight pots, two flagons, three basins, six sets of bowls and eight covered cups, enough for a respectable buffet display, and the dining plate had clearly been selected with due attention to his rank: one of the covered standing cups weighed twice as much as any of the others and must have been for Wolsey's own use; there were two cups of assay and two covered salts; the ten trenchers and five spice plates ('chased about with antiques and wild beasts') ensured appropriate standards of service at the cardinal's board. The list also included a large number of spoons, fifty-seven in all, including three sets of apostle spoons.[97] Not surprisingly, a substantial part of the collection was altar plate, including the usual 'massing plate' and four images. The latter were much smaller (or lighter) than those he had given to the college in Ipswich and were another subtle reminder of his changed circumstances. But these were also signalled by what was *not* included, for there was no gold. Wolsey was a mere archbishop now,[98] no longer the king's chief minister, and – in the king's eyes – had no need of such princely trappings.

If the Cawood inventory gives a view of at least part of Wolsey's plate, other glimpses can be seen elsewhere, principally in a list of plate transferred from the Tower to the court, and in the jewel house inventory of 1532.[99] The list of transferred plate probably dates from December 1530. It is quite badly damaged and parts of it are illegible; in particular, about a third of the weights can no longer be read. The list is written on five folios and comprises nearly 240 items or sets, with the legible weights amounting to nearly 12,500 oz. The total, therefore, would have been considerably more. From the references to their ornament, much of this was clearly Wolsey's and most likely it had all been his. The list divides the plate between the king's standing houses, with a little over half being delivered to York Place and the rest split between Hampton Court, Greenwich, The More and Windsor. Drilling down into the detail, the majority of the gold wares – sixteen pieces in all – went to York Place (soon to be renamed Whitehall), with just four small salts and four spoons going to Greenwich and The More. Other than church plate, of which there was a good deal, nearly everything related to dining. Some pieces were obviously spectacular, such as the very first item, whose only partly legible description reads 'a cup [?] of gold with a cover, the bowl of … the cover garnished with rubies … and great pearls and on the knop [?] … sapphire set in a collet'. As usual, the list gives very little away in terms of appearance, though a number of pieces, significantly, are described as being chased with 'antiques'.

Turning to the 1532 jewel house inventory, very little of which seems to overlap with the other two lists, we find another large body of ex-Wolsey plate. We can be sure (in round numbers) of some 1,900 oz of gold and 4,000 oz of silver and silver-gilt, because the descriptions mention his arms or a cardinal's hat, but there were other items that must have been his too, such as 'two maces or pillars weighing with the timber in them 185 oz' and, perhaps, the ecclesiastical regalia at the end of the list.[100] The church plate new to the jewel house since 1521 is also difficult to account for unless we assume that much of it was Wolsey's. This includes two heavy gold chalices (one with Wolsey's arms and both of which were melted shortly after the inventory was compiled) and an impressive silver-gilt crucifix. The latter weighed 1,020 oz and was described as 'goodly' (a rare term of praise). It featured 'images of Mary and John standing on a gilt mountain' and flying angels catching the blood from Christ's wounds in chalices. Taken together, therefore, these lists suggest some quite dizzying arithmetic: adding together the 9,500 oz sent to Cawood, the 18,000 oz to Whitehall and elsewhere, and the identifiable items in the jewel house produces a speculative total of around 34,000 oz of silver and 2,000 oz of gold. A huge sum although still a long way short of Francesco de' Bardi's reported figure of £40,000 or Ambassador Venier's 300,000 golden ducats.

What light does his plate and other possessions shed on Wolsey? He was undoubtedly acquisitive to an extraordinary degree and he was driven by an overweening ambition that contributed significantly to his downfall. But in terms of his power and his addiction to its trappings he was not unique. His older French contemporary, Cardinal Georges d'Amboise

(d. 1510), straddled Church and state in a similarly grandiose way, as did Cardinal Albrecht of Brandenburg, who was elector and archbishop of Mainz and also archbishop of Magdeburg from 1514 to 1545. Both seem to have used magnificence to support their status.

To a large extent Wolsey's magnificence 'went with the territory'. As the king's chief minister, who 'might be styled the king of England', as the most powerful prelate in the land and the pope's lieutenant, such displays, emblematic of power as they were, were expected and were necessary. Anyway, Wolsey had stated on more than one occasion that he was not accumulating all these possessions for himself but for the king. In 1521, the bishop of Badajoz wrote to Charles V that Wolsey 'had already given [Hampton Court] to the king and his successors' and four years later, in 1525, the imperial ambassador repeated the story.[101] 'Given' surely meant pledged, but it was a resilient story and in February 1530, after his partial return to the king's favour, Chapuys reported to Charles V that 'the cardinal has spent very large sums of money, and said all he accumulated was for the king and [for him] to take administration of it now was not much offence'.[102]

The danger was that such conspicuous displays of wealth and power, whether ultimately for the king or not and whether to reflect on the majesty of the king or himself, could become a focus of resentment. Polydore Vergil addressed the problem directly when he wrote,

> almost at the very moment he gained this dignity [of becoming lord chancellor] he became so arrogant that, imagining himself the equal of sovereigns, quickly started using a gold throne and cushion, to use a cloth-of-gold tablecloth, and to have his cardinal's hat, the badge of his rank, held up aloft by a servant who walked before him, as if it were some kind of idol. And this same hat was placed on the altar of the Chapel Royal during divine services.[103]

The great nobility, such as the dukes of Norfolk and Buckingham, found much to resent in such an 'upstart', but even those not sufficiently elevated to be personally affected by his grandeur found it easy to mock and it was widely accepted at the time that Wolsey was the butt of Skelton's satirical play *Magnificence*, probably written around 1520. But there is no doubt that despite the self-aggrandisement that went with it, Wolsey's greatest achievement was the raising of his king's own magnificence and profile on the international stage. And the apex of that international profile was the Field of Cloth of Gold, the unprecedentedly extravagant meeting of Henry VIII and Francis I in France in 1521.

Nine

The Field of Cloth of Gold

'The Field of Cloth of Gold' is the name given by history to the spectacular meeting between Henry VIII and Francis I near Calais in the summer of 1520. Named for its conspicuous use of this most costly of fabrics, the event was essentially a tournament, but it was a by-word for extravagance in every sense: its sumptuous display, its lavish entertainments, the huge cast of courtiers and attendants who accompanied the two monarchs, and the spectacular encampment erected to stage it. Its huge costs and the poverty of its legacy in terms of long-term political outcomes have led many to dismiss it as the epitome of self-indulgent wastefulness. Yet to do so is to miss an important point: that its *intention* was to seal a lasting peace between traditional adversaries, that preserved honour and equality on both sides. This was only possible within the context of the doctrine of magnificence, which required conspicuous expenditure on a massive scale. But compared with the cost of war, in both human and financial terms, this was modest.

Long-lasting peace was a worthy and Christian aspiration. But it was undermined by the facts that Henry and Francis had never met before and did not entirely trust one another; add to that the facts that they were both relatively young, ambitious and 'greedy for glory' and it became inevitable that they should be rivals. One of Francis's first acts as king in 1515 was to propose a meeting. But there were impediments, not least the unresolved dispute over Mary's dowry after Louis XII's death. Relations warmed following the Treaty of London in 1518 and in the following April Henry became godfather to the duc d'Orleans. Sir Thomas Boleyn was dispatched to stand proxy at the christening, presenting the child with the traditional gifts of a gold salt, cup and layer.[1] But the death of the emperor early in 1519, and the ensuing election for his successor, in which Francis and Henry both had a keen interest, again put things on hold. The election's eventual resolution in favour of Charles Habsburg finally cleared the air and in early 1520 planning for the meeting began in earnest.

Precursors and preparations

The 'interview' between Henry and Francis was preceded by two other royal meetings, one with the Emperor Maximilian and the other with his successor, Charles V. The first, as we have seen, took place in 1513, near Thérouanne in northern France. But this was a brief and spontaneous encounter between campaigning allies and had none of the extravagant spectacle of a formal summit. The meeting with Charles V, held just weeks before the Field of Cloth of Gold, was also hastily arranged but was as magnificent as time allowed. Travelling from Spain to Flanders, the newly elected emperor proposed a meeting with Henry *en route*. It would have been his first with another monarch in his new role and was too important an opportunity for Henry to pass up. But time was short and Francis refused to postpone the date of his own meeting with Henry.

The imperial encounter took place at Canterbury and was effectively a staging post on the road to France. It was a huge undertaking that involved transporting much of the court and its paraphernalia from London to Canterbury, before moving on to Dover. The programme included three splendid services in the cathedral, interspersed with feasting (the account of the ceremonial ablutions at the start of the banquet is quoted on p. 92), a visit to the shrine of Thomas Becket and, most important for the queen, her first meeting with the emperor who was, of course, her nephew.

Meetings between the kings of England and France, traditional enemies trying their hand at friendship, had a special significance, even though they did not always come to pass. Shortly after Louis XII's marriage to Mary Tudor a royal meeting was proposed but was prevented by Louis' sudden death. According to Edward Hall,

> it was intended, that the king in person would pass the sea to Calais, and there on the marches of the same, the French king and queen to come and see the king their brother, and for the same journey many costly works were wrought, and much rich apparel provided for, and much preparation made against the next spring.[2]

The plan sounds almost identical to that which subsequently transpired at the Field of Cloth of Gold and it is likely that both drew on the precedent of a famous earlier meeting that had taken place in 1396. In that year Richard II and Charles VI of France met at Ardres, almost exactly where Henry and Francis were to meet 124 years later. This too had been an extravagant occasion. It inaugurated an extended period of peace with

France, sealed by the betrothal of Charles's daughter, Isabella, to Richard, and was marked by the exchange of lavish gifts of gold plate.[3]

In order to send a message about the importance of his meeting with Francis, Henry elevated the level of his diplomatic delegation by recalling Boleyn and replacing him with Sir Richard Wingfield, a knight of the body in the privy chamber and one of his closest confidants. Initially Wingfield was instructed not to let the scale of the event get out of hand, lest 'excessive expenditure might discourage princes and subjects from meeting again'.[4] But inevitably, as the meeting came to be invested with ever increasing significance, the size of the royal entourages grew larger and larger and, in the end, the English contingent totalled 5,832 people and 3,217 horses; Wolsey alone had 350 attendants and 150 horses.[5] The French party was to be equivalent in every respect.

The challenges of transporting, housing and feeding such a transplanted population were huge. They required an enormous workforce (Hall tells us that as many as 3,000 workers were sent from England to work on the project)[6] and meticulously planned supply lines. They also required an expert administrative team and extraordinary attention to detail. Wolsey was in overall charge, while Wingfield liaised with Francis and his officials to ensure reciprocity and equality across the board. Meanwhile, the work on the ground was supervised by a group of 'commissioners'.

Other than emergency repairs to Guînes Castle, which was in a dilapidated state, the main construction work centred on the tilt-yard, the many tents (some of which were very large) and Henry's extraordinary temporary palace. By April instructions were crossing the Channel on a daily basis as planning became increasingly detailed. As the deadline approached, a note of anxiety started to creep into the correspondence. On 18 April Sir Nicholas Vaux advised Wolsey that Richard Gibson, one of the painters, 'is not yet come, and it is high time his works were in hand, for [the canvas] must be painted on the outside, and after[wards] curiously garnished under with knots and batons gilt and other devices'.[7] A week later they were running into more difficulties: they needed money but had problems agreeing the exchange rate for their English coinage.[8] But it was 'all right on the night' and days before the meeting of the kings things began to relax. Gian Joachino, secretary to the Governor of Genoa, wrote, 'it is said that this palace will be completed on Thursday, or thereabouts, but the English gentlemen charged with its construction and custody receive these French gentlemen with utmost civility, and to all they give drink in large gilt cups'.[9]

Construction was only part of the administrative burden of the event. A major component was the procurement and transport of the vast range of equipment needed to project the maximum degree of magnificence. In part this dovetailed with the meeting at Canterbury and fell to the same teams to organise. The practical arrangements were divided among the household departments, with 'the garnishing of the cupboards with plate' falling to Sir Henry Wyatt, master of the jewel house, 'the garnishing of the chapel' to the dean of the Chapel, and cloth of gold and tapestries to the Wardrobe. At Canterbury the scale of the imperial retinue called for highly detailed planning, with many things to be decided such as whether the imperial party was 'to be provided with house apparel, wine, plate, cooks etc or whether they must bring such with them'.[10]

The issues facing the meeting in France were different, since both sides were accommodated in their own territory, but everything was on a larger scale and, for the English, made more complicated by their supply lines. In terms of plate and 'ornaments', most came from the existing holdings of the jewel house and household, although some new wares were specially commissioned in the months leading up to the event. The most conspicuous category of luxury textiles, of course, was cloth of gold, and this had been stockpiled for some time at enormous expense. Just two purchases, in April, from Giovanni Cavalcanti and Pierfrancesco di Bardi, totalled £3,853.[11] But the unprecedented levels of display required for the Field were such that even the jewel house resources may have been insufficient to the task. While much of the chapel plate at Guînes can be tentatively identified on the 1521 inventory, not all of it corresponds and some may have been borrowed from Westminster Abbey or St George's Chapel. We know, for example, that the resources of the Chapel Royal had to be supplemented by 'the rich copes with the vestments given to the monastery of Westminster by the late king (fig. 5.2) [which] are to be borrowed for this voyage, and afterwards returned'.[12]

Careful provision, shown in various entries in the Chamber accounts, also had to be made for the packing and transport of plate: in April a payment of £20 was made 'for coffers and canvas for trussing jewels and plate to be sent to Calais'.[13] More boxes turned out to be needed and a warrant appears after the event to pay William Rothwell, Sergeant of the Vestry, 16s 4d for 'cases of leather for images' bought at Calais. These cost 2s 8d each, except for the one made for the image of Our Lady, which cost 3s 4d.[14] Transport itself was a significant cost and in June the master of the *Christopher of Hyde* was paid 20s 'for carrying the king's jewels from Dover to Calais'.[15] This was just part of the consignment and the following month a much higher figure of £9 was paid for 'freight of the king's ship with the jewels from Calais to London'. There was also a bill for the carriage of 'eight loads of jewel house stuff from the chapel'.[16]

The Field

All these costly preparations were for a programme of events that lasted just over two weeks, from 7 to 24 June. The events themselves, and the elaborate structures erected for them, are exceptionally well documented. We are also fortunate in the survival of a detailed painting of the Field in the Royal Collection (fig. 9.1), and the remarkably close correspondence between it and the eye-witness accounts means that together they combine to give a fuller picture of what transpired than for virtually any other single event in Tudor history.

The painting is not a contemporary record and dates from perhaps twenty or thirty years later. Like many images of historic events, it compresses both time and space. It shows Henry's arrival at Guînes, as well as his famous wrestling match with Francis which took place several days later. It places Guînes much closer to Calais than it really is and it shows only a few of the many tents that were put up. It also shows the event from an English rather than a French perspective. But it captures its essence: Henry's vast entourage, his extraordinary temporary palace, the tilt-yard with its spectators' gallery, the crowds of people and the extravagance of the tents.

The tents on both sides were made of canvas stretched over wooden

Figure 9.1 *The Field of Cloth of Gold*, British school, c. 1545. Hampton Court Palace. Royal Collection.

Figure 9.2 Designs for royal tents, possibly for the Field of Cloth of Gold, early sixteenth century. British Library (MS Cotton Augustus III, f. 18).

supports; the name Cloth of Gold arose, principally, from the sumptuous fabric that was laid over some of the exteriors. The large English tent in the middle ground of the painting gives a good idea of its richness but very little sense of the quantities that were used: the records show that the most important French tents were covered in some 1,055 *aunes* (nearly 2,000 metres) of cloth of gold.[17] A more detailed idea of the richness and complexity of the English tents comes from a remarkable group of designs in the British Library (fig. 9.2). These show a series of oblong spaces with connecting corridors and round pavilions. They are covered in rich red or blue textile decorated with gold ornament and repeated Garter mottos. Along the carved and gilded ridgeboards are Tudor roses alternating with fleurs de lis and surmounted at intervals with carved and painted royal beasts – dragons, greyhounds, lions, harts and antelopes – each supporting a flag with the royal arms. Other slightly less extravagant tents were covered in the green and white Tudor livery colours. The designs, especially for the red tent, are extraordinarily up to date. The two-handled vase motif at the extreme left of the image is a surprisingly advanced form for 1520, as is the 'candelabrum' pattern on the fabric itself, until one recalls that the rich brocade covering of the tents would all have been imported directly from Italy.

The most prominent and clearly depicted feature of the painting is Henry's temporary palace, which had no French equivalent and which received more comment from those present than anything else. It was designed as a sort of triumphal arch. Built on stone foundations, the lower parts of the walls were of brick and the upper parts formed of a wooden frame covered with canvas and painted to resemble masonry. One of the clearest accounts of the palace is Gian Joachino's, who wrote:

> This palace has a round tower at each corner, and a lofty portal, wide and magnificent [...] placed in the centre of the façade between two handsome round towers, like a fortress, as high as the palace; they are built entirely of bricks and loopholes and battlements defended by statues of armed men, in the act of discharging stones from the 'scapetti' and iron balls from the cannons and culverins. At a distance of some twelve paces from these two towers are two beautiful painted fountains representing images of Bacchus, with very large and handsome basins, into which wine is to flow constantly, in abundance.[18]

What the painting fails to represent correctly is its size, which has also been compressed. According to the dimensions sent to Wolsey in late March it was to be on an enormous scale: the great chamber was to be bigger than that at Whitehall, the second chamber bigger than the largest at Bridewell, and Wolsey was to have three chambers next to the king's.[19] The painting also makes the building appear relatively shallow, whereas in reality it was square; according to Hall, each side was 328 feet long (about 100 metres) and the perimeter measured 1,312 feet.[20] What is most telling about the design of the palace is that it is entirely 'antique' in conception. The notion of a triumphal arch is itself a reference to ancient Rome, as is its decorative language – its strongly accentuated horizontals, its laurel swags above the arch and its scallop shell pediment.

If the palace was Henry's stage, its contents were the props and the accoutrements of magnificence. Unfortunately, we have no images of its interiors, but the written accounts are very rich, especially for the chapel and the great chamber. Edward Hall, who was certainly present,[21] was especially impressed by the chapel and its plate. Part of his description reads:

> Over the high altar was hanged a rich canopy of marvellous greatness, the altar was apparelled with five pair of candlesticks of gold, and on the altar an halpace [ledge or high step] and thereon stood a *corpus domini*, all fine gold, and on the same halpace stood twelve images of the bigness of a child of four years of age all gold [...] Three rich great crosses were there ready to be borne at festival times, and basins and censers, gospellers, paxes, cruets, holy water vessels, and other ornaments all of gold.[22]

He goes on to describe the ornaments of the closets. In the king's was a 'crucifix of fine gold, with an image of the Trinity, an image of Our Lady, and twelve other images all fine gold and precious stones, two pair of candlesticks of fine gold, with basins, cruets, paxes, and other ornaments'. Sanuto's diary, in the Venetian state papers, adds some details to Hall's account: the two gold basins were 'each worth 3,000 ducats' (and therefore must have weighed about 300 oz) and the images on the king's altar were 'more than one cubit [about 18 inches] high'. Sanuto is particularly interested in the images, identifying some of those on the king's altar as jewelled images of St George on horseback and Saints Christopher, Ursula, Katherine and Barbara, as well as a Nativity, and adding that they were all 'worth a world of gold'. He also tells us that the gold images on the high altar represented the apostles.[23] All the accounts mention the 'incredible quantity of jewels' on the altar frontals and one also mentions 'a superb and very beautiful silver organ, with gold ornaments'.[24] The latter is a mystery as it does not seem to be mentioned anywhere else in the records, unless it is to be identified with the 'most excellent instrument' that had been brought to England in 1516 by the organist of St Mark's in Venice and greatly admired by the king.[25]

The other space that received much comment was the banqueting hall. Sanuto described this as 'hung with most beautiful tapestry, such as had never been seen before, worth some 15,000 ducats, representing foliage',[26] while a letter addressed to Pietro Montemerlo, Royal Senator of Milan, focuses on the 'five or six cupboards' around the palace, 'all full of vases and flasks of gold, and sundry other golden vessels, forming the most stupendous sight in the world'.[27]

Setting the stage was important, but the Field was principally about performance and interaction. The minutely choreographed events of June 1520 began with a great procession and a contemporary French account described Wolsey's taste for splendour as he rode to meet Francis I:

> Before [Wolsey] went fifty gentlemen of his household [...] mounted on good horses and clothed in crimson velvet, each with a great gold chain worn scarfwise [...] then fifty gentlemen [...] bearing gold maces as large as a man's head at the one end. After them [...] the bearer of [the cardinal's] double cross of fine gold, with a beautiful crucifix of precious stones [...] then two 'staphiez' or guards of the legate [...] each with a long gold baton in his hand like a poleaxe. Then the legate [...] mounted on a barded mule with headstall, studs, buckles and stirrups of fine gold, and the trappings of crimson velvet.[28]

This was all preliminary to a moment of high drama when the time came for Henry and Francis to meet for the first time. The same account continues: 'the two kings stopped about two casts of a boulle from each other, where they could see each other, when silence was made on both sides. Suddenly the trumpets and other instruments sounded, so that never was heard such joy.' The kings then spurred their horses, galloped towards each other and embraced.

This electric moment inaugurated two weeks of jousts, banquets, religious observance and the exchange of gifts. The jousts were the chivalric heart of the event (although marred by appalling weather) and the focus of the tilt-yard was on the Tree of Honour, visible in the top right corner of the painting (fig. 9.1). The tree was formed of hawthorn and raspberry to signify Henry and Francis; it displayed the arms of the participants and its leaves were of green damask and cloth of gold. No less a focus was the knights themselves with their lavish costumes and their devices, many of which were made of pure gold. Golden ornaments featured in the masked dances too, such as when Henry and his party wore cloth of gold and face masks with beards fashioned out of pure gold wire.[29]

The events that attracted most attention of all, however, were the feasts. These largely followed the pattern already familiar from other royal banquets. But in addition to these large-scale entertainments two rather more intimate dinners took place when each of the queens invited the other king to dine. A delicate issue of protocol lay behind these events, which is explained by Glenn Richardson:

> Neither king could be allowed to offer, or receive, from the other greater or lesser hospitality than he himself provided. It also meant that one could not directly upstage the other by the standard of feasting he offered, nor was there any intimation that in accepting food from each other, either acknowledged the other's 'good lordship' over him. This was particularly important because Henry's formal title still made a claim for him as 'king of France'.[30]

These difficulties were adroitly side-stepped by the queens entertaining the kings. Richardson continues: 'Being received by each other's wife meant that each king was undeniably the highest-status person at the banquet and could accept food as a gift without danger to his reputation as at least equal to the other sovereign.' The two events were doubtless mirror images of each other. They were held simultaneously and the kings travelled by different routes in order to avoid encountering each other on the way.

Amongst the general magnificence of the event, the Mantuan ambassador, who seems to have been present at Katherine's dinner for Francis, was particularly struck by one aspect of the ceremonial:

> amongst other remarkable things [...] were two cupboards, on one of which were many vessels of massive gold, and set with beautiful jewels. From these vessels the king and queen were served. On the other cupboard were vessels, also of massive gold, but not set with jewels, and these were served for the other guests at the royal table. There was besides an infinite number of silver-gilt vessels.[31]

This is one of the most explicit statements we have of the hierarchical symbolism of plate: gold plate with jewels for the king and queen, gold plate without jewels for the others at the royal table and mere silver-gilt for the rest. Hall's account of the same event takes the hierarchy to its logical conclusion by adding that 'all noble men were served in gilt vessel, and all other in silver vessel'.[32]

The spectacular events of the Field concluded, as one would expect, with a great mass and the exchange of gifts. For reasons of strict equivalence, the mass could not be held in either monarch's chapel and had to take place on neutral ground. Equally, one imagines that the altar and processional plate for this great plenary service would have been supplied in similar measure by both sides, but there is no evidence either way. The story is again taken up by the Mantuan ambassador:

> A chapel had been prepared in the field, opposite the stage from which the jousts were viewed. It was very large, with a lofty tribune, on which was the altar, most sumptuously furnished with ten very large silver-gilt images of saints and two large golden candlesticks, all exquisitely wrought; also a large jewelled crucifix entirely of gold, and a large golden basin and two vases [cruets], one for the wine and the other for the water [...] Cardinal Wolsey gave both the Gospel and the Pax to be kissed, to the two kings and to the Cardinal de Vendôme.[33]

Other accounts of the same event focus on different details. For one commentator, the point to capture was the grandeur of the cardinals, especially Wolsey, whose 'apparelling [...] was performed by bishops, [and] who also placed on his feet a pair of very valuable jewelled sandals. The water for his hands was given him by some of the chief noblemen of England.'[34] For another it was the elaborately choreographed deference during the service:

> The Cardinal de Bourbon, who brought the gospel to the kings to be kissed, presented it first to Francis. [Francis] desired Henry to kiss it first, but he refused the honour [...] at the *agnus dei*, the pax was presented to Cardinal Bourbon to take to the kings, who observed the same ceremony as before; then to the two queens, who also declined to kiss it first, and, after many mutual respects, kissed each other instead.[35]

The final event of the Field was the formal exchange of gifts. Some of those exchanged between the two monarchs, such as fine horses, were conventional but others were more unusual. Perhaps the most remarkable was a gold-handled sword which Henry presented to Francis at some stage during the proceedings. This was described as 'of the Spanish fashion, the pommel, haft and chape of gold with a blue girdle well wrought upon with gold and the buckle pendant and other garnishing of gold and enamelled'.[36] We cannot prove it, but it is tempting to believe that this was none other than the magnificent sword given to Henry five years earlier by Ferdinand of Spain and which Wolsey had valued at a huge figure (see p. 120).

Both kings made extravagant gifts of plate and jewels to the principal courtiers of the other side. Henry gave Bonnivet, the French admiral and Wolsey's opposite number, a jewel and gold plate worth 14,000 crowns; to the duc de Bourbon, constable of France, a jewelled gold cup worth 6,000; and to the master of the horse, gold plate and a jewel worth 2,800. He also gave a present of 2,500 crowns to be distributed among the royal household.[37]

From the French side Wolsey, predictably, did better than anyone else. According to the Mantuan ambassador, Francis gave him gold 'vases' worth 20,000 crowns, while Francis's mother, Louise de Savoie, gave him a jewelled crucifix worth 6,000 and he would almost certainly have received substantial gifts of plate from the most senior French courtiers. Twenty thousand crowns, the equivalent of about £4,000, may sound exaggerated but is probably not. Many items formerly belonging to Wolsey appear in the 1532 jewel house inventory and scattered under their different categories is a gold service bearing friars' girdles (one of Francis's badges) and the arms of France. Comprising six bowls with two covers, two covered basins, two covered ewers with serpent spouts, and two flagons, these weighed a total of 1,583 oz which, with an allowance for fashion (see p. 142), would probably not have cost much less than 20,000 crowns.[38] The inventory descriptions make no mention of ornament, other than the arms and girdles, and the service may have been quite plain, perhaps not unlike a pair of silver-gilt bottles, or flagons, made in 1580 and preserved in the Louvre (fig. 6.8).

Another recipient of Francis's largesse was Henry's ambassador, Sir Richard Wingfield, who, according to Gasparo Contarini, received a 'very noble and costly service of silver plate'[39] in acknowledgement of his pivotal role in the planning, although it would not have been anything like as noble and costly as Wolsey's.

Wolsey was also munificent in the gifts he presented himself. To Louise de Savoie he gave – very reciprocally – a jewelled cross with a relic of the True Cross and to Bonnivet he gave 'a very large salt-cellar, all of gold, studded with a number of very beautiful jewels, and surmounted by a St George';[40] he would undoubtedly have given other presents too.

These gifts were all carefully planned, because only in that way could reciprocity and equality be ensured. Less controllable and diplomatically more risky, however, were spontaneous gifts. When Francis decided one morning to pay an unscheduled call on Henry at Guînes, the latter was unprepared – and indeed was not yet fully dressed – but felt obliged to mark the occasion appropriately. 'Having embraced each other the king of England gave [Francis] a collar of jewels and pearls of great value.' Now it was Francis's turn to be wrong-footed. Presumably having nothing else to hand, he 'gave in exchange to the king of England his gold bracelets studded with jewels of great value, [then,] doubting whether the gift was an equivalent for the present received, he sent in addition six coursers of great price'.[41]

The total cost of the Field was enormous, though impossible to calculate exactly. On the English side alone, Henry's palace probably cost around £10,000;[42] the tents and their cloth of gold cost thousands more; as would the many gifts of plate and jewels. Food and drink came to nearly £9,000;[43] transport of goods and people across the Channel would also have cost thousands, and so it went on. In total, Richardson suggests that the direct costs of the Field on the English side came to something of the order of £36,000, compared with basic annual royal household expenses at this time of around £22,000. The contrast is rendered all the more stark when we remind ourselves that the costs related to a period of just two weeks. But equally, the tables turn again when we recall that the Field was meant to be an alternative to war: Frederick Dietz estimated that between 1511 and 1514 the cost of equipping and carrying out Henry's French campaign came to nearly £900,000, while the annual cost of maintaining Tournai after capturing it in 1513 was around £40,000.[44] Compared with such eye-watering sums, long-lasting peace at £36,000 was a snip. Only that was not what happened, as we shall see.

Even in the immediate aftermath of the event commentators seemed to avoid speculation on its major political outcomes and focused instead on superficialities. Once again, Gian Joachino stands for many in his assessment that 'the magnificence of the two kings and their noblemen was great and incredible, but the French excelled the English, both in apparel and horses, although the English had many gold chains, which were not usual in France';[45] Hall made the point more forcefully, saying that

> the marvellous treasure of gold that was worn in chains and bauderickes, so great, so weighty, some so manifold [...] that the gold was too innumerable to my demynge [mind] to be summed, all noblemen, gentlemen, squires, knights, and every honest officer of the king was richly apparelled, and had chains of gold, great and marvellous weighty.[46]

The English obsession with gold chains comes across very clearly in a quite different context, namely Robert Amadas's account with Wolsey, discussed in Chapter 8. A series of entries in the account refer to a quantity of gold chains supplied 'when my lord's grace went to Guînes with the king'. It seems that these were hired specially for the occasion, with Amadas charging for making them but not for the gold itself. One of them, 'a great chain that Mr Page my lord's servant wore at my lord's commandment when my lord went to Calais', contained £200 worth 'of mine own gold which gold I received again'. But not all his servants seem to have been quite so careful and Amadas audited all the chains when they came back to him: four were said to be one link short and one – entrusted to 'Mr Deonyse'[47] – was missing four links. In all, about 10 oz of gold had gone astray.[48]

Other summit meetings

Immediately after concluding the Field, Henry set off to meet with Charles V at Gravelines. This was at the westernmost point of Charles's imperial territories and about twice as far from Calais as Guînes. The meeting was smaller and more business-like than the other; Henry's entourage was about one-quarter the size of that at Guînes and Wingfield wrote charmingly to Wolsey that he had heard that Henry's 'visage and countenance' appeared not 'to be so replenished with joy as they were at the meeting with Francis'.[49] The aim of this second meeting with the emperor, so soon after the first, was to reassure him that his interests had not been undermined by the Field; more significantly, it also laid the groundwork for a higher-profile imperial visit to England that took place two years later in 1522.

This was extremely lavish. Charles embarked for England from Calais with an entourage of 2,000 men and 1,000 horses.[50] Wolsey met him at Dover and Henry at Canterbury. They travelled in stages to London, where he was honoured by a spectacular pageant; jousts and revels were laid on during his visit. But although we know from Charles V's own letters that he was received 'in great triumph', we do not have the detailed anecdotal evidence of Henry's deployment of plate and jewels to impress his ally that we have for the Field.

The emperor's fears that the Field would lead to an anti-imperial pact proved groundless and, despite the weight of expectation laid upon it, little of long-term value emerged from it. The veneer of amity maintained at the meeting very soon wore off and by 1522, at the very time of Charles's visit to England, hostilities once again broke out between England and France and were not finally resolved until the great declarations of perpetual amity forged in 1527. This intermittent animosity was the main impediment to any second meeting between them. Such a meeting did not occur until

1532, twelve years after the first, when the two kings met again at Calais and Boulogne.

Much had happened in the meantime to change the dynamics of European alliances. Not least, the 'great matter' of Henry's divorce had dragged on, putting his relations with the pope and the emperor under strain. To avoid complete isolation Henry needed to rekindle his relationship with Francis and the meeting was a way of doing so. But it differed in several respects from the first. It was shorter, it was not a tournament and the entertainments were on a less lavish scale; it was also cheaper than the other, with many fewer attendants, and made less of an impact on observers. It differed from the other in another important respect too, namely that Henry was accompanied not by the queen but by his paramour, Anne Boleyn, who was created marquess of Pembroke in her own right for the occasion. Indeed, the meeting largely took place at Anne's behest, with the aim of currying Francis's support for the divorce. Much, therefore, hung by it and it required extensive preparations. In August 1532 Chapuys reported to Charles that 'all the lords and gentlemen are making purchases' and that 'yesterday a ship set sail for Calais with tapestries and other royal ornaments'.[51]

Henry was making detailed preparations too and a royal warrant of 20 August instructed Thomas Cromwell, now master of the jewels, to transfer a quantity of jewels and gold plate from the jewel house to the royal goldsmith, Cornelis Hayes, 'to be broken, transposed, changed, set and new made [for the meeting …] according to such devises as we have devised'.[52] The warrant is floridly worded and suggests a lively degree of anticipation, referring to Francis as 'our dearest brother, cousin, gossip and perpetual ally'. The list comprised some forty items weighing nearly 1,150 oz and including gold collars, spoons, chalices, and a 'great ewer'. Two of the most striking objects were 'a corporas case of gold' of 170 oz and a 270 oz 'great cup of gold with a cover', both of which were richly set with stones. In addition to these, Cromwell was instructed to deliver to Hayes various stones that were to be 'taken out' of certain specified pieces of gold plate.

What exactly lay behind these instructions is not certain, but we can guess. Fashion was probably a consideration and it was important that Henry's 'cupboard of gold' be seen to be in the latest styles and as richly set with stones as possible. But other clues emerge from comparing the list with the rather fuller descriptions given in the new jewel house inventory, prepared just a couple of months earlier: the 270 oz 'great cup of gold with a cover' was the largest of all the gold cups in the jewel house at the time and is described in the inventory as being 'set with six letters F', meaning that it was almost certainly an earlier gift from Francis himself. It and the 'great ewer', weighing 129 oz, were very possibly part of the 1,583 oz gold garniture given to Wolsey at the Field of Cloth of Gold. If so, then we can well imagine that Henry was also keen to avoid giving the impression that he could only put on a good show of gold plate by deploying pieces that he had received from Francis (or from Wolsey, for that matter).

Further sensitivities emerge from another inventory description: one of the heavy collars on the 1532 inventory, weighing 88 oz, is described on the warrant as 'our rich collar of gold wherein is set ballasses and great diamonds of sundry fashions'. But the inventory quantifies the stones and identifies one of the diamonds as 'the mirror'.[53] Was this the famous Mirror of Naples, the large stone given to Henry's sister Mary by Louis XII and that had been such a bone of contention after the accession of Francis I? If so, it is more than possible that Henry feared Francis would recognise it and be irritated.

The exact meaning of the 'devices as we have devised' is also unclear. It may simply mean the style of the jewels and plate, or it could refer to specific ornament, such as badges. If the latter, might this be a reference to Anne Boleyn's personal device of a falcon on a tree stump? This is conceivable but would have been indelicate, given that she and Henry were not yet married.

As to the various stones that were extracted from the recycled collars and plate, while some may well have been used to adorn Hayes's new plate, it seems that the best and biggest were probably fashioned into a single new collar, which evidently dazzled the anonymous French author of one account of the meeting. According to this, it had 'fourteen rubies, of which the least was as large as an egg, and fourteen diamonds not so big. Between these stones were two rows of great pearls, and hanging from them a carbuncle as big as a goose's egg.'[54] The author speculates that the collar was worth more than 400,000 crowns or about £90,000. Other stones would doubtless have been set into stunning new jewels to adorn Anne Boleyn and one great collar delivered to Henry on 4 October and modelled with 'friars' knots' was perhaps intended as a gift for Francis.[55]

As before, the meeting was split between French and English territory, with Francis entertaining the English at Boulogne and Henry reciprocating at Calais. The refectory of the abbey at Boulogne was transformed by carpets, canopies embroidered with gold thread, and tapestries depicting the victories of Scipio Africanus and Ovid's *Metamorphoses*. Naturally, the display focused on an impressive display of plate, but for Hall, who also described the event, its most remarkable feature was not so much its quantities as that it was all 'of the new fashion'.[56]

We have a direct insight into what Hall meant by this 'new fashion' through the survival of one major object that was specially made for

Figure 9.3
The St Michael cup, Josse Vezeler, Antwerp, 1532. Gold, enamel, pearls and precious stones. Kunsthistorisches Museum, Vienna.

the occasion, the 'St Michael' cup in the Kunsthistorisches Museum, Vienna (fig. 9.3). This magnificent gold cup was ordered from the Antwerp merchant and goldsmith, Josse Vezeler, and delivered direct to Boulogne, together with other newly made plate, just in time for the meeting.[57] It has a complex, attenuated profile and its strongest decorative feature is the repeated bands of 'antique' flutes and gadroons. Other classical details include pendant husk swags and rams' heads; the embossed frieze around the bowl, depicting scenes of viniculture, is largely composed of naked or classically attired male figures. The cup is further embellished with translucent enamel, pearls and gemstones and is surmounted by the jewelled figure of St Michael, patron of Francis's chivalric order and the French equivalent of Henry's order of St George. An important factor, distinguishing it from earlier works, is that dynastic badges play no part in its ornamental scheme.

Just how different this was from contemporary Italian taste is clear by comparison with an exactly contemporary design for a ewer by the Roman artist Enea Vico (fig. 9.4). The latter is equally full of classical details – acanthus foliage, laurel wreaths, terms and flutes – but it is conceived quite differently. The Vezeler cup is a jewel writ large, its effect depending on intricate surface decoration and a wide variety of techniques and textures, whereas the Vico ewer is conceived architecturally and sculpturally. It has a simpler vase-shaped profile and a smaller foot, introducing a greater sense of tension to the piece; its applied ornament is in higher relief and the upper part of the design is entirely sculptural.

The Vezeler cup weighs just over 80 oz, so would probably have cost (in English money) rather more than £200, plus the value of the stones.[58] But this was just part of the 15,313 livres (£1,530) payment made to Vezeler for 'vaisselle ciselée à l'antique façon de Flandre' (chased vessels in the Flemish antique manner) in December of that year.[59] And this transaction was itself just a small part of a huge number of luxury goods – tapestries as well as goldsmiths' work – that Vezeler supplied to the French court over a decade or more from about 1528. Michèle Bimbenet-Privat has attributed Vezeler's success, in the face of competition from skilled Parisian goldsmiths, to his mobility and the 'commercial organisation' of his business: whenever and wherever the king desired to confer with his Flemish goldsmith, there he

Figure 9.4
Design for a silver ewer, Enea Vico, 1533. Engraving. Private collection.

went and his immediate responsiveness to the king's wishes allowed him to develop a personal relationship with the monarch.[60]

Francis must have been well-pleased with the cup and made a point of exhibiting it at another high-profile summit, his meeting with Pope Clement VII at Marseilles in the following year. Had it remained in France it would eventually have been lost to the melting pot and it owes its survival to the fact that it was given by Charles IX to Archduke Ferdinand of Austria in 1570, when Ferdinand stood proxy for Charles at the time of his marriage to Elizabeth of Austria. From him it descended as part of the Habsburg imperial heirlooms.

On the English side of the meeting, the decoration of Henry's lodgings in the Staple Inn at Calais and of St Mary's church is described at great length by Hall. His chamber, we read, was hanged with cloth of silver, 'raised with gold, and the seams of the same were covered with broad wreathes of goldsmiths' work, full of stone and pearl'. The buffet was much as others, 'seven stages high, all of plate of gold', and the chamber was illuminated with 'ten branches of silver and gilt, and ten branches all white silver, every branch [...] bearing five lights of wax'. Not for the first time, however, Hall's descriptive powers fail to do justice to the richness of the display and he writes that 'to tell the riches of the cloths of estate, the basins and other vessels which was there occupied [...] my wit is insufficient'.[61]

At the end of the meeting, the kings exchanged gifts of 'diverse precious jewels and great horses and to [their] nobles great plenty of plate'.[62] One of the most flamboyant of Francis's gifts to Henry was 'a suit of bed furniture, wrought throughout with pearls on crimson velvet which he purchased lately in Paris of an Italian merchant for 10,000 golden crowns'.[63] In addition, he gave Anne Boleyn a splendid diamond worth 15,000 or 16,000 crowns.[64] The principal courtiers did well too. The dukes of Suffolk and Norfolk were given silver-gilt services and gold cups, as well as being honoured with membership of the order of St Michael; other courtiers received gold chains.[65] Altogether, the nineteenth-century historian, P. A. Hamy, claims that the French gifts cost no less than 100,000 livres, or about £10,000.[66] In return the English gave large sums of money to the French and elaborate horse harnesses.

It is possible that one of the most remarkable pieces of surviving French goldsmiths' work of the period was among the presents given to Henry or to one of his courtiers at that time. Traditionally known as the Royal Clock Salt, this is now in the collection of the Goldsmiths' Company in London (fig. 9.5). It appears to represent a type of sixteenth-century portmanteau object that combined the functions of a salt and a clock, although its subsequent alterations make it difficult to be certain about this. The 'salt' is of silver-gilt and incorporates decorative elements of enamel, shell, agate,

Figure 9.5 The Royal Clock Salt, attributed to Pierre Mangot, Paris or Blois, c. 1530. Silver gilt, glass clockwork, shell, enamel, agate, pearls and precious stones. Collection of the Goldsmiths' Company, London.

pearls and garnets, in addition to the clock mechanism contained within a glass cylinder. Standing on six agate claw and ball feet, the lower part of the object is hexagonal and is set with shell cameo busts carved in high relief. The busts are set on blue enamel plaques embellished with gilding and each side is separated by an architectural pilaster. The next section is the glass cylinder containing the clock and surrounded by free-standing double scroll brackets connecting the upper and lower sections. Above this is an openwork dome incorporating gable-like pediments, standing male nude figures and vase motifs. The top-most surviving elements are a hexagonal knop echoing the form of the base and an open calyx of leaves that formerly supported a now-lost crowning element.

The salt is not marked but it is precisely in the style of a number of surviving pieces by the French royal goldsmith, Pierre Mangot, and can safely be attributed to him. It is exactly the sort of object that would have been described in the sixteenth century as a jewel and is a work of art whose aesthetic impact is multi-layered, contributed to by its gemstones, its virtuosity and its visual complexity. The ornament is largely classically inspired and the carved shell cameos allude to ancient Roman busts, much as the terracotta roundels commissioned by Wolsey for Hampton Court, although in this case with a distinctly Mannerist *contraposto* attitude. But it is not wholly 'antique' and certain distinctly gothic elements, such as the sharply angular gables above the clock mechanism, help give it a somewhat transitional quality.

Jewel-like though it is, however, the clock salt would have appeared even more so at the time. The enamels have mostly deteriorated and their refined gilded surface enrichment is much faded. The whole of the crowning element, which, as we will see, was probably modelled as Jupiter and Ganymede, was replaced in or around the early nineteenth century with a secondary timepiece that has since been removed; the clock mechanism itself has been replaced and the salt dish – if indeed it ever existed – has been lost. Despite its alterations, however, it is very likely that the 'salt' is the same as one described in the 1547 royal inventory. This is described as 'one salt of silver and gilt with a cover standing upon six round balls of jasper with six white agate heads standing in collets of silver[;] within the same a round crystal and therein a clock …'. Moving from bottom to top, the description continues: 'the salt [is] garnished with course stones and certain hanging pearls[,] the cover garnished with small white heads of agate and small counterfeit emeralds[,] having a man sitting upon an eagle upon the top of the cover'.[67] A century later, following the execution of Charles I in 1649, the 'true and perfect inventory of all the Plate and Jewells now being in the Upper Jewel House of the Tower in the charge of Sir Henry Mildmay', includes what appears to be the same piece, now described as 'two [sic] faire large saltes of silver gilt with a clock in it, garnished with six ivory heads about the bottom and enriched with stones in it and little gold heads enamelled[,] with a man upon a Faulcon on the top of it[,] valued at £40'.[68]

Can we be sure that the Goldsmiths' 'salt' is one and the same as that described in 1547 and 1649? And can we be sure that it was a gift in 1532? The answer to the first of these questions is probably, and to the second, not at all.

It is true that there are discrepancies between the object and the earlier descriptions: what was described as a crystal is now glass and there is no receptacle for the salt, despite being called such, but the description of the lower part tallies closely with the piece and its weight in 1547 was given as 108 oz, just eight ounces more than the current weight, again, quite close in view of the alterations.[69] As to whether it was a gift from Francis or a member of his court, this is pure supposition. Given Hamy's detailed account of the French gifts, it is curious that such a significant work of art should not have been mentioned. One thing that is clear, however, is that Henry's coffers returned from France filled with many new acquisitions that were not gifts at all and the privy purse expenses for that year include huge sums spent in Calais on 'jewels'. On 4 November the king authorised payments of about £740 to four French jewellers, and on the following day £1,749 4s 8d to 'Allard Plymmer [Plommier] the jeweller for such jewels as the king's grace bought of him at Calais'.[70]

Allard Plommier was one of Francis I's chief suppliers of luxury goldsmiths' work during the 1530s and purchases between 1534 and 1538

Figure 9.6
Francis I's book of hours, the cover of gold, enamel and precious stones, with a cornelian intaglio, Paris, 1532. Musée du Louvre, Paris.

ranged from gold and jewelled book bindings, to a jewelled cross and a great gold-mounted agate cup set with jewels.[71] One of these, a sumptuously illuminated prayer book with a gold and jewelled cover, dates from 1538 and is now in the Louvre (fig. 9.6). The book is very small and measures just 8.5 cm by 8 cm. It is set on front and back and on the spine with rubies and turquoises and with panels of Latin prayers and antique ornament in black and white enamel. At the centre of each cover is a large oval cornelian panel carved in intaglio, on the front with the crucified Christ with Saints Francis and Jerome, and on the back with the Virgin and child enthroned. It is an astonishingly concentrated work of art.

The year 1532 was not Plommier's first transaction with Henry VIII. In 1529 he had sold him jewels for £569 and in December of the following year a further 7,437 crowns' worth.[72] Between 1529 and 1532 he was much the biggest foreign supplier of jewels and received around £5,400. What exactly he sold him in Calais we do not know; doubtless jewels for the marquess, but the purchases could well have included things like the clock salt too. Indeed, it is more than probable that they did, since Henry owned a number of books with jewelled gold covers, some of whose descriptions in the 1547 inventory sound very similar to Francis's book of hours.[73]

The political outcomes of these costly summit meetings almost always failed to live up to their expectations, for the reasons we have discussed. But their cultural and artistic legacy, although less talked about at the time, was significant. An important concern was that as far as possible everything should be seen to be in the latest fashions. Henry's palace at Guînes in 1520 – unless the painting is seriously misleading – was a bold statement of the 'antique'; some of his goldsmiths' work was in similar vein too. The trappings of Henry's horse, for example, were 'of newly devised fashion [...] of fine gold in bullion, curiously wrought, pounced and set with antique work of Roman figures'.[74]

But there is little doubt, when it came to the antique, that France was ahead of the game. Francis, through his invasion of northern Italy, and from his success in luring Leonardo da Vinci to France, had had direct contact with Italian art in its native habitat, whereas Henry had not. As Richardson explains, the direct contact that Henry and his court had with new French art and design at the Field 'stimulated intellectual and artistic patronage [...] and later helped to keep Henry's court in touch with continental developments in the fine arts, decorative design, military technology and architecture'.[75] Whatever shifts towards Renaissance style were already taking place in England were undoubtedly accelerated thereafter.

Ten

Holbein and the 'Antique'

The main focus of this chapter is on Hans Holbein the younger and his seminal influence on style at Henry's court. But it also considers wider foreign influences on English plate. This was felt partly through foreign plate arriving as diplomatic gifts or purchases, partly through plate being made in London by 'stranger' goldsmiths, and partly through engraved ornament prints, known as pattern books.

Our knowledge of the style of court goldsmiths' work during the first two decades of the reign is limited to the very few surviving royal objects, together with analogous pieces made for other patrons. As a result, these few things have to work very hard; arguably too hard, for it is difficult to know, given the brevity of inventory descriptions, how truly representative the latter are of the things that graced the king's chambers. In this respect the first quarter of the century could hardly stand in greater contrast to the second, for which the equally few real objects are supplemented by a wealth of designs, both in the form of pattern books, informing us of general stylistic trends, and through a remarkable cache of Holbein's designs for actual commissions.

Two objects in particular give us an insight into court style around the beginning of the second quarter of the century, immediately before Holbein's arrival: the so-called Howard Grace Cup in the Victoria and Albert Museum (fig. 10.1), and an instrument case in the collection of the Barbers' Company (fig. 10.2).

The cup's silver-gilt mounts bear London hallmarks for 1525–26 and, despite incorporating an older ivory cup (by tradition associated with Thomas Becket), could have sat well with the presents and display plate seen at the Field of Cloth of Gold. The overall form and decoration of the mounts are entirely contemporary. They are divided into horizontal zones with pierced friezes of masks and foliage around the base and cover, while the finial is formed as a gadrooned vase, itself a distinctly 'antique' motif. Its numerous applied pearls and stones and its finial formed as St George

Figure 10.1
The Howard Grace Cup, London, 1525–26. Ivory, silver gilt, pearls and precious stones. Victoria and Albert Museum, London.

and the dragon mark it out as a courtly object. The original owner of the cup or the circumstances of its commission are not known but it descended through the Howard family from 1614.

At just 18 cm long, the Barbers' Company's parcel-gilt instrument case is quite small, but as a piece of virtuoso goldsmith's work it is extremely impressive. Its origins are not known and the company only acquired it (or reacquired it) in the mid-twentieth century.[1] The instruments it originally contained are lost but were probably surgical, since the ornament of the case incorporates the arms of the Barbers' Company and the cognisance of the Fellowship of Surgeons.[2] It also features the royal arms and a crowned Tudor rose, leading to the conjecture that it was a gift from the king to his surgeon, Thomas Vicary (c. 1490–1561), who was appointed to that role in 1527 and became master of the Barbers' three years later.[3]

Figure 10.2a Reverse of the Barbers' instrument case showing engraving of the murder of Thomas Becket. Collection of the Barbers' Company, London.

Figure 10.2 Instrument case, perhaps given by Henry VIII to Thomas Vicary, serjeant-surgeon to the royal household and master of the Barbers' Company. England, c. 1530. Silver, parcel gilt and enamel. Collection of the Barbers' Company, London.

The iconography of the case is very complex. On the body the Barbers' arms and Surgeons' cognisance are flanked by two saints, identified by their attributes of a urine flask and an albarello as Cosmas and Damian, patron saints of the fellowship. Further down, on the sides, are two further saints, John and Catherine. The four figures are like those found on apostle spoons but are much better modelled. The back of the case is quite flat but is finely engraved with two scenes, St George killing the dragon and the murder of Thomas Becket. No part of the case is left undecorated. In addition to the royal arms, the top of the cover features a cast and enamelled Tudor rose, with supporters and crown imperial, the sides are engraved with panels of Renaissance ornament after or closely related to prints by Heinrich Aldegrever, and at five points the case has applied lions' masks with attached rings for the suspension chain. All the evidence points to the box dating from around 1530. The Aldegrever prints first appeared around 1527 and the royal supporters, the dragon and greyhound, continued to be used in royal heraldry for some years after the adoption of the lion as an alternative to the greyhound around 1525.[4] The most striking features of the engraved decoration are the depictions of St George and the murder of Becket. St George was, of course, the patron saint of England and of the chivalric Order of the Garter, while Becket continued to be one of the most revered saints in England until the king repudiated the cult in 1535. Thereafter any such image on an object with royal associations would have been unthinkable.

Foreign artists and goldsmiths at court

The instrument case is unmarked and we have no idea who made it. But its range of techniques suggest it was a collaborative work involving not only plate workers but also an enameller and a highly skilled engraver. Its exceptionally high standard of workmanship implies that it was made under the supervision, or with the collaboration, of 'stranger' craftsmen. London was full of 'strangers' from 'across the narrow sea' (the term 'foreigners' also referred to Englishmen from other parts of the country). The most prominent of these were the merchants, such as the Italians whom we discussed in Chapter 4 and Hanseatic merchants from north Germany and the Baltic region. The latter mostly occupied the Steelyard, an enclave on the site of Blackfriars Station, but there were also many Flemish and French merchants in and around the City.

Much more numerous than the merchants, however, were the stranger 'artificers'. Some of these were men of repute who enjoyed the protection of patrons like Sir Thomas More or Cardinal Wolsey. But their numbers were swollen by their dependants and servants and a stranger's permission to reside often extended to his workers as well. In 1534 Lucas Horenbout, the king's painter and a native of Flanders, received denization, 'with licence to keep in his service four journeymen, or covenant servants born out of the king's dominions',[5] while in 1528 a goldsmith, John de Colyn [of Cologne], was granted a licence to retain two apprentices and four journeymen 'of foreign birth'.[6]

Alien goldsmiths had much to offer. The training they received in centres like Antwerp, Paris, Augsburg or Nuremberg was more rigorous than in England and the *Wanderjahre* system, whereby an aspirant master was required to spend the final years of his training abroad, encouraged the development of networks and the acquisition of a wide range of skills. In London there was a ready market for such skills and in the early years of the sixteenth century there was a relatively benevolent climate for well-trained immigrant artificers.[7] As a result, the population of settled strangers burgeoned and around the end of the fifteenth century it has been put at about 3,400 people, around six per cent of the total population.[8] Within the crafts this concentration was much higher and in 1529 the wardens of the Goldsmiths' Company claimed that as many as twenty per cent of the householders working in the silver and jewellery trades were strangers.[9] Such numbers inevitably led to tensions, however, most notoriously in the Evil May Day riot of 1517 when apprentices protested against the toleration of stranger artificers. A Venetian account of the riot describes how 'they also sacked a number of houses of French artificers [...] They next went to the houses of the Florentine, and Lucchese, and Genoese merchants, whom they insulted; but, as the dwellings were well supplied with men and arms and artillery, they could not do them any harm.'[10] Over the ensuing years, however, official attitudes hardened and an act of 1523 limited the number of journeymen a stranger master could employ without special licence. Twelve years after the May Day riot, in February 1529, the Spanish ambassador reported that 'to gain the good will of the people [Wolsey] gave orders that no foreign artisan or merchant should be allowed to open a shop here on the plea that English-born operatives and workmen were being thrown out of employment by the great number of foreigners resident here'.[11] Their fate became embroiled with that of Wolsey himself and in the following December Chapuys informed Charles V that 'tomorrow a motion is to be made in parliament [...] that all naturalisations of foreigners granted by the cardinal without the king's sanction be revoked, which is greatly to the prejudice of those who have paid very dear for them'.[12]

With the cardinal's fall it was convenient, because popular, to eject them too. But not if their continued presence was useful to the king and many of Wolsey's artists found themselves instead working directly for Henry. After Wolsey, the sculptors Benedetto da Rovezzano and Giovanni da Maiano transferred seamlessly from working on Wolsey's tomb to that of the king. Or rather, the tomb itself was transferred to the king and the artists went with it. During the early 1530s both were receiving regular payments from the privy purse.[13] An extraordinary survival from this project, very possibly associated with these artists, is a set of four monumental bronze candlesticks in Ghent Cathedral (fig. 10.3). Standing more than two metres high, these bear the royal arms with dragon and greyhound supporters and are composed of a series of vase and baluster elements decorated with motifs drawn from classical architecture: flutes, gadroons, acanthus and guilloche. Superficially they appear entirely Italian, but two sections of ornament are very different. One is composed of Tudor roses and foliage, and the other of bearded masks and palmettes that bear a striking likeness to ornament prints by the Nuremberg artist Hans Sebald Beham.

Beneath the high profile of artists like these and Lucas Horenbout, names of large numbers of stranger merchants and craftsmen regularly occur in surviving privy purse expenses from 1529 to 1532.[14] Covering some 300 pages in its published form, this represents just a small fraction of overall royal expenditure. We have already encountered this source in relation to Henry's purchases of jewels at Calais in 1532 but across the period it projects a lively picture of tradesmen and merchants following the court on its progress around the country. Items of expenditure include tips to the bringers of small presents and purchases from local suppliers or visiting merchants; major capital items are almost entirely absent.[15]

Figure 10.3
Bronze candlestick with the arms and supporters of Henry VIII, England, c. 1525–30. Saint-Bavo's Cathedral, Ghent.

Figure 10.3a Detail of bronze candlestick, showing the arms and supporters of Henry VIII, England, c. 1525–30. Saint-Bavo's Cathedral, Ghent.

Figure 10.3b Detail of bronze candlestick, showing decorative mask, England, c. 1525–30. Saint-Bavo's Cathedral, Ghent.

Most of the jewels were supplied by strangers, such as John Crepye (or Cryspin), Guillaume Ottener, 'John Baptist the Italian jeweller' or John Langues (perhaps identical with Jacques Langeloys, whom we encountered fifteen years earlier, in Chapter 4). The biggest supplier by far, however, was Allard Plommier, the French jeweller whose name occurs repeatedly and who was paid some £5,400 over the brief period covered by the account.

By contrast to the many suppliers of jewels, only four goldsmiths are mentioned by name in the privy purse account, Cornelis Hayes, Robert Amadas, John Freman and Morgan Wolf, and of these only one, Hayes, was a stranger. By this stage Amadas, although still master of the jewels, was nearing the end of his life, while Wolf's relationship with the Crown was just beginning. Hayes, on the other hand, was at the peak of his career. He had been granted denization in 1523, when he was described as a 'native of Holland'.[16] By the early 1530s he had inherited Amadas's mantle as the king's principal goldsmith, supplying the Crown with large quantities of jewels and plate. To do all this work he needed a substantial workshop or network of suppliers and in 1531 he was granted a licence to keep six alien apprentices and twelve journeymen.[17]

But a number of other stranger goldsmiths were supplying the king during the 1530s too, including Hans (or John) of Antwerp and Peter Richardson. Hans of Antwerp seems to have been in London as early as 1511,[18] although nothing more is known of him before the late 1520s, when he attracted the attention of the Goldsmiths' Company for employing stranger servants without consent.[19] Hans becomes much more visible in 1537, the first year from which Cromwell's accounts survive and where we see him receiving regular payments for plate and for setting precious stones. One specific item was a George, perhaps for Cromwell's own Garter insignia.[20] At the end of 1538 he supplied Cromwell's new year's gift to the king: a 52 oz gold cup for which Cromwell supplied the gold and Hans did the work – at a rate of about 7s 5d per ounce. This was nearly 50 per cent higher than the 5s per ounce that Amadas charged Wolsey for a gold cup in 1525 (see p. 142) and suggests an exceptionally high level of workmanship; interestingly, the 51 oz 'layer and trencher of gold' that he supplied a year later, presumably for the same reason, cost just 4s an ounce for the work.[21] Hans's name does not figure in the royal accounts as often as some but he may have been active below the radar, possibly as a subcontractor to one of the more prominent suppliers.

Peter Richardson (clearly an anglicisation) followed a career that was curiously parallel to Hans of Antwerp's and his denization dates from 1541, when he had been resident for eighteen years.[22] By 1536, his first appearance in the state papers, he was clearly already established as a court supplier, since in September of that year he was granted an unusually explicit licence. Described as 'alien goldsmith, a native of Holland, in the Emperor's dominions', he was granted permission to employ six servants, 'natives or foreigners', to make 'jewels, works and devices for Queen Jane'.[23] Whether or not he was officially goldsmith to the queen at that stage we do not know, but he was clearly described as such in 1544, eight years and three queens later, when he was paid £400 'for certain [of the queen's] affairs'.[24] At that time he was apparently also employed by Princess Mary and her own privy expenses show a payment to 'Peter the goldsmith in money to make the king's new year's gift'.[25] At the very end of the reign, in January 1547, we see the near parallel lines of his and Hans's careers actually intersect when a royal warrant is issued authorising the delivery of 80 oz of crown gold to both goldsmiths, 'by them to be employed to your majesty's use'.[26]

A particularly interesting case is Michael Mercator. He first enters the picture in 1527, when he arrived in London from Guelders with two musical instruments.[27] Mercator was a man of many parts. He was reputed to be a skilled goldsmith, an organ maker and a medallist. Between 1527 and 1539 Henry VIII and Count Buren, Stadtholder of Guelders (d. 1539), exchanged a number of letters of which Mercator is both the subject and the bearer. In September 1527 Buren refers to Mercator as 'his goldsmith' and recommends him to Henry's service.[28] Over the next few years he travels between the two courts, apparently in the service of both rulers, and in 1531 his name appears in the Chamber accounts with a small payment as 'organ maker to the king'. Four years later Buren wrote again to the king saying that he is sending Mercator with a gift of a musical instrument.[29] Buren, however, seemed determined to bring Mercator to Henry's attention as a man of more parts than that and in 1538 wrote of him as a man 'whose skill in constructing musical instruments, and in other arts, deserves royal patronage. His dexterity is no less in public and private business, which the count has made trial of him in these disturbances in Lower Saxony.'[30] The point seems to have registered and in 1539 Henry dispatched Mercator on several confidential missions, to Hungary, Brussels and Cleves. It was doubtless for these services, for which he was much more highly paid than as court organ maker, that Henry knighted him. Mercator celebrated this exceptional honour in a most unusual way, by creating a portrait medal of himself (fig. 10.4). The obverse is proudly inscribed 'portrait of the first knight created by the King of the English from Venloo', and the reverse is engraved 'Michael Mercator at the age of 48. Thanks be to God and the king. 1539.' Well might he have celebrated this. His diplomatic missions marked his promotion to the ranks of minor courtiers, a turning point that was signalled by the inclusion of his name amongst those exchanging new year's gifts with the king.[31]

Figure 10.4
Self-portrait medal, Michael Mercator, England, 1539. Silver. British Museum, London (M.6793).

There were more, including those who worked on the fringes of the goldsmith's trade, such as John Demayne, an engraver, Michael Berger, 'goldsmith and seal engraver', Richard Atsill, a stone polisher, and Jerome Benall, carver of precious stones. Some, however, never quite emerge from the shadows, even as far as having a name. One such is referred to in the minutes of a privy council meeting in December 1541, when the wardens of the Goldsmiths' Company, exercising their duty to search out items that contravened hallmarking laws, 'entered a stranger's house within the king's palace at Westminster, and carried away certain pieces of work which they judged forfeit'. This was a seriously ill-judged intervention and the wardens were 'roundly admonished for so malapertly searching what the king had in making'.[32]

Holbein and court style

In a quite different league from other artists and craftsmen at the court of Henry VIII was the German painter, Hans Holbein the younger (1497–1543). The son of a distinguished artist of the same name, Holbein was born in Augsburg and almost certainly trained there under his father. In 1515 he moved to Basel, developing a reputation and eventually becoming a citizen of the city. Holbein first travelled to England under the patronage of Sir Thomas More, to whom he had been recommended by More's friend, Erasmus. When he arrived in London around 1526, More was a rising man. A leading humanist and classical scholar, he was chancellor of the duchy of Lancaster and destined to succeed Wolsey as lord chancellor in 1529. Liking what he saw of Holbein's work, he commissioned one of the artist's most ambitious and original works, the group portrait of his family. This immediately established the credentials that would be his greatest claim to fame, for nothing like the realism and psychological penetration of his portraiture had been seen in England before.

On the strength of such works More was able to recommend Holbein to other patrons, including, it seems, the king himself. Indeed, whether or not he had come to the personal attention of the king by then, Holbein was almost certainly employed on the decoration of the temporary banqueting house at Greenwich in 1527. Various payments for paints in the Revels accounts for that year were made to 'Master Hans' and he is thought to have been responsible, with his fellow countryman, Nikolaus Kratzer, the royal astronomer, for painting a map of the world and the signs of the zodiac on the ceiling (see p. 99).[33] As a jobbing royal artist, ephemeral works like this were just part of the work he was expected to produce and, in addition to immortalising Henry's court through his great legacy of portraits, Holbein produced designs for projects as diverse as interior decoration, ephemeral 'stage sets', plate and jewels.

These designs showed an entirely different side to his talent, namely a masterful command of a new decorative style that is summed up in a single word, 'antique'. We have encountered this word before, but what exactly did it mean to the people who used it? Not at all what we generally mean today; in fact, quite the opposite, for 'antique', in an important sense, meant not old but new. The obvious point of departure is that it is a reference to antiquity which, at that time, meant Rome. But this is not a Rome seen through archaeology or ancient artefacts. Rather, it is a collection of decorative motifs, some of ancient origin, like gadroons and dentils, and others entirely invented, but which collectively evoke a vague notion of antiquity. The word is used both as an adjective and as a noun. Many cups in the 1547 inventory are simply termed 'antique' (meaning with this new range of ornament) but one is described as 'a cup antique gilt with a cover, standing upon three antiques'[34] (meaning, in this case, some specific motif, such as, perhaps, classical busts or figures).

Holbein did not invent this style or even introduce it to England – it had been seeping in through Wolsey's Italian artists, through Campeggio's Italian pillars and through English exposure to Italian-inspired French art at Henry's meetings with Francis I – but he did perfect it.

The contrast between Francis I's highly Italianised court style and Henry VIII's more northern one is epitomised by the two golden seals attached to the French and English copies of the 1527 Treaty of Amiens, the former preserved in the National Archives at Kew and the latter in the Archives nationales in Paris (figs 10.5 and 10.6). Neither seal has been firmly attributed to any particular artist and although Henry's has traditionally

Figure 10.5 Henry VIII's seal attached to the French copy of the Treaty of Amiens, probably designed by Hans Holbein the younger, 1527. Gold. Archives National, Paris.

Figure 10.6 Francis I's seal attached to the English copy of the Treaty of Amiens, France, 1527. Gold. The National Archives, London.

been associated with Lucas Horenbout it has nothing in common with that artist's known works. It does, however, represent the artistic climate of the royal court soon after Holbein's arrival and displays many features of his ornamental style. Indeed, for that reason, an attribution to Holbein rather than Horenbout would make much more sense.

The two seals are superficially alike: both kings are enthroned in majesty and surrounded by a Latin inscription. But they are very different. Essentially, one is the work of a draughtsmen and the other of a sculptor. The English seal is flatter and more stiffly modelled than the French; it is also more highly decorated. The king's throne has an arched and pedimented back, with a scallop motif below the pediment; the pilasters to either side are applied with decorated balusters and flanked by naked putti standing on vases and supporting floral garlands. Beneath the king's feet is a shield supported by putti and charged with a Tudor rose. The French seal, by contrast, is sculptural and dramatic. There is a sense of the two angels having just flung the curtains aside to reveal the person of the king. And this king is much more alive than Henry. His hands grasp and his left knee is thrust out into the space. One can imagine Francis being no less engaged with this commission than he was later on with the gold salt that he commissioned from Benvenuto Cellini in 1540.[35]

Holbein's first visit to England was relatively short. Citizens of Basel were only allowed two years' absence without forfeiting their citizenship and he duly returned there in 1528. By then, however, the city was in the throes of a messy iconoclastic Reformation. It was not a promising environment for an artist and by 1532 he was back in England, this time for good.

The England he found on his return was a changed and changing country: Wolsey was dead; Thomas More, his patron, was 'out'; Thomas Cromwell's star was fast rising and Anne Boleyn was about to become queen. Outside the court itself wheels were in motion that would lead before long to the break with Rome, the ascendancy of the protestant cause and the dissolution of the monasteries. Even so, the next decade, until his death in 1543, was extraordinarily productive. Holbein developed a wide circle of patrons, including members of the German migrant community and others outside the immediate court circle. But his most important work was done for the king and his family. By at least 1537 and probably earlier he was on the regular royal pay roll, receiving an annual salary of £30.[36]

We do not know what exactly Holbein's duties entailed; most probably his salary was a retainer, in exchange for which he was expected to do whatever was asked of him. Not for the first time would a successful court artist find that his role extended beyond the realm of art. Michael Mercator carried out quasi-diplomatic duties, as did Titian and as had Jan van Eyck a century earlier. Holbein found himself joining the elite ranks of artist-diplomats and in 1539 the Chamber accounts show that he was 'sent into the parts of High Almayne upon his grace's affairs'.[37] His mission was to paint the portrait of Anne of Cleves, prospective bride number four, and the costs of his trip came to £40, on top of which was a payment of £13 6s 8d 'for the preparation of such things as he is appointed to carry with him' (presumably the materials for the portrait).[38]

Some of the works which he was paid for were collaborative and a careful reading of the warrant for one such project gives us a fascinating insight into their complexities. This was an elaborate silver cradle delivered to Thomas Cromwell (as master of the jewel house) by Cornelis Hayes, probably in 1534, apparently in preparation for Anne Boleyn's second but, as it turned out, miscarried child:

> A silver cradle price £16. For making a silver plate, altering the images, making the roses underneath the cradle, the roses about the pillars, and new burnishing, 13s 4d. For the stones that were set in the cradle, 15s; for fringes, the gold about the cushions, tassels, white satin, cloth of gold, lining, 'sypars and swadylbands' 13s 6d. Total £18 1s 10d.

On top of this was 'the silver that went to the dressing of the Adam and Eve, the making of all the apples, the gilding of the foot and setting of the coral 33s 4d'. Finally, almost as an afterthought, there was the amount owed to the painter: 'to Hance, painter, for painting the same Adam and Eve

Figure 10.7 Detail of *The Holy Family with Saint Elizabeth, the Infant Saint John the Baptist and Two Angels*, showing a golden crib comparable to one decorated by Holbein, southern Netherlands, c. 1520–30. Bilbao Fine Arts Museum, Bilbao.

20s'.[39] This plethora of detail does not really help us form a clear mental picture of the cradle (beyond the fact that it was sumptuous and visually rich), but what does emerge is that it was not so much new as substantially altered. It had a 'new plate' (perhaps the base); the images (perhaps saints or allegorical figures) were 'altered'; various other parts seem to have been added and it was 'newly burnished'. Holbein's Adam and Eve was a new addition and needed to be 'dressed' (framed) with new silver; gilding was required and the coral had to be set. Finally, 15s worth of new stones were supplied and set. We can imagine, therefore, that the cradle had been made originally for Princess Mary or for a child that had died in infancy. But it has not only been refurbished, it has been brought up to date theologically: Adam and Eve imagery was popular among Lutherans, not only because of its association with original sin – now expiated by faith alone – but as the archetypal symbol of divine approval of the institution of marriage.[40] It is tempting in this to detect the influence of Anne Boleyn.

Forming a mental picture of the cradle requires some imagination, although the depiction of another in a Flemish painting of the Holy Family with St Elizabeth and John the Baptist (fig. 10.7) gives a hint of the aesthetic. It shows one end of a cradle of silver-gilt or carved and gilded wood, decorated with relief foliage, set with a classical cameo bust surrounded by pearls and gemstones and with red flowers or roses to either side. It is a stately object that would not have disgraced either Holbein or the royal nursery.

Holbein's impact on the design of plate and jewels was profound and, thanks to the survival of a remarkable body of original drawings, his work throws a clearer light on the character of English royal and aristocratic plate during the 1530s than at any other time in the sixteenth century. The main repositories of these designs are the British Museum and the Historisches Museum in Basel; these are supplemented by a group of ten seventeenth-century engravings by Wenceslaus Hollar after lost designs by Holbein that had formerly belonged to the earl of Arundel. The material ranges from modestly decorated domestic plate to magnificent royal commissions, from doodles and sketches to highly finished drawings, and from small items of jewellery to massive objects that would have weighed hundreds of ounces.

We know that Holbein's father worked closely with goldsmiths and the younger may well have had a basic training in the craft.[41] Certainly, his designs betray a good understanding of metalworking techniques and some of the drawings are clearly intended as guides to construction. One in the British Museum, for example, depicts the cast stem of a cup in great detail while the bowl and foot are barely suggested (fig. 10.8); another, showing two caryatid figures from different angles that are evidently components of some elaborate object, also includes a sketch of a screw apparently passing through a foot and fixing into the base of the caryatid above (fig. 10.9).

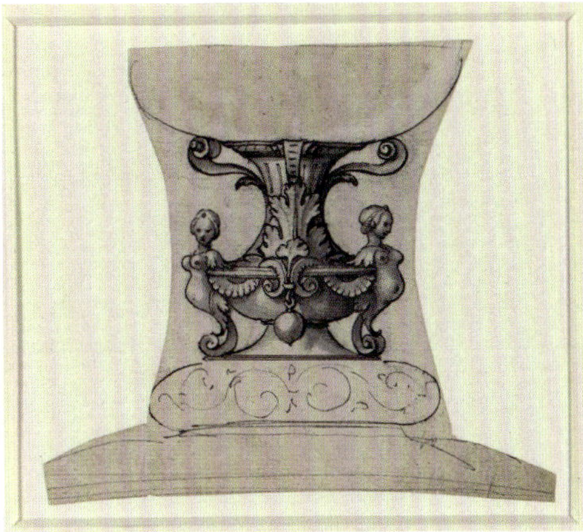

Figure 10.8 Design for the stem of a cup, Hans Holbein the younger, c. 1530–35. Drawing on paper. British Museum, London.

Figure 10.9 Design for elements of a silver vessel, Hans Holbein the younger, c. 1530–35. Drawing on paper. British Museum, London.

A closer look at some of the more spectacular drawings in the two museums, as well as a couple of the Hollar engravings, gives a clear idea of the range and stylistic features of his designs for goldsmiths' work. Several of the Hollar prints depict relatively simple domestic vessels. One is a baluster-shaped ewer or pot with two bands of engraved moresque foliage (fig. 10.10). We do not know exactly when the design dates from but it may have been quite early; a very similar vessel appears in the 1527 More family portrait, standing on the window sill to the right. This has exactly the same profile, including the unusual inverted scroll handle.

The design for a covered cup in Basel (fig. 10.11) is 'off-set': only the left half of the vessel is drawn and the other half is supplied by folding the paper and pressing it down on the still wet ink, printing a mirror image onto the right side of the sheet. The finial, formed as a female figure holding a book and a torch (perhaps representing Truth), is depicted from different angles to guide the goldsmith. The finished cup, if it was ever made, may not have looked exactly like the drawing and sketchy lines around the cover suggest that the goldsmith – or someone else – has tinkered with its profile.

Figure 10.10
Design for a silver jug, Wenceslaus Hollar after Hans Holbein the younger, c. 1645. Engraving after an original of c. 1530–35. Victoria and Albert Museum, London.

The general form of the cup is conventional and the fluted decoration as well as the openwork foliage motif below the bowl can be paralleled by surviving plate from around 1530.[42] What distinguishes it, however, is the assurance of its proportions and the character of its ornament. The frieze below the lip includes several distinctive 'Holbeinesque' elements, namely the vase-shaped motif with basketwork at the centre, flanked by reclining male figures, dolphins morphing into foliage and female demi-figures.

A curious feature of the drawing is the inscription around the cover, the visible part of which reads 'HANS VON ANT'. This has always been taken to refer to the goldsmith, Hans of Antwerp.[43] He and Holbein were friends and Hans was a witness to the signing of Holbein's will in 1543. But it would have been unusual for a cup to be inscribed with the name of its maker, unless he was also its donor, and a possible explanation is that the cup was made in connection with his bid to join the Goldsmiths' Company in 1537.[44] This was an important strategic step for Hans, but his long-term employment of alien journeymen had not endeared him to the company[45] and the successful outcome of his application was probably largely due to a letter of support written by his patron, Thomas Cromwell. Cromwell urged the company to consider his suit, 'in consideration of his long abode here by the space of twenty-six years, and that being married to an English

Figure 10.11
Design for a silver cup inscribed 'HANS VON ANT', Hans Holbein the younger, perhaps c. 1537. Drawing on paper. Kunstmuseum, Basel.

woman by whom he hath many children, he purposes here to continue the rest of his life'.[46] It would have been rash for the company to disregard such a request from the master of the jewel house and lord privy seal and the gift of a fine covered cup would doubtless have sweetened the pill.

Similar ornament to the Hans of Antwerp cup features in the design for a shallow tazza, or perhaps a spice plate (fig. 10.12), but here it is more beautifully worked into a highly finished and animated drawing with relief suggested in pen and ink wash. The design centres on a surprised-looking female satyr, holding two cornucopiae and flanked by scrolling naturalistic foliage. The knop above is bordered by guilloche and decorated with the same basketwork and foliage. Once again, Holbein's practical concerns are hinted at by the nodules on the underneath of the bowl which either represent a circular applied moulding shown in section, or two screws attaching some decorative plate intended to be fixed to the upper side of the bowl.

Other drawings can be more precisely dated because we know what they relate to. Two show what are probably different stages in the evolution of a great fountain given by Anne Boleyn to Henry VIII as her new year's gift in 1534, and a third is the design for the gold cup made to mark Henry's marriage to Jane Seymour in 1536.

The first of the fountain images (fig. 10.13) is lively and energetic and shows the mind of the artist at work. It is very sketchy but has a multi-tiered profile comprising a small shallow bowl superimposed on a larger one and overlaid with a mass of decorative and figural ornament. The fountain stands on a wide shallow basin and the spaces to the side are filled with doodled variant decorative motifs. It would have been a vastly complicated commission, too large or too complicated, perhaps, to be finished in time or on budget. The design was evidently rejected in favour of a simpler solution (fig. 10.14). Unlike the other drawing, this does not include the basin. It shows a vase-shaped vessel on a high stem flanked by standing female figures. The body is divided into horizontal zones decorated with flutes and foliage and with further applied caryatid figures. Sketchily drawn

Figure 10.12 Design for a shallow cup or spice plate, Hans Holbein the younger, perhaps c. 1530–35. Drawing on paper. Kunstmuseum, Basel.

Figure 10.13
Design for a centrepiece or fountain, Hans Holbein the younger, c. 1533. Drawing on paper. Kunstmuseum, Basel.

Figure 10.14
Design for a fountain, Hans Holbein the younger, c. 1533. Drawing on paper. Kunstmuseum, Basel.

on the largest surface is Anne Boleyn's personal badge of a crowned falcon standing on a tree stump, holding a sceptre and with roses before it. The fountain is surmounted by an imperial crown. This, or something like it, is probably the design that was duly fashioned and delivered and appears at the head of the new year's gifts roll in 1534, described as

> a goodly gilt basin, having a rail or board of gold in the midst of the brim, garnished with rubies and pearls, wherein standeth a fountain, also having a rail of gold about it garnished with diamonds; out thereof issueth water, at the teats of three naked women standing at the foot of the same fountain.[47]

Collins observes that it was probably similar in function to one presented to the king by the Merchant Adventurers in 1545 and which was described as a vessel 'which casteth out water running down into a bason [*sic*] made unto the same during the space of two hours'. His conclusion was that it was meant for washing hands during a banquet.[48]

The association of this drawing with the object described on the gift roll has long been accepted,[49] although Eric Ives, in his magisterial biography of Anne Boleyn, dissents, calling it a cup.[50] He argues that to identify the drawing with the 1534 new year's gift 'is unquestionably wrong' since it includes nothing to suggest a basin 'apart from a faint horizontal line and some imagination', nor does the gift list mention the four prominent satyrs. Further discrepancies between the drawing and later inventory descriptions lead him to conclude that there is no connection between the two. But Ives's analysis cannot be right. First, the 'faint horizontal line' is crucial: it and the two sloping lines to either side of the vessel's foot indicate that it is part of an ensemble, and the reason that the basin is not more clearly shown is presumably that it was the subject of a separate drawing (although the point at which the basin engages with the fountain is indicated by the ring of leaf-like motifs at the base of the fountain and that should be read as part of the basin rather than the foot). Secondly, the disparities between the drawing and the gift roll prove nothing: unlike certain other drawings in the Holbein oeuvre, this is not a finished design; it has a sketchy quality and it is rare for finished objects to correspond in every detail with their preliminary designs: complex commissions evolved through dialogue between artist, patron and workshop. Thirdly, Ives's argument that the drawing represents a cup is also hard to accept: the point at which the lip meets the cover is marked by the strong horizontal line above the satyrs' heads and the area immediately beneath this is busy with applied ornament; it could not possibly work as a lip to drink from. Not only that, but the entire form of the object is quite different from other cup designs of the period.

The most famous of Holbein's plate designs is the Seymour cup. It exists in two versions, a working drawing in the British Museum and a more finished – and more beautiful – presentation drawing in the Ashmolean Museum (fig. 10.15). The cup was made of gold, set with pearls and precious stones. It was formed as a vase, carefully articulated into horizontal zones and with each zone given its own distinctive ornament. The bowl is articulated with portrait medallions (reminiscent of those on the Mangot 'clock salt') (fig. 9.5) and bands of grotesques and moresque foliage, all of which were collectively known as 'antiques'. The cup, moreover, is covered with specific royal motifs: at the base of the bowl are the initials H and I, for Henry and Jane, and at the base of the finial is her personal motto, 'Bound to obey and serve'. The shield at the very top, left blank in the drawing, would have been enamelled with the royal arms. The cup itself, which weighed 65 oz, remained close to the king and was among the plate listed at Whitehall in the 1547 inventory.[51]

One of the most splendid of the Basel drawings is for a covered cup

Figure 10.15
Design for the Seymour cup, Hans Holbein the younger, 1536. Drawing on paper. Ashmolean Museum, Oxford.

Figure 10.16
Design for a jewelled gold cup, Hans Holbein the younger, c. 1530–35. Drawing on paper. Kunstmuseum, Basel.

or bowl (fig. 10.16), presumably of gold and set with as many as 230 gemstones (probably rubies and diamonds, the diamonds now showing as black because the silver-rich pigment used to depict them has oxidised), on a ground of intricately chased entwined foliage. Its classical ornament is limited to subtle bands of laurel wreaths (around the foot and lip), guilloche and dentils. As on most of Holbein's designs, there is none of the dynastic ornament that dominated so much of the 1521 inventory and, indeed, continued to have a strong presence on most royal plate throughout the reign. What distinguishes it, apart from the obviously impressive value of its materials, is its beautifully considered proportions and the superbly accomplished craftsmanship that the design calls for.

This is exactly the sort of piece that might have figured at the 1532 meeting between Henry VIII and Francis I, when Francis's buffets were graced with pieces like the St Michael cup in Vienna (fig. 9.3).

Three more drawings must suffice for this brief exploration of Holbein's plate designs: an elaborate timepiece, a jewel-like mount for a drinking vessel, and a diminutive book cover. The design for a 'clock salt' (fig. 10.17) is annotated with a note indicating that it was Sir Anthony Denny's new year's gift to the king in 1545 (old calendar 1544). But Holbein died in late 1543 and the design must have been one of his last. We will be hearing more of Denny later; he was keeper of Whitehall Palace, by the end of the reign Henry VIII's most important residence, and was a powerful courtier. Although the inscription states that it was Denny's gift to the king, it cannot be identified on the 1547 inventory, either because its description is too brief for it to be recognised, or because it was no longer there (perhaps Denny spirited it away after the king's death which, as its donor, he may have decided he was entitled to do and which, as keeper, he would certainly have been *able* to do).

But although always described as a clock salt there is no indication on the drawing itself that it served any other purpose than being an ingenious timepiece. In fact, it tells time in three different ways: by the hourglass contained inside a pair of hinged doors; by the sundial above in which the hour is indicated by the shadows cast by the putti's fingers; and by the mechanical clock on the top. The compass, shown separately to the left and presumably housed flat inside the detachable cover, would have enabled the user to orientate the piece correctly for the sundial to be read. Of course, the very idea of a single object incorporating three different means of measuring time is curious, but as an intellectual conceit it is quite typical of Renaissance princely *Kunstkammer* objects.[52] This is a theme to which we will return in Chapter 14. In terms of its decoration the design is a profusion of 'antiques', with three demi-satyrs indicated at the base, a term figure of Pan on the hourglass, and with goats' masks and putti above. The other ornament is composed of naturalistic and moresque foliage and the piece is surmounted by a crown imperial, the only hint of its intended recipient.

The second image (in fact divided between two plates) comes from the Hollar engravings and appears, from the vessel's profile, to represent the mounts for a Venetian glass (fig. 10.18). Glass had an increasingly conspicuous presence at court during the later years of the reign and a number are listed with gold or silver-gilt mounts, although none that can clearly be identified with this image. The mounts to the foot, unusually for Holbein, are modelled in the form of the royal beasts, a lion, a greyhound and a dragon, each holding a shield that would presumably have borne

Figure 10.17
Design for a timepiece, Sir Anthony Denny's new year's gift to the king in 1545, Hans Holbein the younger, 1543. British Museum, London.

Figure 10.18 Design for the foot of a mounted glass, Wenceslaus Hollar after Hans Holbein the younger, c. 1645. Engraving after an original of c. 1540. Metropolitan Museum of Art, New York.

Figure 10.19 Design for a girdle prayer book, probably for Thomas and Jane Wyatt, Hans Holbein the younger, c. 1534–43. British Museum, London.

the royal arms; the knop is modelled with cherubs and the cover (shown in a second engraving) with stylised dolphins surmounted by a vase and a female figure representing temperance.

The last of these designs is for the cover of a girdle prayer book of around 1540, with moresque foliage against a black background (fig. 10.19). The design may never have been executed but it does relate to a remarkable gold and enamel book cover in the British Museum (fig. 10.20) that is one of the richest surviving examples of courtly goldsmiths' work from the reign. Hugh Tait makes an attractive if not entirely convincing argument for attributing this to Hans of Antwerp,[53] and in addition to its embossed and enamelled panels of the Judgement of Solomon and the 'fyrye serpent', it has very similar moresque foliage on a black enamel ground on the spine and clasps.

Holbein's repertoire of ornament is at the cutting edge of northern European design and in his hands is used to create objects of exceptional balance and visual harmony. The decorative motifs are not, by and large, of his own invention; they come from elsewhere and were gathered in from a variety of sources. These would have included sophisticated objects arriving at court that he had seen with his own eyes, such as the Mangot 'clock salt', as well as what he saw on his travels. But the most important source of inspiration was ornament prints. As Susan Foister points out,

> he combined [these] in novel ways, with clarity and balance and with an extraordinary expressive energy and rhythm. These qualities so animate his decorative designs, whether individual motifs, such as his favoured serpentine mermen and women, or the larger shapes of cups, frames and fountains, that they scintillate on paper even before their transformation into precious metal and stone.[54]

Ornament prints first appeared in the late fifteenth century and by the second half of the sixteenth were universal. Around 1530, however, they were still relatively novel and only a limited number would have been available to Holbein. Foister cites the early sixteenth-century Italian printmakers Zoan Andrea and Antonio Veneziano, the former for the recurring basketwork motif favoured by Holbein and the latter for other elements of his *grotesque* repertoire. But there were others. Holbein must have used his German contacts to ensure he was kept aware of developments there and motifs from a variety of 'Allamayne' printmakers can also be recognised. These include Hans Burgkmair, Daniel Hopfer, Hans Sebald Beham and Heinrich Aldegrever. By the early 1530s the work of the enormously influential Nuremberg artist, Peter Flötner, was starting to circulate through prints. One of Holbein's most ambitious decorative

Figure 10.20 Girdle prayer book, with the judgement of Solomon and Moses and the brazen serpent, attributed to Hans of Antwerp, London, c. 1540. Gold and enamel. British Museum, London.

designs, an elaborate chimney-piece dated c. 1538–40,[55] includes his first use of strapwork, the motif invented by Rosso Fiorentino for Francis I's gallery at Fontainebleau in the late 1530s and disseminated through ornament prints almost immediately. By soon after the middle of the century this had become the most ubiquitous, overworked decorative motif of English plate, but in Holbein's time it was still fresh and new.

The importance of Holbein's contribution to English art and design is impossible to overstate. In portraiture his role was transformative and even though he had no obvious successors in terms of the incisive psychological penetration of his portraits, his legacy of precise draughtsmanship lived on in artists such as Nicholas Hillyard and Isaac Oliver. In plate and jewellery design he set a standard and established a repertoire of ornament that arguably defined not only the rest of the reign of Henry VIII but also much of the rest of the Tudor period. The profile of the Seymour cup, for example, remained the norm for another generation,[56] while the repertoire of ornament continued with relatively little change for much of the rest of the century.

Eleven The Family Silver

The immediate family of a king maintained separate households, subordinate to the king's own but modelled on it. Within these households, princes, princesses and dowagers would be served under the same protocols and would maintain similar (though lesser) jewel houses. This had a multiplying effect on royal plate.

Plate and jewels feature in every aspect of Henry's dealings with his family and in each case they illuminate the relationship. Information varies from one individual to another but we know something even of the plate of Henry's mother and of his redoubtable grandmother, Lady Margaret Beaufort. Unsurprisingly, his long-awaited heir, Edward, accumulated an ever-growing stock of plate almost from the day of his birth. But this contrasts dramatically with Henry's use of gold and silver to manipulate the sense of obligation owed by his sisters, Margaret and Mary, and it contrasts even more starkly with his confiscation of it to humiliate Katherine of Aragon and their daughter Mary when they refused to bend to his will. Katherine had a well-stocked jewel house of her own when the divorce proceedings started; by the end she had very little. The story of Anne Boleyn's plate, enlivened by Holbein's wonderful designs, shows another side of the king's nature through his tendency to thrust greatness on his paramour by inundating her with plate and jewels. Some of her plate, pointedly, comprised the very things taken from Katherine, and some, following their owner, found their way back to the Tower after her fall.

This chapter does not discuss the plate and jewels of all of Henry's family. The documentation is extensive and to tell all the stories would be repetitive. So I have been selective, focusing on his sisters, on Katherine of Aragon and her daughter, on Anne Boleyn, and on the two royal sons, Henry duke of Richmond and Edward prince of Wales. The interest of these stories lies less in the plate and jewels themselves than in what their ebb and flow tells us of Henry's impetuousness, and of his greed and cruelty, traits that we shall see increasingly clearly as the reign unfolds.

French queen and queen of Scots

The story of Henry VIII's younger sister Mary's (1496–1533) betrothal and marriage to the aged Louis XII of France has been told in Chapter 7, as has the story of her dowry plate and the besotted Louis showering his bride with jewels. Now the story moves to the next stage. Louis died within months of their marriage and was succeeded by his cousin, Francis I. This presented the English with a delicate situation. The marriage contract had provided for such an eventuality and allowed for the return of both bride and dowry. But possession being what it was, this inevitably called for cool and careful negotiation.

Francis proposed returning just half the gold plate (worth 50,000 crowns) and half the jewels, on condition that Henry acknowledge that this was not done out of obligation but as a free gesture of goodwill. This was quite unacceptable to Henry and the duke of Suffolk was dispatched to negotiate a solution.

The greatest bone of contention was the spectacular jewel known as 'Mirror of Naples'. Hugely valuable, this was worth haggling over and Francis argued that 'the new queen having such a mind to it [...] he will never be satisfied without it, for it is the same thing that is said should never go from the queens of France'.[1] The Mirror had been described in Wyatt's 1514 inventory as 'a great table of diamond with a fair hanging pearl and a small chain given by the most Christian King of France and sent to England to the lady'; it weighed more than two ounces and according to the Italian merchant, Lorenzo Pasqualigo, had been valued when it was in London at 60,000 crowns.[2]

In sending Suffolk the king was taking a risk. Mary and Suffolk were known to be close and in her present circumstances she was vulnerable. Suffolk had assured Wolsey he would do nothing to abuse Henry's trust and the plan was for him to escort Mary back to England as a widow before seeking royal consent to marry. But the young couple were clearly worried that Henry might have other ideas and that Mary might once again be made party to a political marriage. They decided to take no chances and were married secretly in France. This was a mistake. Unaware how quickly events were moving, Wolsey had written to Suffolk saying, 'I assure you the hope that the king hath to obtain the said plate and jewels is the thing that most stayeth his grace constantly to assent that ye should marry his sister; the lack thereof, I fear me, might make him cold and remiss, and cause some alteration.'[3] How right he was. When Suffolk replied that it was too late and the deed was done, Wolsey wrote again in frostier terms. The king, he said, had taken the news 'grievously and displeasantly, not only for that ye durst presume to marry his sister without his knowledge, but also for breaking of your promise made to his grace in his hand, I being present, at Eltham'.[4]

Wolsey goes on to offer a solution, albeit a costly one: 'in this great perplexity, I see no other remedy but first to make your humble pursuits by your own writing', and then to agree to pay dearly. He advises that they undertake 'to pay yearly to the king during the [French] queen's life £4,000 of her dower' (leaving them £6,000 a year on which to live). 'Over and besides this ye must bind yourself to give unto the king the plate of gold and jewels which the late French king had [from Henry]' and to persuade Francis to return the full 200,000 crowns dowry to Henry.

When the delinquent couple and the king met in person shortly after their return to England the terms agreed were slightly more lenient, although still punitive. The plate and jewels were indeed made over to Henry, and Mary bound herself not only to pay back the entire dowry, but also a further £2,000 a year (rather than £4,000), up to a total of £24,000.[5] As a result of their capitulation, the Suffolks were soon forgiven and resumed their places at court, but their debt was not and continued to dog them for the rest of their lives. In 1534, a year after Mary's death, Suffolk still owed £25,853 and asked the king to take in payment 'such jewels as he lately presented to him and Thomas Cromwell, his secretary'.[6] The following year he handed £4,361 worth of jewellery over to the king in part settlement of his debt.

A similar kind of manipulation, if at a lower level, can be seen in Henry's dealings with his other sister, Margaret (1489–1541). She had married James IV of Scotland in 1503, when she was fourteen, and had been sent north with a magnificent dowry. But the peaceful relations that the marriage was meant to ensure proved short-lived and by 1513 relations were strained as Henry adopted a more aggressive policy towards Scotland's ancient ally, France. In an early instance of his use of plate and jewels as an instrument of policy, Henry had evidently delayed the transfer of certain jewels, 'our father's legacy', to Margaret in order to send a pointed message to her husband; Margaret complained that James 'knows it is withheld for his sake [and] we are ashamed therewith'.[7] Months later England and Scotland were at war; James was killed at Flodden and much of the Scottish royal plate and jewels were captured by the English.

This is not the place to tell the extraordinary story of Margaret's life, but her forfeiture of the regency for the infant James V in 1515 and her flight to England put her for a while back at her brother's court, where she was treated with great honour. According to Hall, she was 'richly appointed of all things meet to her estate, both of jewels, plate, tapestry, arras, coin, horses, and all other things of the king's gift and liberty'. A year later it was deemed safe for her to return to Scotland and she departed 'with great riches',[8] including £125 worth of plate newly supplied by John Twyselton and William Holland.[9]

But her reception was not as warm as she had hoped and in March 1518 Lord Dacre wrote to Wolsey saying that 'her [Scottish] jewels have not been delivered, nor her duties levied. She has been obliged to lay in wed [pawn] the plate given her by the king, and is likely to be driven to extreme poverty.'[10] Three months later he paints an even bleaker picture, saying that she 'lies in Edinburgh like a poor suitor and all she had of the king's gift is consumed'.[11] These reports mark the beginning of a series of increasingly desperate pleas that go on and on. Margaret's letters appeal to the king's core values by their continual reference to her plate, the disposal of which would not be 'to her brother's honour'. But are we completely to believe her? Whereas in June 1518 all of the jewels she had from Henry had supposedly gone, by the following April it seems that they have not been entirely 'consumed' after all, although most assuredly they will have to go unless she has help.[12] Miraculously another year passes without her quite having to surrender her jewels and in October 1520 she threatens once more that she 'is in a sore case, [and] if she be not helped by the king and Wolsey [she] is obliged to pawn the jewels given her by the king when she left'.[13] Fourteen months later we read that 'she is fain to put away her jewels'.[14] Only evidently she did not, for in August 1523 she announces that she 'will be compelled to pawn her cupboard [of plate]'.[15] Perhaps she had cried wolf once or twice too often and it seems that her appeals went unanswered. But fortunately, by the following year, James V was invested with his full powers as king and his mother duly rehabilitated.

Queen Katherine and Princess Mary

The circumstances of Katherine of Aragon's arrival in England, her marriage to Prince Arthur and the protracted negotiations preceding it were discussed in Chapter 7. We now pick up the story with Arthur's death in Wales, just months after their wedding. This was catastrophic for Katherine, causing a reduction in her circumstances that continued until Henry VII's death and her marriage to the new king. So long as Arthur lived they enjoyed the revenues of the lands made over to him as prince of Wales, but the moment he died these reverted to the king. Meanwhile, in Spain, Ferdinand and Isabella reacted immediately to the news, instructing Katherine's chamberlain, Juan de Cuero – as we have seen – to 'keep all the gold, silver, jewels etc of the princess with the greatest care. Not the smallest portion of them ought to be sold.'[16]

Perhaps it was envisaged that these difficulties would be strictly temporary, but the widowhood of a young and eligible princess created an opportunity and both sides considered where Katherine might best be placed. Henry VII even briefly considered marrying her himself after Elizabeth of York's death in 1503. The favoured option, however, was that she should marry her brother-in-law. Papal dispensation was sought on the grounds that her marriage to Arthur had not been consummated and a new round of dowry negotiations began. There was no rush for this as although Katherine was now sixteen years old, Henry was just ten and it was agreed that they should not marry until he was fourteen. Meanwhile her eligibility waxed and waned. With Isabella's death in 1504 and Philip of Castile's accession to the principal Spanish kingdom Katherine became a less attractive catch; Philip's death in 1506, however, meant that Ferdinand reasserted himself as effective ruler of Castile and her prospects improved accordingly.

But still the negotiations dragged on, one of the sticking points being a dispute over the valuation of the plate that Katherine had brought to England in 1501. Then, quite suddenly, it seems, the difficulty was resolved by Ferdinand writing in March 1507 that 'if the king of England [...] be not willing to accept the ornaments, plate &c for the price at which they were valued in Spain, he may take them at the price they are worth in England'.[17]

All this time Katherine was essentially an impoverished prisoner. Both her parents and her father-in-law paid lip service to her status as 'beloved daughter', but neither would offer her any financial support because that would be tantamount to accepting responsibility for her maintenance. Much of her correspondence with her father focused on her worsening money problems and the fact that she was unable even to pay her servants. In the end, she had no choice but to liquidate the only significant asset she had, namely her plate. The documents leave no doubt that she did this very reluctantly. In April 1507 she told her father that she '[is] obliged to sell her gold and silver, as there are no other resources left to her'.[18] She begs him to send new plate or money to replace the plate that has been sold. Perhaps it was this desperate action that finally awakened Ferdinand's sense of paternal duty because five months later he sent her 2,000 ducats. Katherine's response to this is revealing: 'I did not know which wants to satisfy, and thought the most necessary was to redeem the plate which I had pledged.'[19] The servants, presumably, remained unpaid.

But pressures on her plate resumed, especially when Katherine came under the spell of her friar-confessor, who appears to have exercised a Rasputin-like influence on her. In 1509 Ferdinand's ambassador wrote complaining that 'the princess behaves towards [de Cuero] as though he had committed the worst treason in the world, and all because he hinders them from selling every day a piece of plate to satisfy the follies of the friar [...] In fifteen days they have sold gold for 200 ducats.'[20]

With Henry VIII's accession and his marriage to Katherine immediately afterwards, her fortunes were transformed. Her store of plate was now secure and, indeed, it was regularly augmented by great new year's gifts from her husband, such as a pair of massive pots weighing 575 oz in 1513.[21]

We do not know a great deal about Katherine's regular dealings with goldsmiths, but one surviving document makes it clear that they were extensive. The addendum volume of *Letters and Papers* includes an item of 1522 under the heading 'goldsmiths' work'. This in fact appears to be a roll of Katherine's new year's gifts for that year that were distributed to a total of ninety named individuals, from the French queen and the archbishop of Canterbury down to household servants (though some obvious names such as Wolsey and the king himself appear to be omitted).[22] Some of these were recycled jewels, but the new plate by seven goldsmiths was supplied at a cost of some £401. Of course, in the same way as we have seen with the king's gifts, the counter value of gifts received would almost certainly have exceeded the outgoing, so the cost is illusory and the real gainers would have been the goldsmiths.

Henry and Katherine were married for twenty-three years, more than half the reign, and it was nearly twenty years before divorce crept into the picture. At first, when this time came, the king was prepared to be magnanimous and in October 1528 Cardinal Campeggio wrote from London that if only she would agree to retire to a nunnery, 'the queen shall have any honourable conditions which she demands, retain her station as queen [...] allowing her dowry, rents, ornaments, and assignments for her support'.[23] But Katherine would not cooperate and things moved slowly. In 1531 she was living in considerable state at The More, one of Thomas Wolsey's former residences. There she was visited by Mario Savorgano, son of a wealthy Venetian aristocrat, who wrote that 'in the morning we saw her Majesty dine: she had some thirty maids of honour standing round the table, and about fifty who performed its service. Her court consists of about 200 persons.'[24]

By now, however, Henry's patience was wearing thin and relations had become visibly frosty. Eustace Chapuys described an extraordinary incident where Katherine provoked Henry by the surprising means of a new year's gift. His account is worth quoting in full:

> The queen, having been forbidden to write letters or send messages to the king, and yet wishing to fulfil her duty to him in every respect, caused to be presented to him on new year's day, by one of the gentlemen of the

> chamber, a gold cup of great value and singular workmanship, the gift being offered in the most humble and appropriate terms for the occasion. The king, however, not only refused to accept the present, but seemed at first very angry with the gentleman who had undertaken to bring it. Yet it appears that two or three hours afterwards the king himself desired to see the cup again, praised much its shape and workmanship, and fearing lest the gentleman of his chamber who had received it from the queen's messenger should take it back immediately – in which case the queen might have it presented again before the courtiers, when he (the king) could not well refuse its acceptance – he ordered the gentleman not to give the cup back until the evening, which was accordingly done, and it was then returned to the queen. The king, moreover, sent her no new year's gift on this occasion, but has, I fear, forbidden the members of his Privy Council, as well as the gentlemen of his chamber, and others to comply with the said custom.[25]

Several things emerge from this story. First, despite Chapuys' candied words about 'humble and appropriate terms', Katherine was a shrewd woman and must have known her gift would irritate the king; she was testing him. Secondly, it shows Henry being torn between strategy and avarice and although he is determined to reject all overtures from his wife, he is drawn by the praiseworthy 'shape and workmanship' of the gold cup and he wanted it. Finally, the story shows that despite her own – and Chapuys' – protestations of poverty, she still had the means to commission 'a gold cup of great value and singular workmanship'. For even if she anticipated that the king would reject it, the cost of its making would still need paying.

This incident was but a prelude. Soon afterwards we see the beginning of a process of attrition. Not satisfied with merely refusing her gifts, the king adopted a strategy of systematically depriving her of the tokens of her status. By now Henry was openly flaunting his new love, Anne Boleyn, and sought to humiliate Katherine by taking away her jewels and giving them to Anne. Things came to a head through Henry's 1532 meeting with Francis I, when he was accompanied by Anne, made radiantly magnificent for the occasion. Once again, we turn to Chapuys for a colourful (if not entirely neutral) account. According to his report, the king dispatched the duke of Norfolk to Katherine with the express purpose of removing her jewels. Her response was bold and remarkable. She refused to part with them on the grounds that 'I cannot present the king with my jewels as he desires, inasmuch as when, on a late occasion I, according to the custom of this kingdom, presented him with a new year's gift he warned me to refrain from such presents in future.' Having scored a clever legalistic point, she then changed tack and made a moral one:

> Besides which […] I would consider it a sin and a load upon my conscience if I were persuaded to give up my jewels for such a wicked purpose as that of ornamenting a person who is the scandal of Christendom, and is bringing vituperation and infamy upon the king, through his taking her with him to such a meeting across the Channel.

But all that said, she would obey; her tirade (doubtless embellished by Chapuys) ends, 'yet, if the king sends expressly for my jewels I am ready to obey his commands in that as well as in all other matters'. Henry was irritated, expressing his astonishment 'at her not having sent her jewels forthwith when he first asked for them, as the queen of France, her sister […] would have done'. But he duly dispatched the written demand, whereupon 'the queen gently pleaded excuse for her former refusal, and sent him the whole of her jewels [and] the king […] is very much pleased and glad at it'.[26]

Later correspondence suggests that the removal of the jewels had been represented as temporary, in other words, a loan. But if that really was the case it soon became clear that they were not to be returned after all. Chapuys wrote again the following February with the news that 'she [Anne] still keeps in her possession the queen's rings and jewels, and there is no talk at present of her restoring them to their legitimate owner'.[27]

Two months later the thumbscrews were tightened. It was announced that Katherine should no longer be called queen, and that from one month after Easter the king would stop providing for her personal expenses or the wages of her servants. Henceforth she was to be known as the princess dowager (in recognition of her undisputed status as the widow of the late prince of Wales). But if Henry imagined that she would be cowed into submission, he miscalculated. It was like 1503 all over again; Katherine had been there before and, according to Chapuys (unless he invented it), she answered resolutely that 'as long as she lived she would entitle herself queen; as to keeping herself [… if] there was nothing left for her and her servants to live upon, she would willingly go about the world begging for the love of God'.[28]

The stakes were raised again. In July 1533, shortly before the birth of Anne's daughter, Elizabeth, Chapuys reports that 'the Lady, not satisfied with what she has already done, has lately importuned the king to ask the queen for a very rich and gorgeous piece of cloth, which she herself brought from Spain, as an ornament robe for a christening, and of which the Lady is very desirous'. And once again, Katherine's answer was blunt: 'God forbid that I should ever be so badly advised as to give help, assistance, or favour, directly or indirectly, in a case so horrible and abominable as this.'[29]

Just how quickly and dramatically did Katherine's material fortunes decline? This is not easy to judge, especially because much of the evidence is anecdotal or biased. Chapuys, in particular, is not always reliable. Most of the reported depredations up to 1533 focused on her 'jewels' (which may, of course, include jewelled objects as well as items of adornment) but an inventory dating from after April 1533 appears to give us a picture of her plate holdings at that time.[30]

The document is headed 'parcels of plate remaining with the princess dowager for her daily service'. It comprises about sixty separate entries, all arranged under their locations. The chapel plate (in 'her closet') corresponds almost exactly to that in her closet back in 1521 (see p. 75).[31] The domestic plate is divided between eight locations, although most is kept in the pantry, cellar, and ewery. The pantry holds salts and spoons (twelve salts, one of which is gold and weighs 12 oz, and twenty-one spoons, again, one of gold); the cellar contains mainly bowls and pots (twelve of each, weighing around 1,200 oz) but also a single silver-gilt covered cup and a cup of assay; the ewery, as its name implies, is the place for ewers and basins. The other locations are the chaundry (for candlesticks), the 'confessionary' (for spice plates), and the scullery and sawcery (for 'vessel'). A few odd items are also kept in the pitcherhouse. Altogether the weighed items come to just under 2,900 oz, but that is far from the total since, curiously, the items in the last five locations were not weighed.[32]

But impressive though these holdings might appear, they were barely sufficient to maintain her dignity as queen. The domestic plate entrusted to her household was carefully calculated: the single gold salt and spoon are clearly for her personal use, as are the single covered cup and cup of assay in the cellar, while the twelve pots, twelve bowls and two flagons would have been barely enough, by royal standards, to dress a buffet. Indeed, even though not all weighed, the total quantity must have fallen well short of the 12,500 oz or so that Katherine brought with her in 1501. Equally, many individual items on the princess dowager's list are lighter than those listed as 'the queen's plate' in 1521, when she had two gilt pots of 331 oz, a pair of 86 oz gold candlesticks and a pair of huge flagons weighing 457 oz. So there is little doubt that her plate had been somewhat downgraded in the meantime.

Late in 1533, however, we have what looks like evidence of a planned raid on her plate, in the form of a chilling note on Cromwell's 'to do' list reminding him 'to devise that the rest of the plate, not necessary for the Princess Dowager, may be brought to the jewel-house'.[33] What exactly was taken away as a result we do not know, but the action was probably taken well before her death and possibly as early as February 1534, when a rumour reached Rome that 'they have taken away all her servants, male and female, and the little silver left to her for her use'.[34]

Whenever taken, much of the plate that had formerly been Katherine's evidently met its end as part of a large quantity of royal plate consigned to the mint after July 1536 and listed in a document headed 'estimate of the value of certain plate to be delivered to the mint to be coined'.[35] The wider significance of this document is discussed in Chapter 12, but among the enormous quantity of gold and silver plate scheduled for coining are three discrete parcels, one 'from the Lady Dowager', another 'from the Lady Mary' and a third 'from the [late] duke of Richmond'. The Lady Dowager's comprised 163 oz of gold, 2,959 oz of silver-gilt and 63 oz of parcel-gilt and white plate. Its total value came to £956 10s 11d, more than her daughter's but less than the duke of Richmond's.

But even if it had been Cromwell's intention to deprive her of all her plate (though the wording of his note implies that he did not mean to go quite so far), he probably did not succeed and it seems that her servants managed to hide some of her plate away before the inventory was compiled. That this was probably the case is suggested by Sir Edward Bedyngfield's letter of January 1536 to Cromwell, written shortly after Katherine's death, in which he said that 'the persons who had the custody of her jewels, plate, and apparel, have given us a just and plain declaration, containing much more than we could see or know before'.[36] This surely means that some of her chattels had been concealed when the inventory clerks made their previous visit.

Given the close surveillance under which Katherine lived and the dangers of being seen to act against the king's wishes, such concealment could only have been carried out by an especially loyal servant and a clue to his identity is provided by a curious passage in an anonymous Spanish chronicle in which it is stated that

> one of the Spaniards, called Francesco Felipe, had in his possession much plate and jewels belonging to the blessed lady, and the king was told of this; whereupon the king sent for him. 'Felipe, you must give up what you have belonging to the princess'. Felipe, who is a very bold man, answered: 'Sir, may it please your majesty, I have nothing belonging to the princess, unless you order me to give it up to her, for to her it comes by right.'[37]

Felipe was indulging in a dangerous game of semantics here, for by 'princess' the king means Katherine, the princess dowager, whereas for Felipe this can only refer to Mary, since Katherine was not princess but queen. We might suppose that the plate entrusted to Felipe was from the original dowry plate that Katherine had brought with her from Spain and to which she had repeatedly demonstrated an almost religious sense of attachment, recalling the reluctance with which she had been forced to sell some of it in her youth and her keenness to repurchase it when her father finally sent her some money.

The reduction in Katherine's final circumstances is reflected in the simplicity of her will. Among its few bequests are small gifts of cash to some of her servants and 'the collar of gold which I brought out of Spain', which she leaves to Mary. She also makes specific provision for her goldsmith, that 'he be paid his wages for the year coming and all that is due to him besides'.[38] But as a final coda to the saga, Henry (perhaps egged on by Anne Boleyn), was not prepared to let her will stand and sought to overturn it. The attorney general, Richard Rich, counselled against this, arguing that after her divorce she should be classified as a 'sole woman, having full authority by law to dispose of her goods'; he advised that 'the king therefore cannot seize her goods unless there be some other cause' (although, weasel-like, he goes on to propose various ways in which the king might use his position as Supreme Head of the Church to legitimise such an action).[39]

Princess Mary, as we have seen, was the subject of a number of failed matrimonial negotiations and she was destined to remain a 'sole woman', as it were, throughout her father's reign. But for the first twenty years of her life she was the heir apparent and, even as a small child, a prime focus of court attention. As early as 1518, when she was just two years old, she received her first group of new year's gifts, a gold cup from Wolsey, a gold pomander from her aunt, the French queen, a gold spoon from the countess of Devon and more.[40] By November 1525, now nine years old, she had her own household and, as we have also seen (p. 98), Mary's chamberlain, the bishop of Exeter, wrote to Wolsey asking his advice about the protocols that they should follow for Christmas. The significance of this letter, apart from the specific guidance it seeks, is that it shows the princess's household was conceived on the same model as the king's, just on a smaller scale.[41]

Over the next few years Mary's fortunes stood high and we may assume that her plate holdings were substantial. We have no inventory from this period but, as in her mother's case, later annotations to the 1521 jewel house inventory (probably dating from around the time of the bishop's letter) give an idea of at least some of the plate assigned to her use. The range of wares is similar to Katherine's: chapel plate, one gold salt (and others in silver-gilt), one covered cup and a cup of assay, bowls, pots, spoons, ewers and basins, and 'vessel'.[42] But the quantities are smaller. Whereas Katherine had six images weighing 400 oz, Mary had two, weighing 84 oz, and whereas Katherine had twelve pots weighing nearly 1,000 oz, Mary had six weighing just 330 oz.[43] The message is clear: status was finely graded and plate was one of its measures. Just like Katherine's, Mary's household was modelled on the king's, and just as Katherine's was on a smaller scale than her husband's, so Mary's was smaller again.

All this changed as she became tainted by the deteriorating relationship between her parents. The stripping of Katherine's royal title was followed by her divorce and the birth of Mary's half-sister, Elizabeth, as a consequence of which Mary was declared illegitimate. She was punished in the same way as her mother and was systematically stripped, not only of her title, but of her assets and tokens of status. Deliberately separated from her mother, Mary was moved to Beaulieu in Essex, and in August 1533 Cromwell sent Lord Hussey there to retrieve her jewels and bring back an inventory of her plate. When he arrived, he was told that no inventory could be found. Mary's reaction, it seems, was the same as her mother's and Hussey told Cromwell that she 'brought forth the jewels [but] will not deliver [them] unless you obtain the king's letters to her in that behalf'. Clearly Hussey was not given an easy time of it and the letter ends, 'would to God that the king and you did know what I have had to do here of late'.[44] But Mary was evidently prevailed upon to yield up her plate because Cromwell's note to himself about Katherine's plate also included a reminder that 'those things with my Lady Mary, which are not meet for the princess [that is, not suitable to be transferred to the infant Elizabeth], to be also brought thither [to the Tower]'.[45] The 1536 'estimate of the value of certain plate to be delivered to the mint to be coined' included 100 oz of gold and 2,467 oz of silver and silver-gilt from Princess Mary.[46]

Deprivation was followed by humiliation. Mary was placed in Anne Boleyn's household and forced to serve as a lady-in-waiting. The following March, Chapuys wrote to the emperor that 'yesterday the duke of Norfolk went to [the Lady Mary] and besides the ordinary threats took away her principal ornaments, saying she was not a princess and her pomp and pride must be abated'.[47] Contrast this with the attention being paid a month later to the little Princess Elizabeth by the visiting French ambassadors. This was more than Chapuys could swallow: 'the king's bastard daughter', he wrote, 'was brought out to them splendidly accoutred and dressed, and in princely state, with all the ceremonial her governess could think of'.[48]

The nadir of Mary's humiliation came in the months following Katherine's death in January 1536. She had not been permitted to see her mother during her final illness. Now she was denied the consolation of receiving the few bequests that Katherine had left her. One of these was a gold cross which Henry, again according to Chapuys, had decided to pre-empt:

> by the king's command and in his name, [Cromwell] sent for a cross which the queen, her mother, had bequeathed to her. I fancy that the cross is not set with precious stones, and that the gold of it is not worth ten crowns, but that there is inside a piece of the True Cross – an object of great devotion and consolation to the princess.[49]

A month later there was a twist to this unpleasant little story; Chapuys wrote again to say that 'Cromwell, finding that the cross which he re-demanded of the princess [...] was not so rich as he thought, and had only the relic, to which these men attach no importance, has sent it back to her.'[50] In other words, it was worthless, so she could have it.

The reduction in Mary's circumstances continued throughout Anne's reign but was suddenly reversed by her stepmother's execution, by Henry's marriage to Jane Seymour, and by Mary's pragmatic decision (encouraged by Chapuys) to assent to the Act of Supremacy and thereby recognise the king as head of the Church in England. By 26 May 1536, five years after their last meeting and just a week after Anne's death, there was a reconciliation: 'the king has sent for the princess, made much of her, and given her many jewels belonging to the unjust queen'.[51] Once again, Mary knew instinctively how to handle the situation and in June she wrote Cromwell a touching letter that was clearly meant to be shown to the king: '[since] I may perceive his grace of his princely goodness and fatherly pity [has] accepted my letter and withdrawn his displeasure towards me, that nature moveth me to be so bold and send his grace a token, which my servant, this bearer, hath to deliver to you'. She begs he will find a way to persuade the king to send her a reciprocal token, which will be her greatest comfort until she is permitted to come to his presence.[52] We do not know what exactly that token was, but it was almost certainly a ring or small jewel. A month later Chapuys wrote to the emperor's secretary that

> the queen [Jane] presented her with a very fine diamond ring, and the king himself put into her hand a check for about 1,000 crowns for her 'menus plaisirs', all the time exhorting her not to trouble herself in future about money for her private expenses, for she would get as much as she wanted merely by applying to him. At dinner, and in her own rooms, the princess was served with greater solemnity and pomp than she had ever been before.[53]

The improvement in Mary's circumstances was further bolstered by the death of the duke of Richmond, in July 1536, resulting in her brief reinstatement as heir presumptive (Elizabeth's star having waned in parallel with her mother's). Chapuys wrote that 'her father's affection for her increases daily' and reported that Cromwell, mightily relieved by her signing of the Act of Supremacy, had commissioned a medal to present to her. The medal does not survive but Chapuys described it: on one side it depicted the king and queen in relief and on the other the princess.[54] It also bore a Latin inscription which, in translation, read:

> Obedience is the mother of unity. Unity of soul is the mother of calm and constancy. Truly, constant calm of soul is an inestimable treasure. He had regard for humility who left us in his Son a perfect example of humility: he was created obedient to the Father. And indeed his very nature taught the duty of obedience to parents and to country.[55]

Unfortunately for Cromwell, the king thought the medal was so excellent that he decided to give it to Mary himself, leaving Cromwell to find some other, presumably less inspired present.

In October 1536 the French ambassador, Cardinal du Bellay, painted a picture of perfect rehabilitation: 'Madame Marie is now first after the queen and sits at table opposite her.'[56] And so it continued for the rest of the reign. Her rehabilitation is clear from the 1539 new year's gift roll, where she is second only to Prince Edward in receiving 123 oz of gilt plate from her father.[57] Four years later, in January 1543 Chapuys reports approvingly of the king 'addressing her in the most endearing terms, and making her valuable gifts, having on this last new year's day presented her with rings, silver plate, and other jewels, among which are two rubies of inestimable value'.[58]

The anecdotal reports of Mary's rehabilitation are confirmed by the more concrete evidence of her privy expenses and an inventory of her jewels. Princess Mary's privy expenses from 1536 until 1546 include numerous payments to goldsmiths. Some of these were royal goldsmiths whose names we have encountered before, such as Hans of Antwerp, Peter Richardson and Cornelis Hayes, and others not.[59] Richardson was paid £30 in 1544 to make the king's new year's gift,[60] but most of the plate orders for these gifts were supplied by Hayes. Mary's new year's gifts over this period seem to have cost her around £80 a year, but once again this would have been more than compensated by the value of incoming gifts. We have no lists of the latter, but the rewards paid out to thirty servants bringing gifts in 1537 suggest that their total value was considerable.[61]

The inventory of her jewels, dated to 1546, paints a telling picture of her circumstances by the end of the reign.[62] It lists around 200 jewels containing hundreds of precious stones and pearls. Many of the jewels were emblematic. A few had classical subjects, like Piramus and Thisbe, but many more were biblical: 'the history of Jacob being asleep', 'the history of Moses striking water out of the rock', 'the history of how Christ healed the man of the palsy' and so on. Much like Wolsey's plate, this was not a fixed asset but a resource to be drawn upon and annotations to the list show many incoming gifts from her father and others later being given away, as new year's gifts, christening presents or as gifts to ladies of court.

Anne Boleyn

Contrasting Anne Boleyn's situation with Katherine of Aragon's at new year in 1532, when Henry rejected Katherine's gold cup, Chapuys writes to Charles V that Henry 'has not been so discourteous to the Lady [...] He gave her a room hung with cloth of gold and silver, and crimson satin with rich embroideries. She is lodged where the queen used to be, and is accompanied by almost as many ladies as if she were queen.'[63]

The affair between them had been simmering for a long time and a letter of five years earlier, written in August 1527, suggests a considerable degree of intimacy between them. Henry thanks her for a jewel which was rich with symbolic imagery, perhaps a peace offering after a lovers' tiff, even though they were not yet lovers in the way that Henry would have wished. His letter continues, 'for a present so beautiful that nothing could be more so I thank you most heartily, not only for the splendid diamond and the ship in which the solitary damsel is tossed about, but also for the pretty interpretation and too humble submission made by your benignity'.[64] Eric Ives describes the jewel's message as 'transparent', writing that 'for centuries the ship had been a symbol of protection – the ark which rescued Noah from the destroying deluge; the diamond – as the *Roman de la Rose* had said – spoke of a "heart as hard as a diamond, steadfast and nothing pliant." Anne was saying "yes."'[65]

In 1527 their liaison was a closely guarded secret, but by 1531 it was being spoken about quite openly and 'the Lady', of whom Chapuys had a low opinion, becomes a regular topic in his dispatches to the emperor.

Henry may have had six wives, but he was only truly infatuated with one, and he expressed that infatuation by showering Anne with gifts. Gifts of jewellery were easy for Henry and need not have been as costly as they seemed since they could simply be 'issued' from his store. It goes without saying, especially in the case of Henry's wives, that their recipients had only a lifetime interest and the jewels could be – and indeed often were – recycled to their successors. Their true value, of course, lay in their stones, which would often be reset before presentation. A list of jewels delivered to the king by Cornelis Hayes during the year beginning August 1530 includes rings and other items 'delivered to Mistress Anne at Beaulieu'; a stream of further items follows over the succeeding months: 'a diamond in a broach of Our Lady of Boulogne', 'nineteen diamonds for her head', 'two bracelets for her', 'garnishing a little book with crown gold for her' (as a new year's gift) and so on. On 18 January is an item, 'graving &c two arms in a basin and ewer, for Mistress Anne'.[66]

A key moment in the formalising of her position was Henry's second meeting with Francis I. Immediately prior to this event he created her marquess of Pembroke in her own right and when he introduced her to Francis she was queen in all but name. Chapuys wrote that

> though on this matter of the journey and interview the courtiers appear cold and indifferent, certain it is that the Lady thinks otherwise, for knowing very well how to make hay while the sun shines, she has not been slack to provide herself with rich and most expensive dresses and ornaments, which the king has ordered to be bought for the occasion.[67]

Throughout 1532 Anne was in high favour with the king, as were the French. A telling if inconsequential anecdote, told by a frustrated Chapuys who was perhaps resentful of the greater royal access enjoyed by the French ambassadors, concerned a visit to the jewel house. The king happened to be at the Tower with Anne when the French ambassador arrived. The ambassador having delivered his message, the king conducted all three into the jewel house to inspect the treasure, 'when, either in consequence of the good news brought by the ambassador, or to please the Lady, the king presented the former with one of the finest cups therein stored'.[68]

Henry and Anne were secretly married in January 1533. There was good reason for secrecy, since his marriage with Katherine was not yet formally annulled. But behind the scenes this gave rise to a flurry of activity in the jewel house. Cromwell's remembrances in late 1532 include a note to arrange for 'a cupboard for my lady marchioness out of the Tower by Draper',[69] one of the yeomen of the jewel house. Typically, no time was lost in acting on this and the result was a service weighing 5,243 oz and valued at £1,188 11s 10d, presented to Anne in December. We have a full list of what it comprised.[70] Unsurprisingly, it is similar in range to the domestic items in Katherine's and Mary's households, except that Anne has more. At the time of the princess dowager's list Katherine had just one covered cup, while Anne has three (plus two double cups); Katherine had twelve pots, Anne has twenty; Katherine had twelve bowls, Anne has twenty-nine, and so it goes on. But none of this plate (or rather little of it, anyway) was new. It mostly comprised second-hand wares and would not have made a particularly homogeneous display. Some of the cups were described as 'Spanish fashion' or 'of Almain making'; the trenchers were 'of Flanders touch' and three of the salts 'of Paris touch'. Some of it was plain but others had widely differing ornament, including roses, daises, feathers, scallop shells and beasts. Most was doubtless taken directly from the shelves of the jewel house, but not all: 1,488 oz – nearly a quarter of it – had formerly belonged to Sir Henry Guildford, comptroller of the household, and Sir William Compton.[71] Guildford had died earlier in 1532 but had opposed the Boleyn marriage; for Anne to 'inherit' his plate would doubtless have seemed to her an appealing form of revenge. Compton, groom of the stool until 1526, had died of sweating sickness in 1528 and it was presumably only after his death that the royal plate he had embezzled (see p. 17) came to light.

Two months later Anne invited the king to dinner, evidently with an invited audience, since Chapuys wrote to Charles V as if he were present:

> on St. Matthias' Day [24 February] the Lady received the king at dinner in her chamber richly ornamented with tapestry, and the most beautiful sideboard of gold that ever was seen [...] During dinner the king was so much occupied with mirth and talk that he said little which could be understood; but he said to the duchess of Norfolk, 'Has not the marchioness got a grand dote and a rich marriage, as all that we see, and the rest of the plate belongs to the Lady?'[72]

Presumably what Chapuys saw on display was Anne's newly acquired service, in which case it was not gold but silver-gilt and Chapuys was either misinformed or was deliberately hyping the rhetoric. But there is no doubt that even for such a jaded court watcher as he, this was an impressive display, especially since he seldom bothers to remark on plate.

Less than three years separated Anne's coronation in June 1533 from her execution in May 1536. This was a period of high expenditure and Ives suggests that more than 120 items on the 1547 inventory can be linked with the queen, through her arms, her falcon badge or the combined royal initials HA that gave rise to so much mirth at the time.[73] Other than the fountain and basin that she gave to Henry in 1534 (see p. 192), the more impressive items include a pair of highly wrought chained bottles bought at new year 1536 and a number of pots and bowls.[74] Works of a more artistic or jewel-like character appear as well, such as 'a glass of birrall garnished with gold with the late Queen Anne's arms upon the cover' and 'a layer of mother of pearl garnished with gold enamelled with H and A knit together and with the queen's arms in the top of the cover'.[75] But as Ives points out, 'what is not clear is whether this was plate which Anne had owned and to which the king's arms had [later] been added, or vice versa, or whether it was acquired for joint use'.[76] But Cromwell, as ever, was concerned about expense and one of his to-do lists from late 1533 includes

Figure 11.1
The Boleyn Cup, London, 1535–36, maker's mark three flowers. The finial formed as Anne Boleyn's personal badge, a falcon standing on a tree stump. Silver gilt. Church of St John the Baptist, Cirencester.

a note 'to remind the king of the expense of the queen's new year's gifts, and the rewards given for new year's gifts'.[77]

None of the objects described above survives but one piece that almost certainly did belong to Anne does, namely a silver-gilt goblet at Cirencester parish church (fig. 11.1). This is hallmarked for 1535–36 and has a maker's mark of three flowers; it is 31.5 cm high and weighs 18 oz 13 dwt. It lacks the detail and complexity of Holbein's designs, but is closely related to a woodcut in a book of goldsmiths' designs by Hans Brosamer, printed around that time (fig. 11.2). Its sharply angled, V-shaped bowl recalls contemporary Venetian glass, and the acanthus foliage and fluted decoration would both be described as 'antique'. Its most significant feature, however, is the finial, which is in the form of Anne Boleyn's personal badge of a falcon on a tree stump. By tradition the cup was left to the church by Elizabeth I's physician, Richard Martin, who owned the former lands of Cirencester Abbey and was a regular recipient of royal new year's gifts during that reign.[78] Perhaps this was the route by which it came to the church, but there is no proof

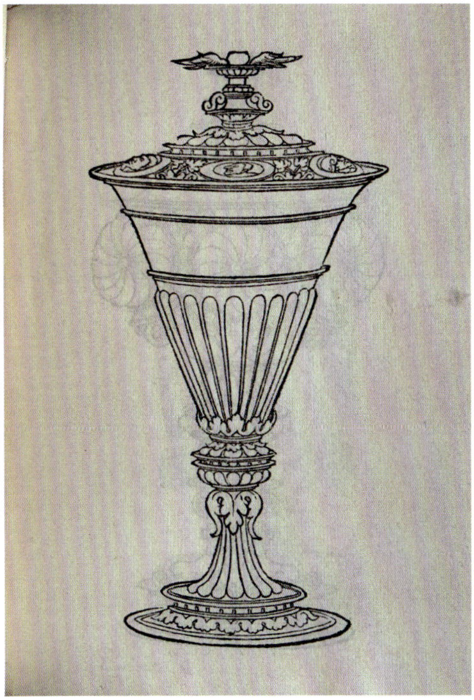

Figure 11.2
Design for a cup, from Hans Brosamer's *Neu Kunst-Büchlein*, c. 1530. Woodcut. Private collection.

of this and it is equally possible that its early history was quite different. In any event, the falcon badge is strong evidence that it did once belong to Anne. Not only that, but a number of cups on the 1547 inventory are described as 'glass fashion', one of which weighed almost the same and was chased with the HA initials.[79]

Jane Seymour and the later queens

Compared with the stories of Katherine and Mary, of the king's use of plate and jewels to control and humiliate, and of its equally deliberate use – in Anne Boleyn's case – as a token of ennoblement, there is much less to say about Jane Seymour and the three queens who followed her.

Jane did two things her predecessors had failed to do: she provided Henry with an heir and she died before he had time to tire of her. For this reason, he loved her in death as much as in life and chose eventually to be buried alongside her. None of this has anything to do with the fact that the most spectacular of Holbein's plate designs happens to be for the gold cup made to celebrate their union (fig. 10.15), but the tragic event that came so soon after the birth of Prince Edward in 1537 gives it a special poignancy.

There is no evidence of Jane or of any of her successors having great quantities of plate formally made over to them like Anne Boleyn, but we must assume they were provided with sufficient to allow their households to function with appropriate dignity. For jewels, however, there is evidence aplenty. The 'Boke of the Queen's Juelles' is dated 1537 and may have been compiled immediately after Jane's death.[80] It is of similar extent to Mary's and lists just under 200 items. Like Mary's, it is also annotated with the names of subsequent recipients. 'The Lady Mary' and 'the Lady Elizabeth' appear several times and some of the jewels were passed on as new year's gifts. It is a more orderly document than Mary's, with the material carefully listed under headings like 'pairs of beads' (rosaries), girdles, brooches and 'borders' (stones and pearls set in goldsmiths' work and sewn onto strips of fabric for stitching onto clothes). Once again, we suspect that the list is incomplete – there are, for example, no rings – but even so, it gives a good idea of the sort of personal magnificence that enveloped the person of the queen. Some, perhaps, of the very items listed are depicted in Holbein's portrait of Jane in Vienna (fig. 11.3), but while the portrait shows us what some of them may have looked like, the inventory shows how vastly more there were than that.

A surprisingly large group comprises 'books of gold', sumptuous gold bindings for devotional texts, such as those discussed in Chapters 9 and 10. Other objects standing on the margins of jewels in the modern sense are 'tablets' and 'coffers'. We might get a sense of the 'table of gold enamelled with the passion in it' from a cover illustrated in fig. 10.20, while the 'little coffers of gold' – one of which bore a depiction of the Magi – were presumably precious boxes for jewels. One particularly intriguing item is 'a glass [presumably a mirror] with the images of the king, his father and others as appeareth with two lambs on the outside'.[81]

The story of Henry's last three wives adds little to our narrative. Once again, we have no inventories of their plate and even if we did they would be unlikely to add much to the pictures we have already formed. But a few interesting details emerge even so.

The high hopes invested in Anne of Cleves, fuelled by fulsome verbal reports and by Holbein's beautiful portrait, are clear from the preparations made for her arrival. In October 1539 the French ambassador reported that the queen's side of Whitehall Palace was being repaired and newly 'ornamented'[82] and the following month Cromwell made a note to himself to organise quantities of plate to be provided at Calais, Dover, Canterbury 'and all other places' along her route so that she could be received in suitable splendour.[83] Nor was Cromwell alone in paving her path with plate: shortly before her arrival Archbishop Cranmer told Cromwell that 'if he can compass it' the town of Canterbury would present her with fifty gold

Figure 11.3
Jane Seymour,
Hans Holbein the younger,
1536–37. Kunsthistorisches
Museum, Vienna.

angels in a cup.[84] And as we have seen, the ambassadors accompanying Anne to England were handsomely rewarded with plate (see p. 119).

All of these expectations, of course, were dashed from the moment Henry first set eyes on her and within half a year they were divorced. But Anne's pliant submission was the key to her survival and, indeed, to an honourable and comfortable retirement, outliving her husband by a full decade. The terms of her settlement are a hint of the status that Katherine of Aragon might have enjoyed had she submitted to the king's will: Anne was to be known as the king's sister and she was to have precedence over all at court save the queen and the king's children. Not only that, but she was provided with two fine manors, an annual income of £4,000 and an allowance of £500 for her servants. Plate, hangings, furniture and jewels were also provided.[85] We have no list of these, but given the level of income she was to enjoy, they were doubtless of a quantity and quality appropriate to her status.

Anne's cordial relations with Henry included the exchange of new year's presents and in 1542, rather than the standard offerings of plate, she gave the king some fine cramoisy cloth, and he gave her glassware.[86] Glass was doubtless cheaper than plate but it was not considered an inferior material. Quite the opposite: rather like porcelain in the eighteenth century, it was seen as a technical and aesthetic wonder that was exciting princes all over Europe, as we shall see in Chapter 14.

The currency of Henry's gifts to Katherine Howard, for whom his feelings were altogether more passionate, was jewels rather than glassware. She was sixteen and he forty-nine, almost exactly the age difference between Mary and Louis XII when they married in 1514, and Henry deluged his bride with jewels, much as Louis had nearly thirty years earlier. Some of the items on a long list of jewels given to Katherine by Henry[87] also appear in Jane Seymour's jewel book, showing that after the latter's death he had retained them and 'reissued' them to his new bride. One, apparently not listed in the jewel book but very clearly depicted in Holbein's portrait of Jane (fig. 11.3), is a diamond brooch of letters IHS; this is very likely identical with one Henry gave to Katherine at Christmas 1540 and which is described on her list as 'a Jesus of gold containing xxxij diamonds having three pearls pendant at the same'. But not all of Katherine's jewels were recycled and several, like an enamelled gold book cover, or a gold pomander, incorporated little clocks. There is nothing like these in the Seymour book and they were probably new.

When Katherine was charged with adultery, however, her jewels became the barometer of change. The French ambassador, Charles de Marillac, picked up the first ominous sign when he heard that an inventory of her jewels had been taken in 1541, 'which, if true, there can be no doubt as to the rest',[88] and when she was first placed under house arrest at Sion, Cranmer was told that her jewels were to be taken away and that the clothes she was left with were 'all of them to be without stone or pearl'.[89] As we have seen before with the first Katherine and with Mary, degradation and deprivation went hand in hand.

And jewels once again, this time by their presence rather than their absence, were a measure of the favour enjoyed by Henry's last wife, Katherine

Parr. She was of a different stamp from her immediate predecessors; she had a sharp and independent mind but soon learned that, where her husband was concerned, deference rather than challenge was the more prudent approach. A widow herself, she was thirty years old and was more likely to give the king comfort than arouse his passions. But still the jewels came, or so it would seem. Like Anne of Cleves, the third Katherine survived her husband and there was never cause to compile an inventory. But a grant in November 1546, three years into the marriage and weeks before the king died, issues a licence to the Parisian jeweller, Allard Plommier, to import 'all manner of jewels, pearls, precious stones [...] for the pleasure of us, of our dearest wife the queen, our nobles, gentlemen and others'.[90] It is a general licence but it is surely significant that the queen is specified as the recipient of at least some of these imported trifles.

Henry Fitzroy and Edward, Prince of Wales

Henry Fitzroy, duke of Richmond (1519–36), the elder of the two half-brothers, was Henry's illegitimate son by his mistress, Elizabeth Blount. In the absence of an heir he was extremely important and in 1525, at the age of just six, he was appointed knight of the Garter and made a double duke, as Richmond and Somerset. Still hoping for a legitimate son, however, Henry never declared him his heir, but the honours and training for a possible future role as king kept coming. In that same year, 1525, he was dispatched to Yorkshire as the titular head of the council of the north and set up with a full-scale household, with a range of officers including gentlemen ushers, cupbearers, a carver and sewers. Interestingly, when – again to expand his range of experience as a possible future monarch – Richmond was sent to reside at the court of Francis I for a year in 1532, his household was effectively mothballed and certain of its members placed for the time being in religious houses. In November of that year he wrote from Calais (during his father's meeting with Francis) to the prior of Tutbury that 'it is determined that such of my servants who remain behind in England shall be established in religious houses [...] of whom Robert Amyas, clerk of my jewel-house, is appointed to abide at your monastery'.[91]

A jewel house of his own, with an appointed clerk, suggests significant holdings of plate, which was indeed the case. The duke died unexpectedly on 23 July 1536 and just two days later Cromwell's servant, John Gostwick, was on hand to prepare an inventory of his possessions.[92] The list of plate is broadly similar to Katherine of Aragon's, comprising 107 oz of gold and 5,517 oz of silver, three-fifths of which is gilt. The gold includes some intriguing pieces, including a salt modelled as a black dragon and set with

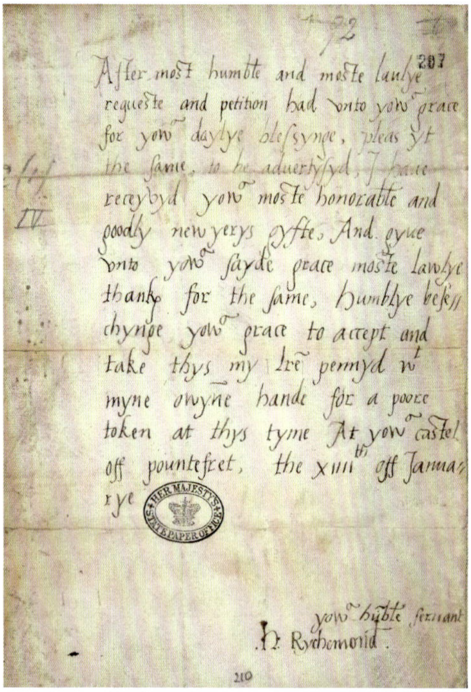

After most humble and moste lawlye requeste and petition had vnto your grace for your daylye blessynge, pleas yt the same, to be aduertysyd, I have receyvyd your moste honorable and goodly new yerys gyfte, And gyve vnto your sayde grace moste lawlye thanks for the same, humblye besechynge your grace to accept and take thys my lre pennyd wt myne owyne hande for a poore token at thys tyme At your castel off pountefret, the xiiii off Januarye

your humble servant
H. Rychemond

Figure 11.4
Letter from Henry Fitzroy, duke of Richmond, to Henry VIII thanking the king for a new year's gift in 1527. The National Archives (SP 1/40, fol. 207).

gems, another of gold-mounted birral and a third 'supposed to be of an unicorn's horn'. The altar plate comprises the usual array of liturgical objects and six images, the same number as Katherine had.

Much of this plate was assigned to the duke from the Tower jewel house, presumably when his household was appointed in 1525, and about a quarter of the items – mostly chapel plate – correspond to entries on the 1521 inventory, later annotated 'with the duke of Richmond'; more may have come from other stores of royal plate and the holdings were further enhanced by an annual inflow of new year's gifts. A gold spoon came from the earl of Northumberland, a gold salt, cup and spoon came from his godfather, Cardinal Wolsey, and other pieces from the king. The king regularly gave silver-gilt drinking vessels and pots and at least some of these must have been quite new, since their economical descriptions include the words 'antique work' and one is described as 'a great jug with cover, gilt, engraved with letters H and A crowned and two ears of serpents'.[93] By happy chance one of the young duke's thank you letters to his father survives, written in 1527 when he was eight and signed in his own hand (fig. 11.4). Part of it reads:

> I have received your most honourable and goodly new year's gift. And give unto your said grace most lowly thanks for the same, humbly

> beseeching your grace to accept and take this my letter penned with mine own hand for a poor token at this time. At your castle of Pontefract, the 14th of January. Your humble servant H. Richmond.[94]

But the inventory also reveals the same lack of sentimentality towards plate that we have noticed elsewhere; plate that came in by way of gift, even from the king himself, was sent straight out again if expedient to do so. A standing cup given by his father in 1534 'was sent incontinently [immediately] to the duchess of Norfolk for her new year's gift' and a little salt, given by the queen, 'was given to Mistress Jennye the same year, when the duke christened [stood godfather to] her son'.[95]

The plate having been listed, no time was lost in putting it to work. On 28 July Gostwick wrote to Cromwell saying that he had delivered the plate to the jewel house 'in four coffers sealed'.[96] From there, it – or most of it – was sent to the mint, and the list mentioned above (in relation to Katherine of Aragon's and Mary's plate) of 'certain plate to be delivered to the mint to be coined' includes '90 oz gold, 2,994 oz gilt plate and 2,262 oz parcel-gilt and white, from the duke of Richmond', valued at a melt-down figure of £1,218 11s 6d.[97]

The reason that Henry never declared Richmond his heir was that he never gave up hope that he would one day be granted a legitimate son. And with the birth of Prince Edward in 1537 his most cherished wish was granted. But it was a close-run thing. Richmond died in July 1536 and Edward was not born until October 1537, so for about fifteen months Henry had no male heir at all. Edward's fundamentally different status from any of his half-siblings (being not only legitimate but also a boy) was reflected from the start in the way he was provided for. His christening at Hampton Court was not essentially different from Elizabeth's, but his gifts were more impressive and while Elizabeth's godparents gave her three gold cups and three standing bowls, Edward received a gold cup, six great bowls, six great pots and two great flagons.[98]

Death and attainder being the great triggers for Henrician inventories, we have no inventory of Edward's plate as prince, but we do have other windows into his holdings, from which a sense of greater abundance emerges than for his siblings. New year's gifts started immediately[99] and we happen to have lists of those he received over the first three years of his life, from 1538 to 1540.[100] These varied from year to year. Charmingly, his two sisters gave clothes and the shirt that Elizabeth gave him (when she was just six years old) was, we are told, 'of her own making'. Some were quite unusual, like the earl of Southampton's '"ullffes" [wolf's] tooth set in gold […] with four little bells' (presumably a teething piece and rattle) and the earl of Shrewsbury's elaborate and bespoke silver-gilt mounted crystal salt, 'enamelled blue with three ostrich feathers set in a coronet and E P garnished and set with [stones and pearls] and a shepherd on the top'. Most, however, were standard wares, although 'antique' and so presumably not recycled. The inner circle of royal councillors – Chancellor Audley, Cranmer, Cromwell and the dukes of Norfolk and Suffolk – were regular donors, although several others were named each year. In all, the prince received between 400 oz and 500 oz of plate each year, the lion's share coming from the king, who always gave around 200 oz. Like his half-brother, Edward wrote pious thank you letters and one from 1546, written in August for a group of presents, gives the general flavour:

> I also thank you that you have given me great and costly gifts, as chains, rings, jewelled buttons, neck-pins, and necklaces, garments [...] However, you grant me all these, not that I should be proud [...] but that you might urge me to the pursuit of all true virtue and piety.[101]

If kept up consistently through the rest of his father's reign, which they doubtless were, new year's gifts alone would have amounted to around 5,000 oz by the time Edward ascended the throne. But there was more, as we can glean from the 1547 inventory. This lists many items of plate coming 'from the prince's side', referring to Edward's apartments at Whitehall. Some of these had surely come as new year's gifts but others, like altar plate, almost certainly had not.

Twelve

Cromwell, the Tower and the Goldsmiths

This chapter continues the story of the jewel house from the time of Thomas Cromwell's appointment as master, but it also brings together two other institutions, the mint and the Goldsmiths' Company. In terms of their functions, these three organisations were quite separate, but when we look at the people that ran them a different picture emerges. The principal Tudor mint, at the Tower of London, was nominally headed by a courtier, but was in practice run by goldsmiths; equally the jewel house was a department of the royal household but was supplied by goldsmiths and for part of the reign was headed by one too, Robert Amadas. In addition to that, the Goldsmiths' Company acquired a role as independent quality controller of the coinage, its members performing the assay and providing the jury at an annual event called the trial of the pyx. To add to the mix, the involvement of certain members of the company with the mint and jewel house went in both directions. Amadas and Martin Bowes had both been prime wardens of the Goldsmiths' Company, suppliers of royal plate *and* deputies at the mint. But, independent though the company might have sought to be as an institution, it, no less than the jewel house or the mint, frequently felt the compelling authority of the king through his principal servant, Thomas Cromwell.

The 1532 jewel house inventory

Cromwell was not yet 'master of everything' when he succeeded Amadas at the jewel house in 1532 and his appointment was another stepping stone towards the almost unlimited power he enjoyed towards the end of his life. His arrival in office was marked by the taking of a new inventory, showing us exactly what was in the jewel house at the time or was on its books and allocated to the household.[1] The inventory follows the order of the previous one, omitting items no longer present and adding new ones at the end of

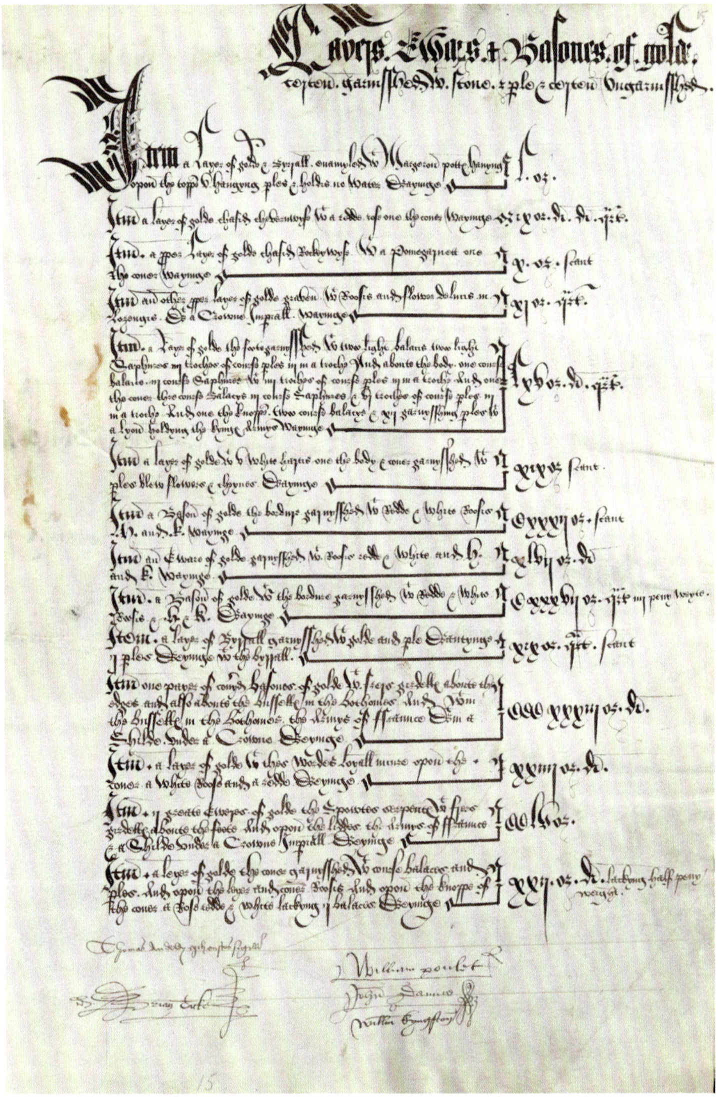

Figure 12.1
A folio from the 1532 jewel house inventory, detailing 'Layers, ewers and basones of golde'. National Archives (E 36/85, fol. 15).

each section. But it is very different from the other. The 1521 inventory, as we have seen, was a working copy, full of additions and annotations showing movements of plate from one place to another. The 1532 list gives us none of that colour, though it is an impressive document (fig. 12.1). Written on both sides of forty-five folios and bound in vellum, it is a painstakingly written fair copy and each page is signed at the bottom by the commissioners who oversaw its compilation: Sir Thomas Audley, Sir William Paulet, Sir William Kingston, Sir Brian Tuke and Sir John Dauntesey. This was no randomly selected group of courtiers and their own principal roles were all closely connected, physically or administratively, with the jewel house. A few weeks before the inventory was commissioned Audley was appointed keeper of the Great Seal and Paulet comptroller of the household; Kingston was constable of the Tower, Tuke was treasurer of the Chamber, and Dauntesey a senior official under Tuke. Audley and Tuke were also co-commissioners, together with Cromwell, of the Tower treasury, which was set up in October 1532. So, each had a strong interest in knowing that the jewel house and its contents were secure and properly accounted for.

First impressions are that its holdings were not much different in 1532 from what they had been eleven years earlier and the total weights are very similar: around 128,000 oz of precious metal in 1521 and 127,000 in 1532.[2] But when we look more closely it becomes clear that there had also been a good deal of 'churn'. Many items listed in 1521 had gone in the meantime and many new ones had arrived in their place. And the changes turn out to have affected some areas more than others, with some growing and others shrinking. Gold (apart from the regalia) rose from 4,800 oz to 6,580 oz,[3] while other, hefty, categories like bowls, pots and 'vessel' shrank (vessel, in particular, weighed around 29,000 oz in 1521 – nearly a quarter of the entire inventory – but just 21,000 oz in 1532).

When we look at numbers rather than weights, a clearer picture starts to emerge. The total number of entries grew from 888 to 970, but because many of the 888 had been culled since 1521, the number of new items in 1532 was close to 350, more than a third of the total. A hint of this volatility can be gleaned from a few specific categories in gold and silver-gilt. Of the twenty-three gold cups and bowls listed in 1521, thirteen had left the jewel house by 1532, while twenty new ones had arrived; and of the thirty gold salts listed in 1532, eight were new. Silver-gilt was even more volatile. In 1532 there were seventy-three cups, sixty-two of which were new, and 278 bowls, slightly more than half of which were new. In short, like the picture we formed through Wolsey's running account with Amadas, the holdings in the jewel house were constantly evolving. Nor did this stop in 1532 and we have already seen (p. 166) how just two months after the inventory was compiled some forty objects were sent off to Cornelis Hayes to be 'new made'.

What drove this constant exchange? The jewel house was a revolving door. On the *extra* side, old or damaged objects were sent to the mint, while others might be refashioned for the king's own use or to provide bullion for a fresh batch of new year's gifts. On the *infra* side, many new year's gifts were dispatched straight to the jewel house, as they had been previously, and new consignments of plate continued to arrive through attainder.[4] Wolsey was in a class of his own in this respect and just as Buckingham was the biggest named source in 1521, so Wolsey's former plate, discussed in Chapter 8, added at least 6,000 oz, greatly swelling the list.

Cromwell and the jewel house

The regular work of the jewel house continued much as it did before Cromwell. As before, this focused on the protection of a major royal asset, on its safe and secure transport, and on repairs and procurement. In terms of status and influence, the position of the master was not particularly elevated. He was subordinate to the chamberlain and he did not have a seat on the privy council. But for the rising Cromwell its potential as a staging post was immediately clear. He had first come to notice as a servant in Wolsey's household, where his skills as an administrator and his command of Italian had made him the perfect man to manage the cardinal's dealings with Italian artists, and after the latter's fall he became useful as a conduit between Wolsey and the king. Now, with the vacancy created by Amadas's death, these same skills help to explain his appointment as master of the jewel house. This was a turning point in his career, perfectly depicted by Holbein's portrait in the Frick Collection (fig. 12.2). Painted at almost exactly that time, it exudes confidence, professionalism and order, but it shows little hint of luxury. Cromwell is surrounded (but not overwhelmed) by letters and documents demanding his immediate attention. This is the portrait of a man on the rise and the only hints of material success are an expensive ring on his finger and a sumptuously bound book on the table, with gilt edges and clasps and mounted with a gemstone.

The jewel house was a busy department, its transactions were immensely detailed and its work involved the regular movement of valuable assets. Approached actively rather than as a sinecure, it had several attractions for Cromwell. It brought him income, partly through its £50 salary but probably more significantly through 'the usual profits';[5] it gave him powers of patronage, both in relation to goldsmiths and to courtiers; and it gave him a direct involvement with royal finance. But its most important advantage, as he must have seen immediately, was that it gave him direct access to the king. Indeed, one of the letters on the table in Cromwell's portrait is from the king and is addressed 'To our trusty and right well biloved Counsaillor Thomas Cromwell, Maister of o[u]r Jewell House'.

For any prince, the state of the royal jewels and plate, their security and their availability, would have been a high priority, but for a king as interested in display and possession as Henry VIII it would have been especially so. And for Henry, Cromwell's command of detail and his energetic transaction of business would have made him a particularly safe pair of hands. This comes across in many of the documents. In August 1532, just three months after he took over, there was a flurry of activity leading up to Henry's second meeting with Francis I, when, as we have seen, a quantity of plate and jewels were sent from the jewel house to

Figure 12.2
Thomas Cromwell, after Hans Holbein the younger, early seventeenth century copy of a work of 1532–33 now in the Frick Collection. The National Portrait Gallery, London.

Cornelis Hayes to be 'broken, transposed, changed, set and new made'.[6] Two months later and just before the meeting, the king consigned a further group of jewels to Cromwell for repair.[7] There was clearly some urgency to this but what is remarkable is not so much how quickly it was done as Cromwell's personal involvement with the job: the king consigned the jewels to him in person at Greenwich and Cromwell returned them in the same way. Each of these was listed with a careful count and identification of all the stones and pearls.[8] Plate too was constantly needing repair or 'amendment'. The clearest picture of this is tacked on to the end of some plate lists from the mid-1530s.[9] These show dozens of repair jobs parcelled out to the royal goldsmiths during the course of the year and plate was sent in from most of the household departments for mending, regilding, reburnishing or having arms changed.

Efficiency apart, Cromwell's influence on the jewel house was most apparent in its financial management, particularly the handling of payments. There was no rigid distinction between expenses paid out by the jewel house and by the Chamber; as Michael Everett points out, 'who paid what, and when, probably depended more on convenience than established procedure [...] Perhaps, as much as anything, it was dependent on who possessed sufficient funds at the required time.'[10] This flexibility is shown very clearly in the warrants for payments to the goldsmiths for new year's gifts in 1533 and 1534.[11] The 1533 warrant stipulated that the total sum of £993 was to be paid out of funds held by Sir Brian Tuke, but the next year it was split between the jewel house and the Chamber, with Cromwell paying £600 19s 1d to John Freman, and Tuke paying the remaining £467 1s 11d to the other three goldsmiths.[12]

Such flexibility was essential, given the amount of refashioning of the royal plate and jewels undertaken during Cromwell's years at the jewel house. But it would be a mistake to attribute the initiation of this process too directly to Cromwell. The king undoubtedly had his own ideas, as did Anne Boleyn. And Holbein's talents as a designer may also have been a stimulus for change. But Cromwell was the man who made it happen. Another catalyst may have been the visit the king paid to the jewel house with Anne Boleyn and the French ambassador in December 1532 (see p. 218).[13] It is not clear what prompted this visit and it is still less clear why, according to Chapuys, Henry then returned just a few days later 'with a small retinue' to inspect it again.[14] Perhaps he was pleased by what he had seen and perhaps this was because Cromwell had reorganised the contents so that they looked more impressive, or orderly, than before. But it might also have been apparent to the king that much of the plate was starting to look decidedly old-fashioned.

Such speculation aside, it seems that over the following year refashioning gathered pace. Cromwell's 'to do list' provides an occasionally tantalising, if abridged, insight into his plans: in December 1533 he makes a note to himself concerning 'the translating, changing and selling certain plate out of the Jewel-house, to be converted into plate of other fashion for the king's use'.[15] It is also clear that Cromwell was much involved in what these 'other fashions' might be, even to the extent of micro-managing certain commissions. In September 1532 he wrote to the king about a new collar, saying, deferentially, that he 'has caused patterns [presumably working drawings or *modelli*] to be made, after the king's device, but has desired the goldsmith not to proceed to the finishing of them till the king's pleasure be further known, for which he will repair to him on Saturday night or Sunday morning'.[16] He adds that he is sending by the bearer the pattern of the king's collar of balases and diamonds 'drawn according to your Grace's first device'. Does this mean that Henry himself had sketched out or indicated what he wanted before the patterns were made? It is very possible, and another letter, written the following day by Cromwell's servant Stephen Vaughan, suggests that the king and Anne Boleyn were both taking a keen interest in what was being made: Vaughan had shown the king 'a draught [sketch] of the fashion of his chain, which he called my lady Marquess to look at, and liked very well'. Henry was looking forward to Cromwell bringing draughts of other jewels but wanted to make sure that not all the jewels were being delivered to the goldsmith at once: '"Yea, but," said his Grace, "he hath not delivered so great a charge unto him at once?"' Vaughan reassured him: 'Not yet; the jewels would be delivered according to Cornelis' [Hayes] need of work, but that he had taken a draught of all.'[17]

A third meeting between Henry and Francis, planned for 1534 but which never actually came to pass, seems to have been yet another catalyst for modernisation. According to Chapuys,

> the king [...] is having a quantity of silver and gold plate of all kinds and forms wrought, at which all the smiths of this city are daily working without daring to undertake any other work. And I am told by a man who has seen the list of the plate, as well as of the persons in France to whom it is destined for presentation, that no less than 12,000 marks weight of it have been commanded.[18]

Administration, patronage and finance all came directly into play with the large-scale procurement exercises that were a regular part of the jewel house's work. These are most revealingly seen in some of the events surrounding ambassadorial gifts. Although very costly, these were not generally of bespoke design and, when properly planned, did not usually run into problems. The long list of plate presented to the noblemen accompanying Anne of Cleves to England in 1539, for example, as far as we know, was all delivered on time.[19] But difficulties sometimes did arise. One such concerned plate for the Scottish ambassadors attending James V's installation by proxy as a knight of the Garter in August 1535. This led to an ill-tempered dispute over who should supply it, which plays out in a three-way correspondence between Cromwell, John Gostwick and Stephen Vaughan. Gostwick was Cromwell's right-hand man and was in charge of the commission, Vaughan was the middleman, and Cromwell needed to be kept informed. Vaughan wrote to Cromwell that

> I gave your letters to Mr Gostwick and John Freman [the goldsmith], telling them what sort of gilt plate it was your pleasure should be given to the ambassadors of Scotland. [But] it seems that Mr Gostwick would prefer some other friend of his to the sale thereof instead of Freman.[20]

This evoked howls of protest from Freman. He thought the job was his and claimed that Cromwell had instructed him already, but Gostwick told Cromwell that he had placed the order elsewhere and 'will deliver it to [the ambassadors] tomorrow'.[21] He adds that 'Freman is very angry because he did not get the making of it; but he would have been too dear'. The preferred supplier was Robert Trappes, who came in at 2d under 5s per oz (perhaps because his plate was second-hand).[22] This was not the first time there had been friction between Gostwick and Freman and the previous October the goldsmith had written direct to Cromwell to complain of Gostwick being 'malicious against him'.[23]

If the problem here was deciding between two willing suppliers, on other occasions it was struggling to find any supplier at all in the time available. Two years after the Scottish incident there was a panic to deliver other diplomatic gifts on time, this time for French ambassadors. On 14 August 1537 Robert Lorde wrote to Cromwell that

> pursuant to your letter received yesterday evening, I went today to all the goldsmiths of London except Bowes and Trappes, who were not in town. Sent for Trappes ten miles out of the city, and of him and Robert à Lathom had such as your lordship wrote for, as near the value as I could get, as you wished them by tomorrow.[24]

Perhaps there was some glitch, however, because three days later Lorde wrote to Cromwell again: he had managed to corral together 1,170 oz of plate at 5s per oz (a total cost of £292 12s 6d). But a sense of the urgency of the situation is conveyed not so much by the letter itself as by its sign-off: '5 a.m. – with speed. Haste post haste'.[25]

The other critically important task of the jewel house, as before, was the procurement of new year's gifts. By Cromwell's time the ceremony had evolved. It was no longer held in the royal bed chamber but in the privy chamber and the cast of givers and receivers had grown. An engaging description of the proceedings on 1 January 1538 has come down to us in a well-known letter from John Husee to his master, Lord Lisle:

> I delivered on New Year's Day your gift to the king [...] and as soon as I was within the chamber of presence [...] my lord Privy Seal [Cromwell] smiled and said to the king's grace 'Here cometh my lord Lisle's man!' and the king spake merrily unto him again, but what his Highness said I cannot tell. So that, after I had done my duty, his Grace received it of me smiling, and thanking your lordship did ask heartily how you and my lady did [...] The king stood leaning against the cupboard, receiving all things; and Mr Tuke at the end of the same cupboard, penning all things that were presented.[26]

This was an informal and intimate gathering, allowing each of the donors the briefest of audiences with their prince, albeit by proxy through their servants, who, like Husee, would be expected to report back exactly what had been seen and been said. Others, such as foreign ambassadors, who normally attended important court ceremonies, were not invited.[27] But it was also an event of major political importance and a barometer of who was in and who was out. The gifts to the king were displayed for others to see and Maria Hayward quotes a document from 1532 recording a payment to the king's carpenters for 'trestles and boards for the king's new year gifts to stand upon but also trestles and boards for the lady marquess of Pembroke's new year gifts likewise to stand upon'.[28]

Brian Tuke's list of 'all things that were presented' that day has not survived. Very few have. Of those that do, the gift rolls of 1534 and 1539 are especially valuable, since they include complete lists of gifts, both given and received.[29] The 1534 list of 'gifts out' is very informative.[30] It includes the names of the recipients, the suppliers (John Freman, Cornelis Hayes, Morgan Wolf, and Thomas Trappes) and the weights and types of plate that were given. In all, there were 197 recipients, ranging from bishops, nobles and ladies of court to minor courtiers and unnamed domestic servants such as 'the king's master cook' and 'the mistress nurse'. The total weight of all the gifts came to 3,778 oz. All of these were charged at a standard rate of 5s 2d an ounce (2d more than in 1513) and cost £1,023 6s 11d altogether. But the work was very unevenly split, with Freman supplying 2,095 oz and Trappes just 139 oz. Quite how these allocations were determined is not clear and they differed from year to year. In 1533, when the king gave a similar quantity of plate, Freman and Hayes each supplied around 1,500 oz. In 1539, when the number of recipients had increased to 252 and the total weight to 5,328 oz, the work was again evenly split between two, this time Hayes and Wolf.[31]

The incoming gifts are in marked contrast to the outgoing ones. They were more varied and, in the case of the 'great', generally more valuable. Thomas Cranmer, the new archbishop of Canterbury, gave a gilt cup weighing 97 oz (but only received a 30 oz cup in return) and the duke of Norfolk gave a pair of pots weighing 224 oz (but received a cup and a cruse of just 43 oz). Some, notably the bishops, gave money and did poorly in the exchange: Winchester gave 100 marks and received a 36 oz cup, while Lincoln gave £40 and received a 29 oz bowl.

Another contrast would have been artistic. The gifts given by the king came in a narrow weight range and, with few exceptions, were of just four types: pots, bowls, cups and 'cruses'. Cruses are not a form we have encountered before and it is not totally clear what they were. The term hardly occurs in the 1521 inventory[32] but over forty appear in 1532. They mostly weighed around ten to fifteen ounces and some are described as having two 'ears', or handles. It is possible that a cup of 1533–34 at Corpus Christi College, Oxford, weighing 13 oz 4 dwt,[33] is the sole survivor of the form (fig. 12.3). In contrast to these, the presents that the king received were much more varied. There were shirts and bonnets, greyhounds and geldings; there were paintings (such as 'a goodly table of Hercules') and there was artistic goldsmiths' work. The duke of Suffolk gave 'a book garnished with gold having therin a clock', the earl of Worcester gave 'a bonnet velvet garnished with goldsmith's work', and Richard Atsill, the king's 'polisher of stones', gave 'a tablet of gold with a devise of Venus and Cupid'. The most spectacular of the incoming presents that year was probably Cromwell's, described as 'a layer of mother of pearl garnished with gold' and weighing 34 oz. This must be the piece more fully described in the 1547 inventory as being enamelled with H and A knit together and with the king's arms on top of the cover.[34]

The 1539 gift roll shows a strengthening of a trend that is already evident in 1534. Some courtiers continued to give plate (notably Cromwell's gift of a gold cup weighing 53¾ oz), but many were moving away from this and, when not giving money, presented luxurious items of clothing instead, such as shirts and handkerchiefs. These were less easy to value than plate but we may safely assume that the shift was not about saving money, or

Figure 12.3
Cruse, London, 1533–34, maker's mark an arbalist (crossbow). Silver gilt. Corpus Christi College, Oxford. By permission of the President and Fellows of Corpus Christi College, Oxford.

Figure 12.4
Henry VIII, Hans Holbein the younger, c. 1537. Museo Nacional Thyssen-Bornemisza, Madrid.

about moving entirely away from precious metal either. For these things were 'garnished with gold', 'wrought with gold and silver' or 'edged with Venice gold' and were costly, as is clear from the gold embroidered collar depicted in Holbein's 1537 portrait of the king in the Thyssen-Bornemisza Collection (fig. 12.4).

A further revealing insight from the list of incoming presents is what was done with them. In 1534 most things, certainly those of precious metal, went in one of three directions. They were sent to the jewel house, they were entrusted to Henry Norris (groom of the stool and 'keeper of the king's usual jewels and money'), or they were retained 'with the king's grace'. And a pattern seems to emerge. Things smacking of jewellery or clothing went to Norris; all the gifts of money stayed 'with the king's grace'; and most of the silver-gilt went to the jewel house. Things of artistic or intellectual interest, such as pictures, Suffolk's gold book with a clock, or Sir William Fitzwilliam's 'compass silver and gilt', tended to stay with the king. As it happens, Cromwell's exotic mother-of-pearl layer did not make the cut and was dispatched to the jewel house, although by the time the 1547 inventory was compiled the layer had found its way back to Whitehall.[35]

From this account of jewel house procurement, the master's powers of patronage as far as goldsmiths were concerned will have emerged very clearly. But these powers were felt, to a lesser extent, on the other side of the equation too. Not all courtiers received new year's gifts and someone had to decide who was in and who was out. Although we have no proof of this, it would seem likely that the master had considerable influence on this matter. That, at least, is the impression we get from a letter written by Sir George Lawson to Cromwell in 1537 to complain that he had always had a new year's gift from the king, but 'this year had none'.[36] On a happier note, it also appears that for those in the master's good books, they could, if they wished, choose what sort of plate they would like to receive (within the permitted weight) and in February 1540 Husee wrote to Lord Lisle that he had heard from the jewel house that he can have his new year's cup 'made according unto your own desire'.[37]

A rather curious and low-level activity of the jewel house that continued throughout the reign was the procurement and distribution of 'cramp rings'. By virtue of being hallowed by the king, these were supposedly invested with a spiritual power to ease various conditions such as birth pains, epilepsy and cramp. They were traditionally blessed on Good Friday and, according to a document of 1521, after the king had 'crept' to the cross before the high altar, 'the master of the jewel house shall be there ready with the cramp rings in a basin or basins of silver'. The hallowing followed a prescribed liturgy, during which the king rubbed the rings between his hands, saying '*sanctifica domine annulos*'.[38] A remarkable image of Mary I performing this office survives in an illuminated prayer book of about 1550 at Westminster Cathedral (fig. 12.5).

Among the many references to cramp rings in the state papers, an exchange between the humanist scholars Thomas Linacre and Guillaume Budé is particularly telling: in June 1518 Linacre sent some rings to Budé in France, 'consecrated by the king against spasms'. Budé replied saying he had distributed them to various women, telling them they were annulets against slander and calumny.[39] Another correspondent wrote from Berwick claiming to have 'relieved a man lying in the falling sickness, in sight of much people' and saying, unsurprisingly, that the rings are 'now in great request'.[40] Many such requests came from abroad and were addressed direct to the king, to Wolsey or to Cromwell. Lady Lisle's correspondence from Calais makes it clear that their distribution was one of the functions of the jewel house. In 1536 her agent wrote to her that he had managed to obtain nine silver rings 'with much ado of John Williams [clerk of the jewel house]. He says he never had so few of gold as this year, as the king had most himself, but next year he will make you amends.'[41] But the clearest indication of the sheer numbers of cramp rings being ordered is the payments to the goldsmiths. For example, in 1521 William Holland received £94 6s 3d for gold and silver cramp rings[42] and in 1542 Cornelis

Figure 12.5
Mary I blessing cramp rings, from a manuscript bound into a prayer book of c. 1550. Westminster Cathedral Treasury (Manuscript TMS 8, fol. 3v).

Hayes was paid for 50 oz of gold cramp rings at 45s 4d the ounce and 140 oz of silver ones at 4s 4d.[43] They presumably did not weigh more than about a third of an ounce each, so there must have been a great many. Nothing that has been clearly identified as a cramp ring has survived so we do not know exactly what they looked like. They were probably of very simple design, such as those placed on a dish in the prayer book image of Mary I.

Cromwell's goldsmiths

The 1530s saw a new generation of up and coming goldsmiths. More than a dozen are mentioned in the state papers during Cromwell's time as master, the most prominent being Cornelis Hayes, Morgan Wolf, John Freman and Robert Trappes. A fifth, Martin Bowes, was arguably the most important of all, but for different reasons and we will turn to him at a later stage.

We know less about Robert Trappes than the others but he is one of the few goldsmiths of the period for whom we have a likeness. His portrait at Goldsmiths' Hall (fig. 12.6) is dated 1554, when he was seventy-five years old and had still another six years to live. There is no hint of the working craftsman in this image; he is depicted as prosperous and richly dressed, wearing gold rings and a chain, and he holds a finely bound prayer book that is partly open, revealing a fragment of text: 'in vayne tak not … name

Figure 12.6
Robert Trappes, Alderman, unknown artist, 1554. Collection of the Goldsmiths' Company, London.

of …', presumably a version of the third commandment, 'Thou shalt take not the name of the Lord thy God in vain.' His prosperity is if anything understated: he had been profitably supplying the Crown since at least 1519 and in the 1541 subsidy roll his estate was valued at the huge sum of 5,000 marks. His nephew, Thomas Trappes, was also one of the jewel house suppliers but he was not nearly so wealthy.

We have considered Cornelis Hayes's status as a settled stranger already (see p. 181), but he had a long career, both before and after his denization in 1523. He was in London by at least 1515, when he was fined by the Goldsmiths' Company for employing a stranger without licence, and he seems to have lived until 1547.[44] His poor start with the company, however, was evidently forgiven and he was admitted to its freedom in 1529, followed eight years later by promotion to the livery and later to the post of renter.[45] By this stage Hayes was prosperous and busy. In 1531 he was employing six apprentices and twelve journeymen and he continued to supply the king with plate up to a year before his death. In 1541 his estate was assessed at £400 and his will includes bequests of 'my lands and houses beyond the sea'.[46] But Hayes seems to have been prone to disputes over money. Several are noted in the court minutes of the Goldsmiths' Company, and he also had a serious run-in with the clerks of the Chamber, which went before the Star Chamber. The story has been told by G. R. Elton.[47] Briefly, Hayes claimed that the clerks had cheated him of part of the money owing to him for the new year's gifts he supplied in 1537. These had cost a total of £766 18s 11d and by the following May he had been paid most of what he was due. But around June or July he claimed to have been defrauded of £100 by being tricked into signing a receipt for the money when he had not actually received it. This was strenuously denied by the Chamber clerks. In Elton's view, he was almost certainly guilty of bringing a false charge, but Hayes enjoyed Cromwell's protection, a factor that probably influenced the council's failure to resolve the matter either way. As a result, Hayes continued in his role as favoured royal goldsmith.[48]

As far as we know, none of Hayes's work has survived. Like the 'feather pots' discussed in Chapter 4, however, it is just possible that a couple of early seventeenth-century objects are in fact copies of earlier ones and give us a hint of the grandeur of court commissions at this time. In 1604, when the newly enthroned James I had to sacrifice some of the most impressive plate from the jewel house as ambassadorial gifts,[49] he presciently commissioned drawings so that replicas that were 'answerable in weight and fashion according to the several patterns' could be made later.[50] The replicas were duly delivered and include a pair of massive water pots that later formed part of a gift to Tsar Mikhail Romanov of Russia (fig. 12.7). These are hallmarked for 1604–05; they weigh a total of 732 oz and stand 64 cm

Figure 12.7
Water pot, London, 1604–05, maker's mark of William Jefferies, possibly a copy of one of about 1530. Silver gilt. Kremlin Armoury Museum, Moscow.

high. They have a somewhat inelegant profile but powerfully modelled dragon spouts and serpent handles and are chased with flame-like ornament and royal emblems.[51] They also have lion thumbpieces which, taken with the spouts, might be taken as allusions to the late Henrician supporters. Amongst the many silver-gilt pots listed in the 1547 inventory is one entry that reads 'two great gilt pots or layers with handles and spouts late made by Cornelius Heyes weighing DCiiij^{xx}ix [689] oz'.[52] The replicas, if that is what they are, are a little over five per cent heavier, close enough to be 'answerable in weight'. Moreover, it is clear from another 1547 entry that dragons were part of Hayes's repertoire, since it describes a pair of bottles incorporating dragons that had been 'bought of Cornelis Hayes' in 1536.[53]

Morgan Wolf (also listed as 'Morgan Fenwolf' and 'Morgan Phelippe alias Wolfe') was Welsh.[54] He was roughly contemporary with Hayes but lived longer, dying in 1552, and towards the end of the reign he eclipsed the latter. The first surviving mention of him as a royal goldsmith is in 1522 when he was one of the suppliers of Katherine of Aragon's new year's gifts.[55] By 1529, at the start of the surviving privy purse expenses accounts, he is described as a 'jeweller' supplying 'Paris work'.[56] But by 1531 he was also providing the king with plate and in 1534 he joined the elite group of goldsmiths suppling new year's gifts. In that year he was the junior partner of the group, supplying a quarter as much as Freman,[57] but by

1540 he had the largest share of all court orders for goldsmiths' work, with annual payments regularly exceeding £1,000. A particularly prestigious order came in 1542 when he was entrusted with providing a new great seal of England (fig. 12.8). These impressive objects, some of which survive from the eighteenth and nineteenth centuries, comprised a pair of silver matrices cut in intaglio with representations of the king on both sides and were used to form the wax seals that were appended to official documents issued in the king's name. The quality of the engraving had to be very high and would have been done by a specialist, such as Henry Coldwell, who was paid for cutting a number of seals around this time. Wolf received £17 8s 4d for the 95 oz of silver used in the seal and the high sum of £40 for making it.[58]

We know nothing of Wolf's business structure and it is probable that, like Amadas, he evolved into more of a manager than a working goldsmith. As a native, there were no restrictions on the size of his workshop or the numbers of apprentices and journeymen he could retain. As a result, we have no knowledge of this, although we do have evidence of his getting one of his suppliers, John Gardiner, into trouble in 1538 by rushing him to finish the crown finial for a royal posset bowl without getting it assayed and marked first.[59]

By the latter part of the reign, however, Wolf had diversified. No longer was he just a supplier of plate and goldsmiths' work on a substantial scale; he was also a minor courtier, described from around 1540 as one of the stewards of the Chamber, and an official in the increasingly important Court of Augmentations. This placed him well to benefit from the redistribution of lands following the dissolution of the monasteries[60] and, unsurprisingly, he rose to become one of the wealthier citizens of London.

We have already encountered John Freman, one of Amadas's former apprentices, who, by his own claim, had been supplying plate to the

Figure 12.8
Engraving of the impression of Henry VIII's third great seal, made by Morgan Wolf in 1542. Illustration for *The Pictorial History of England* (W. & R. Chambers, 1858).

Crown since 1527.[61] But his feud with Gostwick did not seem to do any long-term damage to his standing as a royal goldsmith and he continues to appear in the records as a regular supplier of new year's gifts until 1540.

Quite apart from his official business, Cromwell had dealings with goldsmiths on his own account too. An inventory of his plate taken in 1527 seems modest enough, even though the items are not weighed: seventeen cups of various sorts (including two of mounted glass and coconut), four salts, three mazers, seven pots and twelve spoons.[62] He also had various images and a small quantity of plate 'on pledge'.[63] This was enough to make him concerned about security and in 1528 he asked Steven Vaughan, who was in Antwerp on business, to look out for a suitable strong box. Vaughan wrote to him in August that 'at last I found one much to my pleasure and meet for your purpose [...] Sir, the chest is all iron, of such strength and cleanly making as doth much content my mind.' He goes on to say that, although not cheap at eight Flemish pounds, it will undoubtedly hold its value, 'besides the pleasure and quietness which you shall have wheresoever you go, remembering such money, jewels, plate and other thing whatsoever by you included in the same, to rest in such surety and safeguard as by you shall be desired'.[64] It is not clear whether Cromwell did eventually snap up this tempting offer, though from a further letter written in December it is evident that he was not rushing to do so. Perhaps he suspected that Vaughan was going to make too much out of the deal himself.

Cromwell did well, not only through the 'usual profits' of his various offices, but also through bribes. A number of quite blatant bribes appear in the records, such as when the keeper of the wardrobe offered him a collar worth £100,[65] or when in 1537 Humphrey Monmouth, alderman of London, offered Cromwell and Lord Chancellor Audley 'each a standing cup of silver worth £10' to ensure the appointment of evangelical preachers who would 'preach sermons quietly to the laud of God, the setting forth of the king's godly purposes, and the extinction of the feigned power of the bishop of Rome'.[66] Clearly it helped to offer the king's councillors a *douceur*, even when the request was entirely in line with official policy.

Plate also entered Cromwell's life – and house – as security for loans. There is a hint of this in his 1527 inventory, but a letter from Lord Leonard Grey of July 1533 suggests that by then this had become part of Cromwell's regular business dealings. The letter shows that the honour of accompanying the king to the 1532 summit in France was not without cost and he had to borrow in order to equip himself properly. For the loan he had turned to Cromwell, securing it on plate. By the time of the letter everything has been repaid and his plate returned, but there had been a clerical error: 'Cromwell's servant Williamson has sent a pair of flagons that were not Lord Leonard's, and he wishes the right pair to be given to his chaplain, Sir William.'[67] So presumably Grey's were not the only flagons Cromwell was holding as security or such a muddle would not have occurred.

Cromwell's successors

Between Cromwell's death and the end of the reign the jewel house had three masters, John Williams, Anthony Rous and Anthony Aucher. All three were Cromwell protégés, but none had the latter's administrative genius and complaints about their accounting were levelled at both Williams and Aucher. Cromwell himself retained the title of master until his death, but continued to add other roles to his portfolio in the meantime, becoming chancellor of the exchequer in 1533, master of the rolls in 1534 and lord privy seal in 1536. In April of that year, perhaps as a result of these pressures, he took a step back in the jewel house, allowing his deputy, Williams, to share the title of master.[68]

Williams had followed Thomas Wyatt as clerk of the jewels in 1531 on a salary of twenty marks[69] and his promotion to co-master would have freed Cromwell from the department's administrative burden, while presumably allowing the other to share the master's £50 salary and the 'usual profits'. On Cromwell's death in 1540, Williams became sole master and a commission was issued to survey and view the king's jewel house 'to certify all jewels and plate [...] delivered to Sir John Williams [...] to the king's use'.[70] Such a commission was (or should have been) normal. But it contains a hint of suspicion by adding that the commissioners 'have power to peruse such accounts and to examine the persons who shall have made such delivery etc and to make process against them under the privy seal'. Presumably the commission was never acted upon because in May 1546 Williams faced a privy council enquiry into his management, when it was noted that no proper survey had been made since Cromwell's day.[71] By then he had moved on, surrendering the mastership to Rous in 1544 and becoming treasurer of the Court of Augmentations. In some ways this move was logical. The court, as we shall see in the next chapter, was set up to administer the influx of assets from the dissolution of the monasteries and its huge liquidity meant that it assumed responsibility for a growing proportion of royal expenditure, including payments for new plate. Towards the end of the reign the accounts of the court, like those of the Chamber earlier, show many payments, both directly to royal goldsmiths and also to the clerks and master of the jewel house.[72]

Anthony Rous, former servant of Cromwell and former comptroller of Calais, was only in the post for a year, his promising career being cut short by his early death, and he was succeeded by Anthony Aucher. Aucher was entirely on the make; he never rendered accounts as master of the jewel house and the historian J. D. Alsop commented that 'in an era of laxity in fiscal accounting Aucher's activities were viewed as unprecedented'.[73]

The mint

The jewel house and the mint were closely related. Just a few yards apart within the precincts of the Tower (fig. 2.2), both belonged to the Crown, both worked with precious metals, and the two had officials in common. There was a reciprocal relationship between them too. In conditions of economic and political stability the jewel house could build up its resources, but in less settled times they could be drawn on to feed the mint. And their purposes were complementary: the holdings of the jewel house supported the regime's prestige and reputation, while the mint provided the Crown with specie to conduct its business as well as facilitating trade in general.

At the head of the mint was the master, whose subordinates included the clerk, comptroller and assayer, and the graver of dies. Some of these positions were sinecures, held by courtiers in plurality with other titles. Lord Mountjoy, also treasurer to Katherine of Aragon, was master for much of the reign, from 1509 to 1533; Sir Henry Wyatt, master of the jewels from 1488, was appointed clerk of the mint in the same year and comptroller and assayer in 1495; and Henry Norris, later groom of the stool, was appointed graver in 1519 in succession to Sir John Sharpe.[74] But neither would ever have picked up an engraving tool; the real work was done by deputies, many of whom were goldsmiths. Robert Amadas, Ralph Rowlett and Martin Bowes were all goldsmiths and served as deputies to Lord Mountjoy.

The deputy system had its advantages, certainly from the master's point of view, since he could collect his salary and his share of the profits without having any routine involvement with the administration. But it depended on trust, without which ugly situations could develop. Mountjoy had appointed Amadas and Rowlett as his deputies and Amadas, in turn, had made Bowes *his* deputy, and when Mountjoy accused the deputies of taking excessive profits at his expense, all three were named. The deputies faced some serious charges: that they were slow at paying for bullion, that their production standards were sloppy, that they did not pay fair prices for foreign coin, and that they 'refuse controlment'.[75] In the end the commission found in Mountjoy's favour and the deputies were replaced, but Bowes and Rowlett got their revenge when Mountjoy died and they were both reinstated. Once again, this outcome may have been influenced by Cromwell, who had been bribed by Bowes with a £30 gold chain 'if his mastership will solicit the king for [them] in this matter'.[76]

The symbiotic relationship between the mint and the jewel house is well illustrated by the commission 'to survey the king's plate and jewels', drawn up in 1546 after Anthony Aucher's appointment as master of the Jewels. The commissioners were to survey

> not only the jewels and plate in the said office [...] but also all that has been in the keeping of Sir John Williams since his entry into the office, [by confiscation, voluntary surrender or gift]; and also all money coming of the coinage of plate delivered to Sir Martin Bowes, then master of the mint, and other goldsmiths, and afterwards redelivered to Sir John Williams in ready money.[77]

In other words, noting that no inventory had been taken since Williams's appointment, it required not only a list but a complete audit of all movement of plate and jewels, drawing on the now lost books of *infra* and *extra*. Of particular interest was a complete picture of the plate sent from the jewel house to the mint. This was sometimes necessary, especially at times of war or national emergency. Royal plate was sent to the mint in 1516, and in 1523, shortly after the outbreak of hostilities with France, £700 worth of chains and plate were taken across the inner ward to the mint.[78] At Easter in 1533 'a mass of vessels', many damaged ex-Wolsey pieces, were ordered to be broken and melted down.[79] The most dramatic of these movements, however, was occasioned by the so called Pilgrimage of Grace of 1536. This rebellion erupted quite suddenly in the north of England, partly triggered by the start of the dissolution of the monasteries. Several thousand disaffected people, poorly armed but marching towards London, presented an alarming threat requiring immediate counter-measures. Troops, ordnance and money had to be raised in very short order and the most obvious way to do that was to draw on the reserves of the jewel house. Events moved quickly and there was a flurry of correspondence between Cromwell, the jewel house and the mint about how to produce and deliver the money as soon as possible. On 9 October it was proposed that 'the king's treasure [money] for safety should come [...] with the ordnance from the Tower, secretly, Roke and others attending to it'.[80] The cash requirement was immense: on 11 October Gostwick wrote from Huntingdon that he had 'in money £8,700'. But this was not enough and specie was running out. A week later Wriothesley, the king's secretary, wrote to Cromwell from

Windsor that 'the king orders you to dispatch to Master Gostwick at least 20,000 marks [£13,333]' for one month's wages. Furthermore, that 'you shall promise them more money shortly after, for which you shall make shift to the utmost, coining plate from the jewel house'.[81]

This, in theory, was exactly the sort of situation for which its resources existed and Cromwell knew it. But he also knew that he needed to consult the king before deciding what should be melted. Wriothesley reassured the king 'that you [Cromwell] will not meddle with his plate till you came',[82] but after this consultation had taken place an enormous swathe of plate was conveyed to the mint: 4,128 oz of gold and 42,943 oz of silver, raising a total of £17,008 13s 2d. Of this, 353 oz of gold and 10,745 oz of silver had conveniently been provided by the recently deceased dowager princess and duke of Richmond, and the very much alive but dispossessed Princess Mary. But the rest came from the existing holdings of the jewel house.[83] Since the total contents of the 1532 jewel house had come to a little under 8,000 oz of gold (including the regalia) and about 120,000 oz of silver, this must have made a considerable dent in its holdings, especially the gold.

The coinage

The story of the coinage during the early Tudor period is complicated and of limited relevance to our theme. It is, however, worth telling in outline because of its bearing on the mint itself, on the jewel house and on the Goldsmiths' Company. Silver coinage had long been made to the same sterling standard as plate (92.5 per cent pure) and the two were directly transferable. With gold the situation was more complicated. At the start of the reign the standard for gold coinage was just over 23 carat, slipping in stages to about 20 carat by its end.[84] But gold plate was made to a lower fineness and from 1478 until 1576 was held at 18 carat (75 per cent).[85] Coins could therefore easily be recycled into plate by adding alloy to the melt and when Thomas Wolsey ordered a gold cup from Robert Amadas, for example, he supplied the bullion in the form of gold coins, to which the goldsmith would have added alloy.[86] But making coin from plate required an intervening refining process which added to the cost.

Henry VII favoured gold coinage. He used it to promote his reputation at home and abroad, and introduced a number of new coins, the most important of which was the sovereign (fig. 12.9). First produced in 1489, this was worth a nominal one pound; it was the largest domination English coin yet made and was very beautiful. The obverse showed the enthroned monarch wearing a closed crown imperial and the reverse the royal arms superimposed on a Tudor rose; its purity of metal, its quality of design

Figure 12.9 Gold sovereign, London, 1485–90. British Museum, London.

and its iconography with the crown imperial were all intended to send a clear message about the standing of the new regime.

Reputation had to be balanced against more practical considerations, however, and the high bullion value of English coins relative to their face value and relative to those of other countries led to them being hoarded or drifting abroad, 'bad money driving out good'. Wolsey attempted to address the negative impact of this imbalance on trade by reducing the fineness of gold coins to 22 carat and marginally reducing their weight too.[87] In 1526 a proclamation was issued, raising their face value by 10 per cent (making a sovereign now worth 22s). But the measure failed to make sufficient impact and further revaluations followed. At the end of 1529 Chapuys summed up the dilemma, writing

> there seems to be a scarcity of gold in the kingdom [and] they want to make a law that no payment in that specie be made to foreigners, and that no Englishman leaving this country be allowed to carry away gold or silver of more value than two crowns, which seems to me to be the best expedient that could be invented to drive away foreigners from this island, and put a stop to trade.[88]

Mixed though the results of these revaluations were, they laid the ground for the catastrophic policy of debasement that plagued the last years of the reign. This appears to have been championed by none other than Martin Bowes[89] and was one of the most disastrous monetary experiments the realm had ever seen. Certain people, most notably the king and the mint masters themselves, did very well out it, but for most it led to a spiralling loss of confidence that had to be expensively redressed in later decades. The programme started around 1542. The king was preparing for war and needed a great deal of money; a loan scheme was promoted in which 'faithful subjects' turned in plate at official rates of 45s per oz for gold, 4s 2d for silver-gilt, and 3s 8d for parcel-gilt and silver.[90] But the result was disappointing and other means of raising money had to be devised. Debasement was an excellent way of generating it out of thin air. It required several measures. The first was for the mint to increase the price offered for bullion (plate or old coins) in order to draw in precious metal. Accordingly, the price was raised to 48s per oz for gold and 4s for silver. In 1545 it was raised again, to 50s and 4s 8d respectively; by the following March silver had reached 5s per oz and in 1547 it stood at 5s 2d. As a result, gold and silver plate flooded into the mint and in 1544–45 new coinage was produced with a face value of £812,000.[91] But the incoming bullion was actually worth much less than that and the difference was made up by dramatically increasing the impurities and reducing the weight of the new coinage.

The twist to the process was that the mint had only one way of paying for the bullion: with new, debased coins, and the trick was to pass the new on as quickly as possible, before it became common knowledge that they were worth even less than the previous issue. This harvest could not go on forever, however, and once confidence had been lost, the supply of bullion dried up. But that was into the next reign. Nevertheless, as a means of raising money for the Crown it was remarkably effective. The cost of Henry's late French and Scottish wars has been estimated at £3.5 million, around £1.27 million of which was raised by the debasement programme.[92]

The implications of all this for plate must have been very considerable. First, although no estimates exist, far less wealth across the land was held in the form of plate by the end of the reign than at its start (in 1545 Wriothesley wrote to the council that 'the plate of this realm [is] molten and coined')[93] and the hugely greater rarity of surviving plate from before about 1560 than after must be a distant echo of the great coining. Nor was the jewel house immune to this destruction. Between 1542 and 1544 the king sent some 72,000 oz of his own plate to the mint[94] and in 1544–46 a further 4,900 oz were sent to the mint from Whitehall Palace.[95] Secondly, the scale of the meltdown must have been reflected in a decline in business for most plate workers. Direct evidence for this is thin but may have been reflected in a drive against stranger goldsmiths in 1546.[96] Thirdly, debasement destroyed the traditional equivalence of silver plate and coin: for not only would specie need re-refining to bring it up to plate-working standard, but since there was now a significant gap between its face value and its intrinsic value, it would not have been economic to use it. Bullion would have to come from other sources, such as mining.[97] But this did not easily make up the shortage. Nor was it a peculiarly English problem and in December 1545 one of the king's councillors. William Paget, who had ordered some plate for himself in Antwerp, was told by his agent that 'the difficulty is in lack of silver, which cannot be had here for money'.[98]

Ultimately, there were only three classes of outright gainers from the debasement programme; one was those who got in early and managed to pass on their newly minted coins before their lower value was recognised, the others were the king and the mint masters. In theory the mint had always generated profit for the Crown. The face value of a coin was marginally more than its bullion value, because it included the cost and profit of making it. Traditionally, the king's share of this had been very modest, but for the mint master (or his deputies) it was much larger. In the year up to September 1509, for example, the king received £217 from the mint and Mountjoy, the master, just £48, but his deputies, the goldsmiths Robert Fenrother and William Rede, received £642.[99] Debasement changed all this and it is thought that the king's profit after just ten months of debasement totalled £36,000.[100] On this basis, even if the deputies' rate had been adjusted downwards by this time, their profits must have been huge. Almost everyone else was a loser, including, it seems, the Goldsmiths' Company.

The Goldsmiths' Company

The third side of this symbiotic triangle was the Worshipful Company of Goldsmiths. Goldsmiths' Hall was situated – as it still is – at the west end of the City, close to St Paul's Cathedral, and its physical distance from the Tower sat well with its role as an independent adjudicator of plate and coinage (fig. 12.10).

The Goldsmiths' Company is one of the ancient trade guilds of London. Later known as livery companies, these originated, in some cases, even before the Norman Conquest. But their most vigorous period of expansion, when they evolved into something like their modern form, was between about 1250 and 1500. During this period around sixty of today's 110 companies were established in one form or another. Livery companies were essentially membership bodies that regulated their trade and its practitioners. Many were established as religious fraternities that looked to the spiritual and human welfare of their members. But an essential role was the promotion and regulation of their trade. They were quick to discipline apprentices or masters who broke the rules or who brought the trade into disrepute and they took a keen interest in controlling prices and the quality of merchandise.

Because plate was money, the Goldsmiths' Company's interest in quality focused primarily on ensuring that anything offered for sale was of lawful

Figure 12.10 Map of London, Georg Braun and Frans Hogenberg, 1572. Engraving. British Library (Maps Crace Port.1.12).

alloy. Workmanship could be judged by eye but the purity of the metal, on which its recoverable value depended, could not and had to be taken on trust unless verified by some means. There were two such means. The normal method, known as the touchstone test, is described by John Forbes:

> The gold or silver article was rubbed on a smooth black stone to produce a narrow streak of the metal. Then a similar streak was made alongside, using an alloy of known purity, called a touch-needle. The colours of the two streaks were compared. Quite small differences could be detected and in this way it was possible to determine whether the article was up to the standard of the touch-needle.[101]

A more accurate test, known as cupellation or fire assay, involved taking a small scraping of metal from the object, accurately weighing it and wrapping it in a small sheet of lead foil before putting in a 'cupel' or vessel made of bone ash and placing the package in the fire. As the metals melted the base metals were absorbed into the bone ash, leaving the silver or gold unabsorbed. Comparing the weight of the original sample with what was left after cooling allowed the purity of the alloy to be determined.

The lawful standards of gold and silver plate were set by statute, but the fraudulent sale of substandard plate was an endemic problem, an ingenious solution to which was Edward I's decree of 1300, which charged the Goldsmiths' Company with the independent testing ('assay') of all gold and silver wares 'set for sale' and striking them with the mark of a leopard's head if found to be of the correct standard. This was the origin of 'hallmarking', known as such because the marks were struck at Goldsmiths' Hall. Subsequent refinements to the system led to the gradual evolution of the modern hallmarking system. The company's status as a 'regulator' was strengthened by its 1327 royal charter, which formally vested it with powers, such as the right to search the premises of goldsmiths suspected of wrong-doing, even if they were not members of the company. This was valuable, since, under statute, substandard wares were forfeit, with the proceeds being split between the company and the Crown.[102]

The expertise of the company's members in all matters to do with precious metals led to it becoming more widely consulted, its most important role outside the trade being to test the coinage of the realm. Maintaining confidence in that was at least as important as it was for plate. But coins could not be hallmarked, so a system evolved in which a representative sample of newly minted coins were formally assayed and verified. The so-called trial of the pyx (named from the 'pyx', or box, of sample coins set aside during manufacture) is first recorded in 1279.[103] This was (and remains to this day) a judicial trial, in which a representative sample of the coinage was tested to check that it was of the correct alloy and weight. During the reign of Henry VIII the trial was held at the exchequer at Westminster Hall. Several trials are recorded in the state papers and were attended by some of the greatest in the land. That in April 1527 was held in the presence of Wolsey (as lord chancellor), the bishops of London and Ely and several senior members of the nobility and judiciary, including the chief justice of the king's bench, together with the chief baron of the exchequer.[104] There is no reference in the papers to the role of goldsmiths on these occasions but we may assume they were on hand to provide the technical expertise for the assay. At around this time (if not earlier) the proceedings were enhanced by a formally constituted jury drawn from the members of the Goldsmiths' Company, in effect, the precursor of a modern 'expert jury'. In 1527 or 1528, for example, this comprised the four wardens and sixteen others, all of whom were members of the company.[105]

The Goldsmiths' Company was chosen not only for its expertise but for its independence from the mint. In terms of personnel, however, the senior members of the company were part of a complex web that bound the three bodies – jewel house, mint and company – together in a way that suggests anything but independence. Take, for example, Sir Martin Bowes (fig. 12.11), who was a crucial link between the mint, the company and the Crown. Apprenticed to Robert Amadas in 1513, he advanced through the ranks of the Goldsmiths' Company, becoming a warden in

Figure 12.11
Sir Martin Bowes, unknown artist, 1566. Collection of the Goldsmiths' Company, London.

1532 and serving three times as prime warden between 1537 and the end of the reign (and fifteen times in all by the end of his life in 1566). But by 1532 he had already been a deputy at the mint for six years and by the time he first became prime warden he was a royal goldsmith too.[106] By 1541 he was a wealthy man and in that year his estate was valued at 5,000 marks.[107] But this was as nothing compared with the wealth he amassed during the debasement and a 1551 commission of enquiry into his management of the mint ruled that he had defrauded the Crown of nearly £30,000.[108] But that was all later; in the 1540s his reputation was very high and in 1545 he added another important string to his bow, becoming mayor of London. It was probably these connections that account for him effectively becoming the company's chief negotiator in sensitive dealings with the king.

In terms of the status of the top members of the company, Bowes was part of a pattern and as the late T. F. Reddaway pointed out, in the early sixteenth century the Goldsmiths' Company was ruled by a small group of powerful and wealthy goldsmith-merchants:

> In the twenty-two years 1507–28, there were only eight different prime wardens. [Thomas] Exmew held the position six times, [Henry] Worley thrice, and [Robert] Fenrother and [John] Mundy four times each. [Robert] Amadas, prevented by his place as a royal servant from

> becoming an alderman, held it only once and [Ralph] Rowlett, though twice a junior warden, did not become prime warden until 1529, but their weight and influence were there.[109]

Several of these also had controlling positions at the mint and, although the overlap is not complete, either ran the jewel house or were prominent suppliers to it. Nor were the connections between the company and the mint restricted to the upper echelons and when the mint was under pressure to increase production the goldsmiths' trade was able to provide a pool of labour to help with refining, weighing and striking. Some, at least, from this pool were likely to have been members of the company.

The company's approach towards higher authority ranged from cooperative to abjectly submissive. At the cooperative end of the spectrum, the company had little choice but to join the other livery companies of the City in submitting to an onerous forced loan of £2,000 in 1522, resulting in the sacrifice of almost all their store of plate.[110] Less onerously, the beadles regularly acted as the king's eyes and ears and in 1542, for example, received a reward 'for their pains in giving warning to the goldsmiths when plate hath been stolen out of the king's and prince's courts'.[111] On other occasions the wardens found themselves bending to Cromwell's will by granting leases of company property to his clients or by acquiescing in Hans of Antwerp's application to join the freedom, and it is a measure of the usefulness of the relationship that two of the yeomen of the jewel house, Robert Draper and John Hallile, both sought, and gained, membership of the company.[112]

Relations were not always so convivial, however. The issue of stranger artificers and the company's protectionist instincts were a potential cause of friction with the king, who gave many immigrant craftsmen licence to operate and to employ compatriot journeymen contrary to normal rules.[113] We have seen, for example, how on one occasion the company overstepped the mark in its diligent war on strangers by 'carrying away' the work of a stranger goldsmith who was working directly for the king within the precincts of Whitehall Palace and was 'roundly admonished' as a result (see p. 183).

The lowest point in relations came towards the end of the reign, when, in 1544, the company was forced to surrender its royal charter. Officially, this was related to charges concerning 'alloying' of gold and silver, but it is more likely to have been due to tensions arising from debasement. Whatever the cause, the company suffered the indignity of having direct rule imposed upon it and having two royal appointees put in place to run the assay office, a situation that continued until after the king's death. It has always been assumed that this dangerous situation is related, in a way

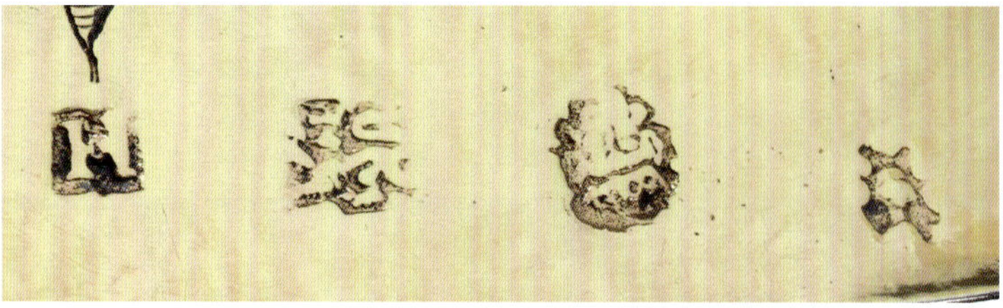

Figure 12.12
London hallmarks for 1545–46, showing the crowned lion passant, taken from a standing cup in the collection of the Goldsmiths' Company, London.

that is not entirely clear, to the introduction of a fourth hallmark that first appeared that year. This mark, formed as a lion passant depicted exactly as it appears on the royal arms but, from 1544 until the end of the reign, with a crown on its head, is difficult to interpret as anything other than a clear statement of royal authority (fig. 12.12).

All this was a far cry from the moment when Anne of Cleves arrived at Blackheath four years earlier and the Goldsmiths were permitted to take part in the reception procession that rode out to meet her, including a delegation of assistants in black livery and gold chains and which included three of the royal goldsmiths, Morgan Wolf, Cornelis Hayes and Fabyan Wethers.

Thirteen Dissolution and Augmentation

The changes that took place in England in the two decades from 1534 were arguably more profound and far-reaching than in any other comparable period in English history. During that time England's ancient ties with Rome were severed, its ways of worship fundamentally changed, and a patchwork of hundreds of religious communities that extended across the country erased. The last of these – the dissolution of the monasteries – was justified by the authorities as a purge of abuse and hypocrisy, but morphed into a smoke screen for the greatest asset grab of the reign.

This chapter is not directly concerned with the break with Rome, nor with the events that gave rise to it, or the royal take-over of the Church that followed it. But the events on which it *is* focused – the confiscation of the vast collective wealth of the monasteries – cannot be entirely disentangled from them. Henry's failure to secure papal consent to the annulment of his marriage led directly to the break and to his own self-elevation as 'Supreme Head of the Church in England'. This, together with his marriage to Anne Boleyn, isolated him on the international stage and raised the threat of invasion by Katherine of Aragon's nephew, Charles V. Such a threat called for a massive and costly strengthening of coastal defences; separately, it was also a contributing factor to the Pilgrimage of Grace. All these things created an urgent need for money, part of which influenced the course of the dissolution itself.

As this chapter opens, Henry was still a loyal son of the Church, basking in his newly awarded title of *Fidei defensor*. In 1524 the recently elected Clement VII sent him another golden rose. It was received with great pomp and ceremony and when, two years later, St Peter's basilica in Rome was desecrated by part of the imperial forces Henry immediately responded by sending Clement 2,500 ducats in aid.[1] The first cracks in the relationship appeared in 1529 with Cardinal Campeggio's ill-starred mission to London to settle the divorce. This was not a success from Henry's point of view and Wolsey rightly foresaw that the long-term consequence of its failure would be that 'the authority of the See Apostolic in this kingdom will be annihilated'.[2] But for the time being Henry could do nothing but suppress his frustrations and keep hoping for the best. Campeggio returned to Rome weighed down with gifts and when the papal nuncio visited England on other business in 1533 the king spoke to him in 'fair and general terms [...] and gave him a cup worth 300 crowns'.[3]

Those opening cracks were systematically widened in the early 1530s by a programme of legislation that moved inexorably towards separation from Rome and suppression of ecclesiastical independence: the offence of *praemunire*, obedience to a foreign power within the realm, was extended from Wolsey alone to the entire Church, which was fined the massive sum of £100,000. This was followed in 1531 by the termination of regular payments to Rome ('annates') and in 1534 by the Act of Supremacy. Subsequent legislation took on an increasingly theological aspect and an act of 1536 not only required that every parish church be provided with an English bible, but also prohibited the display of images and the worship of saints, the first step towards wholesale iconoclasm that continued through the reign of Edward VI.

Dissolution and confiscation

The dissolution of the monasteries was entirely separate from the supremacy and would arguably have taken place anyway (though doubtless differently) if the break with Rome and the subsequent financial crisis had never happened. Monasteries had existed in England for centuries. They provided employment and many were centres of pilgrimage, fuelling local economies. But they were also vulnerable. In the early sixteenth century the number of men and women in religious communities was in decline; their great scholarly and spiritual traditions belonged largely to the past and many houses were impoverished. Long before they were faced with dissolution and confiscation, they met their financial problems in whatever ways they could and as the commissioners conducted their survey of monastic assets they found that certain abbeys had pawned some of their treasures. Visiting Northampton in 1538, they found that 'a piece of St Andrew's finger, covered with silver, [is] now laid to pledge to one of the town for £40'. They decided not to redeem it, presumably because they did not think it worth the money.[4]

To add to the mix, monasteries were also accused of moral decay and corruption, and in 1520 Bishop Fox of Winchester complained to Wolsey that the clergy in his diocese 'and particularly [...] the monks, [are] so depraved, so licentious and corrupt, that we despaired of any perfect reformation'.[5] This was a familiar complaint. Henry VII had used similar arguments to close several inadequate monasteries, and Wolsey would do the same when he sought to divert funds towards his new colleges in Oxford and Ipswich.

There was, therefore, nothing radical in the idea of a partial dissolution. Up until her dramatic fall from grace in 1536 Anne Boleyn had supported a policy of reform that would have transformed, rather than destroyed, many of the religious houses. Following Wolsey's precedent, they would have been converted into educational foundations. It was an enlightened proposal, but it was radically subverted by the king's need for money. Money on the scale he needed was not easy to raise through loans or taxes and other sources had to be tapped. One such, if only he could get his hands on it, was the enormous wealth of the Church. The 800 or so religious houses across the country were collectively one of the greatest landowners in England; they had a vast stock of buildings and possessed astonishingly rich moveable assets, including plate and jewels, bronze (mainly from bells) and lead (moveable once detached from their roofs).

It was Cromwell's great achievement to provide the legal framework for the suppression of the monasteries and the administrative machinery to take possession of their assets. He is often credited with planting this idea in the king's mind, although it is more likely that the immediate precedent for confiscation was provided by Francis I. In 1515 the newly crowned French king needed money and flexed his muscles by seizing a quantity of plate from various abbeys and priories.[6] This was just the start. Further demands were made of the Church and in 1522 he ordered the stripping of the shrine of St Martin of Tours and the melting of (presumably large) silver figures of the twelve apostles. A pious Henry VIII, ironically, was outraged by this assault on the Church and when he dispatched ambassadors to Charles V he instructed them to say that Francis was 'provoking God's indignation against him by such sacrilege'.[7] But by now Francis realised that moveable church assets were there for the taking. In 1528 it was reported to Henry that he was 'extracting from the clergy a third of their goods'[8] and a year later Francis was reported as saying that he could easily raise the ransom to secure his sons' release from captivity 'by taking a chalice from every church in his kingdom'.[9] Whatever else may be said about Henry's policy of church plunder, therefore, it was not original.

The huge *praemunire* fine led Chapuys to speculate that 'the English clergy will be obliged to sell the very chalices and shrines of their churches, as otherwise they would be quite unable to pay one fourth of that sum'.[10] In fact it did not, at that stage, come to that and the payments were spread over several years. Meanwhile, the monasteries and their assets had a reprieve. It took time for the legislative blocks to be put in place, but once done it was possible to embark on a systematic process of attrition. Tacked on to the clause requiring abbots and senior clerics to affirm their assent to the Act of Supremacy was a further obligation that 'each house must be obliged to show their gold, silver and other moveable goods, and deliver an inventory of them'.[11] This was confirmed in the instructions issued to the royal commissioners in 1536, that when visiting the monasteries they should 'make an inventory with the governor of all ornaments, plate [and] jewels [...] and put the whole in safe keeping'.[12]

Corruption was a convenient ground for suppression and the commissioners were encouraged not to hold back in reporting any excesses they encountered. A prime target was so-called holy relics. In some cases these are simply listed without comment, their spuriousness being taken as self-evident. At Bury St Edmunds, for example, they had the shirt of St Edmund, the blood of Christ, parts of the Holy Cross, one of the stones with which St Stephen was stoned and the coals with which St Lawrence was roasted (an interesting survival!).[13] At others the fraudulent use of relics and images to fleece credulous pilgrims aroused a mixture of incredulity and indignation. At Bath, Richard Layton came across the chains of St Peter 'which women put about them at the time of their delivery'. Layton commented that 'it is a very mockery and a great abuse that the prior should carry it on Lammas Day in a basin of silver in procession, and every monk kiss it after the Gospel with great solemnity'.[14] Among the most offensive images was that at Boxley in Kent, where, on

> plucking down the images, [they] found, in the Roode of Grace, which has been held in great veneration, certain engines and old wire, with old rotten sticks in the back of the same, which caused the eyes to move and stir in the head thereof, like unto a lively thing, and also the nether lip in likewise to move as though it should speak.

It goes on, 'considering that the people of Kent had in time past a great devotion to the image' they unveiled the deceit in public at Maidstone market where the people held it in 'wondrous detestation and hatred'.[15] Not even the relics of St Thomas Becket were entirely above suspicion and, according to Wriothesley's *Chronicle*, when they opened the saint's tomb 'they found his head whole with the bones, which had a wound in the skull'. This would have been unsurprising, were it not for the fact that 'the monks had closed another skull in silver richly, for people to offer to, which they said was St Thomas skull'.[16]

But the issues at stake were often more entangled than this, as is shown by the case of the image of Our Lady at Worcester. To feed the royal coffers and to save the people from idolatry, the much-venerated image was stripped of its precious jewels and goldsmiths' work in 1537, probably leaving the wooden sculpture in its original, pre-embellished state. But its impoverished appearance would have dented a valuable income stream for the church, leading one enterprising cleric to try to save the situation by kissing its feet and turning to the people saying 'ye that be disposed to offer, the figure is no worse than it was before'.[17] On one side of the equation, therefore, was valuable income dressed up as meritorious offering, and on the other legalised theft dressed up as reform.

The commissioners (or some of them) were keen that their primary motive should be seen as evangelical zeal, and they went to extraordinary lengths to conceal their rapacity, writing from Winchester in 1538 that 'we intend both at Hyde and St Mary's to sweep away all the rotten bones that be called relics; which we may not omit lest it be thought we came more for the treasure than for avoiding the abomination of idolatry'.[18] But this was not just a smoke screen and many references to fake relics suggest genuine indignation, such as when the bishop of St David's wrote of 'two heads of silver plate enclosing two rotten skulls and a worm-eaten book covered with silver plate'.[19] They were also affronted at the income these so-called relics generated and, in dispatching 'the holiest relic in all North Wales' to Cromwell, Richard Yngworth, bishop of Dover, was clearly delighted that he had thereby deprived the friars of Bangor of 'twenty marks a year'.[20]

Thoroughness verged on fanaticism, particularly towards the end of the dissolution as hearts became hardened. When Dr John London took away the image of Our Lady at Caversham in 1538 his account betrays vindictiveness as well as efficiency:

> [The image] is plated over with silver. I have put it in a chest fast locked and nailed up, and will send it by the next barge to London. I have pulled down the place she stood in, with the lights, shrouds, crutches, images of wax etc about the chapel and defaced the same thoroughly.[21]

Despite all this, the main focus of the commissioners' work was on the assessment, seizure and processing of the moveable (or strippable) assets: plate and jewels, lead and bells. The systematic dissolution started with the poorer houses, defined as those with an annual income of £200 or less, and the harvest of plate from these was predictably modest. Later, at the friaries, the spoils could be disappointing too. In 1538 Yngworth described Greyfriars in Bridgnorth as the poorest house he had seen,[22] where the plate consisted of a chalice and six spoons, weighing in total just 14½ oz.[23] At many of these smaller houses the roof lead and bells were worth more than the plate. At Newsham in Lincolnshire they were valued at £462 10s but the plate at just £115,[24] and at Leicester (where Wolsey had died) the lead came to £1,000 but the plate to just £190.[25] We do not know about the plate at Jervaulx, in Yorkshire, but there was a huge quantity of lead and in May 1537 the duke of Norfolk wrote to the king saying

> it has a barn all covered with lead, the longest, widest, and deepest that ever I saw. The whole lead cannot be worth less than £3,000 or £4,000, and standing near the sea it can easily be carried away.[26]

The larger and wealthier houses yielded much more plate, often in excess of 500 oz, a large part of which was domestic plate from the abbots' or priors' lodgings. Worcester Priory, for example, had twelve great bowls, forty-two spoons, ten mazers, two salts and 'a horn for the wassail, with a cover garnished with silver and stones'.[27] The holdings of the greatest houses were very rich indeed. When Erasmus visited Canterbury and Walsingham he wrote that 'you would say that Midas and Croesus were beggars if you saw that vast assemblage',[28] and in 1535 one of Cromwell's correspondents described Christ Church in Canterbury as 'the richest house in jewels, plate and money in England'. He also said that he 'knows a person who can show Cromwell's visitors, when they come, where the secret treasure is kept'.[29]

The purpose of the visitations was, of course, widely known; rumours quickly spread and those houses further down the list had plenty of time to dispose of their plate surreptitiously rather than handing it over to the commissioners. After all, if it was going to be confiscated anyway, why not hide it, sell it, or embezzle it? All these ruses were tried, with mixed results, but it is clear that from the moment rumours started to circulate, church plate began leaking from the system to the detriment of the Crown. It was easy to find a buyer if you were prepared to sell below the market price, which of course you would be, given the alternative. Richard Layton, as he toured the northern monasteries in June 1535, wrote to Cromwell that religious houses were 'selling their jewels and plate at half their value for ready money'.[30] At the other end of the country, at Abbotsbury in Dorset, the abbot was doing exactly the same thing, and a year earlier Cromwell was receiving reports of churches in Bristol selling their plate.[31]

Apart from the king, the real winners in this process were the dishonest goldsmiths and jewellers who took advantage of clerical naïvety. In January 1536 Layton found himself at the great abbey of Fountains in Yorkshire, where he wrote

> six days before our coming [the abbot] committed theft and sacrilege, getting his chaplain to steal the sexton's keys at midnight, and take out a cross of gold with stones. One Warren,[32] a goldsmith of the Cheap [in London], was then with him in his chamber, and they stole a great

> emerald with a ruby. Warren made the abbot believe the ruby to be a garnet and got it for nothing, paying only £20 for the emerald. He also sold him plate without [taking its] weight or ounces; in fact he is a mere idiot.[33]

This was a real problem and in 1539 another commissioner, Thomas Parry, alerted Cromwell to a similar situation at the convent of St Swithun in Winchester. There,

> diverse precious stones, as emeralds and other, to a great value, taken out of the jewels of the house here privily by the prior and four or five monks of his affinity, without consent or knowledge of the convent, were sold to one Bestyan, a jeweller, who as I hear say, is in London in some family of the strangers there.

Parry then goes on to offer Cromwell some helpful advice:

> Understanding that he hath been in diverse religious houses throughout the realm for a like purpose, in case it pleased your Mastership to command him to be taken and brought before you, he, I suppose, would not only with a little coercion yield again such jewels and treasure as he hath sediciously by his crafty means gotten, but also disclose unto your Mastership things that should be to the King's Highness much profitable and to your right singular pleasure.[34]

A rarer and more public-spirited response to the prospect of confiscation was reported in Hull where they sold the plate ahead of the visitation and 'paved our town withal'. The writer's advice to his correspondent in Louth was to do the same 'and mend your town that is very foul withal'.[35]

A quite different form of leakage was through bestowing plate as bribes to buy favour. Cromwell was offered many, such as when the abbot of Harland sent him a cup worth £22 in 1535, 'desiring you to continue his good master'.[36] But the commonest response to the situation was concealment. All sorts of tricks were tried. In January 1536 the abbot of Coggeshall, in Essex, was charged with swearing his brethren to deny all knowledge of their plate 'that the king might not have it'.[37] The sub-prior of Leominster hid church plate in his house,[38] while the abbot of Colchester was said to have spirited it away to London for safekeeping.[39] The inventory of Christ Church, Canterbury was sent to Cromwell in November 1535 with a cover note to the effect that 'articles to the value of thousands of pounds [had been] skilfully left out',[40] and four years later at Glastonbury, another of the greatest monasteries, the commissioners wrote with evident satisfaction that they had 'found money and plate hid in walls, vaults and other secret

Figure 13.1
The Dolgellau chalice and paten, probably Hereford, 1230–50, signed by Nicholas of Hereford. Silver gilt. Royal Collection, on loan to the National Museum of Wales, Cardiff.

places, and some conveyed to divers places in the country'. They added that they 'have had no time to weigh it, but think it of great value. The abbot [Richard Whiting] and monks had embezzled and stolen as much plate and ornaments as would have sufficed for a new abbey.'[41] Rumours circulated, perhaps exaggerated, that the concealed treasure amounted to some 200,000 crowns,[42] but however much it was, the abbot's concealment of so much of the king's wealth was considered treasonable and two months later, in one of the most gruesome incidents of the entire dissolution, he was hanged, drawn and quartered on Glastonbury Tor.

Occasionally concealment was successful in keeping plate from the Crown and some of the most beautiful surviving English medieval church plate was almost certainly hidden for exactly this purpose. The Dolgellau chalice and paten (fig. 13.1) and the Ramsey Abbey censer and incense boat (fig. 13.2 and fig. 13.3) lay concealed for hundreds of years before being found by chance in the nineteenth century. The chalice and paten, dating from the mid-thirteenth century, were discovered near the site of Cymer Monastery in Merionethshire, which was dissolved in 1536. The paten is engraved with the seated figure of Christ in majesty, surrounded by the four evangelists and is hauntingly beautiful. The cover of the fifteenth-century censer is modelled as a miniature gothic tower, with tracery windows, gables and pinnacles, while the incense boat betrays its origin with its little rebus terminals, modelled as rams' heads. Objects such as these stand as isolated exceptions to the swathes of treasure that was either abruptly destroyed in the melting pots of the mint or that was preserved for a short while longer on the shelves of the jewel house before being sent to meet the same fate.

Figure 13.2 The Ramsey Abbey censer, London or East Anglia, c. 1325. Silver gilt. Victoria and Albert Museum, London.

Figure 13.3 The Ramsey Abbey incense boat, London or East Anglia, c. 1325. Silver gilt. Victoria and Albert Museum, London.

Given what they were up against, the commissioners were remarkably successful in ensuring that as little as possible slipped through the net. And it helped them that the whole issue of dissolution divided communities. Disaffected monks reported embezzlement by abbots and priors, and local people did the same. In Aylsham in Norfolk, a dispute arose in 1537 between the church wardens and the townspeople,

> who, when they heard the king's visitors would come to the town, said they would sell their best cross and other jewels before they came, and commanded the church wardens to deliver the keys of the chest where the cross and jewels lay. The church wardens refused, saying if the king wished to have it he was most worthy.[43]

By late 1540 the last of the monasteries had been suppressed and the last of their gold and silver surrendered. This was not the end of the plundering of the Church, however. Royal sights were soon trained on new targets, although ones that were not fully exploited until the following reign. One was the chantries. These were private chapels erected within parish churches or cathedrals, where masses were said for the souls of the deceased. By the time of their abolition there were over 2,000 of these, mostly endowed with plate, and in 1546 a commission was set up to survey 'and to prevent embezzlement, to make inventories [...] of all plate, jewels, ornaments, goods and chattels'.[44] This set the scene for a further wave of dissolutions and confiscations, although one that largely got under way in the following reign.

The second, potentially no less profitable, vein was the thousands of parish churches across the country and in 1545 the earl of Hertford brought theology to the aid of convenience by arguing that the seizure of surplus parish plate

> is the readiest way to relief and the least chargeable to the king's subjects; for God's service, which consisteth not in jewels, plate or ornaments of gold or silver, cannot thereby be anything diminished, and those things better employed for the weal and defence of the realm; which being well persuaded to the people shall satisfy them.[45]

Hertford was probably right that most people's material lives would be relatively untouched by such a policy, but its wider effect would be to ensure that processions like that described in Wriothesley's *Chronicle* to mark the end of the war in 1546, when seventy silver-gilt crosses from the City parish churches were carried through the streets of London, would soon become a thing of the past.

The great shrines

The greatest prizes of all were the shrines, which were located in the cathedrals and great monasteries. These were beacons to pilgrims and great sources of revenue. In the Middle Ages the most famous shrines of Europe, such as those of St James in Santiago de Compostela, St Peter in Rome or St Thomas in Canterbury, attracted thousands of pilgrims each year, bringing in huge sums, not only around the shrines themselves, but all along the pilgrimage routes. In England, in the context of the gathering momentum of suppression and accumulation, they inevitably became prime targets.

One of the first to go was the shrine of St John of Bridlington in Yorkshire. John of Thwing was a fourteenth-century prior of the Augustinian monastery at Bridlington and was canonised in 1401. His tomb rapidly developed into a major pilgrimage centre and in 1537 was described by the commissioners as being 'in a fair chapel on high, having on either side a stair of stone for to go and come by. Underneath the said shrine be five chapels with five altars and small tables of alabaster and images.'[46] Like all the others, its days were numbered anyway, but its end was probably hastened by the fact that the prior was accused of involvement with the Pilgrimage of Grace. He was taken to London and executed. In May of that year Cromwell wrote to the duke of Norfolk, who was in the area, requesting him to take down the shrine 'that people be not seduced into offering their money, and [to have] all the plate and jewels sent up hither, except such as Norfolk is willing to buy'.[47] Within a month the job was done and Norfolk wrote to the king that he was sending all the gold to London in two coffers. Norfolk mentions several specific items among the gold: 'one proper thing of *radix Jesse* to be set upon an altar' and several wrought tablets. He quips that had he been a thief, he 'would have stolen them to have them sent to the Queen's Grace, but now your Highness having them, may give them unto her without [committing] offence'.[48] As to the silver, amounting to some 3,470 oz, he asks whether he should sell it locally on the king's behalf, adding that 'it is very old stuff and would be better broken up'.

Bridlington was followed in 1538 by Bury St Edmunds, Winchester, Chichester, Lincoln and the most celebrated of them all, the shrine of Thomas Becket at Canterbury. The great Benedictine abbey of Bury was home to the shrine of the Anglo-Saxon martyr King Edmund and was another important pilgrimage centre. Henry VI had visited it in 1434 and a roughly contemporary image of him kneeling before the shrine is in the British Library (fig. 13.4). Its depiction may not be accurate but it shows a gilded architectonic structure on an arcaded stone base. The shrine has

Figure 13.4
Illumination of Henry VI praying at the shrine of St Edmund, late fifteenth century. British Library (Harley 2278, f. 4v).

a steeply pitched roof and gabled ends. It has pinnacles or candle holders at the corners and the sides are divided into panels, each set with gems and pearls. Perhaps the closest surviving shrine today is the Cosmas and Damian shrine of around 1400 in Munich.[49] The commissioners' report in February 1538 is coldly matter-of-fact: 'we found a rich shrine very cumbrous to deface. Have taken in the monastery over 5,000 marks in gold and silver besides a rich cross with emeralds and stones of great value; yet have left the church, abbot and convent well furnished with silver plate.'[50] This leniency was later reconsidered and in November of the following year Sir Richard Rich visited the abbey and wrote that they had 'taken into their own custody, for the king, the plate and best ornaments of the house and sold the rest'.[51]

The shrines at Chichester, Winchester and Lincoln were among the richest. St Swithun's, behind the high altar at Winchester, was covered in silver and garnished with stones, although the commissioners were less impressed by it than they had expected. In September 1538 they told Cromwell that 'about three o'clock this Saturday morning, made an end of the shrine here at Winchester'. (Are we really to understand that they were working through the night to complete the task?) 'There was no gold, no ring, nor true stone in it, but all great counterfeits; but the silver alone will amount to 2,000 marks.' The cathedral did yield up other treasures, however, for the letter continues: 'Have also received the cross of emeralds, the cross called Jerusalem, another gold cross, two gold chalices, and other plate.'[52]

Three months later the commissioners reported from Chichester that the shrine of St Richard de Wych had yielded up fifty-five silver-gilt images and that they were shipping up coffers full of plate and jewels and fifty-seven pieces of silver and gilt 'in a long coffin, wherein bishop Richard's bones were'.[53] The profane requisitioning of the saint's coffin as a convenient packing case shows to what a low level respect for the dead, let alone the revered dead, had sunk.

Lincoln's turn did not come until June 1540 but it was a rich harvest. The cathedral as a whole (not just the shrine) yielded 2,599 oz of gold and 4,309 oz of silver, together with many pearls and precious stones.[54] The cathedral boasted two shrines, St Hugh's, which was apparently of gold, and the silver one of St John of Dalderby.[55]

By far the greatest of the English shrines was Becket's, in the monastery of Christ Church at Canterbury, and to which people had been making pilgrimage for centuries; Erasmus's famous description of the shrine, from his own visit in 1514, is quoted on p. 67. Like others, this had evolved over centuries and been continually enriched with gifts. One of the most famous on Becket's was a jewel known as the Royal of France, said to have been given by Louis VII in 1179, just six years after Becket's canonisation.[56] The tradition continued and in an undated letter Archbishop Warham thanked Wolsey for the rich jewel that he had given to the shrine.[57] Most gifts, however, were of money and in December 1530 Henry himself had sent a gift of 20s.[58]

Once the suppression was fully under way there can have been no doubt that Becket's turn would come. Ironically, the shrine was very nearly accidentally destroyed in 1535. Fire broke out in part of the monastery, but Richard Layton was on hand to take charge and protect the shrine from the flames or – if that proved impossible – to salvage as much as possible: 'I sent for the abbot of St Augustine's to be there within a readiness to have taken down the shrine, and to have sent all the jewels into St Augustine's; but as it chanced, there is no harm done more than those three chambers. No plate nor nothing lost.'[59]

The dismembering of the shrine was a major undertaking. Henry himself took a personal interest and is thought to have been present to oversee its destruction in September 1538.[60] According to Stow's account in the *Annales*,

> the timber work of this shrine on the outside, was covered with plates of gold, damasked with gold wire, which ground of gold was again

> covered with jewels of gold, as rings, ten or twelve, cramped with gold wire into the said ground of gold, many of those rings having stones in them, brooches, images, angels, precious stones, and great pearls. The spoil of which shrine, in gold and precious stones, filled two great chests, such as six or seven strong men could do no more than convey one of them at once out of the Church.[61]

Henry's presence, if he really was there, would not have been by chance. At some stage between his last recorded gift to the shrine and the start of the dissolution Henry's conventional veneration for the saint morphed into hatred. Becket had defied Henry II by defending the rights of the Church against the Crown. And now, some 360 years later, the saint became a rallying point for opponents of the royal supremacy. For the present Henry, this was a direct provocation and he became obsessed with erasing every trace of his memory. As Wriothesley's *Chronicle* puts it, all images of the saint were to be destroyed 'so that there shall no more mention be made of him never'.[62] The other shrines were taken down partly to discourage 'idolatry', but mostly for profit; in Becket's case it was more personal and the king took a special pleasure in pre-empting the Royal of France and having it converted into a finger ring for himself, a potent symbol of his 'triumph'.[63] His final act of desecration was to order the saint's bones to be publicly burned, like a heretic, and the ashes scattered to the wind.[64]

Processing the spoils

The dismembering of Becket's shrine touches on several important factors, namely transport, storage and the ultimate destiny of the treasures. Worn out or broken plate tended to be sold off locally wherever possible, but much of it went to London. Transporting it was not easy and was often complicated by the need to avoid arousing local opposition. In Ipswich around 1537, for example, the commissioners took no chances with the gold-mounted image of Our Lady which was 'conveyed into the ship that very few were privy to it'.[65]

Where exactly the goods went to in London depended on what was to happen to them and where there was room to store them. At first the default destination was the Tower, either the jewel house or the mint, while some was temporarily stored elsewhere for convenience and some was sold directly to goldsmiths. Morgan Wolf alone bought over 11,000 oz and a further 15,000 oz went to Fabian Wethers and Cornelis Hayes.[66] Another important recipient was the king himself, particularly those items deemed to be most beautiful or valuable. Cromwell's instructions to the

Figure 13.5
The tower of Elsyng Spital, part of an Augustinian hospital and priory until 1536 and subsequently part of the home of John Williams, master of the jewel house.

commissioners repeatedly point out that they should be mindful of those 'principal jewels, plate, ornaments and other things as shall be thought meet for the king's majesty'.[67] So, when the Canterbury plate arrived in London it went first to the house of one of the officials, 'thence to the king at Westminster and thence to the master of the jewel house'.[68]

At the height of the dissolution shipments of plate and jewels were arriving on an almost daily basis. Processing it all was a headache and, as events gathered pace, it became increasingly difficult for the regular jewel house staff to handle it all. Cromwell's solution was the Court of Augmentations, an entirely new finance department set up in 1536. Its main role was to administer and receive the revenues and eventual sale proceeds of the monastic buildings and lands, but it also dealt with the allocation and disposal of plate, jewels and other moveable assets. In 1540 a payment of £30 was made to Edward North, treasurer of augmentations, for 'making a strong new treasure house and purchasing iron chests'. But capacity must have been stretched at times. John Williams's house at Elsyng Spital, Cripplegate, part of which survives to this day (fig. 13.5), was used both as the jewel house office and as an extra storage facility. But on 24 December 1541 fire broke out, with the result that 'divers jewels and goods of the king's and also of his [Williams] were embezzled and conveyed away'.[69]

The king's personal interest in choice monastic plate and jewels had been clear from the start and in September 1535 Henry had taken the opportunity on his summer progress to visit Winchester Cathedral and to inspect its 'mete' treasures. That month Chapuys wrote to Charles V that 'on his arrival at Winchester, where he is holding his court, this king had an inventory taken of the treasure in its cathedral church, and appropriated to himself certain very fine unicorn horns, besides a large gold cross set with precious stones'.[70] In such cases he had only to demand and it was granted. As Supreme Head of the Church, it could hardly be otherwise. Earlier that year a canon of St Paul's wrote to Sir Edward Baynton, the queen's vice chamberlain, concerning 'a precious little cross with a crucifix of pure gold and a rich ruby in the side, garnished with four great diamonds, four great emeralds, four large balaces, twelve great orient pearls, amongst the jewels of our church'.[71] Henry had clearly admired it and two months earlier Cromwell made a note to himself 'to remember [...] especially the cross of emeralds at St Paul's'.[72] Now the screw was turned. The canon's letter continues:

> upon the king's high affection and pleasure of the sight of the same, I, with other of my brethren residentiaries, were yesterday commanded by Mr Secretary [Cromwell] in the king's name to be with the king with the said cross tomorrow [... So] his Grace shall have his pleasure thereon, and receive the same of our free gift, trusting in his charitable goodness to our church of St Paul.[73]

His choice of words is euphemistic and for 'high affection and pleasure', we should read 'covetousness and greed'. But he recognises that the king's will is irresistible and just hopes that their abject compliance will at least result in some reciprocal 'charitable goodness'. What happened to the emerald cross subsequently we do not know. There is no sign of it on any of the late royal inventories and it was probably broken up and the stones reused.

Sir John Williams kept a record of monastic plate and jewels received at the jewel house and notes a number of those pre-empted by the king.[74] This includes treasures from Glastonbury, Canterbury, Ely and Winchester. Among the most remarkable were 'a superaltar garnished with silver and gilt and part gold, called the great sapphire of Glastonbury', 'a staff garnished with silver, called Thomas Becket's staff' and (from Ely) 'a folding table [a diptych or triptych] for an altar, the inner part thereof plated with gold and garnished with sapphires, balaces, small sparks of emeralds, and small course pearls', weighing 424 oz.[75] Others appear to be secular. Among the Glastonbury hoard were 'a great piece of a unicorn-horn', 'a piece of mother of pearl, like a shell' and 'eight branches of fair coral'.[76] A sumptuous jewel, probably from Winchester, was 'an eagle of gold' garnished with emeralds, balases, sapphires and pearls and weighing an impressive 77½ oz.[77] Some of these, like the gold and silver 'images' discussed below, required further embellishment. Cornelis Hayes was provided with the necessary gold 'for trimming and garnishing of a cup called an Agate' and Peter Richardson was commissioned to garnish four 'camewes or anticks' that probably came from Lincoln.[78] Other less coveted items were handed over to the goldsmiths to be melted down and remade into useful wares.

Record-keeping from the king's side was no less careful and a telling document, linking together all the key departments in this process, is the 'discharge' issued on 20 April 1544 for the plate, jewels and vestments brought to the king by Sir Antony St Leger, 'one of the gentlemen of our privy chamber'. This also came from Christ Church, Canterbury and must have been from a second sweep. It is addressed to 'our chancellor and treasurer of our Court of Augmentations, and to our treasurer of our Chamber, and the master of our jewelhouse, and to all other our officers and ministers'. It lists twenty-six items of plate and many costly vestments which St Leger had received from Sir John Williams. The implication is that the king retained all those items listed, since they are followed by a separate, shorter inventory of things deemed 'not mete for his Grace's use'.[79]

The plate on the St Leger list was all liturgical and some of it must have been very beautiful, such as 'one great chalice with the paten gilt, and upon the foot the Trinity enamelled, and the image of our Lord holding his hand upon our Lady's crown on the paten enamelled', or 'one great chalice the foot thereof garnished with skuchings [escutcheons] and enamelled with divers pictures and flowers, and upon the paten the Trinity with the xii apostles enamelled set about the edges'. It is hard for us to form more than the vaguest ideas of the actual appearance of such treasures, but a hint, for example, of the Glastonbury sapphire may be gleaned from the Master of St Giles's *Miraculous Mass of St Giles*, in the National Gallery (fig. 13.6). This shows a magnificent silver-gilt retable, divided into three parts. The central panel is embossed in high relief with Christ in Majesty, set with large stones, and flanked by two further panels with depictions of saints. The retable is surmounted by a large jewel-encrusted cross.

It is also difficult to arrive at a reliable estimate of the total quantity of plate and jewels seized from the monasteries and cathedrals during the last decade or so of the reign. Regional estimates show how variable concentrations of monastic plate were, but are only available for some parts of the country. The totals extracted from the state papers are finely calculated to the last ounce or, in some cases, fraction of an ounce. But even so, they should be treated with caution and are almost certainly incomplete. Nevertheless, the numbers are impressive. From the northern monasteries the total harvest was 24,410 oz. This was made up of 766 oz

Figure 13.6
Mass of St Giles, Master of St Giles, c. 1500. National Gallery, London.

of gold plate set with stones, 17,324 oz of silver-gilt, 946 oz of parcel-gilt and 5,373 oz of white silver.[80] This is in marked contrast to just five East Anglian monasteries – Bury St Edmunds, Ely, Ramsey, Peterborough and Crowland – which provided a total of 2,047 oz of gold and 22,793 oz of silver, with Bury alone accounting for 1,553 oz of the gold. The richest hauls of all came from Glastonbury and Canterbury: 13,601 oz from the former and 15,545 oz from the latter, of which no less than 4,994 oz was gold, twice as much as any other monastery. According to one account the precious materials from Becket's shrine alone filled twenty-six wagons.[81] Sir John Williams's account only starts in 1537 but records a total of 289,768⅞ oz of plate surrendered to the Crown between then and the end of the reign. That was about nine tonnes, or more than double the contents of the jewel house in 1532. Of this, 14,531 oz (about 5 per cent) was gold. Williams also shows how the assets were distributed: around 84 per cent (about 250,000 oz) went to the mint or was sold to goldsmiths; the rest was retained by the king, with about 30,000 oz going to the jewel house and between 13,000 oz and 14,000 oz directly into his own hands. According to Maria Hayward, the total value of all assets brought into the Court of Augmentations between 1536 and 1547 was £415,005 6s 10½d.[82]

Religious observance at court

The dissolution, and the enormous influx of liturgical plate that resulted from it, is an appropriate context in which to consider religious observance at court during the latter part of the reign. Henry VIII's religious attitudes shifted during the 1530s. The ebbs and flows of his theology are not always easy to follow, nor is it the aim of this book to explore what J. J. Scarisbrooke refers to as 'that febrile, wayward mechanism, Henry's mind'.[83] His holdings of church plate, anyway, throw little light on these issues. They do, however, corroborate what we know from other sources of his conservatism in worship, both in private and in public.

On a personal level, minor pointers to his continued traditional attitudes can be seen in the privy purse expenses from the early 1530s, such as buying rosaries, making offerings to the Virgin before and after crossing the Channel, and paying a reward of twenty shillings to the abbot of Westminster's servant for bringing 'relic water' to him in Chertsey.[84] Among more public manifestations are a series of events during the late 1530s, by which time dissolution and confiscation were in full swing. In June 1536 Henry and Jane Seymour marked the feast of Corpus Christi by leading an elaborate procession from Whitehall Palace to Westminster Abbey,[85] and during the following December, when the river was frozen and the king had to travel to Greenwich by land, the streets of the City were lined with friars in copes, holding crosses, candlesticks and censers. In a gossipy letter written to Lord Lisle in Calais in May 1539 we read that

> this present Holy Thursday eve [...] the high altar in the chapel was garnished with all the apostles upon the altar, and mass by note and the organs playing, with as much honour to God as might be devised [...] His Grace receives holy bread and holy water every Sunday, and daily uses all other laudable ceremonies.[86]

Finally, Henry's will, although mostly concerned with the succession, is entirely traditional in its religious provisions. It invokes the Virgin Mary and all the company of saints, it gives lengthy instructions for his burial and it provides for perpetual masses to be said for his soul.[87]

Henry seems always to have had a certain veneration for consecrated vessels[88] and from anecdotal evidence to this effect we should not be surprised that, despite the culling of religious images across the country and despite the outlawing of saintly veneration, the royal stock of images remained high and, indeed, even increased. The 1547 inventory shows that while the number of silver images stored in the jewel house declined from previous levels, there were many more elsewhere: twenty-two at Whitehall and twenty-five distributed among the other standing houses. From other sources we know that many of these were recent appropriations and that significant sums were spent on refurbishing them. Sir John Williams's records include a number of entries relating to 'new trimming, burnishing, and mending [images] from sundry late abbeys'. The goldsmith, John Barnes (a name not encountered elsewhere), was paid a total of £54 5s 8d for 'new trimmings' (additions and renovations) made to five gold images, including one of 'the Father of Heaven'.[89] These were in the jewel house in 1547 and weighed between about 90 oz and 170 oz each. Meanwhile Morgan Wolf was given the much bigger task of refurbishing and embellishing forty-three silver-gilt images for which he was paid the huge sum of £912 6s 10d. They had probably been in a poor state of repair when they left their monasteries, but Wolf's embellishments must have been transformative, adding a further 2,300 oz to their original 1,460 oz and raising their average weight from 34 oz to 87 oz. The modifications are carefully listed in the record and included new backs and bases, and the addition of collets, stones, crowns, sceptres and other 'signes', together with 'pieces of timber to put within the same images'. Such a costly make-over would hardly have been undertaken if they were not intended to be used and visible.[90] As to why Henry needed so many extra images in addition to those he already possessed, the explanation probably lies in a combination of factors: greed and aesthetic appeal might be two ('high affection and pleasure', as the canon of St Paul's had put it when he surrendered the jewelled cross); a third might be that a number of existing images had been allocated to the various satellite households that we considered in Chapter 11.

From the 1547 inventory we also have a reasonably clear idea of the other royal holdings of church plate. Apart from images, little of the altar plate at this stage was of gold, although four gold crosses are listed, two in the jewel house, one at Whitehall and one at Hampton Court. The Whitehall one, on three gold feet, was set with many emeralds, balases and pearls and may have been one of those taken from Winchester Cathedral in 1538.[91] At 26 oz it was slightly heavier than the Hampton Court one and was probably the more impressive of the two, since the latter is just described as 'garnished with stone and pearl'. The two in the jewel house were both much larger. One was the 74 oz crucifix that survived from Richard II's treasury and which we discussed on p. 29; the other was the great 'cross of gold called Jerusalem'. This was in fact a complete Calvary scene, with Christ between the two thieves, each enamelled in white; it was enriched with balases and the foot was further set with 'certain small images of gold garnished with stone and pearl'. The entire object weighed 359 oz, including its 284 oz silver-gilt foot. The figures and their crosses were detachable because they were separately weighed at 75 oz. It must have been a sumptuous object.[92]

Altogether the church plate listed in the 1547 inventory runs to 249 objects. It includes virtually the full range of traditional religious paraphernalia: chalices and patens, crosses, monstrances, candlesticks, holy water buckets, cruets, paxes, pyxes, censers, incense boats and bells.[93] Ninety-three of these were in the jewel house, but at least one of each category (and often more) was kept at the 'standing houses', with the majority of the rest at Whitehall. The only reasonable conclusion to draw from this is that the performance of the mass in the Chapel Royal remained entirely traditional. The same is suggested by the fact that despite the removal of certain feast days from the liturgical calendar by Act of Parliament in 1536, their celebration by the Chapel Royal continued as before and the following year a frustrated Archbishop Cranmer wrote to Cromwell complaining that 'if in the Court you do keep such holy days and fasting days [...] when shall we persuade the people to cease keeping them? For the king's own house shall be an example unto all the realm.'[94]

Only one category of church plate is absent from the 1547 inventory: reliquaries. We saw in Chapter 5 that relics were conspicuously displayed in Henry VII's time at Richmond and that Henry VIII kept a small coffer with relics in his closet at the time of the 1521 inventory. A list of jewels in Sir William Compton's keeping in 1519 includes 'a St George full of relics' and Richard Rex argues that given Compton's position as groom of the stool this was presumably something that the king kept close to his person.[95] That he still venerated (or engaged with) relics in the early 1530s is clear from his gift to St George's Chapel in 1533 of a piece of the True Cross. But that all changed soon afterwards, probably under the influence of Anne Boleyn. In 1535 he consented to the removal of the 'Blood of Hailes', a famous relic of the blood of Christ at Hailes Abbey which had been deemed spurious. Later he authorised Sir Thomas Pope to 'deface' any monastic relics that he encountered.[96]

Did these developments reflect Henry's personal religious journey? Very possibly, and if so, the absence of relics from his possessions at the end of the reign is surely significant. Further evidence of a sort for a changing attitude can perhaps be found in the jewellery depicted in Henry's portraits from the 1530s: this varies from picture to picture, but one piece in particular appears repeatedly, suggesting that he wore it regularly. This is a small circular gold pendant hanging from a chain (fig. 12.4). Relatively simple, it is engraved or chased with foliage, set with a sapphire and suspended from a black enamelled gold chain with letters H. If this is a normal jewel, it is an unusually modest one for Henry and another possibility altogether is that it is an amulet containing a relic. Such an interpretation is not implausible, especially given that it is set with a sapphire, a stone redolent with religious symbolism. If so, then it is surely significant that it is no longer to be seen in his final portraits (fig. 14.1).

The dissolution and the harvest of plate and jewels that accrued to the king is revealing in several ways. On one level, it shows the 'affection and pleasure' Henry took in the finest works of church art and reinforces the view that the Chapel Royal was probably at least as splendidly equipped at the end of the reign as at any other time. On another, the whole story throws a chilling spotlight on the changing character of the king: the carefully planned legislative framework that preceded the dissolution shows Henry's respect for due process, but the ensuing events showed that, once put in place, this gave him licence to do almost anything he chose. It traces his metamorphosis from a conventionally pious prince who was outraged at Francis I's appropriation of church treasures and who prayed at Becket's shrine with Charles V in 1520, to a cruel and vindictive despot who plundered the shrines and relics – genuine or otherwise – of saints, and judicially murdered those who stood in his way. The desecration of Becket's remains and the appropriation of one of the shrine's principal embellishments to adorn the royal finger shows a petty and triumphalist 'revenge' that is deeply unattractive. Hardly less so is the obsessive level of personal covetousness that clouded his judgement and superseded almost everything else. Opinions differ as to when exactly the moment came that tipped Henry VIII from 'virtuous prince' into 'most avaricious of men'. Very possibly there was no such moment; we have seen hints of avarice from very early on and we have noted the merging of greed with manipulation in his appetite for attainder and in his callous treatment of various members of his family. But the dissolution stimulated this trait as never before and drove the unrelenting acquisitiveness that coloured the final years of his reign.

Fourteen 'Most Avaricious of Men'

By 1540 the king was getting older. But his decline from the statuesque solidity of Holbein's full-length portrait to the bloated, piggy-eyed king depicted in Cornelis Matsys's 1544 engraving was gradual. The year 1536 has been seen as a watershed and in January of that year Henry had a near fatal jousting accident that left him unconscious for two hours. Whether or not this led to a sea-change in his character, as some have argued,[1] it certainly marked the end of his jousting days and the end of regular vigorous exercise, probably accelerating his advance towards obesity. But against this backdrop of advancing age, life at court continued much as ever, remaining magnificent to the end. The king's jousting days may have been over but hunting and hawking continued, as did splendid receptions, banquets and munificent diplomatic gifts. Hall's description of Henry's first meeting with Anne of Cleves at Blackheath in 1539 shows that although less dashing than before, he was still able, with the help of his goldsmiths, to cut an impressively magnificent figure, not much removed from the older and heavier monarch depicted in an anonymous portrait in the National Portrait Gallery (fig. 14.1):

> His person was apparelled in a coat of purple velvet [...] all over embroidered with flat gold of damask [...] the sleeves and breast were cut, lined with cloth of gold, and tied together with great buttons of diamonds, rubies and orient pearl, his sword and sword girdle adorned with stones and especial emeralds [...] but his bonnet was so rich of jewels that few men could value them. Beside all this he wore in balderick wise a collar of such balises and pearl that few men ever saw the like.[2]

No less marked than his changing appearance, however, were the changes in his behaviour, most notably his increasing tendencies towards excess, unpredictability, cruelty and avarice. Charles de Marillac, the French ambassador, captured two of these, writing in March 1541 that

Figure 14.1
King Henry VIII, unknown artist, early seventeenth century after a work of c. 1542. National Portrait Gallery, London.

he is 'marvellously excessive in drinking and eating'[3] and a year earlier that 'this prince [...] is so covetous that all the riches in the world will not satisfy him'.[4] Two years even before that another French observer in England described him as 'one of the most avaricious men in the world'.[5]

It is not the purpose of this chapter to decide whether Henry was or was not a monster, although his greed for plate and jewels and the manner of their acquisition undoubtedly add to such a view, as they do to less morally weighty issues, such as royal taste and the role of precious objects in the king's life. In exploring this subject we will make use of the same kinds of evidence that we did earlier: tapestries, documents, and a vanishingly small number of surviving objects. Tapestries help fill the gaps in our knowledge of style; documents, including the extraordinary inventories of

1542 and 1547, record the incredible quantities of gold and silver owned by the ageing king; while surviving objects, and one in particular, help flesh out the dry inventory descriptions.

War, finance and jewels

The dizzying acquisitions of jewels and plate in the latter part of the reign took place against a backdrop of international instability. For much of the reign England was at peace with its neighbours. But the threat of war with France or Scotland was seldom far away and in 1543 Henry found himself fighting on both fronts. Hostilities lasted nearly three years and proved ruinously expensive, but for Henry it was an opportunity to relive the glories of his youth and evoke the magnificence of his 1513 French campaign. Arriving at Calais in July 1544, he was received in great state; he took prodigious quantities of plate and jewels and at least six members of the jewel house staff to look after it.[6] When he returned to England in November no fewer than eight carts were needed to get it all back to London.[7]

The two campaigns made just one territorial gain, Boulogne, and cost in all more than two million pounds.[8] Chapuys wrote in March 1544, unsurprisingly, that the king does not want 'to touch his own treasure' but would rather raise the money by other means.[9] These included loans and the wholesale disposal of monastic lands. But as costs mounted, new avenues had to be explored, and in 1544 Stephen Vaughan, Henry's commissioner in Antwerp, was charged with raising money from the international markets. Vaughan approached a number of potential lenders, including the wealthy merchant, Jasper Dowche. Dowche had the money but was slippery and mendacious. In August Vaughan was about to secure a loan for £21,000 at 14 per cent interest when Dowche suddenly shifted tack, demanding that part of the sum be taken not in cash but in jewels of equivalent value. This was a shrewd idea, getting around Charles V's ban on the export of gold coin and at the same time playing on Henry's well-known weakness for precious objects. But for Vaughan it was a nightmare. Under Dowche's proposal, if the jewels were factored into the deal at his valuation, the interest on the money would be generously reduced to 10 per cent. But this was only generous if the valuations were correct. The jewels, it turned out, belonged to the powerful Augsburg banking house of Fugger, and Vaughan was deeply suspicious. Negotiations dragged on and when in the following June he was invited to inspect the jewels, he declined, writing to London that he 'would bring a skilful person to view it, not naming [him] lest the Fugger should corrupt him beforehand'. Unsurprisingly, Vaughan's valuer, Peter Vanderwall (or van den Wale), considered the valuations excessive. He valued, for example, a gold and jewelled dagger at 6,000 crowns, 2,000 less than Fugger. Factoring in the necessary adjustments meant that, in Vaughan's estimation, the effective rate of interest of the whole deal was closer to 18 per cent.[10]

The Fugger jewels comprised, in addition to the gold dagger, a jewelled collar and a gold ewer and basin, also set with stones and pearls. But a final twist emerged as the deal was being concluded when it transpired that the basin was not yet ready. That can only mean that it was being specially made, presumably in Antwerp or Augsburg. Vaughan, therefore, had little choice but to accept the Fuggers' undertaking to deliver it within two months, coupled with the cold comfort that 'the king need have no doubt, for the Fuggers are the "famost" house of merchants in all Christendom'.[11]

We must assume the basin was eventually delivered, and some months later Vaughan went to considerable lengths to ensure the safe transport of the consignment to England. His expenses, submitted around the end of the year, itemise 'five firkins to put the Fuggers' money in [...] three cases to put the said jewels in, for cotton "searyng" of the said cases, and for a hogshead, mats, canvas, ropes and trussing and binding of the same'. All of this came to 23s 4d and the hire of a wagon from Antwerp to Calais cost a further £4.[12] On 21 December Vaughan, having accompanied the precious cargo to England, presented the jewels to the king in person and 'had two large hours talk and pleasant hearing of his majesty'.[13] During that conversation he would surely have shown the king his purchases and indeed several items on the 1547 inventory seem to have more or less strong claims to be the pieces in question: a 114 oz gold basin set with diamonds, rubies, emeralds and pearls, and a 40 oz layer with a serpent spout, set with rubies and pearls;[14] and two obviously magnificent jewelled gold daggers, one of which had a gold-mounted bloodstone handle.[15]

By the middle of January, Vaughan was back in Antwerp, busily negotiating further loans. By now news of the Fugger-Dowche deal must have spread because later in the month Vaughan wrote to Paget saying that he had met with another merchant, John Carolo, who had shown him

> a tabled diamond set in an owch of gold [...] which I think is the greatest sort that lightly is to be found. If the thickness answered the length and breadth, it were a jewel of wondrous price. He holds it at 40,000 crowns. It hath a great fair and orient round pearl hanging thereat.[16]

Vaughan goes on to report that if Henry took the jewel, money would follow at a reasonable rate of interest. But, acting on the king's behalf, he continued to negotiate with Carolo: 'I made him a cold answer, but will tomorrow try whether he will deliver money without jewels.'[17] The crucial letter followed a week later. Vaughan had clearly been unsuccessful in negotiating a jewel-free loan and by now the price of the jewel had mysteriously risen to 50,000 crowns, the purchase of which was a necessary condition for a loan of 100,000. Vaughan was at his wits' end, writing that

> the time is unmeet to pester the king with jewels, who already has more than most of the princes of Christendom, and therefore, although I told him that I would send the pattern to the king, I send it only to you [...] If it be known that the king receives jewels with the empruncture [loan] of money, I shall never get any money without them.[18]

The drawing Vaughan refers to survives in the National Archives (fig. 14.2) and shows a jewel at the absolute forefront of fashion. The large table diamond and 'orient pearl' are coloured with a silver-bearing paint that has oxidised and blackened, but the depiction of the enamelled gold setting is

Figure 14.2
Drawing of a jewel offered for sale to Henry VIII and enclosed in a letter from Stephen Vaughan written at Antwerp in 1545. National Archives (SP 1/213 fol. 167).

perfectly preserved. It is designed *à la antique* as a demi-faun and satyress, emerging from scrolls, with a fantastical horned mask below and with another mask above set against ultra-modern blue enamelled strapwork.

Did Paget bring the jewel to Henry's attention and did the king buy it? We cannot tell for sure, but it is very possible that he did and one entry in the 1547 inventory, the first of a group headed 'the Queen's jewels in a coffer', might answer to it: 'First, one owche or flower containing a fair diamond tabled holden by antiques with a large pendant pearl.'[19]

Dowche continued to offer loans contingent on jewel purchases, but his demand in March 1546 that a loan of 600,000 crowns be guaranteed by Act of Parliament was an affront to the king's dignity, who instructed the privy council to reply that 'his Highness will not [...] seem unto the world to be brought so low as he should need, for that sum, to make them assurance by Act of Parliament'.[20] By now there was a financial crisis and even finding the money for interest payments was not easy. In many cases repayments were financed through further loans. Nor was Vaughan helped by debasement of the English coinage, and the Fuggers made it clear that they would not accept payments in English coin.

Dealings with Jasper Dowche did not end with Henry's death. One of the most celebrated of all medieval jewels, the 'Three Brothers' (fig. 14.3), had been under negotiation along with the other loans, but was not finally purchased until 1551.[21] This extraordinary jewel, composed of three large and closely matched balase rubies around a pointed diamond and with four large pearls, had belonged to Philip the Good of Burgundy but was lost at the battle of Grandson in 1476. Falling into the hands of the magistrates of Basle, it was sold to Jakob Fugger in 1504 and held as an investment for over forty years. After its acquisition in Edward VI's reign it became one of the most prized of English royal jewels. It appears in the 'Ermine portrait' of Elizabeth I and was worn as a hat badge by James I.

The end of hostilities in 1546 was marked with huge celebrations, the negotiation of reparations from France and some relief from the financial chaos of the previous years. It so happened that the peace coincided with the birth in July of the dauphin's daughter, Isabel de Valois, presenting a perfect opportunity to affirm restored Anglo-French amity. Henry was invited to be godfather and sent rich gifts, dispatching Sir Thomas Cheney as his proxy. Cheney was treated with great honour; he sat on the French king's left and was served with covered dishes and a covered cup 'as [if] the king's majesty were here himself'.[22] For his pains, Cheney received, according to Jean de St Mauris, the imperial ambassador to France, 'a sideboard of plate worth five or six thousand crowns'.

Cheney did not present Henry's gifts until two days later. St Mauris describes them quite specifically as 'a jasper cup, a clock with a crystal

Figure 14.3 Watercolour of the Three Brothers jewel. Historisches Museum, Basel.

cover, and a gold saltcellar on a chased gold stand, and with a chased gold cover upon which stags and other animals were carved'.[23] The delay may have been because one of the king's gifts had somehow been damaged *en route* to Fontainebleau.[24] As a result, Cheney 'must have tarried [in Paris] for the mending of the king's chief present, the salt; which could not be finished before Wednesday, so that Allard had to follow with the cover to Melun'.[25] This was presumably Allard Plommier, the French jeweller who had sold jewels to Henry at Calais in 1532 and who had been granted favourable terms for importing plate into England.[26]

It is obviously impossible to assess these gifts on the basis of such brief descriptions but it is clear that they were more than just 'wrought bullion'. The main interest of the jasper cup, even though doubtless embellished with precious mounts, would probably have lain in the rarity and beauty of the polished deep red stone; the clock with its crystal cover resonates with a number of items on the 1547 inventory, and the gold salt, described as the 'chief present', may have been so-called on account of its size, but even so, its description as having 'stags and other animals carved' (presumably chased) on the cover suggests that it was not without artistic interest as well. A privy council warrant to Sir John Williams, master of the jewel house, for £911 2s 5d 'expended at christening of the dolphin's daughter'[27] probably includes the presents, although numerous other costs accrued too, such as £104 spent on gold chains and girdles given to Princess Isabel's nurses.[28]

Unabated avarice

The covetousness and avarice noted by the French ambassadors was reflected as much in Henry's appetite for plate and jewels as it was in anything else. And it was satisfied, as it always had been, through confiscation, gift and purchase.

As a branch of confiscation, attainder continued to be significant and even though there were no big fish of the likes of Buckingham or Wolsey, the quantities added up. In all, thirty-four courtiers were charged with treason between 1532 and 1540, of whom twenty were executed and attainted.[29] Cromwell himself was the subject of an act of attainder in 1540 and, according to Marillac, the inventory of his goods included £7,000 in money and a good deal of plate. Much of this doubtless went directly to the mint but a number of choice Cromwellian objects are identified on the 1547 inventory. Three aristocratic victims of attainder in the last years of the reign were Henry Courtenay, marquess of Exeter (executed in 1538 for his part in the Western Rebellion), Margaret Pole, countess of Salisbury (executed in 1541 at the age of sixty-seven, for the crime of being the last of the Plantagenet line within Henry's grasp), and Henry Howard, earl of Surrey and heir of the duke of Norfolk. Surrey was executed in 1546 and when his father was accused of treason too, royal servants were immediately dispatched to list his plate.[30] That he narrowly escaped his son's fate was due to Henry dying himself within hours of the time appointed for Norfolk's execution.

In contrast to the swathes of confiscated bullion sucked in to feed the mint, the normal business of new plate purchases continued much as before. There was the annual round of new year's gifts, there were ambassadorial gifts and there was the purchase and maintenance of household plate. In 1540, to take just one year, chamber payments to Morgan Wolf, John Freman and Martin Bowes came to more than £2,940.[31]

It is difficult, in the absence of a meaningful sample of royal plate from the period, to form any real idea of what the wares these goldsmiths were supplying were like. Much of it would doubtless have been sparingly or routinely decorated and when the privy council ordered a hundred marks' worth of plate 'of the best and slightest fashion' from Morgan Wolf as

Figure 14.4a Cover of the Barber-Surgeons' Cup, London, 1543–44, maker's mark illegible. Silver gilt. Collection of the Barbers' Company, London.

Figure 14.4 The Barber-Surgeons' Cup, London, 1543–44, maker's mark illegible. Silver gilt. Collection of the Barbers' Company, London.

a gift for a foreign visitor in 1541, this is probably what was meant. But Holbein was still alive in 1543 and the style of plate seen in his drawings was still at the forefront of fashion. One surviving object that belongs in this genre and that is perhaps typical of jewel house issue at this time is a covered bowl or cup belonging to the Barbers' Company (fig. 14.4). Hallmarked for 1543–44, this is traditionally said to have been a royal gift to the company.[32] There is no documentary evidence to support this[33] but its ornament is certainly royal: the cover is chased with portcullises, fleurs de lis and roses (fig. 14.4a) and is surmounted by the royal arms with lion and greyhound supporters.[34] It is not entirely in its original state, however. The bowl itself is a replacement, probably for one made of turned wood,[35] and the foot rim and knop seem to have been modified; the crown imperial above the arms is probably a replacement too. The inside of the cover is engraved with an inscription dated 1678, indicating that the cup was given (or returned) to the company in that year, so perhaps the crown was added then. The pendant bells are an intriguing feature, but may well be original and were not unique.[36]

We do not know who made the Barbers' bowl and the maker's mark is illegible. Its overall design is broadly Holbeinesque, but is prosaic and unimaginative in comparison with the master's drawings. If truly representative of the general quality of plate issued by the jewel house at this stage of the reign, then it is not surprising that Henry sought to buy artistically more interesting plate from abroad, for which he employed agents to scout out opportunities. One such was William Lock, who wrote from Antwerp in August 1538 that

> I had knowledge that there was come to this town certain plate of the Cardinal of Luke [Liege] to be [sold] to certain goldsmiths of Paris for the French king [...] When I saw it I thought much of it so meet for your grace and so stately that I could not find in my heart to suffer it to go in to France, so [...] I laid out my money for twelve parts of it all for one cupboard after one making in all sorts such as I do think no Prince christened hath the like of it in stateliness which I do intend to bring home with me. Sir, there is much more of it which I do intend to stop if I [can] unto such time as your grace hath seen this that I have bought.[37]

Even though we do not know what it looked like, it is easy to see why this set would have appealed to Henry: Lock's use of the word 'stately' implies that it was grand and of exceptional quality, while being 'after one making', suggests that they were all *en suite*. On top of this, a decisive factor in Lock's mind (and perhaps in the king's too) must have been that Henry, through his agent's speedy intervention, had got one over Francis.

Seven years later another of Henry's Antwerp agents offered him an impressive object, 'a goodly fountain of silver all gilt and set with certain stone and pearl'. It was described as 'casting out water above, running down into a bason [*sic*] made unto the same during the space of two hours'. It weighed 97 marks (776 oz) and cost about £260 (around 6s 9d per ounce), but 'looks double that value'.[38] Henry seems to have succumbed to the offer, since the description corresponds quite closely to a 'curiously wrought' fountain listed at Whitehall in 1547 and which weighed 785½ oz, perhaps after some minor modification.[39]

The deciding factor in both these purchases seems to have been their quality, one being described as 'stately' and the other as 'goodly', and a hint of the artistic appeal they had for the king may be found in an exceptional survival at Emmanuel College, Cambridge. The Mildmay bowl (fig. 14.5) was made in Antwerp in 1541–42 and was presented to the college by its founder, Sir Walter Mildmay, one of Henry's councillors. The bowl is a

Figure 14.5 The Mildmay Bowl, Antwerp, 1541–42. Silver gilt. Emmanuel College, Cambridge.

masterpiece of design. Taut, disciplined and superbly executed, it is also totally up to date and some of its details, such as the free-standing faun-like figures supporting the bowl, correspond to newly published ornament prints by the Antwerp artist, Cornelis Floris (fig. 14.6).

The bowl is a sophisticated example of an aesthetic that would have been quite familiar at court, to judge from the number of bowls and cups in the 1547 inventory that are described as German or 'of Flaunders making'. The same aesthetic is also well represented in the Abraham tapestries at

Figure 14.6
Design for a ewer, Cornelis Floris, Antwerp, c. 1540. Engraving. Private collection.

Hampton Court, which were made in Brussels and which Henry acquired at great expense around 1543.[40] One of the tapestries in particular, *The Return of Sarah by the Egyptians* (fig. 14.7), shows a variety of vessels sent by the pharaoh as a gift to Abraham. These include a jug, a pair of footed bowls and various large and impressive covered drinking vessels emerging from handsome coffers. All of these pieces, mostly parcel-gilt, are in the 'antique' style. The large vessel held by a kneeling figure has a strong horizontally zoned structure – like the Mildmay bowl – and is decorated with foliage around the base, with a profusion of flutes and gadroons and with free-standing scrolls on the cover that spring from applied cherubs. The large covered beaker further to the right, which a servant is struggling to lift, is more ambitiously decorated in relief with a frieze of figures reminiscent of Italian Renaissance *cassone*. As a final example, a two-handled bottle or flagon depicted in another tapestry from the series, *The Meeting of Abraham and Melchizedek* (fig. 14.8), is elaborately decorated with cherubs, foliage and tendrils.

Plate supplied by the royal goldsmiths or procured by agents abroad is only part of the story, and not the greater part either, for the money it cost was completely overshadowed by the sums Henry spent directly with foreign merchants. We have seen the feeding frenzy that took place when the king

Figure 14.7
Detail from *The Return of Sarah by the Egyptians* from *The Story of Abraham* series, attributed to Pieter Coeck van Aelst and Wilhelm Pannemaker, Brussels, c. 1540. Tapestry. Hampton Court Palace. Royal Collection.

Figure 14.8
Detail from *The Meeting of Abraham and Melchizidek* from *The Story of Abraham* series, attributed to Pieter Coeck van Aelst and Wilhelm Pannemaker, Brussels, c. 1540. Tapestry. Hampton Court Palace. Royal Collection.

was in Calais in 1532 (see p. 173) and in order to continue his access to such rich sources he offered favoured merchants licences to import luxury goods free of duty, normally on condition that the king should have 'first choice of all'.[41] Such licences were granted to Jerome Harbrott of Germany, Peter Vanderwall of Antwerp, and Allard Plommier and Jehan Lange (or de Langey) of Paris, the last of whom 'did give your highness a ring with a fair sapphire' to seal the deal.[42] The licences give an interesting insight into the diverse business interests of some of these merchants. Plommier, for example, was given licence in 1542 to import 400 tuns of Toulouse wool and Gascon wine and to export 400 tuns of beer,[43] while Francis Barnardo of Venice was permitted to bring into the realm 'all manner of plate and vessel of gold and silver or of silver of what fashion soever it be', as well as jewels, tapestries, textiles, furs and 'munitions of war'.[44]

The incentive to give the king first refusal was high, not least because he was a voracious buyer. In July 1546 Henry signed an obligation to Lange for £1,750 for 'certain plate and jewels', followed a month later by a further bill for £7,000. At the same time Peter Vanderwall was owed the colossal sum of £12,057.[45] Equally impressive bills were settled by Anthony Denny in his capacity as keeper of Whitehall Palace, and between 1542 and 1548 the Italian merchants Domenico Erizo and Anthony Carsidony received a total of £16,360 for 'jewels, plate [and] rich cloth of gold silver tissue'.[46]

But the life of an enterprising merchant was not always easy. Lange worried about pirates and highway robbers. Encounters with customs officials were not always straightforward either. In 1545 Jerome Crikelman, an Antwerp goldsmith, had 8,000 crowns' worth of jewellery seized at Calais, despite claiming to have a safe conduct from the king.[47] Nor were their troubles always over when they reached the royal presence. Henry was a tricky customer and in 1537 Lange wrote to a business associate that 'I find the king much disinclined to buy, for he has told me that he has no more money'.[48] But Henry's poverty was usually a negotiating stance rather than an economic condition and it did not prevent Lange eventually selling him goods for 5,000 crowns. Henry clearly drove a hard bargain and Lange wrote to another correspondent on the same day that 'I have been doing business with the king but have made no profit [...] I hope to show him the rest of the wares in three weeks, for I wish to let him rest'.[49]

Nor is it any wonder that Henry was cautious, for the merchants were up to every trick in the book and used their connections to maximise their opportunities. Lange appears to have been the brother of the French ambassador at the time[50] and his strategy was to ingratiate himself with the king by making presents of jewellery to the rising Anne Boleyn 'and then to sell to the king many fine jewels that he has brought with him'.

But the best laid plans did not always work out and in 1536 John Panner, another foreign merchant, complained to Cromwell that

> they sent the king the picture of a certain golden cross adorned with pearls and precious stones and received answer that [he] desired to buy it. [So] they brought it into England and offered it to the king, first of all princes of the world, much below its original price. The king, however, refused to buy it. In consideration of the danger and expense of bringing it, and the depreciation it has suffered by being shown abroad [that is, offered around], they beg Cromwell to obtain some token of the king's liberality, such as a licence to export thirty sacks of wool.[51]

Our knowledge of what exactly these 'jewels' were is very limited and, with the exception of the Fugger jewel drawing or an actual surviving object, our mental pictures are largely dependent on inventory descriptions and on analogous surviving objects. But one such object does survive. Its description in the 1547 inventory reads as follows:

> Item one bowl of crystal the foot and brim garnished with gold the foot also set with three small diamonds and vi pearls and certain writings in three places upon white enamelled upon the brims thereof there is certain antique work of gold enamelled wherein is set a goodly ruby and an emerald in collets of gold being very curiously wrought and garnished v roses of diamonds and v places written enamelled white the top of the cover being crystal and gold garnished with a ruby and diamond and an emerald and three pearls in the top of the same is two pearls in one and one great pearl lower set in gold and three small pearls pendant at the same poiz togethers xxxviii oz iij quarters.[52]

The description is not easy to follow, especially without punctuation, and while it is obviously a sumptuous object, with its crystal, enamel and precious stones, it is impossible to visualise with any clarity or to evaluate artistically. Except that the object is preserved in the Schatzkammer of the Residenz in Munich, and it is quite extraordinary (fig. 14.9). The crystal bowl is hollowed out to an exceptional thinness and is carved on the outside with spiralling flutes (fig. 14.9a). Like many rock crystals mounted in the sixteenth century, it is much older than the mounts and probably dates from the fourteenth century.[53] The foot mount is decorated with polychrome enamel, chased with a laurel wreath, modelled with harpies and set with stones; the lip is chased with exquisitely refined fleurs de lis and foliage; and the handle is modelled and enamelled with a female mask with an elaborate headdress of fruit. The cover is immensely complex (fig. 14.9c). Modelled around a circle of five convex crystal discs, the spaces

Figure 14.9 The 'Holbein bowl', possibly southern Germany, c. 1545. Gold, rock crystal, enamel, pearls and precious stones. Schatzkammer der Residenz, Munich.

Figure 14.9a and b View of the inside of the 'Holbein bowl' and detail of central disc.

Figure 14.9c Cover of the 'Holbein bowl'.

Figure 14.9d Underside of the lid of the 'Holbein bowl'.

Figure 14.10
Still Life, Willem Kalf, 1678. National Gallery of Denmark, Copenhagen.

between are filled with the 'five roses of diamonds' set within extremely elaborate cartouches, all of which are composed of different motifs. This zone surrounds a domed ring enamelled with polychrome arabesques and 'certain writings' on white shields with strapwork surrounds. The treatment of the inside of the cover is hardly less intense and it is completely covered with an intricately engraved carpet of Moresque foliage centred around a polychrome enamelled disc (fig. 14.9d). In comparison with all this, the finial, formed as a turned crystal 'capstan' with stones and pearls around its base, seems muted. But this is not how it was when it was in Henry VIII's possession and a still-life painting by Willem Kalf of 1678 (fig. 14.10) reveals the full extent of the finial, which rose to about three times its present height in a series of stages, each embellished with pendant pearls. The final point to mention is the 'certain writings'. These are a series of Latin inscriptions on the foot and cover, all of which relate to the virtues of moderation in drinking alcohol.

How did Henry acquire this marvellous jewel and where was it made? Known in Munich as *die Holbeinschale* (the Holbein bowl), it was clearly associated with Henry's court artist from an early date, since Kalf's otherwise painstakingly accurate depiction substitutes one of the Latin 'writings' with 'Holbein fe[cit]'. But the bowl does not fit particularly with the style of Holbein's known designs and the spell-binding refinement of the goldsmith's work is in a different league from anything else that can confidently be attributed to an English workshop. Far more likely is that it was one of Henry's many extravagant but unspecified purchases from foreign merchants around the end of the reign, such as the 'certain plate and jewels' that he bought from Jehan Lange for £1,750 in July 1546. We are unlikely ever to know exactly where the bowl was made, although a south German court goldsmith is a strong possibility. One feature of the bowl we have not yet mentioned tantalisingly nods in this direction: on the underneath of the centre of the bowl, clearly visible through the crystal, is a disc decorated in the *verre eglomisé* (reverse painted glass) technique with an elaborate decorative design (fig. 14.9b). The paint and gilding have partly detached from the crystal and only the outer part is still legible. But enough remains for its structure to be seen: a concentrical design of three birds with spread wings, probably eagles, alternating with baskets of fruit. At the centre appears to be some sort of scroll motif or cartouche. But what sat within, we cannot tell. It may have been a mark of ownership or affinity, but the spread eagles suggest the German cultural region.

The late inventories

With the two inventories from the last decade of the reign we have a different order of information from those that came before. The 1521 and 1532 jewel house inventories are just that: lists of plate and other items in the care of the master of the jewel house. The 1542 Whitehall Palace inventory and the inventory of the late king's possessions commissioned after his death in 1547 are fundamentally different and enormously larger. The Whitehall inventory includes some 4,100 entries across all media and itemises around 8,000 objects, while the 1547 one runs to nearly 18,000 entries and a total of some 50,000 objects. As such, from our point of view, they have a double significance, not only presenting a full (or fuller) quantum of the king's plate but also giving us an idea of its context.

These essential differences pan out in at least two ways. First, they give us real evidence of how much plate was *not* in the jewel house, but secondly, as we read them (and especially the later one), a picture unfolds of a range of goldsmiths' work that was different in kind from most of what was kept in the Tower. In the 1547 inventory we see, for the first time, an abundance of the sort of objects that we know from the great princely *Kunstkammers* of Dresden, Munich and Vienna: mounted rock crystals and hardstones, natural curiosities like nautilus shells, sophisticated clocks and scientific instruments, and even the wondrous material that was newly available in the West and that was taking the courts of Europe by storm, high-quality glass.

In total, the weighed plate in the 1547 inventory amounts to an astonishing 192,000 oz (nearly six tonnes). But that is not all and many clearly substantial items were, for one reason or other, not weighed, so it would have been even more. Most of this material is organised into familiar categories – salts, cups, bowls, pots and so on – and within these divisions is listed under location. These locations will act as our guide as we navigate our way through the list.

We will start with the jewel house, the central store mostly frequented and managed by middle-ranking and senior royal servants attached to the Chamber. Then we will proceed to Whitehall Palace and the other 'standing' (permanently furnished) houses, visiting them as a courtier might. And, finally, as only the most privileged royal servants or honoured guests would be permitted to do, we will enter the inner sanctum, the privy chamber itself.

For the jewel house at the end of the reign we rely entirely on the 1547 inventory. John Hallile had been a yeoman of the jewel house during the 1530s and was still in post at the end of the reign. He would have witnessed much continuity over that time, but many changes too. The quantum of plate in the jewel house (termed in the document 'the Remayne') was little changed – the roughly 126,000 oz kept there amounted to around 65 per cent of the whole – but, as we noticed when comparing the earlier inventories, there was a good deal of replacement in the intervening years. Many new objects had arrived, many others had left, and it clearly continued to perform its role as a 'current account'.

An interesting though possibly not very significant shift related to gold: between 1532 and 1547 the number of gold items held there fell from 192 to 89, a decline of more than 50 per cent. This has led some to conclude that holdings of gold plate were declining. But this is not necessarily the case. First, in terms of weight the decline was smaller – from 7,680 oz in 1532 to around 5,100 oz in 1547 – but secondly, when we look at the later inventory we see the total in all locations rise to 182 items and over 7,000 oz, so perhaps the overall decline was not so marked.

Travelling up river from the Tower towards Whitehall, we need to draw on both inventories to understand what was there. The two documents present a completely different picture. The 1542 inventory contains over 10,500 oz of plate, largely made up of familiar domestic or liturgical types but also including drinking glasses, musical instruments and other works of art with gold or silver mounts. Of particular interest is a group of about fifty items purchased from Morgan Wolf in March 1545 and which seem to have been in the latest styles. Their descriptions do not reveal much and it is not clear how the flagons 'with oaken leaves' differed stylistically from their predecessors, but it is telling that most of the ornament is described as 'antique' and a number of pieces had specific classical motifs, such as 'a woman in the top holding a man's head in the one hand and sword in the other hand', representing Judith and Holofernes.[54] Also included are things not encountered before, like stoneware pots with evidently sophisticated mounts.[55]

In sharp contrast to this, the 1547 inventory lists 53,000 oz of plate at Whitehall, five times the quantity in the other list. To understand how such disparities can be, we need to understand the limitations of both documents. Whitehall Palace – the only one of Henry's many residences to be graced with the title palace – was not a building but a sprawling complex that covered, broadly speaking, most of the area between Westminster Abbey to the south and Charles I's Banqueting House to the north and between the river to the east and St James's Park to the west. It was Henry's principal residence during his final years and compared with what was kept there, the quantities of plate listed at his other standing houses – Hampton Court, Greenwich, Windsor and Oatlands – were negligible. One of the most important officials at Whitehall was Sir Anthony Denny, keeper of the palace, and the 1542 inventory was effectively an indenture listing everything 'in his charge'. The contents of the palace were constantly evolving and Denny's 'book of issue' (the equivalent of the jewel house 'book of *extra*' referred to before) shows him, for example, sending 4,900 oz of plate to the mint in 1545,[56] but replacing it with around 6,000 oz of new plate too. Moreover, despite his all-encompassing title, Denny was not responsible for the entire palace. Specifically, his writ did not extend to several important areas, such as 'the glass house', 'the secret jewelhouse' and 'the little study called new library'. One of these, at least, was an area where we would have expected to find a good deal of plate, jewels and other precious objects. Most of the plate in Denny's charge was for dining and Maria Hayward suggests that the trenchers, vessel and serving pieces would have been sufficient for about twenty diners.[57] This, in other words, was the plate in daily use.

Given the comprehensive plan of the posthumous inventory, one might have expected it to fill these gaps. And so it does. But even this, extraordinary though it is, is almost certainly incomplete. The inventory was not commissioned until September 1547, seven or eight months after the king's death, during which time many changes could have taken place; it was a vast undertaking which took several years to complete and the finished document was not presented to the council until 1551. Within its beautifully written pages there is a sense here and there of hurry and poor housekeeping, particularly in the entries covering the secret jewel house.[58] Apparently unrelated things are jumbled together and it appears that the compilers of this part of the inventory were less familiar with plate than the jewel house clerks: many are unweighed, their descriptions are cursory and getting a sense of their size or appearance is not easy.

Despite the Tudor obsession with record-keeping, the evidence suggests that some things probably went astray during this time. Our suspicions have already been aroused by the facts that Denny's 1545 new year's gift to the king (fig. 10.17) cannot be found on the list and that next to no gold 'vessel' is recorded either. As we noted in Chapter 6, just one gold trencher is listed, described as having 'a salt at the one corner [and] standing upon vj antique men of gold'.[59] This was clearly an elaborate and fashionable object, but its singularity is what makes it extraordinary. And squaring this with the anecdotal evidence to the contrary led us to consider three possibilities: one, that all the gold dining wares had been dispatched to the mint to fund the late wars; two, that its existence had been a myth from the start, with ambassadors and others being duped into believing that mere silver-gilt was in fact gold; and three, that it was spirited away from Whitehall in the immediate aftermath of the king's death. Arguably the most plausible of these is the last. To have sent his personal dining plate to the mint would surely have been too great an indignity for the king to bear, and for the whole world to have been consistently and continually misled seems unlikely. The king was, in any case, still providing his goldsmiths with gold bullion to make new treasures at the very end of his life, as we shall see. And opportunities for pilfering surely existed in early 1547. Immediately following the king's death, the duke of Somerset seized control and with that he also created a number of exclusion zones around the palace. A note inserted at one point in the inventory says that these areas remained in his 'only custody [...] until the time of his trouble' in October 1549, meaning, probably, that the inventory clerks had no access until after his fall.[60]

The quantities of domestic wares listed at Westminster in 1547 are enormous. Taking just three categories – silver-gilt pots, salts and cups – there were some fifty pairs of pots (in addition to about a hundred pairs in the Tower), fifty-five salts, and about 190 covered cups (again, in addition to the main jewel house holdings). All of these were spread across several locations. About sixty of the cups are headed 'at Westminster' and were almost certainly in the privy chamber; just fourteen were in Denny's charge (the same number that he held in 1542) and the care of most of the rest was divided between three privy chamber servants, William Fitzwilliam, John Gates (Denny's brother-in-law) and William St Barbe. Two further groups were 'parcel [part] of the night plate found in a square house in the long gallery' and thirty-five were kept in 'the king's secret jewel house in the old gallery next the privy garden'.[61]

It is difficult, on the basis of their descriptions, to know how these groups differed from each other. Certain general distinctions do emerge, however. The cups in the care of Denny, St Barbe and Fitzwilliam seem to be relatively standard and within a fairly narrow weight range of about twenty to thirty ounces. In contrast, those 'at Westminster', in the secret jewel house and with Sir John Gates include much more varied and interesting material. They came in a much wider range of weights, they had different origins and incorporated different materials. Some were German, Flemish or Spanish and others incorporated precious materials like rock crystal and agate. Among the most extraordinary items in Sir John Gates's keeping was a massive cup 'of Flanders making' weighing 337 oz and described as being set with pearls and enamels and fitted out, almost like an elaborate picnic set, with twelve trenchers, four goblets, three cups of assay, twelve spoons, two jewelled and enamel salts and a candlestick with two sockets. Apparently attached to the outside, but perhaps within ('standing upon the sides'), were twelve forks, each embellished with three pearls. On top of the cover was a clock with a finial in the form of a woman.[62]

Exploring the holdings of this single category of plate at Whitehall has led us beyond the threshold of the privy chamber and into the realm of the king's private space. But before we penetrate further into this very different area, let us retreat and stay for a moment in the world of domestic, or ceremonial plate. In virtually every category of domestic plate we observe the same pattern that we have seen in cups: the vast majority of the material was split between the jewel house and Whitehall but – as far as we can tell – with the more decorative or jewel-like material tending to be retained at Whitehall, either in the secret jewel house or in the privy chamber itself. The relatively few items in Denny's charge tended on the whole to be of an apparently lower artistic order. While most of the plate in the inventory is organised under function, a more random selection appears towards the end of the plate lists, headed 'certain parcels of plate of divers sorts, silver-gilt and parcel-gilt'. This must have been the result of a mopping up exercise, after most of the list had been compiled. It includes some extraordinary objects we have encountered before, like 'the king's great alms dish gilt', weighing 547 oz (but apparently 559 oz in 1521 and 1532, so perhaps it had lost some detachable parts), 'one gilt alms dish [of 314 oz] made like a ship having two plain plates upon the sides wherein the king's arms is set', or 'one alms ship gilt', weighing 305 oz.[63] It also includes a mysterious object, 'a great Gertayne of silver' which, at 558 oz, was one of the largest single items of plate in the whole inventory but the nature of which is entirely unknown.[64] The king's great alms dish and the one 'made like a ship' were both in the Tower, as they were before, implying that they were not in regular use, but the second 'alms ship' (and the 'Gertayne') were at Whitehall, so were perhaps at least in occasional use. To give these two ships some sort of visual reference, the Schlüsselfelder nef, made in Nuremberg around 1500 and which is preserved in the Germanisches National Museum, is the largest of all surviving medieval nefs. It stands 78 cm high and weighs nearly six kilograms;[65] Henry's two, by contrast, weighed more than nine kilograms each, so they must have been very substantial indeed.

The dragon's lair

In April 1544 the duke of Alburquerque visited England on his way to Spain. At a time when England was at war with France the duke was an ally and was treated with great honour. Chapuys describes his reception as extraordinary, writing to Charles V that

> no other foreign nobleman ever met with half the honour and hospitality that has been lavished upon him [the point being that he was visiting in a personal capacity rather than as an ambassador]. The duke has visited no less than six or seven royal manors [...] where feasts and carousels have been ordered for his entertainment, exhibiting before his eyes the best part of the gorgeous furniture and silver plate belonging to the king.[66]

Did the 'honour and hospitality lavished upon him' extend beyond the crossed halberds of the gentlemen pensioners guarding the entrance to the privy chamber at Whitehall? We do not know, but if it did he would have entered a very different world, filled with extraordinarily sumptuous and exotic works of art. These objects are described in the 1547 inventory, but the descriptions are often minimal and their appearance, and the way they were deployed, are difficult to reconstruct. This is partly because the typological arrangement of the inventory dissolves any sense of context and partly because the usual commentators on whom we depend for so much of our knowledge of court life were not admitted to this most private area. Its inaccessibility, even when the king was not present, made it possible for an extraordinary density of precious contents to accumulate. And it is with these contents, particularly those headed 'at Westminster' and 'in the king's secret jewel house', that we start to understand what Henry was spending these prodigious sums on as he grew older.

The floor plan of the privy chamber at Whitehall has been partly reconstructed by Simon Thurley. The term 'privy chamber' is misleading as these inaccessible parts of the palace were an extensive area rather than a single room. It became 'an entire palace within the palace',[67] including the closet, the king's bedroom and a series of rooms adjoining the privy gallery. Some of those specifically housing works of art included the study, the library and 'the king's secret study called the chair house'.[68] For a sense of the lavishness of their decoration we have only to look at the fictive group portrait of Henry with Jane Seymour and Prince Edward in the Royal Collection (fig. 1.3): the floor is inlaid with costly coloured marbles, the cloth of estate is intricately embroidered with gold thread, the king's feet rest on a similar cushion, which in turn sits on the sort of Turkey carpet normally reserved for tables, and the columns and wall panels are elaborately worked with gilded relief ornament.

One of the few fixtures of the privy chamber that we know much about was in the room which housed Holbein's lost mural of the family of Henry VIII.[69] This extraordinary creation is described in the inventory:

> There is set into the wall in the privy chamber a thing artificially made like a rock wherein is many devices of 'friers'[70] and diverse other things having in it a fountain of alabaster which is sore decayed and upon the top of the fountain a round ball of crystal wherein was three heads of gold which are gone and xiij stones made like heads also gone which are supposed to be cameos being set about in a border every one of the compass of a groat all which fountain and rock is locked up with two leaves like windows the which leaves are garnished with pearl and gold thread pearled.[71]

This grotto-like confection had evidently been allowed to fall into a somewhat dilapidated state by the time the inventory clerks got to it. It was 'sore decayed', some of its gold elements had gone missing and the cameos, each about the diameter of a groat (25 mm), had been extracted. Such 'decay' would have been most unlikely while the king was occupying this room and surely occurred later. What else was displayed in this room we do not know, but it would have set the tone for a remarkable journey of discovery for anyone privileged enough to inspect the privy chamber as a whole.

The only surviving object from the end of the reign that we can be sure belonged to Henry and which is listed as 'at Westminster' is the Munich rock-crystal bowl (fig. 14.9). It is, as we have discussed, one of the most astonishing jewels of the sixteenth century. Relatively few other objects in the king's possession can possibly have matched it for quality but even if just the tiniest fraction of his goldsmiths' work was anything close to it in terms of precious virtuosity, the contents of the privy chamber would truly have been 'a marvel to behold'.

As a whole these objects fell into three main groups: hardstones (like rock crystal), natural exotica (like mother of pearl, coconuts and shells), and man-made materials or contrivances (like glass and clocks). We will return to the rationale for these classifications shortly, but for the moment we shall sample just a few of the objects in each of these broad categories.

Given the number of rock crystals listed in the inventory, it is not surprising that two of the surviving Henrician objects are of that material. Rock crystal had a very special place in lapidary lore. This was the only known perfectly transparent naturally occurring material and a special mythology grew up about it that went back at least to Pliny the elder. Following Pliny, the fourteenth-century scholar, Konrad von Megenburg, wrote that 'rock crystal is formed from ice, that has hardened over many years'; other writers carried the myth into the sixteenth century.[72] More than sixty items of goldsmiths' work incorporating rock crystal are listed and, of those, more than fifty were at Whitehall. Some of these would have been old and remounted, as they were in the case of the San Lorenzo and Munich pieces, and the supply of old rock-crystal vessels was boosted in the second quarter of the sixteenth century by the dissolution of the monasteries in England (and the Reformation elsewhere) making countless medieval rock-crystal reliquaries available for repurposing and remounting after their former mounts had been stripped off. But others would have been of more recent manufacture and the second quarter of the sixteenth century saw a marked expansion of rock-crystal production in centres such as Freiburg-im-Breisgau and Milan.

Rock crystal was the dominant hardstone in the collection, but many others were represented too, such as agate, serpentine, jasper, prasinus and birrall. Agate was found in quite large matrices that could be ground down on a wheel and made into substantial vessels. With its translucent and variegated colour range and its capacity to take a high polish, it had been a highly valued material since ancient times. Serpentine had come into favour much more recently. The dull, greenish grey stone was mined in Saxony and most vessels made of it were probably fabricated there before being exported for mounting. An elaborately conceived spice plate, described as being made of 'grey stone', very possibly serpentine, was mounted in silver-gilt, 'standing upon four antique heads with horns' and with a cover set with heads carved in agate, in 'purselyne' and in 'mother of emerald';[73] others included 'beer cups of serpentine' with jewelled mounts.[74] A more difficult category to assess was birrall. The word occurs many times in the inventory but not always with the same meaning. In some cases it seems to mean beryl but in others some sort of glass is probably indicated. Occasionally the inventory clerks were not sure and hedged their bets, such as 'a silver-mounted drinking glass or birrall'.[75]

Natural exotica must have been prominent in the privy chamber displays but the vagaries of nomenclature mean that it is not always easy to know what we are dealing with. The commonest such material is mother of pearl, which is partly explained by the fact that the second half of the reign coincided with the development of a substantial export trade, largely through Portugal, of wares from Gujarat formed of mother-of-pearl tesserae. Many were enriched with gold or silver mounts after they reached Europe and some of the earliest are attributed to Francis I's goldsmith, Pierre Mangot. A large coffer of 1532 in the Louvre (fig. 14.11), mounted in silver-gilt and set with numerous small gemstones and 'antique heads', may have resembled one of those in the secret jewel house, described as a 'coffer of mother of pearl garnished with silver and gilt' and which was large enough to contain forty jewelled collars and chains.[76]

The term mother of pearl was probably applied more broadly, referring also to whole shells, polished to reveal their underlying iridescent nacre. One such was a layer (or ewer) described as 'of mother of pearl being a shell' and was presumably a large polished turban shell or similar. It had a handle 'being an antique man of gold' and it had a gold lip and spout. Its description runs to more than 250 words, most of which enumerate the many precious stones that embellished it: eleven diamonds, twenty-nine rubies, eighteen emeralds, three sapphires and twenty pearls. It weighed 160 oz and must have been a dazzling piece.[77]

Nautilus is not a term that appears in the inventory but these fabled chambered shells, made by cephalopods rather than snails, had been

Figure 14.11
Coffer, Pierre Mangot, Paris, 1532–33. Silver gilt, mother of pearl and precious stones. Musée du Louvre, Paris.

Figure 14.12
The Burghley nef, Paris, 1527–28. Silver gilt, nautilus shell and pearls. Victoria and Albert Museum, London.

sought after by European princely patrons since at least the later Middle Ages and it would be surprising if Henry had not owned any. A 'ship of mother of pearl, the foot and upper part of silver gilt with a mermaid under the belly of the ship of like silver gilt'[78] was surely of this kind. We are not told its weight or size but the Burghley nef, made in Paris in 1527 and incorporating a polished nautilus shell (fig. 14.12), corresponds exactly to the description and it is tempting to think of it as a survivor from Henry VIII's collection. Could this have been one of Henry's purchases from the French jewellers in 1532?

Other materials falling into this category include ostrich eggs, coral and horn. These would all, in the second quarter of the sixteenth century, have been considered great rarities. Only one ostrich egg is named as such but others called 'grypes [griffins'] eggs' were probably of the same kind. The mounts to the ostrich egg were enamelled with 'antique imagery', roses and fruit and the enamelled handle was modelled as entwined serpents; it is perhaps the perceived rarity of the egg that explains why the mounts were of gold rather than silver-gilt.[79]

The greatest prize in terms of rarity was the fabled unicorn horn (in fact the horn of a narwhal). We have seen how Henry seized several from Winchester Cathedral in 1536, and the 1547 inventory records even more, at least one of which was mounted with gold.[80] Coral was probably not considered quite so rare, but it was certainly exotic and its form gave it interesting artistic possibilities, such as 'a tree of coral with the images of Adam and Eve, the serpent and other beasts of silver-gilt enamelled with a foot of silver-gilt likewise enamelled'.[81] As a final example of natural exotica embellished with goldsmiths' work, we might take 'a standing branch of gold with five adders' tongues in the tops'.[82] Similar objects survive today in Dresden and Vienna,[83] the 'adders' tongues' in fact being sharks' teeth, which were thought to react to the presence of poison by changing colour.

The other over-arching category was of man-made, or artificial, materials and covered a wide spectrum from clocks and scientific instruments to glass and ceramics.

Glass-making was a transformative new technology. Made in Venice from the late fifteenth century, blown soda glass provided for the first time an alternative to prohibitively expensive rock crystal and was hugely exciting. There is plenty of evidence for glass in England in the early part of the reign and a number of mounted glasses appear in the 1521 inventory. The 1547 one includes a number that were clearly not new, such as a 'silver-gilt mounted glass [...] the Cardinal's arms on the finial'[84] and another, gold-mounted, and set with red roses, fleurs de lis and pomegranates,[85] which must have dated to when Katherine of Aragon was still in favour. But by 1535 it was all the rage. This was the year that Sir Nicholas Poyntz entertained Henry VIII in great style at Acton Court in Gloucestershire and purchased large numbers of glasses for the occasion. Henry was no less susceptible to the enthusiasm and by the end of the reign, in true Henrician style, had accumulated large numbers of glasses of many kinds. By then the glass house at Whitehall contained more than 550 glass vessels.[86] Many, if not most, of these must have been Venetian and references to blue glass with gilded decoration, to glasses 'of jasper colour' or to 'glass all of diaper work' suggest classic Venetian types such as survive in considerable numbers today. Although much cheaper than rock crystal or plate,[87] its novelty and artistic potential accounted for glass being considered a suitable material even for new year's gifts, such as those Henry gave to Anne of Cleves in 1542.[88] It also led to many glasses being embellished with silver or gold mounts.[89] A further sign of the craze for glass was that many of the newer silver-gilt cups in the royal plate were evidently made in imitation of it and were described as of 'glass fashion'.[90] This is not a term that appears in the previous jewel house inventories, and it perhaps refers to vessels like the Boleyn cup (fig. 11.1). One of Holbein's most splendid designs is for the mounts for a conical glass, discussed on p. 198 (fig. 10.18).

More ambiguous as a material is 'pursulane'. The word occurs a number of times and it is tempting to identify it with porcelain, the pure white and miraculously translucent Chinese ceramic that was starting to reach Europe through Venetian and Portuguese traders. But, like mother of pearl, 'pursulane' seems to have had more than one meaning. When used in a 'ship for frankincense [...] with six cameos or porcelains' or a 'standing cup garnished with agate heads and porcelain'[91] it sounds very like shell (as distinct from agate) cameos. But 'a silver-gilt cup and cover of porcelain glass fashion' or a 'silver-gilt mounted porcelain layer' sounds like something different.[92] The most telling entry in this respect is for a 'blue cup, Turkey [turquoise] colour, of a stone called pur-selyne unset and ungarnished [not mounted]'.[93] This, presumably, was not Chinese and so not actually porcelain at all; more probably it was tin-glazed pottery from Isnik in Turkey, which was sometimes mistaken for porcelain in Europe.

Turning from man-made materials to objects of an intellectual bent, Henry VIII clearly had a predilection for scientific instruments and especially for clocks. There were many clocks at Whitehall, including a number with silver-gilt or gold mounts. Some, especially those in precious metal, were not just functional timepieces but were conceived as luxurious works of art. Others formed just part of much more elaborate objects. One, for example, sat on top of the massive Flemish compendium cup discussed above (see p. 303), and another was similarly located on a great jewelled fountain.[94] The description of the latter (which omits its weight) is confusing and the object is difficult to envisage. Essentially, however, it was as follows: it was of silver-gilt and, like the cup, was a portmanteau object, containing a case of knives and three drawers with ring handles. Its main decorative features were depictions in enamel of 'vj of the vij Sciences' (presumably the Liberal Arts, but why just six?). These were placed beneath rock-crystal and silver-gilt terms ('antiques lacking arms'). In some way that is unclear it also incorporated three rock-crystal saltcellars and three boxes. Above all this was the clock 'closed within crystal and borne up by vj antiques' and which was surmounted by 'a man having a snake by the tail', perhaps Hercules. The description ends with the observation that 'all the said fountain is bordered [...] with plates of gold enamelled curiously wrought'. We have no clue of where this extraordinary object was made, although it is tempting to think of the circle of the great Nuremberg goldsmith, Wenzel Jamnitzer (1508–85). But whoever created it, there is no doubt that it must have been one of the most remarkable *Kunstkammer* pieces in the collection.

The most distinctive group within the clocks category comprised so-called clock salts, such as the one discussed in Chapter 9 (see p. 170). Ten of these are listed in the 1547 inventory, nearly all of them precious and jewelled, including two of gold. The most remarkable of these stood on a triangular base with the clockwork above, contained within a rock crystal, and with a saltcellar 'of prasinus [emerald] green' above that. The cover was modelled as a castle, with a green tree whose flowers were diamonds and rubies and 'in the top of the tree [was] a white boy with a scripture [inscription] over his head'.[95]

Henry's interest in matters broadly scientific extended beyond the measurement of time. An early pointer to this was when he bought an elegant walking staff from Cornelis Hayes in 1531, which was 'garnished with crown gold, furnished with a foot measure, a compass, and a pair of tongs',[96] perhaps rather like that depicted in the late portrait of Henry VIII in the National Portrait Gallery (fig. 14.1). A number of precious objects in the inventory reflect a casual interest in astronomy too, such as 'a tablet of gold enamelled black being an instrument of astronomy'[97] and 'a standing clock with diverse conclusions of astronomy'.[98]

Not all of these objects were new, of course, and many would have fallen below the radar in earlier decades because of our very limited knowledge of royal holdings outside the jewel house. But there is no doubt that the royal goldsmiths were kept busy with new *Kunstkammer* commissions right until the end of the reign. Indeed, we have evidence of major commissions being prepared by Everard Everdyes, 'the king's goldsmith and stonecutter', at the time of Henry's death. Everdyes (or Everdyce) only made his appearance at the very end of the reign. He was a stranger, presumably from Antwerp, and is mentioned as a companion of Peter Vanderwall in a grant of July 1546 giving the latter licence to import a vast range of goods. These included 'all manner of jewels set and unset, all manner embroideries [...], all manner of plate of goldsmith's work, arras and tapestry, cloths of gold, of silver [...] harness, weapons, guns, gunpowder and all kinds of artillery and munitions for war'.[99] Two months later Everdyes was given permission to settle in London with his family,[100] so presumably the king had been sufficiently impressed by his work to want to employ him. Only one piece in the inventory is specifically ascribed to him, the gold and enamel-mounted ostrich egg discussed above, but he was certainly engaged on other projects. The 'blue cup of a stone called pur-selyne' that was 'unset and ungarnished' at the time of the inventory had, according to the same entry, been 'delivered to the said Everarde by

Sir Anthony Denny to be made [mounted] for king Henry VIII'.[101] As was normal, the goldsmith had been provided with the metal and the next entry is for 40 oz of gold delivered to Everard by Martin Bowes 'to the garnishing of the same cup'.[102] Presumably the king's death led to the commission being cancelled. But his work for the Crown did not end there and the same inventory includes a late 'memorandum' recording that Everdyes had made Edward VI's personal crown[103] and was still supplying jewels and goldsmiths' work four years later.[104]

The sense of preciousness and sumptuousness that would have struck any visitor to the privy chamber would have been accompanied by another, equally powerful impression, namely muchness. In addition to the enormous numbers of precious vessels and other substantial objects, the quantities of jewellery were incredible. Most of this was stored in a series of coffers, formerly in the keeping of Sir John Gates, that contained hundreds of rings, aglettes, owches, buttons, chains and so on, collectively containing thousands of precious stones. Many of the coffers were themselves highly decorated, some resembling, perhaps, the one shown in the tapestry of the return of Sarah by the Egyptians (fig. 14.7). Others were clearly precious in themselves, such as one of 'silver and gilt garnished with imagery and agates'.[105]

But it was not only jewels that were stored in coffers. Many of the valuable objects that were, presumably, acquired for display were, by the time the inventory was compiled, packed away in coffers, rather like the precious wares in the Sarah tapestry. This contributes to the picture we have already formed of the privy chamber being in a state of reorganisation, rather than how it would have looked when Henry was still alive. But despite the partial dismantling of the old king's arrangements it is still possible to extract certain clues from the inventory. Various sub-lists within the text break the normal pattern of organisation under material and focus on specific locations within the palace of Whitehall. That headed 'in the secret jewelhouse for the furniture thereof' describes the furniture and its relative positions in the room. There was a 'table with a green cloth with four almeries [armillary spheres]' and there were five cabinets 'set in the wall covered with crimson velvet and garnished all over with gold and silver lace'.[106] It sounds here as if we have a hint of the layout of a *Kunstkammer* or 'art cabinet', with furniture for the display of works of art, perhaps not entirely unlike that seen in a seventeenth-century depiction of a *Kunstkammer* at Regensburg (fig. 14.13). But the list makes no mention of contents. Moreover, the room is cluttered with coffers, iron chests and black leather cases filled with a bewildering array of precious objects and with 'empty cases for clocks'. Very similar impressions emerge from the descriptions of the 'study at the end of the long gallery' and 'the king's

Figure 14.13 *Kunstkammer of the Dimpfel Family of Regensburg*, Joseph Arnold, 1668. Museum Ulm (1952.2611).

secret study called the chair house'.[107] The *Kunstkammer*, it seems, has been turned into a storeroom.

But a *Kunstkammer* is very likely what it was. The earliest surviving such space was created by Archduke Ferdinand II of Austria at Schloss Ambras in Innsbruck after 1557. What survives of the collection is now mostly in Vienna but contemporary inventories give a clear impression of an immensely dense display, not unlike the view invited by Henry's inventory.

By the end of the sixteenth century the princely *Kunstkammer* or *Wunderkammer* had become an important cultural phenomenon all over Europe. Precious or 'curious' objects were collected or commissioned in a highly competitive way and were installed in displays based on quasi-scientific classifications. These varied depending on which intellectual principles were adopted or on the relative strengths of the collection, but the most consistent over-arching classifications were *naturalia* and *artificialia*. *Naturalia* might be divided into material from the earth (essentially hardstones) and from the sea (mother of pearl, shells and coral); *artificialia* might be broken into many sub-categories: mechanical objects, scientific instruments, medals and so on. It is tempting to interpret the collections in the privy chamber at Whitehall as being laid out according to such principles. This cannot be proved but it is, at least, clear that the materials to do so were there.[108]

Henry VIII died possessed of more gold and silver than any other English monarch, before or since, and possibly more than any other monarch ever. The astonishing headline figures of quantity are what are easiest to focus on, and the often-repeated accounts of massive displays of magnificence at royal banquets are easy to evoke, if only vaguely, in the mind's eye. These show a monarch with a clear grasp of the use of magnificence in the closely allied arts of impressing and intimidating. But what is much harder to appreciate is Henry as a connoisseur, for this only emerges from the much more private world of the objects he amassed in the privy chamber and the secret jewel house. These were not exceptional in a general sense and accumulations of precious and 'curious' objects were very much part of the princely ethos. We get a sense of such objects from the inventory of Richard II, some of which were still in existence in Henry's time, and we find similar artfully mounted hardstones in the collection of Lorenzo de' Medici (d. 1492).[109] It was also a lively preoccupation of Francis I, whose ability to call on the services of artists like Benvenuto Cellini and Rosso Fiorentino gave Henry much to envy. But what was exceptional was the sheer numbers of such precious objects, made possible partly by Henry's ruthless use of deprivation as a means of accumulation. For the closest equivalents to the huge extent of Henry's collection we must turn to the great dynastic collections of the Wittelsbachs, the Habsburgs and the rulers of Saxony. All of these were later and were accumulated over generations, whereas Henry's were only partly inherited and were almost entirely dispersed and destroyed by the end of the sixteenth century. What exactly happened to this extraordinary legacy is the subject of the last chapter.

Fifteen

'Sic transit gloria mundi': the Fate of Henry VIII's Plate and Jewels

Stand by the road close to Calais, halfway between Guînes and Ardres, facing north-east. What do you see? A flat, featureless agricultural landscape, with the village of Guînes a mile or so to your left and Ardres a similar distance to your right. A plain granite slab marks the spot, inscribed

CAMP DU DRAP D'OR
1520
FIELD OF CLOTH OF GOLD

Other than that, there is not the slightest hint that you are standing on the site of one of the most spectacular and famous events of the sixteenth century. Fabulously expensive, it was also ephemeral and no trace of it survived, even a few years after it took place. A similar, although more gradual, fate awaited the vast hoard of plate and jewels that filled Whitehall and the Tower jewel house as Henry VIII lay dying in January 1547: a century later hardly a trace of it remained. How could this be?

Despite its vast scale, despite the artfulness of many of the pieces in the king's personal keeping and the historic resonance of some of the treasures in the jewel house, it would be a mistake to regard the royal plate as a collection in the modern sense. For plate and jewels were infinitely recyclable and, ultimately, were mainly prized for their intrinsic value. This differentiated them fundamentally from other things and meant that goldsmiths' work, although admired as things of beauty and virtuosity, was primarily seen as a resource. It is for this reason that the inventories are often thin on description but scrupulous in recording weight and counting precious stones.

The destruction of Henry's plate was a continual process. Against the overall pattern of ever-increasing holdings, there were many occasions when the graph dipped and large quantities of plate were dispatched to the mint to meet a national emergency: 57,000 ounces in 1536 at the time of the Pilgrimage of Grace, for example, or some 72,000 between 1542 and 1544 to help fund the war with France. There were also many occasions when royal plate was given away or melted down to be remade in new fashions. So, although some 192,000 ounces of plate were listed in the last inventory of the reign, much of this dated only from the previous decade or two and many of the objects listed in 1521 or 1532 no longer existed by the time of the king's death.

The dispersal of the final holdings – the ones that are included in the posthumous inventory – began immediately after the king's death, with the provisions of his will. This is very different from his father's. While Henry VII's will devoted pages to his bequests of pyxes for parish churches and images for the altar associated with his tomb in Westminster Abbey, Henry VIII's bequests of plate were all personal. He left legacies to his daughters of £10,000 each 'in money, plate, jewels and household stuff'; £3,000 of this was payable immediately and the rest on their marriage 'to any outward potentate'. A few more specific bequests to his executors, to Katherine Parr and others were also included, but the residue was left to his heir, the young Edward VI.[1]

The new king's vast inheritance did not remain intact for long, however, and the start of its erosion can be detected even in the pages of the inventory. We have considered the possibility that some valuable objects were removed from Whitehall even before the final inventory was begun; notes added during its compilation record the modification of certain jewels 'against his coronation taken from the furniture of certain collars and caps of the king's majesty's that dead is',[2] or the sending in July 1547 of 'a great sapphire set in a ring of gold' to Everard Everdyes, which was subsequently returned 'cut in squares'.[3] In 1550 a meltdown of royal plate was ordered and a substantial quantity transferred to the mint.[4] In 1552 a pair of gold flagons was sent 'amongst others' as gifts to the queen of France[5] and in the same year the great jewelled bust of St George, bequeathed by Henry VII to St George's Chapel 'for a perpetual memory there to remain while the world shall endure', was sold off to goldsmiths. Another great loss, from around this time or a little later, was the magnificent gold cross that had survived from the time of Richard II (see p. 29) but which had disappeared by the time of the 1574 jewel house inventory.

During the remaining half-century of Tudor rule the resources of the jewel house, although regularly refreshed with new stock, were gradually depleted and Collins has estimated that just seventy-four of the nearly 900 entries from the 1521 inventory were still extant in 1574. But when we focus on works of art rather than bullion, despite the specific objects just mentioned, a more discerning attitude seems to emerge. A category probably richer in works of art than, say, pots or 'vessel', was gold or gold-mounted cups. These included things like the French royal gold cup, the 'Dream of Paris' cup and Holbein's Seymour cup, and here we seem to detect a tendency to preserve the best: of the thirty-one listed in 1574, fifteen – nearly half – had appeared in the Henrician inventories.

James I, when he came to the English throne in 1604, seems where possible to have adopted a conservative attitude to the royal plate. But such scruples had no choice but to bow in the face of political or financial necessity. Shortly after his accession, the conclusion of the Somerset House Conference, which drew a line under eighteen years of war with Spain, called for munificent gifts to the Spanish ambassadors. Gold plate of recent manufacture and suitable importance was not available, so a number of historic objects – perhaps reluctantly – were selected for the purpose. These included the French royal gold cup (fig. 3.3) and a gold ewer and basin which had been made for Jane Seymour and was perhaps designed by Holbein.[6] In all, the ambassadorial gifts came to 290 oz of gold and nearly 29,000 oz of silver-gilt. Further inroads into the remains of Henry's gold became unavoidable with the visit of James's brother-in-law, Christian IV of Denmark, in 1606.[7]

Charles I did not share his father's fastidiousness in this respect. His reign started with grandiose military ambitions which needed funding, and a warrant of 1625, shortly after his accession, instructed the groom of the jewel house to deliver some forty items of gold plate, much of it jewelled, to the duke of Buckingham and the earl of Holland. It was to be shipped to The Hague and there 'disposed of as we have specially directed them for our service'.[8] Some of this rich consignment (bearing the arms of the king's mother, Anne of Denmark) was evidently of recent manufacture, but at least nine Henrician pieces can be recognised as well. These included the Seymour cup, the fabulous 160 oz jewelled mother-of-pearl layer discussed in Chapter 14, and at least two great historic pieces, namely the 'salt called the Morris dance' and the 'Dream of Paris' cup. This was a two-stage process and Collins traces the final chapters in the story of the Seymour cup: like many older pieces in the jewel house, it was not in perfect condition and by the time it was taken to the Netherlands only one of its pendant pearls remained; once abroad it was not sold but pawned. Four years later it was redeemed and then melted, the remaining gems being separately sold to two Dutch jewellers.[9] The layer was treated in a similar way, being pawned then redeemed and sold, with its great enrichment of gems, for £2,390.[10] But Charles did not only require bullion to fund his military expeditions, he was also the greatest English collector-monarch since Henry VIII and was not satisfied with plate that was in old-fashioned taste. The ewer and basin designed by Rubens and the great altar service commissioned from his goldsmith,

Christian van Vianen, were almost certainly made with bullion provided by old jewel house plate.[11]

The erosion of Henry's holdings accelerated during the Civil War and in 1649, after the regicide, the imperial regalia itself, now surplus to constitutional requirements, was finally destroyed. Rather than run the risk of it falling into the hands of royalists and being treated as relics, all the objects were sent to the mint and the gold coined. The coronation regalia, on the other hand, was sold, the chalice of St Edward fetching £110 15s.[12] Among the few remaining Henrician objects included in the sale of the 'goods and personal estate of the late king, queen and prince' were the French clock salt (fig. 9.5) and the gold salt 'with a cover borne up with a morion', which dated back to the time of Richard III. The gold-mounted crystal bowl now in Munich was among this group, as was the enamelled and gold-mounted ostrich egg supplied by Everard Everdyes at the very end of the reign. They were valued at £120 and £70 respectively.

What by then was left? More, perhaps, than we think. The descriptions on the 1649 lists are brief and imprecise and it is difficult to tie them to the 1547 inventory, especially since their weights have to be inferred from their per ounce valuations. When Collins published his ground-breaking work on the 1574 inventory he was aware of just a single surviving piece from the reign of Henry VIII: the French royal gold cup, which he described as 'the sole relic of the treasure-hoard of Tudor England'.[13] During the 1960s John Hayward identified the Munich rock-crystal bowl, and the Mangot clock salt subsequently emerged as another royal Tudor object. Later still, in the 1990s, I myself recognised the origins of the San Lorenzo vase, bringing the total to four. The Burghley nef, if accepted, would make five and the Halle monstrance, although hugely compromised, would make six. But where several have emerged others might follow, perhaps lurking in one or other of the great European *Kunstkammers*, or even in the rich and largely uncatalogued treasuries of the Spanish cathedrals. With three 'new' objects added to the list in the last half-century, it would be surprising if others did not eventually appear and throw more light on the vanished world of what was surely one of the greatest accumulations of royal gold and silver ever formed.

Notes

Chapter 1

1. Piero Pasqualigo, describing Henry VIII's Garter celebrations in April 1515 (quoted from Frank Mumby (ed.), *The Youth of Henry VIII: A Narrative in Contemporary Letters* (London, 1913), pp. 340–42).
2. For a discussion of the tapestries and the evidence for Henry's ownership of them, see Thomas P. Campbell, *Henry VIII and the Art of Majesty: Tapestries at the Tudor Court* (New Haven and London, 2007), pp. 145–47.
3. Aristotle, *The Nicomachean Ethics*, trans. J. A. K. Thomson, rev. edn (London, 2004), p. 83, lines 24–27; p. 85, lines 28–31.
4. Aristotle, *Nicomachean Ethics*, pp. 82–85.
5. A. R. Myers (ed.), *The Household of Edward IV: The Black Book and the Ordinance of 1478* (Manchester, 1959), p. 86. I am grateful to Dr Lisa Jefferson for her translation of this passage from the Latin.
6. Sir John Fortescue, 'The Governance of England', in *On the Laws and Governance of England*, ed. Shelley Lockwood (Cambridge, 1997), p. 98.
7. Gordon Kipling, *The Triumph of Honour: Burgundian Origins of the Elizabethan Renaissance* (The Hague, 1977), p. 29.
8. Aristotle, *Nicomachean Ethics*, p. 85.
9. According to Campbell (*Henry VIII and the Art of Majesty*, pp. 93–94), ordinary wool tapestry cost around 8d per ell, while the finest Arras with gilt-metal thread was as much as 40s.
10. See Campbell, *Henry VIII and the Art of Majesty*, p. 68.
11. *Chamber Books*, BL, Add. MS 21481, fol. 125. All references to the *Chamber Books* are to the online versions, available at https://www.tudorchamberbooks.org.
12. Maria Hayward, *Dress at the Court of Henry VIII* (Leeds, 2007), p. 120.
13. *LP*, vol. 1, no. 3055.
14. *LP*, vol. 16, no. 276.
15. The quotation, used for the title of this book, comes from Edward Hall's description of a royal banquet at Greenwich in 1527 (Hall, *King Henry VIII*, vol. 2, p. 85).
16. *CSP*, *Milan*, no. 539.
17. *LP*, vol. 2, King's Book of Payments, 1509–18, pp. 1441–90.
18. For example, see *LP*, vol. 15, no. 642 and vol. 18, part 2, p. 127.
19. Thomas Elyot, *The Boke Named the Governour: A Scolar Press Facsimile*, ed. R. C. Alston (Menston, 1970), fol. 106.
20. *CSP*, *Venetian*, vol. 2, no. 887.
21. *LP*, vol. 16, no. 1183.
22. See Chapter 12, p. 249 for a full account of this episode.
23. *Great Chronicle of London*, pp. 311–12.
24. David Starkey (ed.), *Henry VIII: A European Court in England* (London, 1991), p. 174.
25. *LP*, vol. 15, no. 1015.
26. *LP*, vol. 15, no. 954.

Chapter 2

1. Simon Thurley, *Houses of Power: The Places That Shaped the Tudor World* (London, 2017), p. 21.
2. Maria Hayward, *Dress at the Court of Henry VIII* (Leeds, 2007), p. 243.
3. David Starkey, 'The Age of the Household: Politics, Society and the Arts c. 1350–1550', in *The Later Middle Ages*, ed. Stephen Medcalf (London, 1981), p. 255.
4. Thurley, *Houses of Power*, p. 57.
5. A. R. Myers (ed.), *The Household of Edward IV: The Black Book and the Ordinance of 1478* (Manchester, 1959), pp. 183–84. Plate allocated to other departments included 'layers' (in the cellar), candlesticks (in the chaundry) and 'vessel' (in the scullery).
6. Myers (ed.), *Household of Edward IV*, p. 158.
7. Myers (ed.), *Household of Edward IV*, p. 194.
8. *CSP*, *Milan*, no. 527.
9. *CSP*, *Venetian*, vol. 1, no. 662.
10. Myers (ed.), *Household of Edward IV*, pp. 121–22.
11. *The Ryalle Book* names the master of the jewel house as one of the few officials allowed to sit in the great chamber (see Francis Grose and Thomas Astle (eds), *The Antiquarian Repertory: A Miscellaneous Assemblage of Topography, History, Biography, Customs and Manners*, vol. 1 (London, 1807), p. 307).
12. Simon Thurley, in *Houses of Power* (p. 46), uses the term 'deposit account'. Others have used similar analogies: W. C. Richardson (*Tudor Chamber Administration 1485–1547* (Baton Rouge, 1952), p. 80) calls it 'a kind of bank for the Chamber', and A. J. Collins (*Jewels and Plate of Queen Elizabeth I: The Inventory of 1574* (London, 1955), p. 83) a 'current account' (citing the culling of nine out of ten gold cups presented between 1522 and 1529).
13. The grant confirming Henry Wyatt as master in 1513 states that the appointment is 'to be, during good conduct […] with the usual profits and an annuity of £50' (*LP*, vol. 1, part 2, no. 1948.92). The 'usual profits' are not defined but according to Collins (*Jewels and Plate of Queen Elizabeth I*, p. 226) included fees from issuing goldsmiths' warrants, a 'poundage' on new year's gifts and rewards that could be expected from ambassadors and others receiving royal gifts of plate.
14. Claude Blair (ed.), *The Crown Jewels: The History of the Coronation Regalia in the Jewel House of the Tower of London* (London, 1998).
15. This is presumably not identical with the William Tyler identified by Starkey as joint groom of the stool in 1509 with John Sharp.
16. H. D. Sitwell, 'The Jewel House and the Royal Goldsmiths', *Archaeological Journal*, 117 (1960), p. 132.
17. *LP*, vol. 1, no. 20. Robert Draper, one of the key jewel house officials over the first two decades of the reign, is not named on this occasion but was clearly in post as groom by September 1509 when his six-month salary of 33s 4d fell due (*Chamber Books*, BL, Add. MS 21481, fol. 22v).
18. Biographical material from 'Sir Thomas Wyatt', *ODNB*.
19. For instance, in February 1510 Amadas was paid over £450 for plate bought for a 'disguising' at court. The next month he was paid £1,000 towards an obligation of £2,516 8s 5d. *Chamber Books*, BL, Add. MS 21481, fols 22v, 24v.
20. *LP*, vol. 6, no. 924.
21. *LP*, vol. 4, no. 6771.
22. David Starkey, 'The King's Privy Chamber' (unpublished PhD dissertation, University of Cambridge, 1973), p. 256.
23. For instance, in April 1511: 'to John Twyselton of London goldsmith upon his bill signed for cramp rings and mending of plate in diverse offices in the king's house'. *Chamber Books*, BL, Add. MS 21481, fol. 57v. All references are to the online versions of these records available at http://www.tudorchamberbooks.org.
24. Gordon Kipling (ed.), *The Receyt of the Ladie Kateryne*, Early English Text Society, original series, no. 296 (Oxford, 1990), p. 70.
25. Myers (ed.), *Household of Edward IV*, pp. 121–23.
26. *LP*, vol. 5, Treasurer of the Chamber's Accounts, pp. 303, 313.
27. *LP*, vol. 5, no. 1370.
28. *LP*, vol. 5, no. 1589.

29. BL, Cotton MS Titus B I, fol. 57.
30. *LP*, vol. 14, part 2, no. 548.
31. Myers (ed.), *Household of Edward IV*, p. 122.
32. TNA, E36/85. The 1547 inventory of the possessions of Henry VIII (*Inventory of Henry VIII*) includes the contents of the jewel house too, under the heading 'The Remain'.
33. Fletcher Gyles was a bookseller and publisher based in Holborn near Gray's Inn from about 1714 to 1741 (see H. R. Plomer et al., *A Dictionary of the Printers and Booksellers Who Were at Work in England, Scotland and Ireland from 1726 to 1775* (London, 1932). I am grateful to Giles Mandelbrote, Librarian and Archivist at Lambeth Palace for this information)
34. Trollope, 'King Henry VIII's Jewel Book', pp. 155–229.
35. We have to be cautious in relying too heavily on Trollope's transcriptions of weights, since some are misconstrued. This can be seen by comparing weights for corresponding entries in the 1532 inventory, preserved in the National Archives: in some cases, for example, he has evidently read a Roman 'C' (100) as 'D' (for 500), leading to massive overstatements of weights, such as a pair of pots whose weight he shows as 1,596 oz but which are clearly given as 396 oz in the 1532 inventory. If individual weights are wrong, totals will be also.
36. These are very round numbers and prices fluctuated. For most of the reign the price offered by the mint for scrap silver was just over £2 per lb for silver (roughly 3s 4d per oz); fine gold (rather than 18 carat) fetched just over £27 per lb (roughly 45s per oz). C. E. Challis, *The Tudor Coinage* (London, 1978), p. 171.
37. Trollope, 'King Henry VIII's Jewel Book', pp. 158–59, 164, 167.
38. See, for instance, in a warrant for delivery of jewels to Cornelis Hayes in 1532: 'which said parcels be and are of the book of *infra* indenting [...] for the receipt of every part and parcel of the said our jewels [...] and that you do enter these our said letters in our book of *extra*'. TNA, E 101/421/5, no. 11.
39. Trollope, 'King Henry VIII's Jewel Book', p. 201.
40. A schedule of prices, probably dating from about 1520, sets how much the king was to pay for various kinds of goldsmiths' work. 'Making of cups and layers and bowls of gold garnished with stone and pearls' was to be charged at 4s per ounce above the metal, whereas 'all manner of goldsmith's work made in silver and gilt [...] for every ounce making and golding' cost 1s 8d per ounce (TNA, SP 1/232, fols 288–89v). The gilding would have accounted for a significant part of this sum.
41. *CSP*, *Venetian*, vol. 2, no. 1287. For a further discussion of this see p. 237 below.
42. Grose and Astle (eds), *Antiquarian Repertory*, vol. 1, p. 330.
43. *LP*, vol. 1, no. 1549.
44. For this and following references to the Chamber accounts, see *Chamber Books*, BL, Add. MS 21481. See also *LP*, vol. 1, no. 1549.
45. TNA, SP 1/229, fol. 110v.
46. Sometimes the payments were made directly to the goldsmiths and sometimes to the master for onward distribution. One interim payment in November 1509 was made direct 'to diverse goldsmiths of London' but another the following April was to Wyatt. The final payment in January 1511 came to £454 11s 8d, which was 'over and besides the 500 marks paid to Sir Henry Wyatt before hand'. To judge from the Chamber accounts, payments were somewhat irregular; in January 1515 and 1516 the entire cost seems to have been settled in single payments of £806 15s and £1,056 15s 8d respectively.
47. *LP*, vol. 3, part 2, no. 3370.
48. *LP*, vol. 12, part 2, no. 1277.
49. See David Starkey, 'Henry VI's Old Blue Gown', *The Court Historian*, 4, 1 (1999), pp. 1–28.
50. Myers (ed.), *Household of Edward IV*, p. 330.
51. *LP*, vol. 5, Treasurer of the Chamber's Accounts, p. 303; vol. 9, no. 477.
52. The Tudor jewel house accounts have not survived and its financial relations with the Chamber are not directly relevant to our story. Briefly, however, the Chamber seems to have been the principal paymaster for the jewel house, although the picture is complicated by the latter also having had direct access to funds (certainly during John Heron's time as treasurer) through the regular transfer of Chamber surpluses to the Tower. These were apparently used, for example, to pay

the expenses of English ambassadors abroad. But we should not be too clear-cut about this. Alsop argues that the multiple functions of certain officials (such as Heron), often working from their residences rather than at a designated office, blurred the distinction between one department and another. 'This extended so far that on occasion information relating to totally distinct offices was entered into single registers' (J. D. Alsop, 'The Structure of Early Tudor Finance c 1509–1558', in *Revolution Reassessed: Revisions in the History of Tudor Government and Administration*, ed. Christopher Coleman and David Starkey (Oxford, 1986), p. 147).

53. *Chamber Books*, BL, Add. MS 21481, fols 131, 168.
54. *Chamber Books*, BL, Add. MS 21481, fol. 260v; TNA, E 36/216, fol. 21v.
55. *Chamber Books*, BL, Add. MS 21481, fol. 114.
56. *Chamber Books*, TNA, E 36/216, fols 7, 47v.
57. *Chamber Books*, TNA, E 36/216, fols 91v, 101.
58. Starkey, 'The King's Privy Chamber', p. 254.
59. Other documents from later in the reign alert us to old plate that survived from the previous reign, such as an enamelled gold cup with initials H and E (for Henry VII and Elizabeth of York), that is not included in the 1521 inventory (*LP*, vol. 9, no. 909).
60. It is also worth noting that, other than the regalia, jewellery for personal adornment was not kept in the jewel house. A list of items in Sir William Compton's keeping in 1519 (*LP*, vol. 3, part 1, no. 463) is largely made up of jewels: hugely weighty collars and girdles, including several of over 100 oz, brooches, rings and so on. But it also included small items of plate such as a gold spoon and fork, a pair of gold snuffers and 'a silver-gilt box for green ginger, with a dragon on top'. The list hints at the fluidity of royal holdings, with reference to 'a gold toothpick, with a ruby and diamond, given to my lord Cardinal'.

Chapter 3

1. *CSP*, *Venetian*, vol. 1, no. 942. The operative word here is gold: Henry VII preferred gold coinage to silver and took active measures to restrict the export of gold coin. For a further discussion of this see Chapter 12, p. 250.
2. Raphael Holinshed, *Chronicles of England, Scotland and Ireland*, vol. 3 (London, 1808), p. 544.
3. *CSP*, *Milan*, no. 540.
4. For a complete transcript, see Jenny Stratford, *Richard II and the English Royal Treasure* (London, 2012), pp. 145–252.
5. Stratford, *Richard II*, inv. no. R38 and pp. 268–69.
6. A second piece survives from Richard's treasury, though it never belonged to Henry VIII: a beautiful jewelled gold crown preserved in the Schatzkammer of the Residenz Museum in Munich (illus. Stratford, *Richard II*, plates 6 and 7). It left England in 1402 with Princess Blanche, daughter of Henry IV, when she married the Count Palatine, Ludwig of Bavaria.
7. The 1521 description (in Trollope, 'King Henry VIII's Jewel Book', p. 163) reads: 'A crucifix of gold standing upon vj pillars with iiij pinnacles and iij pearls, the base set with an emerald, a sapphire, ij diamonds, and viij other small garnishing pearls, vj white harts upon the base with crowns, ij whole chains and ij pieces of chains of gold about their necks and lxxvj small pearls upon the harts' heads and among the harts v bushes with xxi small pearls and an image of Our Lady of Pity set with a light sapphire, viij stones or glasses of no value and xxxij small pearls and an image of St John Baptist set with a light sapphire, ix glasses or stones and xxxj pearls within the pinnacles and upon the pinnacles ij light rubies and xlij small pearls, ij angels holding a balance garnished with xvj small pearls, upon the foot of the cross Mary and John set with ij xlij small pearls and upon the cross a crucifix set with ij balaces ij sapphires and a hundred small pearls poysant [weighing] lxxiiij oz qrt'. Conflating this with

the description in the 1399 inventory makes for a rather clearer picture of its appearance.

8. The cup was acquired from the convent by Baron Jérôme Pichon in 1891; he sold it for £8,000 to the Parisian dealers, Wertheimer, who in turn sold it at cost price to the British Museum Curator, A. W. Franks. Franks went about raising the money by subscription so that the cup could be acquired by the museum.
9. The 1521 description (Trollope, 'King Henry VIII's Jewel Book', p. 165) reads: 'A cup of gold enamelled with imagery, the knop a crowne imperial and about the border of the cover and foot a crown garnished with lxij garnishing pearls poyzt lxxix oz'. In March 2018 I was given special access to the cup and noted the following technical features: the bowl and cover are double-skinned with the enamel applied to the thin outer sheet. The cup has undergone several interventions in addition to the additions to the stem. The lip has been rehammered, possibly after being dented; underneath the bowl and visible inside the stem is a strange, crudely amputated, square section that is hard to understand; traces of red enamel remain on the engraved sunburst on top of the cover; the top of the cup, where it meets the finial ring, is broken off and is very rough.
10. Trollope, 'King Henry VIII's Jewel Book', p. 160.
11. Account taken from Samuel Bentley, *Excerpta Historica or Illustrations of English History* (London, 1831), pp. 43–44.
12. A. J. Collins (ed.), *Jewels and Plate of Queen Elizabeth I: The Inventory of 1574: Edited from Harley MS 1650 and Stowe MS 555 in the British Museum* (London, 1955), p. 290.
13. Oliver Millar (ed.), *The Inventories and Valuations of the King's Goods 1649–1651*, Walpole Society, vol. 43 (Glasgow, 1972), p. 33.
14. Trollope, 'King Henry VIII's Jewel Book', p. 174. In the absence of a full description it is difficult to tie up objects on the two inventories since the 1521 gives their weight, whereas the 1399 gives their value. Equally, the harts do not necessarily indicate Richard II; Henry VII's standard featured the cross of St George and the same white hart collared with a crown (illus. Claude Blair (ed.), *The Crown Jewels: The History of the Coronation Regalia in the Jewel House of the Tower of London*, vol. 1 (London, 1998), p. 199).
15. Trollope, 'King Henry VIII's Jewel Book', p. 195.
16. Trollope, 'King Henry VIII's Jewel Book', p. 166. The clarification that the sculptural group was on the cover comes from a document of 1629 quoted by Collins (ed.), *Jewels and Plate of Queen Elizabeth I*, p. 278.
17. Collins (ed.), *Jewels and Plate of Queen Elizabeth I*, p. 277.
18. Trollope, 'King Henry VIII's Jewel Book', p. 170.
19. Henry T. Riley (ed. and trans.), *Ingulph's Chronicle of the Abbey of Croyland with the Continuations by Peter of Blois and Anonymous Writers* (London, 1854), p. 475.
20. *Great Chronicle of London*, p. 234.
21. *Great Chronicle of London*, p. 236.
22. According to W. C. Richardson (*Tudor Chamber Administration 1485–1547* (Baton Rouge, 1952), p. 11) no fewer than 122 people lost their estates to the Crown through attainder between 1485 and 1503. For a general, if old-fashioned, account of early Tudor royal finances, see Frederick Dietz, *English Government Finance, 1485–1558* (Urbana, 1921).
23. S. B. Chrimes, *Henry VII* (London, 1972), p. 217. According to Dietz (*English Government Finance*, p. 85) at least £128,441 of this was in his last years.
24. *Chamber Books*, BL, Add. MS 7099, fols 68, 87.
25. *CSP, Spain*, vol. 1, no. 511.
26. *Great Chronicle of London*, pp. 311–12. The figure mentioned by Stow in his account of the same event is £1,200 but since his source was probably the *Great Chronicle* the figure he gives is probably just a mistake. John Stow, *Annals of England to 1603* (London, c. 1605), p. 809.
27. The French royal gold cup is a useful bench-mark against which to imagine the scale of other royal gold plate. At 79 oz, it was one of the heaviest gold drinking vessels on the 1521 inventory. Only three were heavier, the 117 oz 'cup called the Dream of Paris' and two standing bowls at 128 oz and 142 oz. Of the twenty-eight gold salts, only one, the 'salt called Mores dance', was heavier, weighing 147 oz. Compared with some of the colossal silver-gilt

vessels in the jewel house, therefore, the gold plate must all have been relatively small.

28. *Chamber Books*, TNA, E 36/214, fols 10v, 146, 151.
29. See Margaret Condon, 'The Last Will of Henry VII: Document and Text', in *Westminster Abbey: The Lady Chapel of Henry VII*, ed. Tim Tatton-Brown and Richard Mortimer (Woodbridge, 2003), p. 134. The pyxes were evidently well in hand by the time of the king's death and two payments, each for £500, appear in the Chamber accounts for March and April 1509 'for making a certain sum of pyxes'. The goldsmiths named were Nicholas Warley, John Mundy, Robert Amadas and William Kebill. *Chamber Books*, TNA, E 36/214, fols 163, 165v.
30. See Condon, 'The Last Will of Henry VII', pp. 132–33.
31. Illus. Charles Truman (ed.), *Sotheby's Concise Encyclopaedia of Silver* (London, 1993), p. 46.
32. Condon, 'The Last Will of Henry VII', p. 133. It is unlikely that all the provisions of the will were carried out. The tomb does not appear to have been ornamented as instructed, and 'the greatest image of Our Lady that we now have in our jewel house', bequeathed to St George's Chapel, was probably the one weighing 415 oz that was still in the jewel house in 1521.
33. Philippa Glanville, *Silver in Tudor and Early Stuart England: A Social History and Catalogue of the National Collection, 1480–1660* (London, 1990), p. 24. This is an informed guess, based in most cases on the ornament as described in the inventory. Items with red and white roses or pomegranates probably post-dated Henry VII; and those with named donors were probably recent. Very little of the church plate (other than that seized from the duke of Buckingham) can be firmly identified as post-1509.
34. Not necessarily, however, and the roses on the grandstands in the *Westminster Tournament Roll* of 1511 (see Chapter 3) are all red.
35. Trollope, 'King Henry VIII's Jewel Book', pp. 164, 167, 180, 181, 188, 189 and 196.
36. *Inventory of Henry VIII*, no. 74.
37. Trollope, 'King Henry VIII's Jewel Book', p. 187.
38. Trollope, 'King Henry VIII's Jewel Book', pp. 108, 212.
39. *Great Chronicle of London*, pp. 288–89.
40. *Chamber Books*, TNA, E 101/414/6, fol. 36.
41. William Dunbar, 'In Honour of London', in *The Poems of William Dunbar, Collected, with Notes and a Memoir of his Life*, ed. D. Laing (London, 1834), p. 279, lines 53–55.
42. See S. P. Harper, 'Royal Servants and City Fathers: The Double Lives of London Goldsmiths at the Court of Henry VII', in *Medieval Merchants and Money: Essays in Honour of James L. Bolton*, ed. Martin Allen and Matthew Davies (London, 2016), pp. 177–96.
43. Harper, 'Royal Servants and City Fathers', p. 193.

Chapter 4

1. So described by Hall on the title page of the 1548 edition of Edward Hall, *The Vnion of the Two Noble and Illustre Famelies* (London, 1809).
2. Quoted by David Starkey in *Henry VIII: Man and Monarch*, ed. Susan Doran (London, 2009), p. 63.
3. Frank Mumby (ed.), *The Youth of Henry VIII: A Narrative in Contemporary Letters* (London, 1913), p. 127.
4. *LP*, vol. 2, part 1, no. 1653.
5. Hall, *King Henry VIII*, vol. 1, p. 5.
6. Hall, *King Henry VIII*, vol. 1, p. 7.
7. See Claude Blair (ed.), *The Crown Jewels: The History of the Coronation Regalia in the Jewel House of the Tower of London*, vol. 1 (London, 1998), p. 202.
8. Alice Hunt, *The Drama of Coronation: Medieval Ceremony in Early Modern England* (Cambridge, 2008), p. 15.
9. Hunt, *The Drama of Coronation*, p. 29.
10. For a fuller exposition, see Hunt, *The Drama of Coronation*, pp. 29–30.
11. See Blair (ed.), *The Crown Jewels*, vol. 1, p. 269.

12. Illus. Claude Blair (ed.), *The History of Silver* (London, 1987), p. 45.
13. *Great Chronicle of London*, p. 341. A survey of medieval coronations notes that this is the first account of a coronation feast to mention a rich cupboard of plate (Blair (ed.), *The Crown Jewels*, vol. 1, p. 202). It would be surprising if such a universal status symbol had not been used on such occasions before but it is possible that Henry VIII's buffet, reflecting the massive holdings left to him by his father, was on a more remarkable scale than before.
14. These went back at least to the coronation of Richard II (see William Robinson, *Collections Relative to Claims at Coronations of Several of the Kings of England beginning with Richard II* (London, 1820), pp. 1–19).
15. Hall, *King Henry VIII*, vol. 1, p. 10.
16. These included the paneter, the head of the ewery, and the chief butler, all of whom received items related to the role they performed. The barons of the Cinque Ports, who bore the king's canopy, were given the canopy bells, a tradition that continued at least until the late seventeenth century.
17. TNA, SP 1/4, fols 48, 49.
18. When exactly the crown was made is not known, but Lightbown, in Blair (ed.), *The Crown Jewels*, vol. 1, p. 294, notes that all the diamonds are described in the inventory as cut; if they were the original stones the crown could not predate the late fourteenth century (when diamond cutting started) 'and points to the fifteenth or early sixteenth century'.
19. Crown-wearing appears to have been on the decline. Henry VI was said to have worn the crown on six great feast days each year, but Henry VII is thought only to have done so on the feast of Epiphany (see Fiona Kisby, '"When the King Goeth a Procession": Chapel Ceremonies and Services, the Ritual Year, and Religious Reforms at the Early Tudor Court, 1485–1547', *Journal of British Studies*, 40, 1 (January 2001), pp. 59–60.
20. 'Articles ordained by King Henry VII for the regulation of his household' ('The Royal Book'), in *A Collection of Ordinances and Regulations for the Government of the Royal Household* (London, 1790), pp. 109–33.
21. For example, the so-called Russell tapestry of about 1538 and the royal charter portrait commissioned by the Barber-Surgeons Company in 1541. But this is not the same as the one in the jewel house. Moreover, the one in the 1541 portrait is worn, curiously, over a beaver hat (I am grateful to David Starkey for pointing this out).
22. Trollope, 'King Henry VIII's Jewel Book', pp. 158–59.
23. *LP*, vol. 5, no. 1799.
24. Sydney Anglo (ed.), *The Great Tournament Roll of Westminster: A Collotype Reproduction of the Manuscript* (Oxford, 1968), p. 22.
25. Sydney Anglo, *Spectacle, Pageantry, and Early Tudor Policy* (Oxford, 1997), p. 122.
26. *CSP*, *Venetian*, vol. 2, no. 918.
27. The figure given in the calendared version of Chieregato's letter – 300,000 ducats – is scarcely credible, equivalent to more than £65,000, and is treated with scepticism here.
28. *Great Chronicle of London*, pp. 369–70.
29. College of Arms, *Westminster Tournament Roll.*
30. Anglo (ed.), *The Great Tournament Roll of Westminster*, p. 104.
31. I am grateful to Tobias Capwell, curator of arms and armour at the Wallace Collection, for the following explanation: 'A "shapwe" is almost certainly a chapeau, or chapel-de-fer, or as we would say in English, a war hat. English knights routinely owned a sallet, a helmet with a visor, and a war hat, for heavier and lighter armoured uses respectively.'
32. *Chamber Books*, BL, Add. MS 21481, fols 131, 133v, 221.
33. Hall, *King Henry VIII*, vol. 1, p. 22.
34. *LP*, vol. 2, no. 1510.
35. *LP*, vol. 2, no. 1510.
36. Hall, *King Henry VIII*, vol. 1, p. 27. The same story, with slight variations, is told in the *Great Chronicle of London*, p. 374.
37. See M. E. Bratchel, 'Italian Merchant Organization and Business Relationships in Early Tudor London', *Journal of European Economic History*, 7, 1 (1978), pp. 5–32.
38. *LP*, vol. 1, appendix 3. Henry VIII writes to Margaret of Savoy requesting a licence for Jerome Frycobaldi 'to send over certain silver plate which he is having made in Flanders'.

39. *Chamber Books*, BL Add. MS 21481, fols 28v, 34v.
40. *Chamber Books*, TNA, E36/216, fol. 68v. An entry in the King's Book of Payments, February 1519 (*LP*, vol. 3) records a payment of £2,730 'to Sir William Compton, for jewels bought by him from Jenyn Lengram'.
41. Cinzia M. Sicca, 'Consumption and Trade of Art between Italy and England in the First Half of the Sixteenth Century: The London House of the Bardi and Cavalcanti Company', *Renaissance Studies*, 16, 2 (2002), pp. 168–70. The reference to him in the state papers in 1522 as 'an usher of the chamber' (*LP*, vol. 3, no. 2214.20) has been mistakenly taken to refer to Henry VIII's chamber. Cavalcanti regularly supplied the king with luxury goods in the early 1520s.
42. *CSP*, *Spain*, vol. 4, part 2, no. 1076.
43. *Four Years at the Court*, p. 139.
44. *CSP*, *Venetian*, vol. 2, no. 671.
45. *Chamber Books*, TNA, E 36/216, fol. 68v; BL, Add. MS 21841, fol. 168; TNA, E 36/216, fol. 31.
46. Their apprenticeships are recorded in the records of the Goldsmiths' Company. GC, Court Minute Book A, vol. 2, pp. 199, 314, 352, 358.
47. Alfred P. Beaven, 'Chronological List of Aldermen: 1501–1600', in *The Aldermen of the City of London Temp. Henry III – 1912* (London, 1908), pp. 20–47. British History Online, http://www.british-history.ac.uk/no-series/london-aldermen/hen3-1912/pp20-47.
48. GC, Minute Book D, p. 364.
49. TNA, PROB 11/27/118; John Nichols, *The History and Antiquities of the County of Leicester*, vol. 4, part 2 (London, 1811), p. 525.
50. 'William Exmew', *ODNB*; GC, Minute Book F, p. 149.
51. For example, he repeatedly ignored orders not to attend fairs outside London and refused to pay fines for his behaviour. In April 1516 he threatened to leave the livery of the company, claiming the other members spoke 'unfitting and slanderous words' about him in alehouses. GC, Minute Book A, vol. 2, pp. 392, 401, 417, 429, 481; Minute Book C, pp. 137–39.
52. *LP*, vol. 2, no. 284; vol. 3, King's Book of Payments.
53. GC, Minute Book D, pp. 25, 44.
54. *Chamber Books*, TNA, E 36/215, fol. 298; BL, Add. MS 21841, fol. 23v.
55. *Chamber Books*, BL, Add. MS 21481, fol. 40.
56. See, for example, the payments in 1513 and 1514. *Chamber Books*, BL, Add. MS 21481, fols 129v, 143v, https://www.dhi.ac.uk/chamber-books/folio.
57. TNA, PROB 2/486.
58. *Chamber Books*, BL, Add. MS 21481, fol. 153.
59. *Chamber Books*, BL, Add. MS 21481, fol. 30.
60. See C. L. Kingsford, 'On Some London Houses of the Early Tudor Period', *Archaeologia*, 71 (1921), pp. 39–42. The total haul from Dudley appears to have been more than 1,200 oz of silver and silver-gilt.
61. *LP*, vol. 3, part 1, no. 2861.
62. *Great Chronicle of London*, pp. 339–40.
63. *LP*, vol. 3, part 1, no. 1070.
64. Trollope, 'King Henry VIII's Jewel Book', p. 167.
65. *LP*, vol. 3, part 1, no. 1285.
66. Trollope, 'King Henry VIII's Jewel Book', pp. 215–26.
67. The total weight of the former Buckingham plate in the 1521 inventory transcription comes to more than 17,000 oz, but for a note of caution see Chapter 2, note 35.
68. The same badge also appeared on the half groat coin issued by the York mint during Henry VII's reign. G. C. Brooke and L. A. Lawrence, 'The Martlet and Half Rose Groats of Henry VII', *The Numismatic Chronicle and Journal of the Royal Numismatic Society*, fourth series, 19 (1919), pp. 257–64.
69. Not only the motifs of the Beaufort beaker but the pattern they are arranged in is paralleled in the inventory by 'two great gilt pots chased lozenge wise with portcullises and roses'. Trollope, 'King Henry VIII's Jewel Book', p. 189.
70. Trollope, 'King Henry VIII's Jewel Book', p. 185.
71. Trollope, 'King Henry VIII's Jewel Book', p. 199.
72. Trollope, 'King Henry VIII's Jewel Book', p. 190.
73. Of the three surviving pairs, two are in the Royal Collection and one is at St George's Chapel, Windsor. The former are hallmarked for 1660 and 1664; they are 52 cm high and

weigh (as pairs) 377 oz 2 dwt and 420 oz 6 dwt. The St George's pots weigh 414 oz.

74. Trollope, 'King Henry VIII's Jewel Book', p. 189.
75. For a full account of the vase, see Timothy Schroder, 'A Royal Tudor Rock-Crystal and Silver-Gilt Vase', *Burlington Magazine*, 137, 1107 (June 1995), pp. 356–66.
76. Including the relic which it has contained since at least the eighteenth century; the church authorities kindly gave permission for this to be removed in 1995 so that it could be photographed as it was originally conceived. A possibly similar object in the 1547 inventory (*Inventory of Henry VIII*, no. 532), when it was among the plate at Whitehall, is tantalisingly described as a 'cup of crystal the foot and cover of silver gilt garnished with flower deluces and scriptures upon the cover with Saint George on the top thereof' and weighing 83 oz.
77. Trollope, 'King Henry VIII's Jewel Book', p. 199.
78. *LP*, vol 2, no. 4183.
79. David Mitchell, *Silversmiths in Elizabethan and Stuart London: Their Lives and Their Marks* (Woodbridge, 2017), pp. 24–25.

Chapter 5

1. *CSP*, *Milan*, no. 700; and *CSP*, *Venetian*, vol. 2, no. 450.
2. See 'Richard Fox', *ODNB*.
3. *LP*, vol. 5, no. 1799.
4. The following passage is largely lifted from my own essay, 'Gold and Godliness', in *Gold: Power and Allure*, ed. Helen Clifford (London, 2012), p. 66.
5. Abbot Suger, *Abbot Suger on the Abbey Church of St. Denis and Its Art Treasures*, ed. and trans. Erwin Panofsky (Princeton, NJ, 1979), pp. 63–65.
6. Suger, *Abbot Suger on the Abbey Church of St. Denis*, p. 65.
7. Quoted by Sydney Anglo in *Images of Tudor Kingship* (London, 1992), p. 8.
8. Quoted in *Four Years at the Court*, vol. 1, p. 88, n. 5.
9. *Four Years at the Court*, vol. 2, p. 103.
10. *LP*, vol. 1, no. 842.
11. Frank Mumby (ed.), *The Youth of Henry VIII: A Narrative in Contemporary Letters* (London, 1913), p. 137.
12. Hall, *King Henry VIII*, vol. 2, p. 13.
13. Trollope, 'King Henry VIII's Jewel Book', p. 162.
14. For the full inventory, see *Das Hallesche Heiltum: Man. Aschaffenb. 14*, ed. Philipp Maria Halm and Rudolph Berliner (Berlin, 1931).
15. *CSP*, *Venetian*, vol. 2, no. 433.
16. *CSP*, *Venetian*, vol. 2, no. 445.
17. *LP*, vol. 1, part 2, no. 2929.
18. The other two were given to Ladislaus II of Hungary and the Swiss Cantons. See Charles J. Burnett and Christopher J. Tabraham, *The Honours of Scotland: The Story of the Scottish Crown Jewels* (Edinburgh, 1993), p. 19.
19. *LP*, vol. 1, part 2, no. 2688.
20. *CSP*, *Venetian*, vol. 2, no. 1279.
21. *LP*, vol. 3, part 1, no. 433.
22. *LP*, vol. 3, nos. 183, 1016.
23. *LP*, vol. 3, King's Book of Payments, 1519, p. 1538.
24. *LP*, vol. 2, no. 894.
25. Gordon Kipling (ed.), *The Receyt of the Ladie Kateryne* (Oxford, 1990), p. 39.
26. *CSP*, *Venetian*, vol. 3, no. 50. The Italian word translated by the editor of the Venetian state papers as 'pew' is *camaretta*. This evidently gave him some concern and I use the word 'traverse' instead. This was a small temporary enclosure erected in churches on important occasions (see glossary) and is probably what the writer saw.
27. *CSP*, *Venetian*, vol. 2, no. 1088.
28. Charles Wriothesley, *A Chronicle of England During the Reigns of the Tudors from 1485 to 1559*, Camden Society, new series, vol. 11 (London, 1875), p. 46.
29. Trollope, 'King Henry VIII's Jewel Book', p. 175.
30. For a full account of Chapel Royal ceremonial, see Fiona Kisby, '"When the King Goeth a Procession": Chapel Ceremonies

and Services, the Ritual Year, and Religious Reforms at the Early Tudor Court, 1485–1547', *Journal of British Studies*, 40, 1 (January 2001), pp. 44–75.

31. For crucifixes see *Inventory of Henry VIII*, nos. 29, 30, 199–208. Other liturgical plate can be found under the relevant headings.
32. Kipling (ed.), *Receyt of the Ladie Kateryne*, pp. 315–16.
33. Trollope, 'King Henry VIII's Jewel Book', p. 176.
34. Trollope, 'King Henry VIII's Jewel Book', pp. 174–81.
35. Harry Schnitker, 'Margaret of York on Pilgrimage: The Exercise of Devotion and the Religious Traditions of the House of York', in *Reputation and Representation in Fifteenth Century Europe*, ed. Douglas L. Biggs, Sharon D. Michalove and A. Compton Reeves (Leiden and Boston, 2004), pp. 85–90.
36. I am grateful to Mme Anne Renaux of the basilica in Halle, for allowing me to examine the monstrance.
37. Illus. in C. Ellory, H. Clifford and F. Rogers (eds), *Corpus Silver: Patronage and Plate at Corpus Christi College Oxford* (Barton under Needwood, 1999), pp. 61–67.
38. Trollope, 'King Henry VIII's Jewel Book', p. 164.
39. Marian Campbell, 'Bishop Fox's Salt', in Ellory et al. (eds), *Corpus Silver*, p. 81.
40. The museum's figure weighs 3,150 g. My thanks to Regina Palm, Curatorial Assistant at Kimbell Art Museum, for this information.
41. See Chapter 13, p. 278 for evidence of this.
42. Margaret Condon, 'The Last Will of Henry VII: Document and Text', in *Westminster Abbey: The Lady Chapel of Henry VII*, ed. Tim Tatton-Brown and Richard Mortimer (Woodbridge, 2003), pp. 131–32.
43. 'Articles ordained by King Henry VII for the regulation of his household' ('The Royal Book'), in *A Collection of Ordinances and Regulations for the Government of the Royal Household* (London, 1790), p. 126.
44. Hall, *King Henry VIII*, vol. 2, pp. 243–44.
45. Hall, *King Henry VIII*, vol. 2, p. 244.
46. Trollope, 'King Henry VIII's Jewel Book', p. 213.
47. *LP*, vol. 1, no. 674.
48. *LP*, vol. 12, part 2, no. 911. The godparents were Princess Mary, who gave the gold cup, and the archbishop of Canterbury and the dukes of Norfolk and Suffolk, who gave the silver-gilt vessels between them.
49. Ezekiel 16:4.
50. Quoted in David Cressy, *Birth, Marriage and Death: Ritual, Religion, and the Life-Cycle in Tudor and Stuart England* (Oxford, 1997), p. 135.
51. 'The Northumberland Ceremonial', 1501, Bodleian Library, MS Eng. Hist. b. 208, fol. 18v. Quoted extracts here and elsewhere in this book are from a transcript of the manuscript made available to me by Kent Rawlinson. In line with other quoted sources, I have modernised the spelling.
52. *LP*, vol. 2, King's Book of Payments, 1516, p. 1470.
53. Nor does anything plausible appear in the priory's earlier records. £14 was paid to a London goldsmith in 1446 for a silver font, but this cannot possibly have been big enough to have cost so much to transport (C. E. Woodruff and W. Danks, *Memorials of the Cathedral and Priory of Christ in Canterbury* (London, 1912), pp. 320–21).
54. Trollope, 'King Henry VIII's Jewel Book', p. 181. In the 1547 inventory the weight of the same piece is given as 281 oz. *Inventory of Henry VIII*, no. 293.
55. 'The Northumberland Ceremonial', f. 18v.
56. *LP*, vol. 12, part 2, no. 911.
57. John Leland, 'The manner of the christening of the child of the Lady Cecile, wife of John Earl of East Friesland [Frisia] ... which christening was done at the Queen's Majesty's palace of Westminster', *Collectanea*, 2nd edn, vol. 1, part 2 (London, 1770), p. 691.
58. For example, an agate bird garnished with gold and stones with the king's arms is found in *Inventory of Henry VIII*, no. 19.

Chapter 6

1. *LP*, vol. 2, no. 918.
2. *CSP*, *Venetian*, vol. 2, no. 918.
3. Dora Thornton and Michael Cowell, 'The Armada Service: A Set of Late Tudor Dining Silver', *The Antiquaries Journal*, 76 (1996), pp. 153–80.
4. For a general account of its development as a form, I refer the reader to the introduction to the section on saltcellars in my catalogue of *British and Continental Gold and Silver in the Ashmolean Museum* (Oxford, 2009), pp. 300–04.
5. 'The Northumberland Ceremonial', 1501, Bodleian Library, MS Eng. Hist. b. 208, f. 35r.
6. *Inventory of Henry VIII*, no. 69. The inventory notes that some of the stones may in fact have been glass.
7. For a good account of the intricacies and refinement of courtly carving, see Ivan Day, 'The Honours of the Table', in *British Cutlery*, ed. Peter Brown (York, 2001), pp. 32–41.
8. This is a précis of Robinson's description; see *Proceedings of the Society of Antiquaries of London*, second series, vol. XVII, pp. 9–10.
9. David Starkey, 'Henry VI's Old Blue Gown: The English Court under the Lancastrians and Yorkists', *The Court Historian*, 4, 1 (April 1999), pp. 1–28.
10. Eamon Duffy, *The Stripping of the Altars* (London, 1992), p. 281.
11. *CSP*, *Venetian*, vol. 3, no. 50.
12. Trollope, 'King Henry VIII's Jewel Book', p. 201.
13. Hall, *King Henry VIII*, vol. 2, p. 85.
14. 'The Northumberland Ceremonial', 1501, Bodleian Library, MS Eng. Hist. b. 208, f. 18v.
15. Illustrated in Philippa Glanville, *Silver in Tudor and Early Stuart England: A Social History and Catalogue of the National Collection, 1480–1660* (London, 1990), p. 62.
16. A variant on the void was the 'banket' (or 'banquet'). This was a later development of the void; it involved fewer servants and was varied in the range of sweet foods on offer (see Peter Brears, *Cooking and Dining in Tudor and Early Stuart England* (London, 2015), p. 519.
17. Gordon Kipling (ed.), *The Receyt of the Ladie Kateryne* (Oxford, 1990), p. 58.
18. 'Articles ordained by King Henry VII for the regulation of his household' ('The Royal Book'), in *A Collection of Ordinances and Regulations for the Government of the Royal Household* (London, 1790), p. 110.
19. 'The Northumberland Ceremonial', f. 43r.
20. *CSP*, *Venetian*, vol. 2, no. 918.
21. The weight of one pair on the 1521 inventory is given as 1,596 oz, but for a note on why this should be disregarded see Chapter 2, note 35.
22. The actual weights are 99 oz and 102 oz. I am grateful to Michael Carter, Associate Museum Librarian at the Metropolitan Museum of Art (The Cloisters), for this information.
23. R. W. Lightbown, *Secular Goldsmiths' Work in Medieval France: A History* (London, 1978), p. 24.
24. Illus. Timothy Schroder, *The Gilbert Collection of Gold and Silver* (Los Angeles, 1988), cat. no. 2.
25. Hall, *King Henry VIII*, vol. 2, p. 172.
26. Trollope, 'King Henry VIII's Jewel Book', p. 195. Trollope's transcription of the weight as 'iijxlj oz' is unintelligible but the corresponding entry in the 1532 inventory is clear.
27. Trollope, 'King Henry VIII's Jewel Book', p. 195.
28. Measuring 21.5 cm in diameter and weighing just 30 oz each (excluding the cover), the Rochester tazzas would have been at the lower end of the range and many in the inventory weighed more than 100 oz. The Goldsmiths' one, at 27 oz, is lighter still.
29. The inscription on the British Museum's vessels reads 'Benedicamus patrem et filium cum sancto spiritu' (Let us bless the Father, Son and Holy Spirit).
30. My thanks to Lisa Jefferson for this interpretation.
31. A. R. Myers (ed.), *The Household of Edward IV: The Black Book and the Ordinance of 1478* (Manchester, 1959), p. 84.
32. TNA, E36/84. For a further discussion of this question see Chapter 14, p. 303.
33. Henry Ellis (ed.), *Original Letters Illustrative of English History*, first series, vol. 1 (London, 1825), no. 93.

34. *CSP*, *Venetian*, vol. 4, no. 105; and Hall, *King Henry VIII*, vol. 2, pp. 85–86.
35. See Gilly Lehmann, 'Henry VIII's Great Feast at Greenwich, May 1527', *The Court Historian*, 23, 1 (June 2018), pp. 1–12.
36. In fact Henry had two sets on this theme. Thomas P. Campbell, *Henry VIII and the Art of Majesty: Tapestries at the Tudor Court* (New Haven and London, 2007), p. 146.
37. *CSP*, *Venetian*, vol. 4, no. 105.
38. Hall, *King Henry VIII*, vol. 2, p. 85.
39. *LP*, vol. 3, part 1, nos. 3097, 3098 and 3104.
40. BL, MS Add. 45716A, fols 113–21. See Lehmann, 'Henry VIII's Great Feast at Greenwich'.
41. Hall, *King Henry VIII*, vol. 2, pp. 85–86.
42. *CSP*, *Venetian*, vol. 4, no. 105.
43. *LP*, vol. 4, no. 3104.
44. *Inventory of Henry VIII*, no. 9141 etc.
45. *CSP*, *Venetian*, vol. 2, no. 918; also *CSP*, *Venetian*, vol. 4, no. 105.
46. Lightbown, *Secular Goldsmiths' Work in Medieval France*, p. 40. The fact that Burgundian buffets were limited in height did not mean they were small and at the wedding feast of Philip the Good and Isabelle of Portugal in 1429 the five-step buffet was twenty feet long.
47. Kipling (ed.), *Receyt of the Ladie Kateryne*, p. 66.
48. Kipling (ed.), *Receyt of the Ladie Kateryne*, p. 75.
49. *CSP*, *Venetian*, vol. 4, no. 105.
50. Hall, *King Henry VIII*, vol. 2, p. 85.
51. The Court of Chancery shared the south end of Westminster Hall with the Court of King's Bench, each occupying roughly half the width of the hall.
52. Hall, *King Henry VIII*, vol. 2, p. 88.
53. Illus. Timothy Schroder, *English Silver before the Civil War: The David Little Collection* (London, 2015), p. 24.
54. See A. Jeffries Collins (ed.), *Jewels and Plate of Queen Elizabeth I: The Inventory of 1574: Edited from Harley MS 1650 and Stowe MS 555 in the British Museum* (London, 1955), p. 148.
55. 'The Northumberland Ceremonial', f. 34v.
56. Illus. Helen Clifford, *A Treasured Inheritance: 600 Years of Oxford College Silver* (Oxford, 2004), fig. 81.
57. 'The Royal Book', p. 121.
58. BL, MS Sloane 1494. Titled 'A volume illustrative of the duties of a Gentleman of the Royal Household'. This is a seventeenth-century manuscript but includes sections that appear to transcribe early Tudor documents. I am grateful to David Mitchell for bringing this to my attention.
59. Young aristocratic hostages had been taken during Henry's 1513 campaign as guarantees for the fulfilment of the terms of the peace treaty. They spent several years at Henry's court and were treated throughout as honoured guests.
60. BL, MS Sloane 1494, fol. 62v.
61. BL, MS Sloane 1494, fols 63–63v.
62. BL, MS Sloane 1494, fol. 63.
63. BL, MS Sloane 1494, fol. 56.
64. BL, MS Sloane 1494, fol. 64.
65. BL, MS Sloane 1494, fol. 67.
66. BL, MS Sloane 1494, fol. 56.
67. BL, MS Sloane 1494, fol. 72.
68. BL, MS Sloane 1494, fol. 73v.
69. BL, MS Sloane 1494, fol. 74.
70. BL, MS Sloane 1494, fol. 74v.
71. 'Directions for different officers about the court of King Henry VIII [...] drawn up [...] by Henry Fitzalan, Earl of Arundell [...] from 1526–30', in F. Gross, *Antiquarian Repertory*, vol. 2 (London, 1808), pp. 184–207. As David Starkey points out, although issued in 1526, this was a reissue of an earlier set of directions dating from 1494–1501 (David Starkey, 'The King's Privy Chamber' (unpublished PhD dissertation, University of Cambridge, 1973), p. 18).
72. See Chapter 2, p. 12 and note 5.
73. Trollope, 'King Henry VIII's Jewel Book', pp. 168, 169, 172, 173.
74. *Four Years at the Court of Henry VIII*, p. 86.
75. *Inventory of Henry VIII*, no. 182. For a further discussion of this see Chapter 14, p. 300.
76. Trollope, 'King Henry VIII's Jewel Book', p. 182.
77. Trollope, 'King Henry VIII's Jewel Book', p. 189. The entry adds that 'the gold that went to the garnishing of the same [weighed] 9¼ oz'. This amounted to about 6.5 per cent of their total weight, a significant addition, but much less than the cost of making them in solid gold.
78. Collins (ed.), *Jewels and Plate of Queen Elizabeth I*, p. 171 and no. 1578.

Chapter 7

1. Letter dated 26 August 1513 in Niccolò Machiavelli, *Lettere familiari*, ed. Edoardo Alvisi (Florence, 1883), p. 293.
2. *CSP*, *Venetian*, vol. 2, no. 333.
3. See Chapter 3, p. 35.
4. *CSP*, *Venetian*, vol. 2, nos. 86 and 94.
5. *CSP*, *Venetian*, vol. 2, no. 954.
6. *LP*, vol. 3, part 1, no. 161.
7. *CSP*, *Spain*, vols 1 and 2, second supplement, pp. 24 and 41.
8. Trollope, 'King Henry VIII's Jewel Book', p. 213.
9. *LP*, vol. 4, no. 5957.
10. *CSP*, *Spain*, vol. 4, part 1, no. 250.
11. *LP*, vol. 4, no. 6227.
12. *CSP*, *Spain*, vol. 4, part 1, no. 255.
13. Chamber accounts, February 1530 (*LP*, vol. 5, p. 317). The French court was at that time at Bayonne, close to the Spanish border.
14. *LP*, vol. 4, no. 6380.
15. This final episode is described in Annemarie Jordan Gschwend, '*Ma Meilleur Soeur*: Leonor of Austria, Queen of Portugal and France', *Los inventarios de Carlos V y la familia imperial = The Inventories of Charles V and the Imperial Family*, ed. Fernando Checa Cremades, vol. III (Madrid, 2010), p. 2576. I am grateful to Michèle Bimbenet-Privat for bringing it to my attention.
16. *CSP*, *Venetian*, vol. 2, no. 341.
17. *CSP*, *Spain*, vol. 3, part 1, no. 18.
18. Trollope, 'King Henry VIII's Jewel Book', p. 171. A visual sense of battlefield magnificence can be gleaned from the booty captured from the defeated Charles the Bold at the battles of Grandson and Morat in 1476, some of which is preserved at the Historisches Museum in Bern. This includes plate, jewels, tapestries and great copes embroidered with gold and silver thread.
19. Antonio Bavarin, factor of the Pesaro firm in London. *CSP*, *Venetian*, vol. 2, nos. 252 and 283.
20. Hall, *King Henry VIII*, vol. 1, p. 89. This may well be the armour partly preserved at the Tower of London. Given to Henry by the Emperor Maximilian, it was probably decorated by the royal 'harness gilder', Paul van Vreland, a stranger from Brussels. Several contracts and warrants naming Vreland survive. A 1514 warrant to pay him £121 6s 8d for 'certain gold, quicksilver and workmanship' on the king's armour was followed by a £200 contract in 1516 to decorate a bard, 'according to a complete harness which of late he made for our body'. *LP*, vol. 1, no. 3055; vol. 2, no. 1950.
21. *LP*, vol. 1, part 2, appendix 25.
22. *CSP*, *Milan*, no. 651.
23. *LP*, vol. 1, part 2, appendix 25.
24. Hall, *King Henry VIII*, vol. 1, p. 75.
25. F. Gross (ed.), *Antiquarian Repertory*, vol. 4 (London, 1809), p. 346.
26. *CSP*, *Venetian*, vol. 2, no. 283.
27. *CSP*, *Spain*, vol. 3, part 1, no. 405.
28. *CSP*, *Venetian*, vol. 2, no. 918.
29. *LP*, vol. 2, no. 4453.
30. Hall, *King Henry VIII*, vol. 1, p. 168.
31. *LP*, vol. 21, part 2, no. 19.
32. *CSP*, *Venetian*, vol. 2, no. 214.
33. BL, Royal Appendix MS 89, fols 106–10v.
34. TNA, E 36/216, fol. 21v, *Chamber Books*.
35. Hall, *King Henry VIII*, vol. 1, p. 172.
36. *CSP*, *Venetian*, vol. 2, nos. 1088 and 1089. The quotation slightly misrepresents the Calendar, the exact words of which are 'more than five feet (*palmi*) high each'. But it cannot possibly be the case that the vessels displayed on the buffet were five feet high. According to *The Cambridge Italian Dictionary*, the *palmo* varies from region to region but can equal one third of a cubit, or about six inches, which would make five *palmi* equal to about two and a half feet or 75 cm. *The Cambridge Italian Dictionary*, s.v. 'palmo'.
37. *CSP*, *Spain*, vols 1 and 2, second supplement, p. 87.
38. *LP*, vol. 7, no. 1436.
39. *LP*, vol. 7, no. 1507.
40. *CSP*, *Spain*, vol. 5, part 1, no. 1.
41. *CSP*, *Venetian*, vol. 2, no. 446.
42. *CSP*, *Spain*, vol. 2, no. 238.
43. *CSP*, *Spain*, vol. 2, no. 238.
44. *CSP*, *Venetian*, vol. 4, no. 443.
45. *CSP*, *Spain*, vol. 2, part 2, no. 683.
46. *CSP*, *Venetian*, vol. 3, no. 1451.

47. *LP*, vol. 7, appendix, no. 110.
48. *LP*, vol. 4, no. 3169.
49. *CSP*, *Milan*, no. 584.
50. *CSP*, *Venetian*, vol. 3, no. 949.
51. *CSP*, *Venetian*, vol. 2, no. 26.
52. *CSP*, *Spain*, vol. 4, part 2, no. 1132.
53. In 1490, for example, the papal nuncio complained that 'almost everything is dearer than elsewhere, and the high coinage raises the price'. *CSP*, *Venetian*, vol. 4, appendix, no. 1005.
54. *CSP*, *Venetian*, vol. 4, nos. 896 and 956.
55. *CSP*, *Venetian*, vol. 5, no. 53.
56. *CSP*, *Spain*, vol. 4, part 1, no. 228.
57. *LP*, vol. 3, part 1, no. 2774.
58. Writing to the duke of Norfolk. *LP*, vol. 6, no. 159.
59. *LP*, vol. 12, part 2, no. 1077.
60. *CSP*, *Venetian*, vol. 3, nos. 603 and 719.
61. *LP*, vol. 13, part 2, no. 581.
62. *CSP*, *Venetian*, vol. 3, no. 224.
63. *LP*, vol. 3, part 2, no. 1777.
64. *LP*, vol. 3, part 1, no. 2558.
65. *LP*, vol. 4, part 1, nos. 1415 and 1480.
66. *LP*, vol. 4, part 1, no. 1721.
67. *LP*, vol. 4, part 2, no. 3835.
68. *LP*, vol. 5, no. 1564.
69. *LP*, vol. 5, no. 1661.
70. TNA, SP 2/N, fol. 5v.
71. *LP*, vol. 13, part 2, no. 130.
72. *LP*, vol. 15, no. 186.
73. John Williams, *Account of the monastic treasures confiscated at the dissolution of the various houses in England*, ed. W. B. D. D. Turnbull, Publications of the Abbotsford Club, vol. 5 (Edinburgh, 1836), p. 46.
74. BL, Add. MS 5756, fols 256–57.
75. *CSP*, *Spain*, vol. 1, no. 20.
76. *CSP*, *Spain*, vol. 1, no. 163.
77. *CSP*, *Spain*, vol. 5, no. 287.
78. *CSP*, *Spain*, vol. 1, no. 288.
79. *CSP*, *Spain*, vol. 1, no. 321.
80. *LP*, vol. 1, no. 2957.
81. *LP*, vol. 1, part 2, no. 2958.
82. *LP*, vol. 1, no. 3146.
83. *CSP*, *Venetian*, vol. 2, no. 482.
84. *LP*, vol. 1, no. 3171.
85. *CSP*, *Venetian*, vol. 2, no. 500.
86. Hall, *King Henry VIII*, vol. 1, p. 124.
87. The original inventory is preserved in the Bibliothèque Nationale de France in BNF, Trésor des Chartes, J.650 Angleterre XVIII; a nineteenth-century manuscript copy is in the National Archives. TNA, PRO 31/8/137, fols 74–76v.
88. In the National Archives transcript (TNA, PRO 31/8/137) *harsses* is repeatedly misread as 'harttes' (deer). The former is almost certainly a variant spelling of 'herses', meaning portcullises, much more typical early Tudor iconography.
89. BL, Cotton MS Vitellius C XI, fols 150–52. The date of this document is not clear but its numerous annotations and amendments suggest that it was probably drawn up as preparations were reaching an advanced stage, perhaps in the second half of 1513.
90. *CSP*, *Venetian*, vol. 2, no. 507.
91. Henry Ellis (ed.), *Original Letters Illustrative of English History*, second series, vol. 1 (London, 1827), pp. 236–37.
92. *CSP*, *Venetian*, vol. 2, no. 511.

Chapter 8

1. *LP*, vol. 2, no. 1814.
2. *LP*, vol. 2, no. 960.
3. George Cavendish, *Thomas Wolsey, Late Cardinal: His Life and Death*, ed. Roger Lockyer (London, 1973), p. 15.
4. See Sybil M. Jack, 'Thomas Wolsey', *ODNB*.
5. See S. J. Gunn and P. G. Lindley, 'Introduction', in *Cardinal Wolsey: Church, State and Art*, ed. S. J. Gunn and P. G. Lindley (Cambridge, 1991), p. 6.
6. *CSP*, *Venetian*, vol. 4, no. 694.
7. Gunn and Lindley, 'Introduction', pp. 37–38.
8. *Four Years at the Court*, vol. 2, p. 314.
9. *Four Years at the Court*, p. 218.
10. *CSP*, *Venetian*, vol. 4, no. 205.
11. *CSP*, *Venetian*, vol. 4, no. 168.

12. Polydore Vergil, *Anglica Historia (1555 version): A Hypertext Critical Edition*, ed. Dana F. Sutton, bk 27, para. 32, http://www.philological.bham.ac.uk/polverg/27eng.html.
13. Vergil, *Anglica Historia (1555 version)*, bk 27, para. 25.
14. *CSP*, *Venetian*, vol. 3, no. 130.
15. *CSP*, *Venetian*, vol. 3, no. 1.
16. *CSP*, *Venetian*, vol. 4, no. 493.
17. This is confirmed by an entry in Wolsey's account with Robert Amadas, 'paid for the barge hire and carts to Hampton Court when the French ambassadors were there for conveying of certain plate, that is to say, for barge hire to and from and three men's charges waiting upon the same 5s and for a cart to and from 6s 8d and four men's charges going and coming with the said cart, 3s 4d 25s' (J. Gutch (ed.), *Collectanea Curiosa*, vol. 2 (London, 1781), no. 28, p. 326).
18. Cavendish, *Thomas Wolsey*, pp. 101–02.
19. Cavendish, *Thomas Wolsey*, p. 104.
20. *LP*, vol. 4, no. 6184; 'some bought against the King's coming to Hampton Court' in 1520–21 and others bought very specifically on 23 October 1527.
21. The 'bolts of iron in them', included in the weight, meant that the actual silver content of the candlesticks would have been rather less than 880 oz, so perhaps Amadas charged a higher rate than 4s 6d, especially since they were 'most curiously wrought'.
22. Cavendish, *Thomas Wolsey*, p. 104.
23. *CSP*, *Venetian*, vol. 4, no. 156.
24. *LP*, vol. 2, no. 894.
25. Hall, *King Henry VIII*, vol. 2, p. 148.
26. *LP*, vol. 2, no. 1154.
27. Illustrated, for example, in Peter Gwyn, *The King's Cardinal* (London, 1990), opposite p. 443.
28. Cavendish, *Thomas Wolsey*, p. 53.
29. *CSP*, *Venetian*, vol. 3, no. 210.
30. Vergil, *Anglica Historia (1555 version)*, bk 27, para. 34.
31. Hall, *King Henry VIII*, vol. 1, p. 170.
32. Quoted in Gunn and Lindley, 'Introduction', p. 19.
33. Neville Williams, *Henry VIII and His Court* (London, 1971), p. 94.
34. *LP*, vol. 5, no. 1799.
35. For instance, in a description of a mass on 23 June (*CSP*, *Venetian*, vol. 3, no. 50).
36. Gunn and Lindley, 'Introduction', p. 49.
37. *LP*, vol. 2, no. 1013.
38. *LP*, vol. 2, no. 2270.
39. *LP*, vol. 4, no. 2668.
40. *LP*, vol. 2, nos. 159, 282.
41. *Inventory of Henry VIII*, nos. 463 and 728.
42. *LP*, vol. 2, no. 1355.
43. See Diarmaid MacCulloch, *Thomas Cromwell: A Life* (London, 2018), pp. 56–58.
44. *LP*, vol. 4, no. 5743.
45. *LP*, vol. 20, no. 6748; but for a full transcript, see Gutch (ed.), *Collectanea Curiosa*, vol. 2, no. 28, pp. 283–346.
46. The transaction is not dated but appears immediately after certain items supplied for the Field of Cloth of Gold.
47. Gutch (ed.), *Collectanea Curiosa*, vol. 2, pp. 294–96.
48. Gutch (ed.), *Collectanea Curiosa*, vol. 2, p. 313.
49. TNA, E 36/85, fol. 11r.
50. TNA, E 36/85, fol. 10v.
51. TNA, E 36/85, fol. 27r. Martlets are not strictly part of Wolsey's arms and the birds to either side of the rose on the chief are correctly blazoned as choughs. But from their repeated mention coupled with a cardinal's hat it is reasonable to assume that is what is meant.
52. TNA, E 36/85, fol. 25v.
53. TNA, E 36/85, fol. 21r.
54. There were two Sir William Fitzwilliams, one of whom was Wolsey's treasurer and high chamberlain and the other a member of the king's council. 'Sir William Fitzwilliam of the court' is clearly the latter. My thanks to David Starkey for pointing this out.
55. Gutch (ed.), *Collectanea Curiosa*, vol. 2, pp. 287, 318.
56. Gutch (ed.), *Collectanea Curiosa*, vol. 2, p. 284.
57. Gutch (ed.), *Collectanea Curiosa*, vol. 2, p. 322.
58. Gutch (ed.), *Collectanea Curiosa*, vol. 2, p. 313. The price charged for the gold seems low compared with the price normally offered by the mint and may reflect the purity of the alloy used; for the gold of another supplied a little earlier, Amadas charged 34s 4d per ounce (ibid., p. 212).
59. I am grateful to Gareth Harris, goldsmith and silversmith, for explaining these issues to me.

60. Lien Bich Luu, *Immigrants and the Industries of London, 1500–1700* (Aldershot, 2005), p. 225.
61. Several variant spellings are found: Huzor, Huxer or Huxser. There are few references to Huxor in the records of the Goldsmiths' Company, but according to Philippa Glanville (*Silver in Tudor and Early Stuart England: A Social History and Catalogue of the National Collection, 1480–1660* (London, 1990), p. 94) he was a stranger.
62. John Beynarde (or Beynyarde) was apprenticed to John Shaa before 1488 and had a long career, dying after 1542. Most of the works cited in Goldsmiths' Company records were horse harnesses, girdles and spoons. GC, Court Minutes, Book A, vol. 2, pp. 284, 297, 338, 358, 385; Book G, p. 43.
63. Robert Cowper (or Cowpar) (before 1512–42) had a long and fractious relationship with the Goldsmiths' Company, culminating in his ejection from the company in 1530 for challenging the wardens' governance. His earlier business must have been quite active for him to have run up a debt of £20 to Robert Amadas in 1523. GC, Court Minutes, Book D, pp. 159, 302–31.
64. Probably the John van Harlar, Harlyn or Harlem who narrowly escaped punishment by the Goldsmiths' Company in 1514 through the intervention of the duke of Suffolk. He presented five of his alien journeymen to be registered with the company from 1514 to 1521. GC, Court Minutes, Book C, pp. 167, 178; Book D, pp. 60, 113, 122.
65. For a discussion of Hayes, see p. 243.
66. Gutch (ed.), *Collectanea Curiosa*, vol. 2, no. 28, p. 288.
67. Gutch (ed.), *Collectanea Curiosa*, vol. 2, no. 28, pp. 285–86.
68. *LP*, vol. 4, no. 5341.
69. Gutch (ed.), *Collectanea Curiosa*, vol. 2, no. 28, p. 286.
70. Probably shell cameos; for a further discussion of 'porcelain' see Chapter 14, p. 310.
71. Gutch (ed.), *Collectanea Curiosa*, vol. 2, no. 28, p. 289.
72. TNA, E 36/85, fol. 18r.
73. Gutch (ed.), *Collectanea Curiosa*, vol. 2, no. 28, p. 284.
74. See, for example, the new year's gift in 1526 (Gutch (ed.), *Collectanea Curiosa*, vol. 2, no. 28, p. 322).
75. *CSP*, *Venetian*, vol. 2, no. 1287.
76. Gutch (ed.), *Collectanea Curiosa*, vol. 2, no. 28, pp. 298–306, 334–38.
77. Gutch (ed.), *Collectanea Curiosa*, vol. 2, no. 28, p. 289.
78. *CSP*, *Venetian*, vol. 4, no. 519.
79. *CSP*, *Spain*, vol. 4, no. 160.
80. *CSP*, *Venetian*, vol. 4, no. 461.
81. Cavendish, *Thomas Wolsey*, p. 135.
82. *LP*, vol. 4, no. 6029.
83. Cavendish, *Thomas Wolsey*, p. 141.
84. *CSP*, *Venetian*, vol. 4, no. 519.
85. *LP*, vol. 4, no. 6030.
86. *CSP*, *Spain*, vol. 4, no. 232.
87. *CSP*, *Spain*, vol. 4, no. 194.
88. *LP*, vol. 5, Treasurer of the Chamber's Accounts, p. 317.
89. *LP*, vol. 5, Treasurer of the Chamber's Accounts, p. 323.
90. Cavendish, *Thomas Wolsey*, pp. 138–39.
91. Cavendish, *Thomas Wolsey*, p. 160.
92. *LP*, vol. 4, no. 6214.
93. *LP*, vol. 4, no. 6220.
94. *LP*, vol. 4, no. 6447.
95. *LP*, vol. 5, Treasurer of the Chamber's Accounts, p. 324.
96. TNA, E 36/171, fols 1–5v.
97. Two sets of twelve and one of thirteen, including Christ.
98. He was, of course, still a cardinal, but the value of this status was fast draining away with the invocation of *praemunire* and the decline in Anglo-papal relations.
99. It is an assumption, but a reasonable one, that what Henry gave to Wolsey was part of what had been his before. The list of plate and the jewel house inventory are found in TNA, SP 1/56, fols 206–15; E 36/85.
100. The indisputable items include those that are stated to be 'late the Cardinal's', those whose ornament confirms it, and those that are identifiable from other sources. The 880 oz candlesticks, for example, are not identified as such in the inventory but are specifically described by Cavendish; the 1,583 oz gold service given to Wolsey by Francis I at the Field of Cloth of Gold and bearing his badges (see

Chapter 9, p. 163) appear scattered around the gold sections of the list. An area of uncertainty is wares decorated with martlets. These probably refer to the choughs from Wolsey's arms (since many items on the Amadas account have 'martlets' too), but items with this motif that were already in the jewel house in 1521 are not counted in this figure. Many items, however, have been rebranded by erasing Wolsey's arms and replacing them with the king's.

101. *LP*, vol. 3, no. 1913; *CSP*, *Spain*, vol. 3, no. 119.
102. *LP*, vol. 4, no. 6199.
103. Vergil, *Anglica Historia (1555 version)*, bk 27, para. 20.

Chapter 9

1. Unfortunately, the courier from England had an accident on his journey and the cup and layer were both 'injured'. But the christening had to be postponed anyway, so presumably Boleyn was able to have them repaired in time (*LP*, vol. 3, part 1, no. 170).
2. Hall, *King Henry VIII*, vol. 1, pp. 144–45.
3. Glenn Richardson, *The Field of Cloth of Gold* (New Haven and London, 2013), p. 7.
4. *LP*, vol. 3, no. 629.
5. Richardson, *The Field of Cloth of Gold*, p. 82.
6. Hall, *King Henry VIII*, vol. 1, p. 181.
7. *LP*, vol. 3, no. 737. Perhaps Richard Gibson, master of the revels, to supervise the painters.
8. *LP*, vol. 3, no. 750.
9. *CSP*, *Venetian*, vol. 3, no. 60.
10. *LP*, vol. 3, no. 804.
11. *LP*, vol. 3, King's Book of Payments, p. 1540.
12. *LP*, vol. 3, no. 704.
13. *LP*, vol. 3, King's Book of Payments, p. 1540.
14. *LP*, vol. 3, no. 1093.
15. *LP*, vol. 3, King's Book of Payments, p. 1541.
16. *LP*, vol. 3, no. 919.
17. Richardson, *The Field of Cloth of Gold*, p. 51.
18. *CSP*, *Venetian*, vol. 3, no. 60.
19. *LP*, vol. 3, part 1, no. 700.
20. Hall, *King Henry VIII*, vol. 1, p. 200.
21. This is clear from Hall's remark at one point that 'I then perceived …' (Hall, *King Henry VIII*, vol. 1, p. 200).
22. Hall, *King Henry VIII*, vol. 1, p. 192.
23. Most of the chapel plate mentioned in Sanuto's account is plausibly matched by items in the 1521 inventory: there were, indeed, substantial gold and jewelled images of St George and St Christopher (weighing 101 oz and 62 oz respectively), and there were multiple images in silver-gilt of Our Lady and child, St Katherine and St Barbara. But other things – St Ursula or 'the twelve apostles in gold', gold altar candlesticks, basins, incense boats and censers – are not matched in the inventory.
24. *CSP*, *Venetian*, vol. 3, no. 83.
25. *Four Years at the Court*, p. 296.
26. *CSP*, *Venetian*, vol. 3, no. 50.
27. *CSP*, *Venetian*, vol. 3, no. 88.
28. *LP*, vol. 3, no. 869. This account is exaggerated and the cross, unless different from that supplied by Amadas in 1519 (see p. 143) was silver-gilt.
29. See Sydney Anglo, *Spectacle, Pageantry and Early Tudor Policy*, 2nd edn (Oxford, 1997), pp. 150–55.
30. Richardson, *The Field of Cloth of Gold*, p. 145.
31. Soardino, the Mantuan ambassador to France, *CSP*, *Venetian*, vol. 3, no. 81.
32. Hall, *King Henry VIII*, vol. 1, p. 210.
33. *CSP*, *Venetian*, vol. 3, no. 93.
34. *CSP*, *Venetian*, vol. 3, no. 50.
35. *LP*, vol. 2, no. 870.
36. See Maria Hayward, *Dress at the Court of Henry VIII* (Leeds, 2007), p. 376, A309.
37. *CSP*, *Venetian*, vol. 3, no. 94.
38. Richardson (*The Field of Cloth of Gold*, p. 163) suggests that the service described in the 1532 inventory was not Francis's gift to Wolsey in 1520 but to Henry in 1532. But the inventory was commissioned in June, whereas the kings' meeting was in October.
39. *CSP*, *Venetian*, vol. 3, no. 224.
40. *CSP*, *Venetian*, vol. 3, no. 94. There is no sign of such an object in Wolsey's account with Amadas; either it was provided by another goldsmith or Wolsey had it already.
41. *CSP*, *Venetian*, vol. 3, no. 77.

42. A contemporary estimate (*CSP*, *Venetian*, vol. 3, no. 72), supported by Richardson (*The Field of Cloth of Gold*, p. 66).
43. Richardson, *The Field of Cloth of Gold*, p. 141.
44. Frederick Dietz, *English Government Finance, 1485–1558* (Urbana, 1921), pp. 90–91.
45. *CSP*, *Venetian*, vol. 3, no. 60.
46. Hall, *King Henry VIII*, vol. 1, p. 197.
47. Perhaps Wolsey's chamberlain, Mr Dennys. I am grateful to Glenn Richardson for this suggestion.
48. J. Gutch (ed.), *Collectanea Curiosa*, vol. 2 (London, 1781), no. 28, pp. 290, 293.
49. *LP*, vol. 3, no. 913.
50. *LP*, vol. 3, part 3, no. 2288.
51. *CSP*, *Spain*, vol. 4, no. 797.
52. TNA, E 101/421/5, no. 11.
53. TNA, E 36/85, fol. 6r.
54. *LP*, vol. 3, no. 1485.
55. BL, Royal MS 7 C XVI, fols 39–39v.
56. Hall, *King Henry VIII*, vol. 2, pp. 215–17.
57. Michèle Bimbenet-Privat, 'Orfèvrerie et politique: le cas Vezeler', in *François Ier et l'art des Pays-Bas*, ed. Cécile Scailliérez (Paris, 2017), p. 301.
58. The actual weight is 2,490 kg (information from Paulus Reiner). The cost of workmanship for such an elaborate object would have been high. This estimate is based on the 7s 5d per ounce charged by Hans of Antwerp for Cromwell's new year's gift to the king in 1537, but it may have been more.
59. Bimbenet-Privat, 'Orfèvrerie et politique: le cas Vezeler', p. 301.
60. Bimbenet-Privat, 'Orfèvrerie et politique: le cas Vezeler', p. 302.
61. Hall, *King Henry VIII*, vol. 2, pp. 218–20.
62. Hall, *King Henry VIII*, vol. 2, p. 221. Among the specific jewels given by Henry was a jewelled gold cross (*LP*, vol. 5, no. 1546).
63. *CSP*, *Venetian*, vol. 4, no. 822.
64. *LP*, vol. 5, no. 1485.
65. Though not all at the time and two gold chains, presumably those forming part of the St Michael regalia, had to be delivered to England at a later date by Jean de Dintville (Bimbenet-Privat, 'Orfèvrerie et politique: le cas Vezeler', p. 301).
66. P. A. Hamy, *Entrevue de Francois Premier avec Henri VIII à Boulogne-sur-Mer en 1532* (Paris, 1898), p. 73.
67. *Inventory of Henry VIII*, no. 1353. Another, no. 1367 ('one clock within crystal garnished with silver gilt containing a salt in the top and standing upon six balls of agate with six cameo heads', weighing 115 oz), is another, though arguably less convincing, contender.
68. The salt was sold by the Commonwealth government in 1649 and bought by a Mr Smith for £43, after which it appears to have descended to the Sackville family, who sold it at Christie's in 1967. The salt was subsequently purchased by the Goldsmiths' Company to save it from export.
69. The opening reference in the 1649 inventory to '*two* faire large Saltes of Silver Gilt with a clocke in *it*' is strange but it was suggested in Christie's sale catalogue that the clerk, doubtless rushed, has assumed that the lower hexagonal section contained a second salt dish.
70. N. H. Nicholas (ed.), *The Privy Purse Expences of Henry the Eighth* (London, 1827), pp. 270–71.
71. See Philippe Malgouyres, *Le livre d'heures de François Ier* (Paris, 2018), p. 43.
72. *LP*, vol. 5, Privy Purse Expenses, pp. 747–62.
73. For example, *Inventory of Henry VIII*, nos. 2086 and 3523.
74. Hall, *King Henry VIII*, vol. 1, p. 198.
75. Glenn Richardson, '"As Presence Did Present Them": Personal Gift-Giving at the Field of Cloth of Gold', in *Henry VIII and the Court: Art, Politics and Performance*, ed. Thomas Betteridge and Suzannah Lipscombe (Farnham and Burlington, VT, 2013), pp. 62–63.

Chapter 10

1. The case appeared at auction without provenance in 1922 and was bought by Viscount Lee of Fareham; his widow presented it to the company in 1955. I am grateful to Victoria West, archivist of the Worshipful Company of Barbers, for this information.

2. The company and the fellowship formally merged with a royal charter in 1540 as the Barber-Surgeons' Company but, in view of their allied trades, had been closely cooperating for some time.
3. Thomas Vicary's will (TNA, PROB 11/4/86) includes a bequest of 'my best plaister box garnisshed with silver' to Thomas Bayley, warden of the Barber-Surgeons in 1559. Under 'plaster box' the *OED* cites a 1487 reference to 'my plaster box … and the cysars [scissors] therein', suggesting the description could refer to an instrument case. 'plaster, n., C1', *OED Online*, http://www.oed.com/view/Entry/145274.
4. See H. Stanford London, 'The Greyhound as a Royal Beast', *Archaeologia*, 97 (1959), pp. 139–63. Although it is often claimed that the greyhound supporter was replaced by the lion around 1525, London states (at p. 140, n. 4) that it is 'doubtful whether the dragon-greyhound combination was ever completely superseded by the lion and dragon [under Henry VIII]. If it was so superseded this can only have been in the last ten or twelve years of the reign.'
5. *LP*, vol. 5, no. 922.
6. *LP*, vol. 4, no. 4231.
7. I am grateful to Charlotte Berry for giving me sight of a draft of her article, 'The Changing Structure of an Immigrant Community: Alien Goldsmiths in London, 1480–1540', on which part of this section draws.
8. See J. L. Bolton, *The Alien Community of London in the Fifteenth Century: The Subsidy Rolls of 1440 and 1483–4* (Stamford, 1998), pp. 1–10.
9. GC, Court Minutes, Book D, pp. 306–08. My thanks to Charlotte Berry for this reference.
10. *Four Years at the Court*, vol. 2, p. 70.
11. *CSP, Spain*, vol. 3, part 2, no. 629.
12. *CSP, Spain*, vol. 4, part 1, no. 228.
13. *LP*, vol. 5, nos. 32, 558, 1244, etc.
14. N. H. Nicholas (ed.), *The Privy Purse Expences of Henry the Eighth* (London, 1827).
15. An exception is a massive payment of some £1,700 to ambassadors about to depart for Germany (Nicholas, *The Privy Purse Expences*, p. 19).
16. *LP*, vol. 3, part 2, no. 2807.28.
17. *LP*, vol. 5, no. 278. For a further discussion of Hayes see Chapter 12, p. 243.
18. For a biographical sketch of Hans, see Hugh Tait, 'The Girdle-Prayer Book or "Tablet": An Important Class of Renaissance Jewellery at the Court of Henry VIII', *Jewellery Studies*, 2 (1985), pp. 29–57.
19. GC, Court Minutes, Book D, p. 291.
20. For this and the following references to Cromwell's accounts, see *LP*, vol. 14, part 2, no. 782.
21. *LP*, vol. 14, part 2, no 782.
22. 'Peter Richardson, letters of denization', *England's Immigrants*, https://www.englandsimmigrants.com/person/48876; GC, Court Minutes, Book G, p. 34.
23. *LP*, vol. 11, no. 519.17.
24. *LP*, vol. 19, part 2, no. 688.
25. Frederick Madden (ed.), *Privy Purse Expenses of the Princess Mary 1536–46* (London, 1831), p. 170.
26. TNA, SP 4/1, fol. 110.
27. *LP*, vol. 4, part 2, no. 3446.
28. *LP*, vol. 5, no. 3445.
29. *LP*, vol. 8, no. 845.
30. *LP*, vol. 13, no. 617.
31. *LP*, vol. 13, part 2, no. 1280.
32. *LP*, vol. 16, no. 1480.
33. *LP*, vol. 4, no. 3097.
34. *Inventory of Henry VIII*, no. 500.
35. Michèle Bimbenet-Privat and Clèment Blanc-Riel, 'Un chef-d'oeuvre diplomatie et d'orfèvrerie', in *François Ier: pouvoir et image*, ed. Bruno Petey-Girard and Magali Vène (Paris, 2015), pp. 164–65. They note that no firm attribution has been proposed for its design and suggest that it may have been based on already existing royal portraits.
36. The Chamber accounts for the previous years are missing. This salary was slightly less than the £33 paid to Horenbout but, given the outside commissions he also received, Holbein probably earned more. His salary compares favourably, for example, with the £50 paid to senior court officials like the master of the jewel house.
37. *LP*, vol. 14, no. 781.
38. *LP*, vol. 14, no. 781.
39. *LP*, vol. 7, no. 1668. The document is undated but is thought to date from 1534; if from the

previous year, it would refer to the birth of Princess Elizabeth.

40. Kathleen M. Crowther, *Adam and Eve in the Protestant Reformation* (Cambridge, 2010), pp. 3–11.
41. One of the elder Holbein's surviving drawings is a design for a silver figure of St Sebastian; both the drawing and silver figure based on it are preserved in the Victoria and Albert Museum. Many Renaissance artists were trained as goldsmiths, most famously Cellini, but also Albrecht Dürer, Antonio Pollaiuolo and Lorenzo Ghiberti. Closer to home, Nicholas Hillyard was trained as a goldsmith.
42. In particular, a standing cup (cover lost) of 1529–30 (illus. Michael Clayton, *Christie's Pictorial History of English and American Silver* (Oxford, 1985), p. 197, fig. 292).
43. The Holbein portrait in the Royal Collection, dated July 1532 and formerly thought to be of Hans of Antwerp, is now believed to depict a German merchant from the Steelyard.
44. A suggestion made by Susan Foister, *Holbein in England* (London, 2006), p. 63.
45. Indeed, in 1536 the wardens of the company went so far as to imprison him for taking stranger servants without licence from the company (information from Charlotte Berry). GC, Court Minutes, Book F, p. 42.
46. GC, Court Minutes, Book F, pp. 61–62.
47. *LP*, vol. 7, no. 9.
48. A. Jeffries Collins (ed.), *Jewels and Plate of Queen Elizabeth I: The Inventory of 1574: Edited from Harley MS 1650 and Stowe MS 555 in the British Museum* (London, 1955), p. 50.
49. Among others, by Collins (ed.), *Jewels and Plate of Queen Elizabeth I*, p. 50; J. F. Hayward, *Virtuoso Goldsmiths and the Triumph of Mannerism, 1540–1620* (London, 1976), p. 112; David Starkey (ed.), *Henry VIII: A European Court in England* (London, 1991), p. 130; Foister, *Holbein in England*, p. 86.
50. Eric Ives, *The Life and Death of Anne Boleyn* (Oxford, 2004), p. 238.
51. *Inventory of Henry VIII*, no. 55.
52. That it was intended as a working scientific instrument rather than a frivolous toy is evident from a second annotation, apparently by Nikolaus Kratzer, concerning its calibrations.
53. The evidence (Tait, 'The Girdle-Prayer Book or "Tablet"', pp. 39–43) is primarily circumstantial: the English inscription around the edge of the panels is taken from the text of the First Great Bible, printed in 1539; and the panel of the 'Fyrye serpent' relates very closely to one that forms part of a large silver-gilt book cover completed by Hieronymus Mamaker of Antwerp in 1543 (illus. Tait, 'The Girdle-Prayer Book or "Tablet"', fig. 14) and which Tait argues Hans was probably aware of from his travels and his Antwerp contacts.
54. Foister, *Holbein in England*, p. 15.
55. Illus. Foister, *Holbein in England*, cat. no. 102.
56. For a cup and cover of 1561–62, the profile of which is clearly derived from the Seymour cup, see Timothy Schroder, *Renaissance and Baroque Silver, Mounted Porcelain and Ruby Glass from the Zilkha Collection* (London, 2012), cat. 10.

Chapter 11

1. Quoted by Frank Mumby (ed.), *The Youth of Henry VIII: A Narrative in Contemporary Letters* (London, 1913), p. 333.
2. *CSP*, *Venetian*, vol. 2, no. 500.
3. *LP*, vol. 2, no. 203.
4. Preface to *LP*, vol. 2, p. xxvii.
5. Steven Gunn, *Charles Brandon: Henry VIII's Closest Friend* (Stroud, 2015), p. 52.
6. *LP*, vol. 7, no. 1657.
7. Henry Ellis (ed.), *Original Letters Illustrative of English History*, first series (London, 1825), vol. 1, pp. 64–65.
8. Hall, *King Henry VIII*, vol. 1, p. 163.
9. BL, Add. MS 21481, fol. 260v, *Chamber Books*.
10. *LP*, vol. 2, no. 3968.
11. *LP*, vol. 2, no. 4217.
12. *LP*, vol. 3, no. 166.
13. *LP*, vol. 3, no. 1024.
14. *LP*, vol. 3, no. 1919.

15. *LP*, vol. 3, no. 3268.
16. *CSP*, *Spain*, vol. 5, no. 321.
17. *CSP*, *Spain*, vol. 5, no. 502.
18. *CSP*, *Spain*, vol. 5, no. 513.
19. Mumby (ed.), *The Youth of Henry VIII*, p. 87.
20. Mumby (ed.), *The Youth of Henry VIII*, p. 113.
21. *LP*, vol. 1, no. 1549.
22. *LP*, Addenda, vol. 1, part 1, no. 367.
23. *LP*, vol. 4, no. 4881.
24. *CSP*, *Venetian*, vol. 4, no. 682.
25. *CSP*, *Spain*, vol. 4, part 2, no. 880.
26. *CSP*, *Spain*, vol. 4, part 2, no. 1003.
27. *CSP*, *Spain*, vol. 4, part 2, no. 1047.
28. *CSP*, *Spain*, vol. 4, part 2, no. 1061.
29. *CSP*, *Spain*, vol. 4, part 2, no. 1107.
30. Published in 'Original documents relating to Katherine of Aragon', *Gentleman's Magazine*, vol. 42 (December 1854), pp. 572–74. The list is undated but its reference to the 'princess dowager' means it has to date from after April 1533.
31. Just two pieces of chapel plate annotated on the 1521 list as being in the queen's closet appear to be missing from the later list: a pair of images of Mary and John weighing 142 oz and described as 'newly made by [sic] the queen'. From their descriptions it would appear that they were made to complement the 95 oz crucifix described on the princess dowager's list as 'of the Spanish work' and 'of her own plate' and on the 1521 inventory as 'broken'. Trollope, 'King Henry VIII's Jewel Book', pp. 210–12.
32. At a guess, the twenty-five 'chaundelers' and eighty-three scullery and sawcery items probably weighed more than 2,000 oz. By way of comparison, the forty-two chargers, platters, dishes and saucers from the 1521 inventory allocated to Princess Mary weighed a total of 923 oz.
33. *LP*, vol. 6, no. 1382. Undated but placed in *LP* around November 1533.
34. *CSP*, *Milan*, no. 936.
35. *LP*, vol. 6, no. 1612. The dating of this document presents some difficulties. *LP* places it at the end of the 1533 volume but it includes the duke of Richmond's plate, which was not removed until after his death in July 1536; Katherine had already been dead for six months by then.
36. *LP*, vol. 10, no. 41.
37. Anon., *Chronicle of King Henry VIII of England*, trans. Martin A. Sharp Hume (London, 1889), pp. 53–54.
38. *LP*, vol. 10, no. 40.
39. *LP*, vol. 10, no. 128.
40. Frederick Madden (ed.), *Privy Purse Expenses of the Princess Mary 1536–46* (London, 1831), pp. xxi–xxii.
41. According to Madden (ed.), *Privy Purse Expenses of the Princess Mary*, p. xxxix, her household and council amounted to 304 people.
42. Trollope, 'King Henry VIII's Jewel Book', pp. 172, 175, 181, 182, 185 *et passim*.
43. Trollope, 'King Henry VIII's Jewel Book', pp. 178–81, 190, 210–12.
44. *LP*, vol. 6, no. 1009.
45. *LP*, vol. 6, no. 1382.
46. *LP*, vol. 6, no. 1612.
47. *LP*, vol. 7, no. 337.
48. *CSP*, *Spain*, vol. 2, no. 40.
49. *CSP*, *Spain*, vol. 5, part 2, no. 29.
50. *LP*, vol. 10, no. 494.
51. *LP*, vol. 10, no. 973.
52. *LP*, vol. 10, no. 1079.
53. *CSP*, *Spain*, vol. 5, no. 71.
54. *LP*, vol. 11, no. 148. Chapuys' letter was written in French. The calendared version uses the word 'ring' rather than medal, but from the subsequent description it clearly cannot be a finger ring that is meant but something round.
55. 'Obedientia unitatem parit, Unitas animi quietem et constantiam; Constans vero animi quies thesaurus inestimabilis. Respexit humilitatem Qui in Filio nobis reliquit Perfectum humilitatis exemplar. Factus est obediens Patri, Et ipsa etiam natura parentibus Et patrie obediendum docuit.' My thanks to Professor Timothy Wilson for the translation.
56. *LP*, vol. 11, no. 860.
57. Maria Hayward, 'Gift Giving at the Court of Henry VIII: The 1539 New Year's Gift Roll in Context', *The Antiquaries Journal*, 85 (September 2005), p. 144.
58. *CSP*, *Spain*, vol. 6, part 2, no. 90.
59. Such as 'Frauncis', 'Orton', 'Busshe', 'Mabell' and 'Reynolds'.
60. Madden (ed.), *Privy Purse Expenses of the Princess Mary*, p. 170.

61. Madden (ed.), *Privy Purse Expenses of the Princess Mary*, pp. 51–52.
62. BL, Royal MS 17 B XXVIII, fols 112–25v.
63. *LP*, vol. 5, no. 696.
64. *LP*, vol. 4, no. 3325.
65. Eric Ives, *The Life and Death of Anne Boleyn: 'The Most Happy'* (Oxford, 2004), p. 87.
66. *LP*, vol. 5, no. 276.
67. *CSP*, *Spain*, vol. 4, no. 1003.
68. *CSP*, *Spain*, vol. 4, part 2, no. 1033.
69. *LP*, vol. 5, no. 1548.
70. *LP*, vol. 5, no. 1685, and vol. 6, no. 6.
71. *LP*, vol. 6, no. 6.
72. *LP*, vol. 6, no. 212.
73. Ives, *The Life and Death of Anne Boleyn*, p. 233.
74. *Inventory of Henry VIII*, nos. 780, 981, 1046.
75. *Inventory of Henry VIII*, nos. 163, 178.
76. Ives, *The Life and Death of Anne Boleyn*, p. 233. Indeed, A. J. Collins suggests that the mother-of-pearl ewer may have been Cromwell's new year's gift to the queen in 1534 (see A. J. Collins (ed.), *Jewels and Plate of Queen Elizabeth I: The Inventory of 1574: Edited from Harley MS 1650 and Stowe MS 555 in the British Museum* (London, 1955), no. 131).
77. *LP*, vol. 6, no. 1382.
78. See Collins (ed.), *Jewels and Plate of Queen Elizabeth I*, p. 197.
79. *Inventory of Henry VIII*, no. 723.
80. BL, Royal MS 7 C XVI, fols 18–31.
81. BL, Royal MS 7 C XVI, fol. 22v.
82. *LP*, vol. 14, part 2, no. 274.
83. *LP*, vol. 14, part 2, no. 548.
84. *LP*, vol. 14, part 2, no. 753.
85. *LP*, vol. 15, nos. 899 and 925.
86. *LP*, vol. 17, no. 63.
87. *LP*, vol. 16, no. 1398.
88. *CSP*, *Spain*, vol. 5, p. 549.
89. *LP*, vol. 16, no. 1333.
90. *LP*, vol. 3, part 2, no. 467.56.
91. *LP*, vol. 5, no. 1529.
92. *LP*, vol. 11, no. 163. The inventory was published in John Gough Nichols (ed.), *Inventories of the Wardrobes, Plate, Chapel Stuff, etc. of Henry Fitzroy, Duke of Richmond, and of the Wardrobe Stuff at Baynard's Castle of Katharine, Princess Dowager*, Camden Society, old series, vol. 61 (London, 1855), pp. 1–21.
93. *LP*, vol. 11, no. 163.
94. TNA, SP 1/40, fol. 207.
95. *LP*, vol. 11, no. 163.
96. *LP*, vol. 11, no. 174.
97. *LP*, vol. 6, no. 1605.
98. *LP*, vol. 12, part 2, no. 911.
99. The question had evidently not been settled as late as December 1537 when Cromwell made a note to himself 'to know whether the lords will [give] any new year's gifts to my lord Prince' (*LP*, vol. 12, part 2, no. 1151).
100. 1538: TNA, SP 1/128, fol. 5. 1539: BL, Royal Appendix MS 89, fols 410–42. 1540: BL, Add. MS 11301, fol. 12.
101. James Orchard Halliwell (ed.), *Letters of the Kings of England*, vol. 2 (London, 1846), p. 15.

Chapter 12

1. TNA, E 36/85.
2. These headline figures must be taken with some caution. First, the 1521 total is distorted somewhat by Trollope's misreading of some of the larger numbers (see Chapter 2, note 35). Secondly, the weights of around 180 entries on the 1532 inventory are left blank. Most of these weights can be inferred from comparison with the corresponding descriptions in 1521 and relate to objects allocated to the household, but a few remain unknown.
3. In 1521 gold accounted for about 4 per cent of the total weight of precious metal in the jewel house, but by 1532 this had risen to 6 per cent.
4. In June 1535, the king received 2,020 oz of plate from Bishop Fisher, who refused to subscribe to the Act of Supremacy (*LP*, vol. 8, no. 888).
5. See Chapter 2, note 13.
6. TNA, E 101/421/5, no. 11.
7. BL, Royal Appendix MS 89, fols 38–39v.
8. TNA, E 101/421/5, no. 11.
9. TNA, SP 2/N, fols 1–15; and TNA, SP 2/P, no. 1.
10. Michael Everett, *The Rise of Thomas Cromwell: Power and Politics in the Reign of Henry VIII* (London, 2015), p. 171.
11. TNA, SP 2/N, fols 1–15; and TNA, SP 2/P, no. 1.

12. At the very end of the reign we see a bill of £838 for new year's gifts being paid by the Court of Augmentations (*LP*, vol. 21, part 2, no. 775).
13. See Chapter 11, p. 218.
14. *CSP*, *Spain*, vol. 4, no. 1033.
15. *LP*, vol. 6, no. 1382. (The exact same note also appears as no. 1194, dated to September, but other items on the list suggest that December is the more likely date.) This may or may not be connected with the king's order of Easter that year for 'a mass of vessels to be broken' referred to by Collins (*Jewels and Plate of Queen Elizabeth I: The Inventory of 1574: Edited from Harley MS 1650 and Stowe MS 555 in the British Museum* (London, 1955), p. 117).
16. *LP*, vol. 5, no. 1298.
17. *LP*, vol. 5, no. 1299.
18. *CSP*, *Spain*, vol. 5, no. 70. Chapuys admits to being unsure whether the marks were 'English marks, worth two nobles each, or those weighing eight ounces', but it was surely the former. An English noble (or angel) was worth 6s 8d (one-third of a pound), the equivalent of about 2 oz of sterling silver, so two nobles would equal 4 oz. This would have amounted to 48,000 oz – a huge sum in itself – whereas the latter would have come to a scarcely credible 96,000 oz, about 75 per cent of the total weight of the plate in the jewel house at that time.
19. BL, Royal Appendix MS 89, fols 106–10v. This was supplied by Cornelis Hayes and Morgan Wolf at a cost of £1,631 8s (*LP*, vol. 16, no. 745).
20. *LP*, vol. 9, no. 47.
21. *LP*, vol. 9, no. 151.
22. *LP*, vol. 9, nos. 47, 151, 154 and 217.
23. *LP*, vol. 7, no. 1340.
24. *LP*, vol. 12, part 2, no. 516.
25. *LP*, vol. 12, part 2, no. 529.
26. Muriel St. Clare Byrne (ed.), *The Lisle Letters* (Chicago and London, 1981), vol. 5, no. 1086, p. 10.
27. On 30 December 1535 Henry VIII invited Chapuys to call on him 'any day I chose during these festivities, excepting on new year's day' (*CSP*, *Spain*, vol. 5, part 2, no. 246).
28. Maria Hayward, 'Gift Giving at the Court of Henry VIII: The 1539 New Year's Gift Roll in Context', *The Antiquaries Journal*, 85 (September 2005), p. 127.
29. See *LP*, vol. 5, no. 686 for the 1534 roll; the 1539, not calendared in *LP*, is in the Folger Shakespeare Library, Washington DC (Folger MS Z. d. 11).
30. TNA, E 101/421/13.
31. For a full analysis of the 1539 gift roll, compared with those of 1534, 1532 and 1528, see Hayward, 'Gift Giving at the Court of Henry VIII'.
32. One section of the inventory is titled 'goblettis and crusis gilte', but only mentions goblets; at the end of the list the plate left with the duke of Buckingham during his incarceration includes three 'ale cruses'.
33. My thanks to Matthew Winterbottom, Curator of Sculpture and Decorative Arts at the Ashmolean Museum, for weighing it.
34. *Inventory of Henry VIII*, no. 163.
35. *Inventory of Henry VIII*, no. 163.
36. *LP*, vol. 12, no. 968.
37. St. Clare Byrne (ed.), *Lisle Letters*, vol. 6, no. 1643, pp. 19–20.
38. Edmund Waterton, 'On a Remarkable Incident in the Life of Saint Edward the Confessor, with Notices of Certain Rings Hallowed on Good Friday by the Sovereigns of England', *The Archaeological Journal*, 21 (June 1864), pp. 103–13.
39. *LP*, vol. 2, nos. 4223 and 4305.
40. *LP*, vol. 4, no. 2035.
41. *LP*, vol. 10, no. 920. Another of the Lisle letters, dated March 1535, mentions that 'he that keepeth the rings, one of the jewel house, is forth from town' (*LP*, vol. 8, no. 309).
42. *LP*, vol. 3, King's Book of Payments, 1521, p. 1545.
43. *LP*, vol. 18, no. 436.
44. GC, Court Minutes, Book A, vol. 2, p. 503.
45. The practice of the company was to require a liveryman to have served as renter in order to qualify for election as a warden. GC, Court Minutes, Book D, p. 272; Book F, pp. 53, 157.
46. '1541 London Subsidy Roll: Dowgate Ward', in *Two Tudor Subsidy Rolls for the City of London, 1541 and 1582*, ed. R. G. Lang (London, 1993), pp. 62–66. British History Online, http://www.british-history.ac.uk/london-record-soc/vol29/pp62-66; TNA, PROB 11/31/529.
47. See G. R. Elton, 'The Treasurer and the Goldsmith, a Cautionary Story', in *Star*

Chamber Stories, ed. G. R. Elton (London, 1958), pp. 114–46.

48. At new year in 1540 Hayes gave the king 'a shaving cloth wrought with gold' and received a reward of 6s 8d (*LP*, vol. 16, no. 380).
49. The occasion was the Somerset House Conference, when the gifts presented to the Spanish ambassador, Juan de Velasco, included the French royal gold cup (fig. 3.3).
50. See Collins (ed.), *Jewels and Plate of Queen Elizabeth I*, p. 137.
51. The addition of a thistle to the roses would be a perfectly appropriate modification to the original Tudor ornament.
52. *The Inventory of King Henry VIII* (London, 1998), no. 947.
53. *The Inventory of King Henry VIII* (London, 1998), no. 1047.
54. His will states that he was born in Usk. TNA, PROB 11/35/175.
55. *LP*, Addendum volume, no. 367.
56. N. H. Nicholas (ed.), *The Privy Purse Expences of Henry the Eighth* (London, 1827), p. 7 etc. Ambrose Heal (*The London Goldsmiths 1200–1800* (Cambridge, 1972), p. 271) lists him as early as 1520, although without reference.
57. £139 compared with £560.
58. *LP*, vol. 18, part 2, no. 231.
59. Philippa Glanville, *Silver in Tudor and Early Stuart England: A Social History and Catalogue of the National Collection, 1480–1660* (London, 1990), p. 94.
60. He was granted properties in London and Essex in 1540, and in 1543 he appears to have been part of a consortium buying land from the Court of Augmentations for £22,616. As a contributor to the forced loan in 1544 he, along with various other goldsmiths, benefited from grants of royal land issued as security, and the number of properties transferred to him and his wife Elizabeth suggests that he must have been a major creditor.
61. In a letter to Cromwell dated October 1534 he stated that he 'has served the ambassadors for seven years to the king's satisfaction' (*LP*, vol. 7, no. 1340).
62. Cromwell's will, dated 1529, gives a further hint of his holdings at that stage. He leaves a number of specific bequests to his son, Gregory: a basin and ewer, his 'best' salt, his 'best' cup, three 'best' goblets, three others, his twelve 'best' spoons and his three 'best ale drinking pots' (*LP*, vol. 4, part 2, no. 5772). The term 'best' implies, of course, that there were others.
63. *LP*, vol. 4, no. 3197.
64. Henry Ellis (ed.), *Original Letters Illustrative of English History*, third series, vol. 2 (London, 1846), pp. 131–34.
65. *LP*, vol. 8, no. 978.
66. *LP*, vol. 12, part 2, no. 1100.
67. *LP*, vol. 6, no. 857.
68. *LP*, vol. 10, no. 776.1. See also Everett, *The Rise of Thomas Cromwell*, pp. 169 and 312, n. 193.
69. *LP*, vol. 5, no. 278.
70. *LP*, vol. 16, no. 396. The commission is undated but is placed in *LP* in 1540.
71. Diarmaid MacCulloch, *Thomas Cromwell: A Life* (London, 2018), p. 537.
72. *LP*, vol. 21, part 1, nos. 643 and 650.
73. J. D. Alsop, 'Anthony Aucher', *ODNB*.
74. *LP*, vol. 3, part 1, no. 86.
75. *LP*, vol. 4, no. 3867.
76. *LP*, vol. 5, no. 634.
77. *LP*, vol. 21, part 1, no. 970.18.
78. Martin Allen, *Mints and Money in Medieval England* (Cambridge, 2012), p. 279; *LP*, vol. 3, no. 2348.
79. Collins (ed.), *Jewels and Plate of Queen Elizabeth I*, p. 117.
80. *LP*, vol. 11, no. 624.
81. *LP*, vol. 11. no. 768.
82. *LP*, vol. 11, no. 769.
83. See C. E. Challis, *The Tudor Coinage* (London, 1978), p. 157.
84. See Challis, *The Tudor Coinage*, appendix II.
85. T. F. Reddaway and Lorna Walker, *The Early History of the Goldsmiths' Company 1327–1507* (London, 1975), p. 166.
86. J. Gutch (ed.), *Collectanea Curiosa*, vol. 2 (London, 1781), no. 28, p. 290.
87. Allen, *Mints and Money*, p. 163.
88. *CSP*, *Spain*, vol. 4, part 1, no. 228.
89. Challis, *The Tudor Coinage*, p. 89.
90. *LP*, vol. 17, no. 189.
91. Challis, *The Tudor Coinage*, p. 91.
92. Challis, *The Tudor Coinage*, p. 254.
93. *LP*, vol. 20, part 2, no. 366.
94. Allen, *Mints and Money*, p. 279.

95. Maria Hayward, *The 1542 Inventory of Whitehall. The Palace and Its Keeper* (London, 2004), p. 128.
96. See GC, Court Minutes, Book H, pp. 67–76.
97. Mining was often on Henry VIII's mind. An ambitious project concerned a silver mine near Barnstaple around 1528. This was to be a joint venture between Wolsey, the king and a German merchant called Joachim Hochsteter. Hochsteter proposed employing about 1,000 miners (some of whom would be German). The costs (mostly to be borne by the king) would be huge, but Hochsteter estimated the likely profits, after costs, to be between £30,528 and £78,000 a year (*LP*, Addenda, no. 583.2). In October of that year he wrote to Wolsey that he had 'commenced smelting 1,000 lb of ore from each mine [… and that …] truly the king may say his realm contains the richest mines of gold, silver, copper and lead in all the world'. It is unclear whether the scheme ever returned a profit.
98. *LP*, vol. 20, part 2, no. 1004.
99. *LP*, vol. 1, no. 185. It was perhaps the scale of this and other payments that led to Thomas Exmew being appointed to conduct an enquiry in 1512 into 'deceptions' by Fenrother and Rede (*LP*, vol. 1, no. 1083.24).
100. Challis, *The Tudor Coinage*, p. 88.
101. John Forbes, *Hallmark: A History of the London Assay Office* (London, 1999), p. 20.
102. This point drawn from the T. F. Reddaway manuscript at Goldsmiths' Hall library (see note 109 below).
103. The date when the procedure for a regular trial of the pyx was set down. There had been occasional trials of suspect coins before that date, but these were exceptional. (See Allen, *Mints and Money*, pp. 165–66.)
104. *LP*, vol. 4, no. 3150.
105. *LP*, vol. 4, no. 3738.
106. *LP*, vol. 11, 1419.
107. '1541 London Subsidy Roll: Langbourn Ward', in *Two Tudor Subsidy Rolls for the City of London, 1541 and 1582*, ed. R. G. Lang (London, 1993), pp. 87–95. British History Online, http://www.british-history.ac.uk/london-record-soc/vol29/pp87-95.
108. See the entry on Bowes (by C. E. Challis) in *ODNB*.
109. Quoted from the unfinished manuscript of what was intended to be the eighth chapter of Reddaway and Walker, *The Early History of the Goldsmiths' Company 1327–1507*; the manuscript is preserved in the library of the Goldsmiths' Company.
110. Hall, *King Henry VIII*, vol. 1, p. 258.
111. *LP*, vol. 18, part 1, no. 436. See also Collins (ed.), *Jewels and Plate of Queen Elizabeth I*, p. 156.
112. See W. S. Prideaux, *Memorials of the Goldsmiths' Company*, vol. 1 (London, 1896), pp. 49–51.
113. In 1540 the French ambassador, Marillac, reported that 'all strangers in the service of the king [were exempted and] shall remain as long as they shall be in such service'. *LP*, vol. 16, no. 9.

Chapter 13

1. *CSP*, *Venetian*, vol. 3, no. 1427.
2. Quoted from a letter from Campeggio to Clement (*LP*, vol. 4, no. 4881).
3. *CSP*, *Venetian*, vol. 4, nos. 896 and 956.
4. *LP*, vol. 13, part 1, no. 407.
5. *LP*, vol. 3, no. 1122.
6. *LP*, vol. 2, no. 1227.
7. *LP*, vol. 3, no. 2567.
8. *LP*, vol. 3, no. 3898.
9. *LP*, vol. 3, no. 6003.
10. *CSP*, *Spain*, vol. 4, part 2, no. 615.
11. *LP*, vol. 7, no. 590.
12. *LP*, vol. 10, no. 721.
13. *LP*, vol. 10, no. 364.
14. *LP*, vol. 9, no. 42.
15. *LP*, vol. 13, part 1, no. 231.
16. Charles Wriothesley, *A Chronicle of England During the Reigns of the Tudors*, vol. 1, Camden Society, new series, vol. 11 (London, 1875), pp. 86–87.
17. *LP*, vol. 12, part 2, no. 587.
18. *LP*, vol. 13, part 2, no. 401.

19. *LP*, vol. 13, part 1, no. 634.
20. *LP*, vol. 13, part 2, no. 200.
21. *LP*, vol. 13, part 2, no. 367.
22. *LP*, vol. 13, part 2, no. 49.
23. *LP*, vol. 13, part 2, no. 41.2.
24. *LP*, vol. 11, no. 198.
25. *LP*, vol. 13, part 2, no. 211. (This letter says the plate is with John Freman.)
26. *LP*, vol. 12, part 1, no. 1172. Norfolk's remark is curious, since Jervaulx is in fact about sixty miles from the sea. But it is close to the River Ure, which feeds into the Ouse, so it is possible that is what Norfolk meant.
27. *LP*, vol. 9, no. 297.
28. Quoted in Philippa Glanville, 'Cardinal Wolsey and the Goldsmiths', in *Cardinal Wolsey: Church, State and Art*, ed. S. J. Gunn and P. G. Lindley (Cambridge, 1991), p. 135.
29. *LP*, vol. 9, no. 534.
30. *LP*, vol. 8, no. 822.
31. *LP*, vol. 7, no. 692; vol. 9, no. 1081.
32. Lawrence Warren was a member of the Goldsmiths' Company and later assay master at the mint at Canterbury, appointed in 1545 (*LP*, vol. 20, no. 620.38). He joined the Goldsmiths' livery in 1543 and went on to serve as renter of the company. GC, Court Book G, p. 61; Book I, p. 20.
33. *LP*, vol. 10, no. 137.
34. Henry Ellis (ed.), *Original Letters Illustrative of English History*, third series, vol. 3 (London, 1825), pp. 235–36.
35. *LP*, vol. 12, part 1, no. 481.
36. *LP*, vol. 8, no. 569.
37. *LP*, vol. 10, no. 164.
38. *LP*, vol. 7, no. 1678.
39. *LP*, vol. 14, part 2, no. 438.
40. *LP*, vol. 9, no. 881.
41. *LP*, vol. 14, part 2, no. 232.
42. Marillac to Francis I (*LP*, vol. 14, part 2, no. 389).
43. *LP*, vol. 12, part 1, no. 1316.
44. *LP*, vol. 21, part 1, no. 302.
45. *LP*, vol. 20, part 1, no. 1145.
46. John Caley, 'Copy of the Survey of the Priory of Bridlington in Yorkshire', *Archaeologia*, 19 (1821), p. 272.
47. *LP*, vol. 12, part 1, no. 1257.
48. *LP*, vol. 12, part 2, no. 34.
49. Illus. in J. M. Fritz, *Goldschmiedekunst der Gotik in Mitteleuropa* (Munich, 1982), fig. 481.
50. *LP*, vol. 13, part 1, no. 192.
51. *LP*, vol. 14, part 2, no. 475.
52. *LP*, vol. 13, part 2, no. 401.
53. *LP*, vol. 13, part 2, no. 1103.
54. John Williams, *Account of the monastic treasures confiscated at the dissolution of the various houses in England*, Publications of the Abbotsford Club, vol. 5, ed. W. B. D. D. Turnbull (Edinburgh, 1836), pp. 44–45. These numbers differ slightly from those given in *LP*, vol. 15, no. 772.
55. *LP*, vol. 15, no. 772.
56. Wriothesley, *Chronicle of England*, vol. 1, p. 86, n. a.
57. Ellis (ed.), *Original Letters*, third series, vol. 1, pp. 245–47. This was perhaps in 1522 and an entry of that year from Amadas's account with Wolsey (J. Gutch (ed.), *Collectanea Curiosa*, vol. 2 (London, 1781), no. 28, p. 289) reads: 'delivered to George [Huxor] 5 oz crown gold for the roll with scriptures that went about the cross that was offered at Canterbury £9 3s 4d'.
58. *LP*, vol. 5, Treasurer of the Chamber's Accounts, p. 323.
59. Ellis (ed.), *Original Letters*, third series, vol. 3, p. 165.
60. Susan Doran (ed.), *Henry VIII: Man and Monarch* (London, 2009), p. 207. John Husee's letter of 8 September 1538 to Lord Lisle clearly states that the king was in Canterbury on that date (Muriel St. Clare Byrne (ed.), *The Lisle Letters* (Chicago and London, 1981), vol. 5, no 1217).
61. John Stow, *Annals of England to 1603* (London, c. 1605), p. 907.
62. Wriothesley, *Chronicle of England*, vol. 1, p. 87.
63. Wriothesley, *Chronicle of England*, vol. 1, p. 86, n. a.
64. The order to confiscate the treasure of the shrine and publicly burn the saint's bones was pronounced in June 1538 (*LP*, vol. 13, part 2, no. 133).
65. Ellis (ed.), *Original Letters*, third series, vol. 3, p. 78.
66. Williams, *Account of the monastic treasures*, pp. 59, 61.
67. *LP*, vol. 14, part 1, no. 1190.i.
68. *LP*, vol. 16, no. 745.

69. Wriothesley, *Chronicle of England*, vol. 1, p. 133.
70. *CSP*, *Spain*, vol. 5, part 1, no. 205.
71. *LP*, vol. 8, no. 722.
72. *LP*, vol. 8, no. 475.
73. *LP*, vol. 8, no. 722.
74. Two variant versions of this account were published in transcript: Sir John Williams, *Account of the monastic treasures* (full reference above in note 54), and 'Diverse pieces of Gold Plate accrued to the king. Signed by John Williams, Master and Treasurer of the king's jewels (Bodleian MS è Musæo 57)', reprinted in *Monasticon Anglicanum*, ed. William Dugdale, vol. 1 (London, 1846), p. 63 *et seq*. This paragraph draws on both.
75. Williams, *Account of the monastic* treasures, pp. 24, 50–51. The last is clearly identical with item 18 of the 1547 inventory, even though there is a discrepancy in the weights given by the two documents, Williams's list erroneously giving it as 104 oz (iiij^{xx}xxiiij) and the inventory as 424 oz (iiij^{C}xxiiij). Other former monastic goods mentioned in the 1547 inventory include nos. 191–93.
76. Williams, *Account of the monastic treasures*, p. 24.
77. 'Diverse pieces of Gold Plate accrued to the king. Signed by John Williams, Master and Treasurer of the king's jewels', reprinted in Dugdale (ed.), *Monasticon Anglicanum*, vol. 1, p. 63.
78. Williams, *Account of the monastic treasures*, p. 74; Dugdale (ed.), *Monasticon Anglicanum*, vol. 1, p. 63.
79. Thomas Rymer, *Foedera*, 2nd edn, vol. 15 (London, 1725), pp. 35–36.
80. *LP*, vol. 15, no. 139.
81. Neville Williams, *Henry VIII and His Court* (London, 1971), p. 165. But presumably this included the plate and jewels from the monastery itself as otherwise it would not square with Stow's account of 'two great chests' (see note 61, above).
82. Maria Hayward, 'Rich Pickings: Henry VIII's Use of Confiscation and Its Significance for the Development of the Royal Collection', in *Henry VIII and the Court: Art, Politics and Performance*, ed. Thomas Betteridge and Suzannah Lipscombe (Farnham and Burlington, VT, 2013), p. 34.
83. J. J. Scarisbrooke, *Henry VIII* (Berkeley and Los Angeles, 1968), p. 400.
84. N. H. Nicholas (ed.), *The Privy Purse Expences of Henry the Eighth* (London, 1827), pp. 81, 148, 272.
85. Diarmaid MacCulloch, *Thomas Cromwell: A Life* (London, 2018), p. 346.
86. *LP*, vol. 14, part 1, no. 967.
87. Suzannah Lipscomb, *The King Is Dead: The Last Will and Testament of Henry VIII* (London, 2015), pp. 107–11.
88. When Henry wrote to Charles V in 1526 expressing his shock at the attack on St Peter's he said: 'We are informed [that] imperial soldiers despoiled and plundered the Church of St Peter and other temples and houses consecrated to God, and made most abominable use of vases and ornaments of the same, such as was never seen before [...] to the notable dishonour of the Apostolic See' (*CSP*, *Spain*, vol. 2, no. 588).
89. Williams, *Account of the monastic treasures*, p. 96.
90. Williams, *Account of the monastic treasures*, pp. 97–98.
91. Unfortunately, the Winchester inventory printed in John Strype, *Memorials of Archbishop Cranmer* (Oxford, 1848), pp. 360–66, is thin on detail: the five gold crosses, for example, are clustered together in a single entry and economically described as 'five crosses of gold, garnished with precious stones'.
92. *Inventory of Henry VIII*, no. 27.
93. Some of this, like the images, must have been monastic appropriations, since Williams's Court of Augmentations account records a payment of £102 3s 11d to Fabyan Wethers for 'mending of diverse and sundry parcels of plate', including gilt crosses, candlesticks, cruets, holy water stocks, and an incense boat (Williams, *Account of the monastic treasures*, pp. 75–78).
94. Quoted by Fiona Kisby, '"When the King Goeth a Procession": Chapel Ceremonies and Services, the Ritual Year, and Religious Reforms at the Early Tudor Court, 1485–1547', *Journal of British Studies*, 40, 1 (January 2001), p. 71.
95. Richard Rex, 'The Religion of Henry VIII', *The Historical Journal*, 57 (2014), pp. 1–32.
96. Rex, 'The Religion of Henry VIII', pp. 17–19.

Chapter 14

1. See Suzannah Lipscomb, *1536: The Year That Changed Henry VIII* (Oxford, 2009).
2. Hall, *King Henry VIII*, vol. 2, p. 298.
3. *LP*, vol. 16, no. 590.
4. *LP*, vol. 15, no. 954.
5. *LP*, vol. 13, part 1, no. 1102.
6. The Chamber accounts show per diem payments to jewel house staff Robert Draper and John Kirkby and four servants for 'attending upon his personage' in France (*LP*, vol. 19, part 2, no. 524).
7. A warrant issued by the duke of Suffolk (*LP*, vol. 20, part 1, no. 19) authorises payment of £27 7s 6s to Anthony Rous, master of the jewels, 'for conveying eight loads of plate and jewels from Calais castle to the Tower of London in November [1544]'.
8. Frederick Dietz, *English Government Finance, 1485–1558* (Urbana, 1921), p. 147.
9. *LP*, vol. 19, part 1, no. 206.
10. *LP*, vol. 20, part 1, no. 1008.
11. *LP*, vol. 20, part 2, no. 362.
12. *LP*, vol. 20, part 2, no. 957.
13. *LP*, vol. 20, no. 1025.
14. *Inventory of Henry VIII*, nos. 162 and 158.
15. *Inventory of Henry VIII*, nos. 2753 and 2754.
16. *LP*, vol. 21, part 1, no. 95.
17. *LP*, vol. 21, part 1, no. 95.
18. *LP*, vol. 21, part 1, no. 127.
19. *Inventory of Henry VIII*, no. 2619.
20. *LP*, vol. 21, part 1, no. 354.
21. For a full account, see Roy Strong, 'Three Royal Jewels: The Three Brothers, the Mirror of Great Britain and the Feather', *The Burlington Magazine*, 108, 760 (July 1966), pp. 350–53.
22. *LP*, vol. 21, part 1, no. 1200.
23. *CSP*, *Spain*, vol. 7, no. 294.
24. A curious case of history repeating itself (see Chapter 9, note 1 for a similar incident in 1519).
25. *LP*, vol. 21, part 1, no. 1185.
26. *LP*, vol. 21, part 1, no, 1535.57. See also above pp. 173–74.
27. *LP*, vol. 21, part 1, no. 1367.
28. *LP*, vol. 21, part 1, no. 1212.
29. Thomas Campbell, *Henry VIII and the Art of Majesty* (New Haven and London, 2007), pp. 241–42.
30. *LP*, vol. 21, part 2, no. 548.
31. *LP*, vol. 16, no. 380.
32. The portrait of Henry VIII, attributed to Holbein, granting the royal charter to the merged company of Barber-Surgeons in 1540 shows the company basking in royal favour.
33. The inside of the cover is engraved with an inscription dated 1678 indicating that the cup was given (or returned) to the company in that year.
34. This is an unusual combination (see p. 55 for a discussion of the royal supporters). However, H. Stanford London ('The Greyhound as a Royal Beast', *Archaeologia*, 97 (1959), p. 140) notes that the same combination also appears on a seal of the Court of Common Pleas of 1542.
35. The construction of the cup, with vertical straps enclosing the bowl and connecting the stem to the lip, would have been unnecessary if the bowl had originally been of silver.
36. A covered cup with 'five hanging bells of silver' is included in an inventory of Skinners' Company plate compiled in the late sixteenth century (see manuscript volume held in the Guildhall Library called the 'Register Book of Evidences … and Implements Appertaining to the Worshipful Company of Skinners'. London Metropolitan Archives, CLC/L/SE/A/005/MS30817, fol. 41).
37. BL, Cotton MS Galba B X, fol. 82v.
38. *LP*, vol. 20, part 2, no. 1004.
39. *Inventory of Henry VIII*, no. 1491.
40. See Campbell, *Henry VIII and the Art of Majesty*, p. 277. We do not know exactly how much the set cost but according to Campbell (pp. 282–83) it was valued at over £8,000 in the Commonwealth sale in the seventeenth century, by far the most valuable in the Royal Collection.
41. *LP*, vol. 21, part 2, no. 332.48.
42. *LP*, vol. 21, part 1, 1539; part 2, no. 475.
43. *LP*, vol. 17, no. 220.3.
44. *LP*, vol. 21, part 2, no. 332.48.
45. *LP*, vol. 21, part 1, nos. 1382.34, 1535.54, 1535.55.
46. Maria Hayward (ed.), *The 1542 Inventory of Whitehall. The Palace and Its Keeper* (London, 2004), vol. 1, p. 78.

47. *LP*, vol. 20, part 1, no. 1202.
48. *LP*, vol. 12, part 1, no. 11.
49. *LP*, vol. 12, nos. 47.2 and 11.
50. This information comes from Chapuys (*CSP*, *Spain*, vol. 4, part 1, no. 252). The title he uses for the ambassador is 'the Sieur de Bayonne', referring either to Jean du Bellay, bishop of Bayonne (often called Monseigneur de Bayonne), or his brother Guillaume du Bellay, seigneur de Langey, both of whom were ambassadors to England around this time.
51. *LP*, Addendum, vol. 1, part 1, no. 1173.
52. *Inventory of Henry VIII*, no. 61.
53. A group of very similar crystal bowls, with mounts of varying periods, is illustrated in H. Hahnloser and S. Brugger-Koch, *Corpus der Hartsteinschliffe des 12–15. Jahrhunderts* (Berlin, 1985), figs 449–57.
54. Hayward (ed.), *1542 Inventory of Whitehall*, vol. 2, no. 3719.
55. Hayward (ed.), *1542 Inventory of Whitehall*, vol. 2, no. 3726. We cannot be certain that these 'stone' jugs were stoneware (a high-fired dense ceramic produced in Germany in the sixteenth century) but a number of hints support this, such as one being described as 'stone tawney' and another as 'stone with an armentes berde' (*Inventory of Henry VIII*, nos. 1317 and 1319) suggesting the kind of early to mid-sixteenth-century stoneware pots known as 'Bartmankrugs'.
56. Hayward (ed.), *1542 Inventory of Whitehall*, vol. 1, pp. 118, 128.
57. Hayward (ed.), *1542 Inventory of Whitehall*, vol. 1, p. 29.
58. *Inventory of Henry VIII*, nos. 2029 onwards.
59. *Inventory of Henry VIII*, no. 182.
60. *Inventory of Henry VIII*, immediately following entry no. 10544.
61. *Inventory of Henry VIII*, nos. 530–738.
62. *Inventory of Henry VIII*, no. 631.
63. *Inventory of Henry VIII*, nos. 1923, 1927 and 1984.
64. *Inventory of Henry VIII*, no. 2004.
65. My thanks to Dr Heike Zech, director of the Germanisches National Museum, for this information.
66. *CSP*, *Spain*, vol. 7, no. 69.
67. See Simon Thurley, *Houses of Power: The Places That Shaped the Tudor World* (London, 2017), p. 132. For a plan of the palace towards the end of the reign, see pp. 134–35.
68. Hayward (ed.), *1542 Inventory of Whitehall*, vol. 1, p. 28.
69. The picture was destroyed in the devastating fire of 1698 but is known to us from a seventeenth-century copy.
70. This is a strange term and suggests the friar's knot motif that was one of Francis I's badges. Could this extraordinary confection have been a gift from Francis?
71. *Inventory of Henry VIII*, no. 16922.
72. See H. Hahnloser and S. Brugger-Koch, *Corpus der Hartsteinschliffe des 12.–15. Jahrhunderts*, p. 10.
73. *Inventory of Henry VIII*, no. 1118. What exactly 'mother of emerald' was is not clear, unless it refers to an emerald-bearing matrix.
74. *Inventory of Henry VIII*, nos. 729, 730, etc.
75. *Inventory of Henry VIII*, no. 513.
76. *Inventory of Henry VIII*, no. 2171.
77. *Inventory of Henry VIII*, no. 167.
78. *Inventory of Henry VIII*, no. 3024.
79. *Inventory of Henry VIII*, no. 3676.
80. *Inventory of Henry VIII*, no. 3244.
81. *Inventory of Henry VIII*, no. 3244.
82. *Inventory of Henry VIII*, no. 3166.
83. See, for example, Dirk Syndram, *Gems of the Green Vault in Dresden* (Leipzig, 2005), p. 24.
84. *Inventory of Henry VIII*, no. 463.
85. *Inventory of Henry VIII*, no. 177.
86. *Inventory of Henry VIII*, nos. 10,894–11,034.
87. A payment in 1546 of £30 for thirty-three glasses of various sorts is recorded. *LP*, vol. 20, part 2, no. 650.
88. *LP*, vol. 17, no. 63.
89. For gold-mounted glasses see *Inventory of Henry VIII*, nos. 52, 67, 171–73, 10955, etc.
90. *Inventory of Henry VIII*, nos. 592, 556, 527, etc.
91. *Inventory of Henry VIII*, nos. 417 and 541.
92. *Inventory of Henry VIII*, nos. 611 and 1597.
93. *Inventory of Henry VIII*, no. 3674.
94. *Inventory of Henry VIII*, no. 1494.
95. *Inventory of Henry VIII*, no. 92.
96. *LP*, vol. 5, no. 276.
97. *Inventory of Henry VIII*, no. 3308.
98. *Inventory of Henry VIII*, no. 3287.
99. *LP*, vol. 21, part 1, no. 1383.11.
100. *LP*, vol. 21, part 2, no. 199.5.
101. *Inventory of Henry VIII*, no. 3674.
102. *Inventory of Henry VIII*, no. 3675.

103. *Inventory of Henry VIII*, no. 3279.
104. *Inventory of Henry VIII*, p. 98.
105. *Inventory of Henry VIII*, no. 2210.
106. *Inventory of Henry VIII*, nos. 10427–33.
107. *Inventory of Henry VIII*, nos. 10434–44.
108. There is a considerable literature on the princely *Kunstkammer*, much of it in German. For general English language introductions, see J. F. Hayward, *Virtuoso Goldsmiths 1540–1620* (London, 1976); and Géza von Habsburg, *Princely Treasures* (London, 1997).
109. Some of Lorenzo's treasures are preserved in the Pitti Palace (Museo degli Argenti) and the church of San Lorenzo in Florence.

Chapter 15

1. See Suzannah Lipscomb, *The King Is Dead: The Last Will and Testament of Henry VIII* (London, 2015).
2. *Inventory of Henry VIII*, no. 3279.
3. *Inventory of Henry VIII*, no. 3281.
4. C. E. Challis, *The Tudor Coinage* (London, 1978), p. 162.
5. *Inventory of Henry VIII*, no. 3371.
6. See A. J. Collins, *The Jewels and Plate of Queen Elizabeth I: The Inventory of 1574: Edited from Harley MS 1650 and Stowe MS 555 in the British Museum* (London, 1955), p. 136.
7. *Inventory of Henry VIII*, no. 46.
8. Thomas Rymer, *Foedera*, 2nd edn, vol. 18 (London, 1725), pp. 236–40.
9. Collins, *The Jewels and Plate of Queen Elizabeth I*, p. 279.
10. Collins, *The Jewels and Plate of Queen Elizabeth I*, p. 300.
11. The van Vianen altar service was not destined to survive long and was an early victim of the financial crisis of the Civil War.
12. Collins, *The Jewels and Plate of Queen Elizabeth I*, p. 191.
13. Collins, *The Jewels and Plate of Queen Elizabeth I*, p. 198.

Bibliography

Please see also the List of Abbreviations.

Primary sources – manuscript and unpublished

BL, MS Add. 11301, Various papers including new year's gifts to Prince Edward, 1540

BL, MS Add. 45716 A, 'The book of the new ordinary of the king's most honourable household', 1539–44

BL, MS Cotton Galba B X, Records and papers concerning England and Burgundy, 1531–46

BL, MS Cotton Titus B I, Various state papers of Henry VIII, sixteenth century

BL, MS Cotton Vitellius C XI, Collections relating to royal marriages, sixteenth century

BL, MS Royal 7 C XVI, Various state papers of Henry VIII, sixteenth century

BL, MS Royal 17 B XXVIII, Book of the expenses and plate of Lady Mary, 1536–44

BL, MS Royal Appendix 89, Various state papers of Henry VIII, fifteenth to seventeenth centuries

BL, MS Sloane 1494, 'A volume illustrative of the duties of a Gentleman of the Royal Household', seventeenth century

BNF, Trésor des Chartes, J.650 Angleterre XVIII, Inventory of jewels for Mary, Queen of France, 1514

GC, Court Minutes, Books A–I, 1444–1557

London Metropolitan Archives, CLC/L/SE/A/005/MS30817, 'Register Book of Evidences … and Implements Appertaining to the Worshipful Company of Skinners', 1578–c. 1640

TNA, E 36/84, Inventory of the jewels of Henry VI, c. 1440–64

TNA, E 36/85, Inventory of the jewel house, 1532–33

TNA, E 36/171, Inventory of goods of Thomas Cardinal Wolsey at Cawood, 1530

TNA, E 351/2077, Mint accounts, 1544–50

TNA, E 101/421/5, no. 11, Warrant to Cornelius Hayes, 1532

TNA, E 101/421/13, New year's gifts given by and to Henry VIII, 1533–34

TNA, PRO 31/8/137, Transcripts from the Archives du Royaume, nineteenth century

TNA, PROB 2/486, Probate inventory of Robert Amadas, 1533

TNA, PROB 11/27/118, Will of John Mundy, Goldsmith and Alderman of London, 1537

TNA, PROB 11/31/529, Will of Cornelius Hayes, Goldsmith, 1547

TNA, PROB 11/35/207, Will of Morgan Wolf, Goldsmith, 1552

TNA, PROB 11/45/86, Will of Thomas Vicary, Serjeant of the Surgeons, 1562

TNA, SP 1/4, Letters and Papers from the Reign of Henry VIII, 1513–31

TNA, SP 1/40, Letters and Papers from the Reign of Henry VIII, 1526–27

TNA, SP 1/56, Letters and Papers from the Reign of Henry VIII, 1529–30

TNA, SP 1/128, Letters and Papers from the Reign of Henry VIII, 1538

TNA, SP 1/229, Letters and Papers from the Reign of Henry VIII, 1509–13

TNA, SP 1/232, Letters and Papers from the Reign of Henry VIII, 1516–21

TNA, SP 2/N, Letters and Papers from the Reign of Henry VIII, 1533

TNA, SP 2/P, Letters and Papers from the Reign of Henry VIII, 1534

TNA, SP 4/1, Letters and Papers from the Reign of Henry VIII, 1545–47

Primary sources – printed and online

Anglo, Sydney, ed., *The Great Tournament Roll of Westminster: A Collotype Reproduction of the Manuscript* (Oxford, 1968)

Anon., ed., 'Original Documents Relating to Katherine of Aragon', *Gentleman's Magazine*, second series, vol. 42 (December 1854), pp. 572–74

Anon., *Chronicle of King Henry VIII of England*, trans. Martin A. Sharp Hume (London, 1889)

Aristotle, *The Nicomachean Ethics*, ed. and trans. J. A. K. Thomson, rev. edn (London, 2004)

Bentley, Samuel, *Excerpta Historica or Illustrations of English History* (London, 1831)

Bergenroth, G. A., P. de Gayangos, M. A. S. Hume and R. Tyler, eds, *Calendar of State Papers, Spain*, 16 vols (London, 1862–99)

Brewer, J. S. and J. Gairdner, eds, *Letters and Papers, Foreign and Domestic, of Henry VIII*, 21 vols (1862–1920)

Brown, Rawdon, ed. and trans., *Four Years at the Court of Henry VIII: Selection of Despatches Written by the Venetian Ambassador, Sebastian Giustinian, and Addressed to the Signory of Venice, January 12th 1515, to July 26th 1519*, 2 vols (London, 1854)

Brown, Rawdon, G. Cavendish Bentinck, Horatio F. Brown and Allen B. Hind, eds, *Calendar of State Papers Relating to English Affairs in the Archives of Venice*, 38 vols (London, 1864–1947)

Caley, John, 'Copy of the Survey of the Priory of Bridlington in Yorkshire', *Archaeologia*, 19 (1821), pp. 270–75

Cavendish, George, *Thomas Wolsey, Late Cardinal: His Life and Death*, ed. Roger Lockyer (London, 1973)

Checa Cremades, Fernando, ed., *Los inventarios de Carlos V y la familia imperial – The Inventories of Charles V and the Imperial Family*, 3 vols (Madrid, 2010)

Collins, A. Jeffries, ed., *Jewels and Plate of Queen Elizabeth I: The Inventory of 1574: Edited from Harley MS 1650 and Stowe MS 555 in the British Museum* (London, 1955)

Condon, M. M., S. P. Harper, L. Liddy, S. Cunningham and J. Ross, eds, *The Chamber Books of Henry VII and Henry VIII, 1485–1521*, http://www.tudorchamberbooks.org

Dugdale, William, ed., *Monasticon Anglicanum*, vol. 1 (London, 1846)

Dunbar, William, *The Poems of William Dunbar, Collected, with Notes and a Memoir of his Life*, ed. D. Laing (London, 1834)

Ellis, Henry, ed., *Original Letters Illustrative of English History*, 3 series (London, 1825–46)

Elyot, Thomas, *The Boke Named the Governour: A Scolar Press Facsimile*, ed. R. C. Alston (Menston, 1970)

Fortescue, Sir John, *On the Laws and Governance of England*, ed. Shelley Lockwood (Cambridge, 1997)

Grose, Francis and Thomas Astle, eds, *The Antiquarian Repertory: A Miscellaneous Assemblage of Topography, History, Biography, Customs and Manners*, 4 vols (London, 1807–09)

Gutch, John, ed., *Collectanea curiosa; or miscellaneous tracts, relating to the history and antiquities of England and Ireland*, 2 vols (Oxford, 1781)

Hahnloser, H. and S. Brugger-Koch, *Corpus der Hartsteinschliffe des 12.–15. Jahrhunderts* (Berlin, 1985)

Hall, Edward, *The Vnion of the Two Noble and Illustre Famelies* (London, 1809)

Hall, Edward, *King Henry VIII*, 2 vols, ed. Charles Whibley (London, 1904)

Hayward, Maria, ed., *The 1542 Inventory of Whitehall. The Palace and Its Keeper* (London, 2004)

Hinds, Allen B., ed., *Calendar of State Papers and Manuscripts in the Archives and Collections of Milan* (London, 1912)

Holinshed, Raphael, *Chronicles of England, Scotland and Ireland*, 6 vols (London, 1807–08)

Kipling, Gordon, ed., *The Receyt of the Ladie Kateryne*, Early English Text Society, original series, no. 296 (Oxford, 1990)

Lang, R. G., ed., *Two Tudor Subsidy Rolls for the City of London, 1541 and 1582* (London, 1993), British History Online, https://www.british-history.ac.uk/london-record-soc/vol29

Leland, John, *Collectanea*, 2nd edn, 6 vols (London, 1770)

Machiavelli, Niccolò, *Lettere familiari*, ed. Edoardo Alvisi (Florence, 1883)

Madden, Frederick, ed., *Privy Purse Expenses of the Princess Mary 1536–46* (London, 1831)

Millar, Oliver, ed., *The Inventories and Valuations of the King's Goods 1649–1651*, Walpole Society, vol. 43 (Glasgow, 1972)

Mumby, Frank, ed., *The Youth of Henry VIII: A Narrative in Contemporary Letters* (London, 1913)

Myers, A. R., ed., *The Household of Edward IV: The Black Book and the Ordinance of 1478* (Manchester, 1959)

Nicholas, N. H., ed., *The Privy Purse Expences of Henry the Eighth* (London, 1827)

Nichols, John Gough, ed., *Inventories of the Wardrobes, Plate, Chapel Stuff, etc. of Henry Fitzroy, Duke of Richmond, and of the Wardrobe Stuff at Baynard's Castle of Katharine, Princess Dowager*, Camden Society, old series, vol. 61 (London, 1855)

Orchard Halliwell, James, ed., *Letters of the Kings of England*, 2 vols (London, 1846)

Ormrod, W. Mark et al., eds, *England's Immigrants: 1330–1550*, http://www.englandsimmigrants.com

Prideaux, W. S., *Memorials of the Goldsmiths' Company*, 2 vols (London, 1896)

Riley, Henry T., ed. and trans., *Ingulph's Chronicle of the Abbey of Croyland with the Continuations by Peter of Blois and Anonymous Writers* (London, 1854)

Rymer, Thomas, *Foedera*, 1st edn, 20 vols (London, 1704–35)

Society of Antiquaries of London, ed., *A Collection of Ordinances and Regulations for the Government of the Royal Household* (London, 1790)

St. Clare Byrne, Muriel, ed., *The Lisle Letters*, 6 vols (Chicago and London, 1981)

Starkey, David, ed., *The Inventory of King Henry VIII: Society of Antiquaries MS 129 and British Library MS Harley 1419*, vol. 1 (London, 1998)

Stow, John, *Annals of England to 1603* (London, c. 1605)

Strype, John, *Memorials of Archbishop Cranmer* (Oxford, 1848)

Suger, Abbot, *Abbot Suger on the Abbey Church of St. Denis and Its Art Treasures*, ed. and trans. Erwin Panofsky (Princeton, NJ, 1979)

Thomas, A. H. and I. D. Thornley, eds, *The Great Chronicle of London* (London, 1938)

Trollope, Edward, 'King Henry VIII's Jewel Book', *Lincolnshire Diocesan Architectural Society*, 17, 2 (1883–84), pp. 155–229

Vergil, Polydore, *Anglica Historia (1555 version): A Hypertext Critical Edition*, ed. Dana F. Sutton, http://www.philological.bham.ac.uk/polverg/

Williams, John, *Account of the monastic treasures confiscated at the dissolution of the various houses in England*, Publications of the Abbotsford Club, vol. 5, ed. W. B. D. D. Turnbull (Edinburgh, 1836)

Woodruff, C. E. and W. Danks, eds, *Memorials of the Cathedral and Priory of Christ in Canterbury* (London, 1912)

Wriothesley, Charles, *A Chronicle of England During the Reigns of the Tudors from 1485 to 1559*, 2 vols, Camden Society, new series, vols 11, 20 (London, 1875–77)

Reference works cited

Beaven, Alfred P., *The Aldermen of the City of London Temp. Henry III – 1912* (London, 1908), British History Online, http://www.british-history.ac.uk/no-series/london-aldermen/hen3-1912/

Heal, Ambrose, *The London Goldsmiths 1200–1800* (Cambridge, 1972)

Oxford Dictionary of National Biography, http://www.oxforddnb.com

Oxford English Dictionary Online, http://www.oed.com

Plomer, H. R., et al., *A Dictionary of the Printers and Booksellers Who Were at Work in England, Scotland and Ireland from 1726 to 1775* (London, 1932)

Robinson, William, *Collections Relative to Claims at Coronations of Several of the Kings of England beginning with Richard II* (London, 1820)

Truman, Charles, ed., *Sotheby's Concise Encyclopaedia of Silver* (London, 1993)

Secondary sources

Allen, Martin, *Mints and Money in Medieval England* (Cambridge, 2012)

Alsop, J. D., 'The Structure of Early Tudor Finance c. 1509–1558', in *Revolution Reassessed: Revisions in the History of Tudor Government and Administration*, ed. Christopher Coleman and David Starkey (Oxford, 1986), pp. 135–62

Anglo, Sydney, *Images of Tudor Kingship* (London, 1992)

——, *Spectacle, Pageantry, and Early Tudor Policy* (Oxford, 1997)

Bimbenet-Privat, Michèle, 'Orfèvrerie et politique: le cas Vezeler', in *François Ier et l'art des Pays-Bas*, ed. Cécile Scailliérez (Paris, 2017), pp. 298–309

Bimbenet-Privat, Michèle and Clèment Blanc-Riel, 'Un chef-d'oeuvre diplomatie et d'orfèvrerie', in *François Ier: pouvoir et image*, ed. Bruno Petey-Girard and Magali Vène (Paris, 2015), pp. 164–65

Blair, Claude, ed., *The History of Silver* (London, 1987)

——, *The Crown Jewels: The History of the Coronation Regalia in the Jewel House of the Tower of London*, 2 vols (London, 1998)

Bolton, J. L., *The Alien Community of London in the Fifteenth Century: The Subsidy Rolls of 1440 and 1483–4* (Stamford, 1998)

Bratchel, M. E., 'Italian Merchant Organization and Business Relationships in Early Tudor London', *Journal of European Economic History*, 7, 1 (1978), pp. 5–32

Brooke, G. C. and L. A. Lawrence, 'The Martlet and Half Rose Groats of Henry VII', *The Numismatic Chronicle and Journal of the Royal Numismatic Society*, fourth series, 19 (1919), pp. 257–64

Burnett, Charles J. and Christopher Tabraham, *The Honours of Scotland: The Story of the Scottish Crown Jewels* (Edinburgh, 1993)

Campbell, Marian, 'Bishop Fox's Salt', in *Corpus Silver: Patronage and Plate at Corpus Christi College, Oxford*, ed. Clive Ellory, Helen Clifford and Foster Rogers (Barton under Needwood, 1999), pp. 129–73

Campbell, Thomas P., *Henry VIII and the Art of Majesty: Tapestries at the Tudor Court* (New Haven and London, 2007)

Challis, C. E., *The Tudor Coinage* (London, 1978)

Chrimes, S. B., *Henry VII* (London, 1972)

Clayton, Michael, *Christie's Pictorial History of English and American Silver* (Oxford, 1985)

Clifford, Helen, *A Treasured Inheritance: 600 Years of Oxford College Silver* (Oxford, 2004)

Condon, Margaret, 'The Last Will of Henry VII: Document and Text', in *Westminster Abbey: The Lady Chapel of Henry VII*, ed. Tim Tatton-Brown and Richard Mortimer (Woodbridge, 2003), pp. 99–140

Cressy, David, *Birth, Marriage and Death: Ritual, Religion, and the Life-Cycle in Tudor and Stuart England* (Oxford, 1997)

Crowther, Kathleen M., *Adam and Eve in the Protestant Reformation* (Cambridge, 2010)

Dietz, Frederick, *English Government Finance, 1485–1558* (Urbana, 1921)

Doran, Susan, ed., *Henry VIII: Man and Monarch* (London, 2009)
Duffy, Eamon, *The Stripping of the Altars* (London, 1992)
Ellory, Clive, Helen Clifford and Foster Rogers, eds, *Corpus Silver: Patronage and Plate at Corpus Christi College, Oxford* (Barton under Needwood, 1999)
Elton, G. R., 'The Treasurer and the Goldsmith, a Cautionary Story', in *Star Chamber Stories*, ed. G. R. Elton (London, 1958), pp. 114–46
Everett, Michael, *The Rise of Thomas Cromwell: Power and Politics in the Reign of Henry VIII* (London, 2015)
Foister, Susan, *Holbein in England* (London, 2006)
Forbes, John, *Hallmark: A History of the London Assay Office* (London, 1999)
Fritz, J. M., *Goldschmiedekunst der Gotik in Mitteleuropa* (Munich, 1982)
Glanville, Philippa, *Silver in Tudor and Early Stuart England: A Social History and Catalogue of the National Collection, 1480–1660* (London, 1990)
——, 'Cardinal Wolsey and the Goldsmiths', in *Cardinal Wolsey: Church, State and Art*, ed. S. J. Gunn and P. G. Lindley (Cambridge, 1991), pp. 131–48
Gunn, Steven, *Charles Brandon: Henry VIII's Closest Friend* (Stroud, 2015)
Gunn, S. J. and P. G. Lindley, eds, *Cardinal Wolsey: Church, State and Art* (Cambridge, 1991)
Hamy, P. A., *Entrevue de Francois premier avec Henri VIII à Boulogne-sur-Mer en 1532* (Paris, 1898)
Harper, S. P., 'Royal Servants and City Fathers: The Double Lives of London Goldsmiths at the Court of Henry VII', in *Medieval Merchants and Money: Essays in Honour of James L. Bolton*, ed. Martin Allen and Matthew Davies (London, 2016), pp. 177–96
Hayward, J. F., *Virtuoso Goldsmiths and the Triumph of Mannerism, 1540–1620* (London, 1976)
Hayward, Maria, 'Gift Giving at the Court of Henry VIII: The 1539 New Year's Gift Roll in Context', *The Antiquaries Journal*, 85 (September 2005), pp. 126–75
——, *Dress at the Court of Henry VIII* (Leeds, 2007)
Hoyle, R. W. and J. B. Ramsdale, 'The Royal Progress of 1541, the North of England, and Anglo-Scottish Relations, 1534–1542', *Northern History*, 41, 2 (September 2004), pp. 239–65
Hunt, Alice, *The Drama of Coronation: Medieval Ceremony in Early Modern England* (Cambridge, 2008)
Ives, Eric, *The Life and Death of Anne Boleyn: 'The Most Happy'* (Oxford, 2004)
Kingsford, C. L., 'On Some London Houses of the Early Tudor Period', *Archaeologia*, 71 (1921), pp. 17–54
Kipling, Gordon, *The Triumph of Honour: Burgundian Origins of the Elizabethan Renaissance* (The Hague, 1977)
Kisby, Fiona, '"When the King Goeth a Procession": Chapel Ceremonies and Services, the Ritual Year, and Religious Reforms at the Early Tudor Court, 1485–1547', *Journal of British Studies*, 40, 1 (January 2001), pp. 44–75
Lehmann, Gilly, 'Henry VIII's Great Feast at Greenwich, May 1527', *The Court Historian*, 23, 1 (June 2018), pp. 1–12
Lightbown, R. W., *Secular Goldsmiths' Work in Medieval France: A History* (London, 1978)
Lipscomb, Suzannah, *1536: The Year That Changed Henry VIII* (Oxford, 2009)
——, *The King Is Dead: The Last Will and Testament of Henry VIII* (London, 2015)
Luu, Lien Bich, *Immigrants and the Industries of London, 1500–1700* (Aldershot, 2005)
MacCulloch, Diarmaid, *Thomas Cromwell: A Life* (London, 2018)
Mitchell, David, *Silversmiths in Elizabethan and Stuart London: Their Lives and Their Marks* (Woodbridge, 2017)
Nichols, John, *The History and Antiquities of the County of Leicester*, 4 vols (London, 1795–1815)
Rex, Richard, 'The Religion of Henry VIII', *The Historical Journal*, 57 (2014), pp. 1–32
Richardson, Glenn, *The Field of Cloth of Gold* (New Haven and London, 2013)
——, '"As Presence Did Present Them": Personal Gift-Giving at the Field of Cloth of Gold', in *Henry VIII and the Court. Art, Politics and Performance*, ed. Thomas Betteridge and Suzannah Lipscomb (Farnham and Burlington, VT, 2013), pp. 47–64
Richardson, W. C., *Tudor Chamber Administration 1485–1547* (Baton Rouge, 1952)
Scarisbrooke, J. J., *Henry VIII* (Berkeley and Los Angeles, 1968)
Schroder, Timothy, *The Gilbert Collection of Gold and Silver* (Los Angeles, 1988)

——, 'A Royal Tudor Rock-Crystal and Silver-Gilt Vase', *Burlington Magazine*, 137, 1107 (June 1995), pp. 356–66

——, ed., *Treasures of the English Church* (London, 2008)

——, *British and Continental Gold and Silver in the Ashmolean Museum* (Oxford, 2009)

——, 'Gold and Godliness', in *Gold: Power and Allure*, ed. Helen Clifford (London, 2012), pp. 59–73

——, *Renaissance and Baroque Silver, Mounted Porcelain and Ruby Glass from the Zilkha Collection* (London, 2012)

——, *English Silver before the Civil War: The David Little Collection* (London, 2015)

Sicca, Cinzia M., 'Consumption and Trade of Art between Italy and England in the First Half of the Sixteenth Century: The London House of the Bardi and Cavalcanti Company', *Renaissance Studies*, 16, 2 (2002), pp. 163–201

Sitwell, H. D., 'The Jewel House and the Royal Goldsmiths', *Archaeological Journal*, 117 (1960), pp. 131–55

Stanford London, H., 'The Greyhound as a Royal Beast', *Archaeologia*, 97 (1959), pp. 139–63

Starkey, David, 'The King's Privy Chamber' (unpublished PhD dissertation, University of Cambridge, 1973)

——, 'The Age of the Household: Politics, Society and the Arts c. 1350–1550', in *The Later Middle Ages*, ed. Stephen Medcalf (London, 1981), pp. 225–90

——, ed., *Henry VIII: A European Court in England* (London, 1991)

——, 'Henry VI's Old Blue Gown: The English Court under the Lancastrians and Yorkists', *The Court Historian*, 4, 1 (April 1999), pp. 1–28

Stratford, Jenny, *Richard II and the English Royal Treasure* (London, 2012)

Syndram, Dirk, *Gems of the Green Vault in Dresden* (Leipzig, 2005)

Tait, Hugh, 'The Girdle-Prayer Book or "Tablet": An Important Class of Renaissance Jewellery at the Court of Henry VIII', *Jewellery Studies*, 2 (1985), pp. 29–57

Thornton, Dora and Michael Cowell, 'The Armada Service: A Set of Late Tudor Dining Silver', *The Antiquaries Journal*, 76 (1996), pp. 153–180

Thurley, Simon, *Houses of Power: The Places That Shaped the Tudor World* (London, 2017)

Waterton, Edmund, 'On a Remarkable Incident in the Life of Saint Edward the Confessor, with Notices of Certain Rings Hallowed on Good Friday by the Sovereigns of England', *The Archaeological Journal*, 21 (June 1864), pp. 103–13

Williams, Neville, *Henry VIII and His Court* (London, 1971)

Index

Abbeville, France 129
Abbotsbury, Dorset 264
Act of Supremacy 215, 216, 260, 262, 340n.4
Acton Court, Gloucestershire 309
Adders' tongues 309
Agate 306
Albrecht, cardinal of Brandenburg 69, 112, 152
Alburquerque, third duke of 304
Aldegrever, Heinrich, artist 177, 201
Alexander VI, pope 68–9
Alloys for precious metals 250–1, 254
Alms dishes 98, 303–4
Amadas, Robert, royal goldsmith and deputy of mint
  Deputy master of the Mint 248
  Goldsmith to Thomas Wolsey 140, 148, 149, 165, 181
  Master of the jewel house 16–17
  Probate inventory 52–3
  Royal goldsmith 24, 38, 47, 71, 119
Ambassadors, resident 121–2 (*see also* Embassies; Gifts, Diplomatic)
  Allowances of plate 124–5
  Gifts on retirement 122–3
  Living conditions 121–4
Amboise, Georges d', French cardinal 151
Amiens, Treaty of, seals for 184–5
Amyas, Robert 225
Andrea, Zoan, print maker 201
Anne Boleyn, queen of England (*see* Boleyn, Anne)
Anne of Cleves, queen of England 222–4, 258
Anne of Denmark 317
'Antique' 99, 144, 146, 168, 175, 184, 220
Antwerp 168, 178, 246, 253, 283–4, 290
Aristotle 4
'Armada Service' (British Museum) 88
Arnold, John, royal goldsmith 51
Arras (*see under* Tapestry)
Arthur, prince of Wales 34, 37, 68, 72, 126–7, 206–7
Artificialia 313
Arundell, Sir Thomas, courtier 148, 330n.71
Assay (of food and wine) 106–7
Assay (of precious metals) 254–5
Atsill, Richard, stone polisher 183, 238
Attainder 21, 53, 231, 288, 323n.22
Aucher, Anthony, master of the jewel house 248–9
Audley, Sir Thomas, keeper of the great seal 228, 230–1, 246
Augmentations, court of 247, 273–6
Aylsham, Norfolk 268

Badges 33, 36, 55, 59, 112, 163, 347n.70
Badoer, Andrea, Venetian ambassador 69, 112, 122
Bainbridge, Christopher, cardinal 64
Banquets 85–110, 161 (*see also* Assay (of food and wine); Buffet of plate; Garter Feast; Void)
  Entertainments at 48, 98–100
  Eucharistic character of 91
  Handwashing at 91–2
  Temporary structures for 99
Baptist, John, Italian jeweller 181
Barber-Surgeons' Company (now Barbers' Company) 176–7, 289–90
Bardi, Pierfrancesco di, merchant 148, 156
Barnardo, Francis, merchant 294
Barnes, John, goldsmith 278
Basins 81–3, 91–2, 105, 284 *et passim*
Baynton, Sir Edward, vice chamberlain to Anne Boleyn 274

Beakers 56, 61, 96
Beaufort, Henry, cardinal 31, 32
Beaufort, Margaret, mother of Henry VII 36, 55, 56, 89, 203
Becket, Thomas, archbishop of Canterbury and saint 175, 177, 262, 272, 274 (*see also under* Shrines)
Bedford, duke of (*see* John of Lancaster, duke of Bedford)
Bedyngfield, Sir Edward 212
Beham, Hans Sebald, artist 179, 201
Bellay, Jean du, cardinal bishop of Paris 120, 148, 216, 347n.50
Benall, Jerome, gem carver 183
Bergavenny, Lord (*see* Nevill, George)
Berger, Michael, goldsmith and seal engraver 183
Berry, Jean, duc de 28, 29, 31
'Bestyan', jeweller 265
Beynarde, John, goldsmith 143, 334n.62
Birrall 109, 306
Black Book of the Household 4–5, 11, 14, 22
Blanche, daughter of Henry IV of England, and wife of Ludwig of Bavaria 322n.6
'Blood of Hailes' (relic) 279
Blount, Elizabeth, mistress of Henry VIII 225
Blount, William, Baron Mountjoy, master of the mint 17, 39, 248–9, 253
Boke Named the Governour 8, 67
Boleyn, Anne, queen of England 209, 213, 217–21, 261
  Exchanges gifts of jewels with Henry VIII 217–18
  Receives jewels and plate from Henry VIII 218
  Entertains Henry VIII to dinner 219
  Created marquess of Pembroke 166
  Accompanies Henry VIII to France in 1532 166
  Marries Henry VIII 218
  Coronation 88
  Badge and arms 194, 219, 220
  Holdings of plate 218–20
  New year's gifts 192–4
  Patronage 188, 235
Boleyn, Sir Thomas, courtier 153, 155, 335n.1
Bonner, Edmund, bishop and ambassador 124–5
Bonnivet, Guillaume, French admiral 118, 119, 163
Bonvixi, Lorenzo, merchant 49
Bourbon, cardinal 162
Bourbon, duc de, constable of France 163
Bowes, Martin 236, 248, 251, 255–6, 288, 312
Bowls 21, 35, 104, 141, 289–92 *et passim*
Boxley, Kent 262
Brandon, Charles, duke of Suffolk 92, 170, 204–5, 228, 238
Brice, Hugh, royal goldsmith 37–8, 51
Bridlington, shrine at 269
Brosamer, Hans, artist 220
Bruges 143
Bryan, Sir Francis, courtier 114, 124–5
Buckingham, duke of (*see* Stafford, Edward)
Budé, Guillaume, French humanist 240
Buffet of plate 100–4, 105–6, 160, 170, 330n.46 *et passim*
Bullion, gold and silver 20, 142, 231, 248, 250–3, 288, 321n.36, 333n.58
Buren, Count, Stadtholder of Guelders 182
Burghley, Lord (*see* Cecil, William) 110
Burghley nef 308, 318
Burgkmair, Hans 201

Cameo 43, 172, 188, 310
Campeggio, cardinal, papal legate 71, 143–4, 146–8, 208, 259–60
Capon, William, master of Wolsey's college in Ipswich 149
Cardinal College, Oxford 145, 148
Carolo, John, merchant 284
Carsidony, Anthony, merchant 294
Carving knives 91, 105
Castellesi, Adrian, cardinal 119
Cavalcanti, Giovanni, merchant 50, 156, 326n.41
Cavallari Antonio, merchant 49, 140
Cavendish, George, Wolsey's gentleman usher 9, 104, 132, 133, 135–6, 145–9, 334n.100
Cawood, bishop of York's palace 149–51
Cecil, William, Lord Burghley 110
Cellini, Benvenuto, artist 185, 314, 338n.41
Censers 266
Chabot, Philippe de, French ambassador 120
Chains, gold 45, 72, 122–3, 164–5, 336n.65
Chalcedony 109
Chalices 41, 67, 75, 77–8, 266 *et passim*
Chamber accounts 35, 47, 49–50, 71, 234, 321n.52
Chantries 268
Chapel Royal 73–9, 277–9 (*see also* Christenings, royal)
  Closets 74–5
  Department of household 74
  Plate 75

Chapuys, Eustace, imperial ambassador 9, 113–14, 122, 123, 132, 219, 251, 261, 339n.54, 341n.18, 347n.50 *et passim*

Chargers (*see* 'Vessel')

Charles I, king of England 317

Charles V, Holy Roman Emperor

Betrothed to Princess Mary, sister of Henry VIII 127

Betrothed to Princess Mary, daughter of Henry VIII 126

Elected Holy Roman Emperor 153, 154

Meetings with Henry VIII 92, 165

Recovers the Fleur de lis from Henry VIII 114

Bans export of gold coinage 283

Charles VI, king of France 31, 154

Charles IX, king of France 170

Charles the Bold, duke of Burgundy 36, 112, 331n.18

Cheney, Sir Thomas, courtier 286–7

Chichester, shrine at 270–1

Chieregato, Francesco, papal nuncio 45, 85, 87, 94

Christ Church monastery, Canterbury 264, 265, 271, 275 (*see also* Becket, Thomas)

Christ Church, Oxford (*see* Cardinal College)

Christenings, royal 79–83 (*see also* Gifts, Christening)

Christian IV, king of Denmark 317

Church (*see also* Chapel Royal)

Church plate 20, 73, 75–9

Insignia 64, 138–9

Relationship with Crown 63–4

Royal church services 72

Clement VII, pope 61, 68, 170, 259

Clock salts 170–3, 198, 200, 311

Clocks 303, 310

Cloth of gold and silver 50, 64–6, 116, 156, 158

In church 72

Cost of 5–6, 156

Coggeshall, Essex 265

Coinage 250–3, 322n.1

Debasement 251–3

Coldwell, Henry, seal engraver 245

Colyn, John de, goldsmith 178

Compton, Sir William, groom of the stool 17, 21, 219, 279, 322n.60, 326n.40

Contarini, Gasparo 138, 163

Coral 309

Coronation claims 325n.16

Corpus Christi College, Cambridge 93

Corpus Christi College, Oxford 22, 56, 61, 64, 77, 79, 92, 238

Court of Augmentations (*see* Augmentations, court of)

Courtenay, Henry, marquess of Exeter 288

Cowper, Robert, goldsmith to Thomas Wolsey 143, 334n.63

Cramp rings (*see* Rings, cramp)

Cranmer, Thomas, archbishop of Canterbury 124, 222, 224, 228, 237, 279

Crepye, John (or Cryspin), jeweller 181

Crikelman, Jerome, Antwerp goldsmith 294

Cromwell, Gregory 242n.62

Cromwell, Thomas 229–50

Servant to Wolsey 140

Master of jewel house 17, 166, 229–41, 249–50

Receives bribes 246

Takes plate as security for loans 246

Portrait 252

Role in dissolution of monasteries 260–8

Patronage 181, 239–40, 246–7

Plate of 246

Relations with Katherine of Aragon and Princess Mary 211, 214, 216

Relations with Goldsmiths' Company 190

Fall 288

Crowland Abbey, Lincolnshire 276

Crown days and crown wearing 44, 325n.19

Croyland Chronicle 34

Cruses 237–8

Cuero, Juan de, servant to Katherine of Aragon 206, 207–8

Cups 32, 59–61, 88–9, 168, 175–6, 195–8, 220–1, 289–92 *et passim*

Cups of assay 95–6

Cymer Monastery, Merionethshire 266

Dacre, Lord, courtier 206

Dauntesey, Sir John 230–1

Delft, John van, goldsmith 51

Demayne, John, engraver 183

Denny, Sir Anthony, keeper of Whitehall palace 198, 294, 301–4, 312

Dimocke, Robert, the king's champion 42

Dintville, Jean de, French ambassador 336n.65

Diplomacy 117–25 (*see also* Ambassadors, resident; Embassies; Gifts)

Dishes (*see* 'Vessel')

Dolgellau chalice and paten (Royal Collection) 266

Domus Magnificentiae and *Domus Providentiae* (*see* Household, Departments)
Dowche, Jasper, Flemish merchant and financier 283–6
Draper, Robert, yeoman of the jewel house 18, 24, 148, 218, 257, 320n.17, 346n.6
'Dream of Paris' cup 33, 88–9, 317, 323n.27
Dudley, Sir Edmund, minster of Henry VII 37, 39, 53, 326n.60
Dunbar, William, poet 38
Dürer, Albrecht, artist 14, 338n.41

Edward III, king of England 13
Edward IV, king of England 33, 34, 98
Edward, Prince of Wales (later Edward VI, king of England) 227–8
Elizabeth I, queen of England 83
Elizabeth of York, queen of England 36–7
Ely 274, 276
Elyot, Sir Thomas 8, 67
Embassies 85, 118–20 (*see also* Ambassadors, resident; Gifts, Diplomatic)
  Cleves 119
  English 137
  French 118
  Scottish 38, 235
  Spanish 85, 118, 126
Empson, Sir Richard, minster of Henry VII 37, 39, 53
Enamel 29, 32, 36, 59, 77–8, 172, 200, 228, 275, 286, 295–8, 303, 309–11 *et passim*
Erasmus, Desiderius 39, 67, 183, 264
Erizo, Domenico, merchant 294
Everdyes, Everard, royal goldsmith 311–12, 316, 318
Evil May Day riot 8, 178–9
Ewers 92, 105
  Status relative to basins 92, 105
Exmew, Thomas, royal goldsmith 38, 51–2, 256, 343n.99

Falier, Ludovico, Venetian ambassador 134, 146
Fava, Lodovico della, merchant 50
Favri, Nicola di, Venetian diplomat 70, 111
'Feast of Ahazuerius' (*see* Tapestry) 87, 91, 101, 103, 104
Feasts (*see* Banquets)
'Feather fashion' (*see* Plate, Ornament)
Fenrother, Robert, royal goldsmith 51, 253, 256, 343n.99
Ferdinand of Aragon, Spanish king 35, 120, 126, 127, 163, 170, 206, 207
Ferdinand, Archduke of Austria 170, 313
Field of Cloth of Gold (1520) 153–65
  Chapel and church services 159–60, 162
  Cloth of gold at 156, 158
  Cost 164
  Feasts 161
  Gifts 162–4, 170
  Henry VIII's temporary palace 158–9
  Jewel House, role of 156
  Logistics and personnel 155–6
  Painting of 157–8
  Plate and ornaments deployed at 156, 335n.23
  Precursors 154–5
  Tapestry at 160
  Tents 157–8
  Tournament 161
  Wolsey's role and entourage 155, 160, 162
Fillastre, Guillaume 5
Fiorentino, Rosso, artist 202, 314
Fitzwilliam, Sir William, courtier 142, 239, 302–3
Fitzwilliam, Sir William, treasurer to Thomas Wolsey 333n.54
Flagons 103, 301 *et passim*
'Fleur de lis', jewel 112–14
Flodden, Battle 21, 114
Floris, Cornelis, artist 291
Flötner, Peter, artist 201
Fontainebleau 202
Fonts, silver 80–2, 328n.53
Fortescue, Sir John 5
Fountains 192–5, 290, 305
Fountains Abbey, Yorkshire 264
Fox, Richard, bishop of Winchester 64, 105–6, 132, 133, 260
  Bequests to Corpus Christi College, Oxford 56–7, 61, 64, 77–8, 92
Francis I, king of France
  Dispute over Mary's dowry 204
  Confiscates church plate 261
  Defeated at Pavia 114
  Gifts to Henry VIII 120–1, 164, 166, 347n.70
  Meetings with Henry VIII 160–4, 166–73, 198
  Relationship with Henry VIII 121
  Meeting with Clement VII 170
  Royal goldsmiths 168–9, 172
  Taste 6
Freman, John, royal goldsmith 124–5, 181, 234–6, 237, 242, 244, 245–6, 288, 344n.25

Frescobaldi, merchants 49–50
Fugger, house of, Augsburg bankers 283–4, 286, 295

Gardiner, John, goldsmith 245
Gardiner, Stephen, bishop of Winchester 125
Gardyner, Richard, alderman of London 33
Garter Feast (1519) 104–7
Gates, Sir John, courtier 302–3, 312
Gentlemen pensioners 7, 304
Ghent cathedral candlesticks 179
Gibson, Richard, master of the revels 48, 155
Gifts 21 (*see also* Ambassadors, resident; Embassies)
  Administration and cost 23
  Between Henry VIII and foreign princes 120–1, 331n.20
  Christening 80–1, 153, 286–8, 328n.48
  Diplomatic 24, 71, 119–20, 286, 341n.18
  New year's 22–4, 224, 234, 236–9
  Papal 68–70, 259
  Reciprocity 23, 118–19
  Rewards for bringers 23–4
Gilding 6, 110, 142, 330n.77
Girdle books 200
Giustinian, Sebastian, Venetian ambassador 22, 50, 134
Glass 109, 198–200, 224, 309–10
Glass house (at Whitehall) 309
Glastonbury Abbey 265–6, 274
Goblets 54, 57, 59, 103, 109, 220, 341n.31 *et passim*
Gold (*see also* Bullion; Cloth of gold and silver; Gilding; Plate)
  Evidence for use of 109–10, 316–17, 323n.27
  Foil 48, 100
  Thread 5–6, 20, 167, 305
'Golden Horse' reliquary 29
Goldsmiths' Company 253–8 (*see also* Alloys for precious metals; Assay (of precious metals); Hallmarking; Trial of the pyx)
  Prime Wardens 256–7
  Regulation of trade 62, 253–5
  Relations with the Crown 183, 255, 257–8
  Relations with mint 255–6
  Tensions with strangers 183, 190, 257
Gostwick, John, servant to Thomas Cromwell 225, 227, 235–6, 246, 249–50
Grandson, Battle of 286, 331n.18
Great Chronicle of London 34, 35, 37, 42, 45, 54, 323n.26, 325n.13
Greenwich 98–100, 301
Gresham, Richard, financier 124
Grey, Lord Leonard 246–7
Groom of the stool 12, 21, 24, 279
Guildford, Sir Henry, courtier 17, 100, 219
Gujarat, India 307

Hackett, John, courtier 123
Hall, Edward, chronicler 9, 40, 48, 68–9, 80, 92, 98–101, 137, 154, 159, 164, 170, 281 *et passim*
Halle Basilica, near Brussels 75–6, 318
Hallile, John, yeoman of the jewel house 257, 300
Hallmarking 255
Hampton Court 134–6, 140, 151, 152, 227, 301
Hannibal, Dr Thomas 68
Hans of Antwerp, royal goldsmith 181, 190, 200, 216, 257, 336n.58, 338n.45, 338n.53
Harbrott, Jerome, merchant 294
Harlam, John, goldsmith to Thomas Wolsey 143, 334n.64
Hawkins, Nicholas, diplomat and archdeacon of Ely 124
Hayes, Cornelis, royal goldsmith 143, 166, 181, 186, 217, 233, 235, 237, 241, 243–4, 258, 272, 275, 311
Helmets 34, 46
Henry VI, king of England 31
Henry VII, king of England 13–16, 34–8
  Character 27
  Expenditure on plate and jewels 34–5, 323n.23
  Tomb 60, 79, 140, 324n.32
  Will and bequests 35–6, 324n.29, 324n.32
Henry VIII, king of England
  Character
    Acquisitiveness and avarice 148–9, 209, 281–2, 288
    Changing character 10, 281
    Connoisseurship 314
    Identifies with David, King of Israel 1
    Liberality 48
    Religious attitudes 1, 68, 73, 261, 277–9, 345n.88
    Vindictiveness 272, 280
  Life
    As duke of York 72
    Coronation 40–2, 325n.13
    Wealth and liquidity 39, 111–12
    Crown wearing 43–4
    Relations with pope 68–71, 259–60
    Loans to foreign princes 112

War 114–17, 164
Takes plate and jewels on campaign 114–17, 283
Meeting with Emperor Maximilian 116–17
Meetings with Charles V 92, 165
Visits shrine of Becket 154, 272
As godfather 153, 286–8
Meetings with Francis I 160–4, 166–73, 198
Relationship with Francis I 121
Visits Tower jewel house 218
Progresses 8
Will and bequests 277, 316
Armour 116
Buying luxuries abroad 50, 290, 292–5
Expenditure on plate and jewels 24–5, 49–53, 179–81, 219–20
Gifts to Francis I 121, 164, 167, 173
Inheritance 27, 36–7, 322n.59
Interest in plate and jewels 117, 235, 273
Personal domestic plate 108, 109, 322n.60
Magnificence 1, 116
Portraits of 6, 239, 281, 305, 311, 325n.21
Tomb 179
Henry Fitzroy, duke of Richmond, illegitimate son of Henry VIII 144, 225–7
Henry, prince, son of Henry VIII 45
Heron, John, treasurer of chamber 16, 23, 37, 321n.52
Hertford, earl of (*see* Seymour, Edward) 268
Hippocras 42, 80, 83, 93, 106, 107
Hochsteter, Joachim, mining expert 343n.97
Holbein, Hans the younger, court artist 99, 107, 183–202, 338n.41
First sojourn in England 183
Works for Thomas More 183–4
Designs for ephemera 184
Exponent of the 'antique' 184
Returns to Basel 185
Second sojourn in England 186
Duties and remuneration as court artist 186
Designs for plate and jewels 9, 188–200, 310, 317
Diplomatic role 186
Portraits 7, 184, 186, 305
'Holbein bowl' (Schatzkammer, Munich) 295–9
Holinshed, Raphael, chronicler 27
Holland, William, royal goldsmith 23, 24, 51, 71, 82, 114, 119, 206, 240
Hollar, Wenceslaus, engraver 188–9, 190, 198, 200
Holtesweller, Henry, stranger goldsmith 51
Hopfer, Daniel, artist 201
Horenbout, Lucas, court artist 178, 179, 185, 337n.36
Horse harnesses 45–7
Household, Royal 11–15, 203 (*see also* Chapel Royal)
Allocations of plate 12–13
Departments 11–12, 83, 108, 211, 325n.16
Distinguished from Court 11–12
Size and personnel 11
Howard, Henry, earl of Surrey 288
Howard, Katherine, queen of England 224
Howard, Thomas, duke of Norfolk 152, 170, 228, 237, 264, 269, 288
Howard Grace Cup (Victoria and Albert Museum) 175–6
Huntsman salt (All Souls College, Oxford) 90
Husee, John, servant to Lord Lisle 236, 237, 240, 344n.60
Huxor, George, goldsmith to Thomas Wolsey 143, 144, 145, 334n.61

Images 72–3, 75, 79, 260, 262, 272 (*see also* Henry VII, Will and bequests)
Evidence for in Chapel Royal 156, 159–60, 278
Henry VIII acquires from monasteries 277–8
Incense boats 79, 266, 279
Inventories, royal 9, 19–22, 24–5, 109–10
Richard II (1399) 28–31, 322n.6
Princess Mary's dowry plate (1514) 128
Jewel House (1521) 19–22, 36–7, 320n.35, 324n.33, 340n.2
Jewel House (1532) 151, 229–31, 340n.2
Whitehall (1542) 278, 299–304
Inventory of the king's possessions (1547) 278–9, 283, 291, 295, 299–314, 321n.32
Isabella, queen of Castile 206
Isabella de Valois, French princess 155

James I, king of England 317
James IV, king of Scotland 75, 114–16
Jamnitzer, Wenzel, German goldsmith 311
Jane Seymour, queen of England (*see* Seymour, Jane)
Jasper 306
Jenyns, Sir Stephen, mayor of London 42
'Jerusalem', gold cross 271, 278–9
Jervaulx monastery, Yorkshire 264, 344
Jewel House 11–25, 320n.12
Administration 15, 24, 320n.11

Allocation of plate to household 108–9
Inventories of (*see under* Inventories, royal)
Lending plate to English ambassadors 125
Masters 15–17, 247–8, 320n.13
Responsibilities and procurement of plate 17–19, 22–5, 232, 235–6, 321n.46, 346n.7
Secret jewel house, Whitehall 303, 312
Tower jewel house 13
Westminster 13
Jewels 1–4, 34–5, 43, 49–50, 64, 112–13, 117, 127–9, 216, 222, 234–5
As asset 7–8
As component of plate 20
Depiction in portraits 7
Henry VIII's 'rich collar' 167
Quantum 322n.60
Refashioning 167
Joachino, Gian, secretary to governor of Genoa 155, 158–9, 164
Jocquin, Jehan, French ambassador 121
John de Colyn, stranger goldsmith 178
John of Antwerp, royal goldsmith (*see* Hans of Antwerp)
John of Lancaster, duke of Bedford 31–2
John of Thwing, St (*see* Bridlington)
Julius II, pope 64, 68, 70, 116

Kalf, Willem, artist 298
Katherine of Aragon, queen of England 206–13
Life
Betrothal and dowry 126, 207
Arrival in England and marriage to Prince Arthur 71–2, 126–7
Death of Arthur 206
Letters to her parents 120
Sells plate 207
Marriage to Henry VIII 208
Household 208
Deprivation 209–10
Divorce 146, 208
Death and bequests 213
Chapel plate 75, 211
Inventory and fate of plate 211–12
New year's gifts 208–9
Katherine Howard, queen of England (*see* Howard, Katherine)
Katherine Parr, queen of England (*see* Parr, Katherine)
Kebill, William, royal goldsmith 51, 324n.29
King David tapestries (Musée de la Renaissance, Ecouen) 1–4
King Henry VIII's College (*see* Cardinal College)
Kingston, Sir William, constable of the Tower 230–1
Kirkby, John, yeoman of jewel house 346n.6
Knives, carving (*see* Carving knives)
Knyvet, Sir Thomas, courtier 48
Kratzer, Nikolaus, royal astronomer 184, 338n.52
Kunstkammer 83, 109, 198, 300, 311, 312–13

Lange, Jehan, merchant 294, 299
Langeloys, Jacques (or John Langues) French jeweller 50, 181
Lathom, Robert à, royal goldsmith 236
Laude, Paolo de, Milanese ambassador to Emperor Maximilian 117
Lawson, Sir George, courtier 240
Layton, Richard, church commissioner 262, 264, 271
Leather cases for plate 61, 156
Lengeam, Jenyn, merchant 50
Leo X, pope 61, 69–71, 112, 118, 132, 133, 144
Liber Regalis 41
Liberality 4
Liege, cardinal bishop of 290
Linacre, Thomas, humanist scholar 240
Lincoln, shrines at 269, 270, 275
Lisle, Lord (*see* Plantagenet, Arthur, Viscount Lisle)
Lock, William, merchant 290
London, Dr John 263
London, Treaty of 118, 153
Lorde, Robert, servant to Cromwell 236
Louis VII, king of France 271
Louis XII, king of France 111, 116, 129
Louise de Savoie 163
Luneburg, town council plate 97
Lyberd, John, royal goldsmith 51

Machiavelli, Niccolò 111
Magnificence 1–10
Aristotelian doctrine 4–5
In church 67
On battlefield 114–17, 283, 331n.18
Maiano, Giovanni da, Florentine sculptor 139–40, 179
Mangot, Pierre, goldsmith to Francis I 172, 195, 200, 307, 318
Margaret of Austria, regent in Netherlands 114

Margaret, countess of Richmond (*see* Beaufort, Margaret)
Margaret Tudor, queen of Scotland, sister of Henry VIII 205–6
Marillac, Charles de, French ambassador 10, 224, 281–2, 288
Martin, Richard, physician to Elizabeth I 220
Martlets 333n.51, 334n.100 (*see also* Badges)
'Mary Rose' (warship) 88
Mary Tudor, queen of France, sister of Henry VIII 127–9, 204–5
- Life
  - Betrothal to Charles of Habsburg 127, 128
  - Marriage to Louis XII 127–9
  - Dispute over dowry 153, 204–5
  - Marriage to Duke of Suffolk 204
  - Relationship with Henry VIII 204–5
- Dowry 127–8
- Gifts of jewels from Louis XII 129

Mary Tudor, daughter of Henry VIII, later queen of England 213–17, 240–1
- Life
  - Betrothed to dauphin (1518) 126
  - Betrothed to Charles V 126
  - Household 98, 213
  - Deprived of plate and jewels 214
  - Declared illegitimate 214
  - Restored to favour 215–16
  - Privy expenses 216
  - Patronage 182
- Inventory of jewels 216–17
- New Year's gifts 213, 216
- Plate 213–14

Maryne, Jacques, French merchant 50
Mass for the Holy Ghost 73
Masters of the Jewel house (*see* Jewel House, Masters)
Matsys, Cornelis, artist 281
Maximilian, Holy Roman Emperor 14–15, 127, 153, 154, 331n.20
- Borrows money from Henry VII 112
- Meets Henry VIII (1513) 116–17

Medici, Lorenzo de' 60, 314
Megenburg, Konrad von 306
Melanchthon, Philip 10
Mercator, Michael, Flemish goldsmith 182, 186
Merchants, foreign, in London 178
Mildmay, Sir Henry, master of the jewel house 172
Mildmay, Sir Walter, courtier 290–1
Mining 343n.97
Mint, Tower 248–9
- Administration 248
- Dispute over profits 248–9
- Relationship with Jewel house 249

Miraculous mass of St Giles 275
'Mirror of Naples' (jewel) 128, 167, 204
Monasteries, Dissolution of 260–8
- Earlier dissolutions 261
- Plate 264
- Wealth 261
- Inventories ordered 262
- Destiny of plate and jewels 272–6

Monmouth, Humphrey, alderman of London 246
Monstrances 75–7
More, Sir Thomas, lord chancellor 21, 178, 183–4
'Moresdaunce' salt 33, 89–90, 317
Morton, John, archbishop of Canterbury 37
'Moryon' salt 33, 318
Mother of pearl 307
Mountjoy Lord (*see* Blount, William, Baron Mountjoy)
Mowbray, Thomas, duke of Norfolk 31
Mundy, John, royal goldsmith 38, 51–3, 256, 324

Nanfan, Sir Richard 133
Narwhal horn 226, 274, 309
Naturalia 313
Nautilus shell 300, 307–8
Nefs 98, 128, 304, 308 (*see also* Ships)
Nevill, George, Baron Bergavenny, courtier 21, 46
New year's gifts (*see* Gifts, New year's)
Nicomachean Ethics 4
Norfolk, duke of (*see* Howard, Thomas)
Norris, Henry, groom of the stool 24, 149, 239, 248
North, Edward, treasurer of augmentations 273
Northumberland Ceremonial 81–2, 89, 92, 93, 102–3
Northumberland, earl of (*see* Percy, Henry)
Nuremberg 310–11

Oatlands 301
Orio, Lorenzo, Venetian ambassador 122
Ornament prints 201
Ostrich egg 28, 308–9, 311, 318
Ostrich feathers 228
Ottener, Guillaume, French jeweller 181
Oxford, earl of (*see* Vere, John de)

Pace, Richard, courtier 123

Pageants and revels 47–9
Paget, William, courtier 253, 284–6
Panner, John, merchant 295
Papal rose and sword (*see* Gifts, Papal)
Parish churches 268
Parker, Matthew, archbishop of Canterbury 93
Parr, Katherine, queen of England 224–5, 316
Parry, Thomas, church commissioner 265
Pasqualigo, Lorenzo, Italian merchant 127, 204
Pasqualigo, Piero, Venetian ambassador 1
Paulet, Sir William, comptroller of the household 230–1
Pavia, battle 114
Paxes 79, 162
Percy, Henry, earl of Northumberland 95, 117, 226
Peterborough Abbey 276
Philip of Castile 207
Philip II, king of Spain 114, 126
Philip the Fair, duke of Burgundy 111
Philip the Good, duke of Burgundy 286, 330n.46
Pilgrimage of Grace 8, 249–50, 259, 269, 316
Plantagenet, Arthur, Viscount Lisle 125, 236, 240, 277, 341n.41, 344n.60
Plate (*see also* Alms dishes; Basins; Beakers; Bowls; Carving knives; Chargers; Chapel Royal; Church; Cruses; Cups; Cups of assay; Dishes; Ewers; Flagons; Fountains; Goblets; Nefs; Platters; Pots; Salts; Saucers; Spice plates; Spoons; Trenchers; 'Vessel')
  Coining of 250, 252
  Cost and value of 8, 20, 23, 142, 321n.40
  Domestic 88–91, 302–3 *et passim*
  Fashion charge 142, 181
  Hierarchical symbolism 161–2
  Ornament 55–8, 61–2
  Plate for king's personal use 107–9
  Procurement 22–5, 235–40, 325n.38
  Quantity owned by Henry VIII 21
  Recycling 315–16
  Refashioning and repairing 166, 233, 234–5
  Relative quantities in gold, silver-gilt and silver 20, 231, 300, 340n.3
  Security 17, 102, 246
  Transportation 18–19, 24, 156, 284, 333n.17, 346n.7
  Ubiquity at court 7, 9
Platters (*see* 'Vessel')
Pliny the elder 306
Plommier, Allard, French royal goldsmith 173–4, 181, 225, 287, 294
Pole, Margaret, countess of Salisbury 288
Pope, Sir Thomas, church commissioner 279
Porcelain ('pursulane') 310
Portinari, Guido, merchant 50
Pots 94
Poyntz, Sir Nicholas, courtier 309
Praemunire 147, 149, 260, 261, 334n.98
Prasinus 306, 311
Privy chamber 49, 107, 304–5
  Privy dining 107–9
  Works of art in 304–14
Privy purse 179–81
Puebla, Dr de, Spanish ambassador 126
Pyx, trial of (*see* Trial of the pyx)
Pyxes 35, 324n.29

Raimondi, Raimondo de', Milanese ambassador 122
Ramsey Abbey, censer and incense boat 79, 266, 276
Receyt of the Ladie Kateryne 18, 72, 74, 93, 101
Rede, Bartholomew, royal goldsmith 37–8, 51
Rede, William 253, 343n.99
Regalia
  Coronation 13, 41, 318
  Ecclesiastical 64
  Imperial 20, 41, 42–4, 318, 325n.18
Relics and reliquaries 260, 262–3, 279–80
Rich, Sir Richard, attorney general 213, 270
Richard II, king of England 28–31, 33, 154–5, 278, 314, 316 (*see also under* Inventories)
Richard III, king of England 34, 318
Richardson, Peter, royal goldsmith 181–2, 216, 275
Richmond, duke of (*see* Henry Fitzroy)
Richmond Palace 8, 36, 48, 74, 87, 101, 279
Rings, cramp 240–1
Rochester tazzas (British Museum) 97, 104
Rock crystal 59–60, 306, 310
Rome, break with 259–60
Rothelin, marquis de 127
Rothwell, William, Sergeant of the Vestry 156
Rous, Anthony, master of jewel house 248, 346n.7
Rovezzano, Benedetto da, Florentine sculptor 140, 179
Rowlett, Ralph, goldsmith and deputy mint master 248, 249, 257
Royal finances 27, 259, 261, 283–6 (*see also* Chamber accounts)
'Royal gold cup' (British Museum) 31–2, 317, 318, 323n.8

Ryalle Book, The 23, 41, 44, 80, 93, 104

St Alban's Abbey 145, 148
St Barbe, William, courtier 302–3
St Catherine 177
St Cosmas 177
St Damian 177
St George, patron saint of England 20, 36, 59, 160, 163, 175, 177, 279, 316
St George's Chapel, Windsor 35, 36, 74, 156, 279, 316, 324n.32, 326n.73
St Hugh of Lincoln (*see under* Shrines)
St John 177
St John of Bridlington (*see under* Shrines)
St John of Dalderby (*see under* Shrines)
St Lambert, golden reliquary of (Liège Cathedral) 36
St Leger, Sir Antony gentleman of privy chamber 275
St Martin of Tours (*see under* Shrines)
St Mauris, Jean de, imperial ambassador to France 286
St Michael cup (Kunsthistorisches Museum, Vienna) 168–70, 198
St Michael, Order of 170
St Paul's Cathedral 69, 138, 274
St Richard de Wych (*see under* Shrines)
St Swithun (*see under* Shrines)
St Thomas of Canterbury (*see* Becket, Thomas; Shrines, St Thomas Becket) 128, 262, 269
Salt, symbolism of 81, 91
Salts 89–91, 329n.4
Sampson, Richard, courtier 123
San Lorenzo vase (Church of San Lorenzo, Florence) 59–62, 71, 306, 318, 327n.75
'Sapphire of Glastonbury' 274
Saucers (*see* 'Vessel')
Sauche, Jehan de la, imperial ambassador 120
Schloss Ambras, Innsbruck 313
Schlüsselfelder nef (Germanisches National Museum, Nuremberg) 304
Serpentine 306
Seymour, Edward, earl of Hertford and duke of Somerset 268, 302
Seymour, Jane, queen of England 221–2
Seymour cup, drawing (Ashmolean Museum) 195, 202, 215, 221, 317
Shaa, Edmund, royal goldsmith 51
Shaa, Sir John, royal goldsmith and mayor of London 35, 37–8, 51
Sharpe, Sir John, courtier 248
Sheen, fire at 74
Ships 98, 303–4 (*see also* Nefs)
Shrines 269–72
  St Edmund at Bury 262, 269–70, 276
  St Hugh of Lincoln 271
  St John of Bridlington 269
  St John of Dalderby 271
  St Martin of Tours 261
  St Swithun at Winchester 265, 269–70
  St Thomas Becket 67, 154, 262, 269, 271–2, 276, 280
Silver foil 100
Skelton, John, playwright 5, 152
Smyth, John, royal goldsmith 53
Solozano, Saravia and Pedro de, servants to Katherine of Aragon 127
Somerset, duke of (*see* Seymour, Edward)
Somerset House Conference 317
Spangles 7, 10, 45, 48, 52, 100, 117
Spice (*see* Void)
Spice plates 96–7
Spinelli, Anthony 139
Spinelli, Gasparo, Venetian diplomat 98, 100, 101, 121
Spinola, Agostino, merchant 122
Spoons 12, 20, 55, 77, 109, 150, 177 *et passim*
Stafford, Edward, duke of Buckingham 73, 92, 117, 138, 141, 152, 231, 288, 326n.67
  Attainder plate 53–4
  New year's gifts 54
Stafford, Henry, earl of Wiltshire 53
Standing houses 74, 151, 278–9, 301
Star Chamber, court of 243
Staves 75
Steelyard, London 178
Stoneware 347n.55
Strangers 51, 53, 62, 178–9, 181
  Population in London 178
  In royal service 183, 311, 343n.113
  Size of workshops 181–2
Suffolk, duke of (*see* Brandon, Charles)
Suger, Abbot of St-Dennis 41, 66–7
Supporters (in heraldry) 55, 142, 177, 244, 289, 337n.4, 346n.34
Surian, Antonio, Venetian ambassador 135
Surrey, earl of (*see* Howard, Henry)

'Tablet of Bourbon' 32–3

Tapestry 1–4, 87, 91, 97, 99, 104, 116, 167, 291–2
  Arras 5
  Cost of 5, 319n.9
Thérouanne 117
'Three brothers' (jewel) 286
'Tiger' nef 28, 29, 31
Tissue (*see* Cloth of gold and silver)
Toison d'Or 5
Torrigiano, Pietro, sculptor 60, 139–40
Tournai 76, 117–18
Tournaments 44–7 (*see also* Field of Cloth of Gold)
  Tournament for birth of Prince Henry (1511) 45–7
Tower of London (*see* Jewel House, Tower)
Trade guilds 253
Trappes, Robert, royal goldsmith 236, 242–3
Trappes, Thomas 237, 243
Treaty of Amiens (*see* Amiens, Treaty of)
Treaty of London (*see* London, Treaty of)
Trenchers 88, 109, 188, 302
Trial of the pyx 255
Trollope, Edward, bishop and antiquarian 20
Tuke, Sir Brian, treasurer of the Chamber 124, 230–1, 234, 236
Twyselton, John, royal goldsmith 24, 51–3, 119, 206, 320n.23
Tyler, Sir William, master of jewels 15

Unicorn horn (*see* Narwhal horn)

Vanderwall, Peter (or van den Wale) 283–4, 294, 311
Vaughan, Richard, courtier 123
Vaughan, Stephen, servant to Cromwell 235, 246, 283–6
Vaux, Joachim de, French diplomat 114
Vaux, Nicholas 155
Velasco, Juan Fernández de, Spanish ambassador 32
Veneziano, Antonio 201
Venier, Marc Antonio, Venetian ambassador 134, 151
Vere, John de, earl of Oxford 42
Vergil, Polydore, historian 132, 134, 135, 152
'Vessel' 88, 124, 142, 231 *et passim*
Vezeler, Josse, goldsmith to Francis I 168, 169
Vianen, Christian van, royal goldsmith 318, 348n.11
Vicary, Thomas, royal surgeon 176, 337n.3
Vico, Enea, artist 169
Void 93–4, 106–7, 329n.4
Vreland, Paul van, royal armourer 6, 51, 331n.20

Wallop, Sir John, courtier 6, 124–5
War, costs of 164, 252, 283
Warham, William, archbishop of Canterbury 24, 64, 68, 73, 133, 137, 271
Warley, Nicholas, royal goldsmith 38, 51, 256, 324n.29
Warren, Lawrence, goldsmith 264–5, 344n.32
Westminster Abbey 40–1, 72
  Lends plate and copes to Henry VIII 156
Westminster Palace (*see* Whitehall)
Westminster Tournament Roll (College of Arms) 46–7, 122
Wethers, Fabyan, goldsmith 258, 272, 345n.93
Whitehall 301–14 (*see also under* Inventories)
Whiting, Richard, Abbot of Glastonbury 266
Williams, John, master of the jewel house and treasurer of court of augmentations 240, 247, 273–6, 288
Winchester Cathedral 273–4, 278, 309, 345n.91
Windsor Castle 74, 104–7, 151, 301
Wingfield, Sir Richard, courtier 124, 139, 155, 163
Wingfield, Sir Robert, courtier 124
Wolf, Morgan, royal goldsmith 181, 237, 244–5, 258, 272, 278, 288, 303, 342n.60
Wolsey, Thomas, cardinal
  Life
    Early career 132–3
    Ecclesiastical preferments 133
    Income and expenditure 133–4, 148
    Building projects 134
    Foundation of colleges at Ipswich and Oxford 145, 148
    Magnificence 135–9
    King's minister 98, 133, 179, 204, 255
    Fall 146–51
  Banquets 135–6
  Gifts 136, 144–5, 149
    From Venice 135
    To St Alban's Abbey and colleges 145, 148
  Goldsmiths (*see* Amadas, Robert; Beynarde, John; Cowper, Robert; Harlam, John; Hayes, Cornelis; Huxor, George)
  Inventories and plate lists 147, 150–1
  Patronage of Italian artists 139–40

Plate
Decoration 141–2
Holdings 134–6, 150–1, 231, 334n.100
Regalia 137–9, 143
Sources of luxury goods 134–5, 139
Tomb 144, 179
Worcester 262, 264
Worley, Henry, royal goldsmith 256
Wotton, Nicholas, courtier 119
Wriothesley, Thomas, secretary to Henry VIII 123, 249, 250, 252
Wriothesley's *Chronicle* 268
Wyatt, Sir Henry, courtier 15–16, 19, 24, 35, 37, 128, 156, 204, 248, 320n.13, 321n.46
Wyatt, Thomas, poet and courtier 16, 100, 247

Yngworth, Richard, bishop of Dover 263
York, royal progress to 8